The Muslim Veil in North America

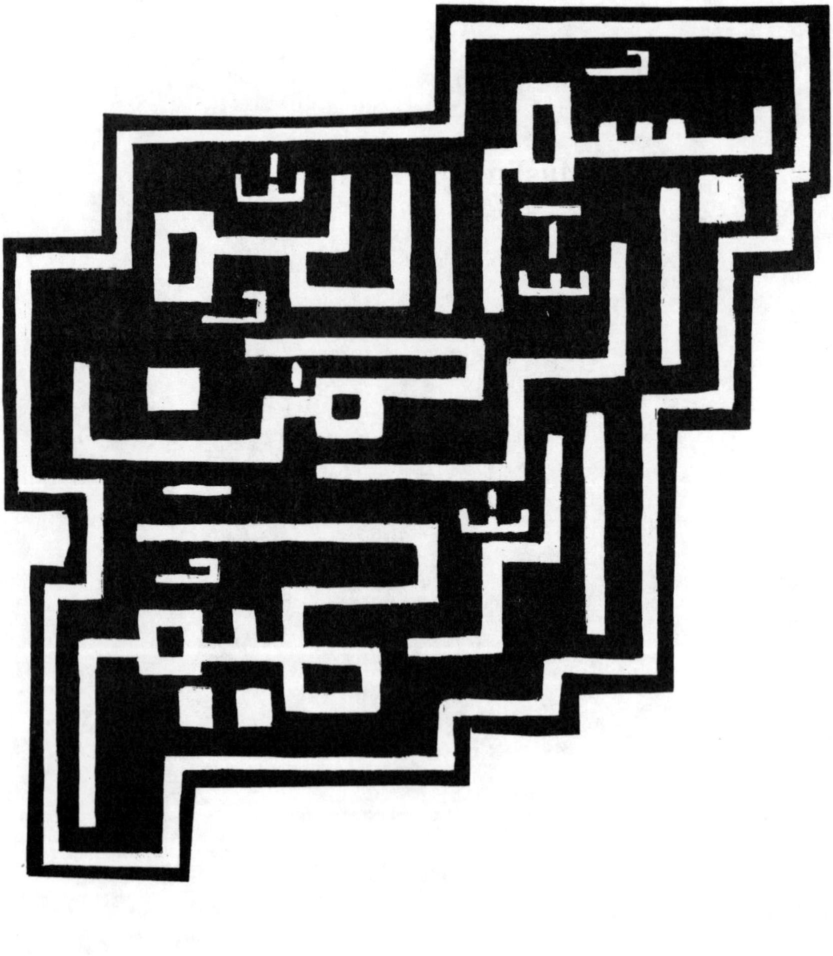
بسم الله الرحمن الرحيم

The Muslim Veil in North America

Issues and Debates

Edited by

Sajida Sultana Alvi, Homa Hoodfar
and Sheila McDonough

Women's Press / Toronto

The Muslim Veil in North America: Issues and Debates
Edited by Sajida S. Alvi, Homa Hoodfar and Sheila McDonough

First published in 2003 by
Women's Press
180 Bloor Street West, Suite 801
Toronto, Ontario
M5S 2V6

www.womenspress.ca

Women's Press gratefully acknowledges financial assistance for our publishing activities from the Ontario Arts Council, the Canada Council for the Arts, and the Government of Canada through the Book Publishing Industry Development Program (BPIDP).

National Library of Canada Cataloguing in Publication Data

The Muslim veil in North America : issues and debates / edited by Sajida S. Alvi, Homa Hoodfar and Sheila McDonough.

Includes bibliographical references.
ISBN 0-88961-408-3

1. Veils—Social aspects—Canada. 2. Islam—Canada—Customs and practices. 3. Muslim women—Costume—Canada. I. Alvi, Sajida S. (Sajida Sultana), 1941– II. Hoodfar, Homa III. McDonough, Sheila

GT2112.M88 2003 391.4'3 C2002-905275-0

Cover design by Zack Taylor
Cover art by Tehzib Morad
Text design and layout by Susan Thomas/Digital Zone
Inscription illustrations by Tehzib Morad

04 05 06 07 08 6 5 4 3 2

Printed and bound in Canada by AGMV Marquis Imprimeur Inc.

ONTARIO ARTS COUNCIL
CONSEIL DES ARTS DE L'ONTARIO

The Canada Council for the Arts since 1957 | Le Conseil des Arts du Canada depuis 1957

Canada

To Muslim Women in Diaspora

Table of Contents

Acknowledgements

We are grateful to the many Muslim women who agreed to be interviewed, and who shared their concerns and interests with us. We also deeply appreciate the stimulus and the financial support given to this work by the leadership of the Canadian Council of Muslim Women. They started us off by asking questions on the topic of *ḥijāb,* and they were unfailingly helpful and supportive as we struggled to provide the answers. We are also thankful to the Institute of Islamic Studies, McGill University, for its material support to this project from its inception. Tehzib Morad has added much to our volume by introducing the word *ḥijāb* to the cover and as well writing three Qur'anic inscriptions inside the work in beautiful Arabic calligraphy. We greatly appreciate her contribution. In preparing this volume for publication, we are greatly indebted to Stephen Millier for his editorial assistance, and for painstakingly incorporating the changes the contributors made to the text.

Note on Transliteration: Most words and names originally written in Arabic script have been romanized according to the Library of Congress rules for transliterating Arabic, Persian and Urdu.

Note on the Inscriptions

Cover	The word in the cover design is *ḥijāb* in Arabic script. For the interpretation of the word *ḥijāb* and its derivatives in the Qur'an, see Chapter 7, pp. 183–184.
Inscription I (page ii)	Meaning: "In the Name of God, Most Gracious, Most Merciful." This statement is used in the beginning of each chapter of the Qur'an, and uttered by Muslims as a general invocation before undertaking any task.
Inscription II (page 2)	Meaning: "[God] the Knower of the invisible and visible, all-mighty, all-wise." (Qur'an, Chapter 64, verse 18)
Inscription III (page 144)	Meaning: "Whatsoever is in the heavens and the earth sings the praises [of God]. And He is all-mighty, all-wise." (Qur'an, Chapter 57, verse 1)

Introduction

Homa Hoodfar, Sajida S. Alvi and Sheila McDonough

The final touches to this manuscript were made in the aftermath of the September 11 tragedy, which, in addition to its many other ramifications, has brought the issue of Muslim dress codes and veiling under greater scrutiny by the general public in the West, and has raised many concerns for the Diaspora Muslim community. Ironically, some of the initial impetus for our project arose ten years ago as a consequence of the 1991 Gulf War. That conflict, too, resulted in harassment of and discrimination against Muslim individuals and communities, particularly veiled women. This occurred throughout the West and included Canada despite its official multicultural policy (Hoodfar 1997; Kashmerier 1991). Muslims born and raised in the West, and imbued with the doctrine of individual rights, liberty and freedom of religion, were as shocked then as they are today to realize that not only are they identified as "other" (read, not belonging) but also as an enemy within. This created a crisis in the Diaspora Muslim community, particularly in North America and among young Muslims, many of whom identified as Canadian, American, British or French. For many Muslims in the Diaspora, the Gulf War was a turning point. It was a wake-up call to the post-Cold War reality of the demonization of Islam and, by implication, Muslims (Esposito 1995;

Halliday 1999; Huntington 1993) with grave implications for Diaspora Muslim communities everywhere.

Strategies to cope with this heightened awareness of "Muslimness" have varied, particularly among the younger segment of the community. They include the formation of many formal and informal Muslim groups or associations, as well as establishing more mosques. Homa Hoodfar, in a post-Gulf War study of the Muslim community in Canada (1992–1997), broadly distinguished four distinct but overlapping coping responses and strategies. The first of these was dissociation: a sizable number of Muslims, particularly the more secular, attempted, not always successfully, to disassociate themselves from the Muslim community and remove any outward signs of Muslimness. At times, they went as far as changing their names and creating fictitious origins. The second response was escape: many Muslims simply withdrew from the wider society to their own communities to minimize contact with non-Muslims as much as possible (Hoodfar 1997).

Other Muslims opted for a third response: self-assertion. Frustrated by what they viewed as unjust exclusion and negative stereotyping, many Muslims chose to claim their space in society by declaring their presence and raising their grievances at every opportunity. Since clothing is a very potent channel of symbolic communication, many chose to adopt a dress code associated with Islam by the general public. For women this has meant adopting the veil; for men it is wearing the Palestinian scarf, growing a beard and sometimes adopting non-Western clothing. This silent self-assertion has made dominant ethnic groups somewhat uncomfortable, despite living in a postmodern society where differences are expected to be tolerated, if not understood and celebrated.

The wider Western society has found it difficult to relinquish old colonial images of the veil and the idea of oppressed, choiceless Muslim women, and has responded to this bluntly different style of clothing with more extreme stereotyping of Muslims. The considerable harassment of Muslim individuals and communities in North America since September 11 (despite some efforts on the part of public officials and civil libertarians within our committed civil societies to prevent this) is thus a repetition of the recent past. Unfortunately, these widespread incidents often convince even more Muslims of the hypocrisy of the Western world concerning freedom of expression and individual liberty, further poisoning the relationship between Muslims and non-Muslims.

The fourth and most prevalent response (adopted by the broadest, if silent, segment of the Muslim community) has been, on the one hand, to try to understand the preoccupation of the wider society with stereotyping Muslims and, on the other, to attempt to differentiate the cultural practices of their communities of origin from Islamic tenets. This process, they hope, will enable them to see themselves as Muslim-Canadians, Muslim-Americans, Muslim-British, etc. (Metcalf 1996; Waardenburg 1988). It is in this context that beliefs concerning dress codes and the veiling of women have mushroomed into controversy for young Muslim women (Bloul 1996; Hoodfar 1991, 1997b; Zuhur 1992). Cultural evidence of the historically diverse forms of women's dress — from the *sari* (commonly worn on the Indian subcontinent) to the Sudanese *tobah*, the Egyptian *jalabīyah* and *'abā'ah*, and the *burqa'* among the Pushtun of Afghanistan — demonstrates that Muslimness has had little to do with a particular dress code.

Clearly the history of Muslims in the Diaspora indicates that the idea of a specific dress code for women (often calling for long, loose dresses), with an emphasis on the *ḥijāb,* found a consensus among Muslim religious leaders in North America and Europe only within the last twenty years. Many Muslims are trying to comprehend the process by which this consensus came about, given the near absence of public discussion in the community. They are trying to understand why public discussion of the *ḥijāb* is curtailed and branded as "un-Islamic," if not blasphemous. After all, many Muslims believe they have been blessed with a religion that encourages them to understand their religion rather than just obey rules; they have taken pride in not needing an intermediary between them and their God, in contrast to Christianity. Thus, they question why discussion of the veil has been discouraged, if not completely declared off limits, by some conservative Muslim leaders.

This said, veiling in the Diaspora is not a phenomenon isolated from economic and cultural development in the Muslim world, extending from Morocco to the Bay of Bengal, from Algeria to the Archipelago of Indonesia, and from Mongolia to Somalia.[1] While Saudi Arabia, the only "fundamentalist" Muslim state, had long ago taken it upon itself to enforce the veiling and segregation of women through its "morality police," it wasn't until shortly after 1973 that the modern veiling movement, as a political statement among the urban middle classes in Egypt, first caught the attention of social scientists (El-Guindi 1981; Hoodfar 1991; Zuhur 1992).[2] However, it was not until the success of the Iranian revolution in 1979 and the imposition of dress codes for women (and men) that veiling emerged as a preoccupation of Muslim as well as Western societies. Added to this complex backdrop was the American humiliation by the hostage-taking in Iran and the end of the Cold War. The tendency of Western media and political leaders to reduce legitimate grievances in Muslim nations to religious fervour and to associate Islam with terrorism (Said 2001) aggravated the situation. All of this has discouraged a quest for more open discussion of Islam and modernity, particularly the question of veiling (Halliday 1999; Said 1997).[3]

Clearly, for many Muslims, veiling signifies their piety and spirituality, and they are unhappy with both the wider society's demonization of the veil as a symbol of oppression, and the elevation by some Muslims of the veil as a symbol of Muslim identity, resistance, and even *jihād*. As well, there are women who have adopted the veil for personal reasons stemming from their particular social contexts. Some wish to prevent alienation from their parents and community as they engage in "unconventional" pursuits such as higher education and careers, which may entail mingling with men, living alone and travelling to distant places. Other women are using Islam, including practices such as veiling, to help break away from certain practices of their community's patriarchal cultural traditions, such as arranged marriages, which they find unacceptable (Hoodfar in this volume). In short, for some women veiling can be empowering and in some contexts even subversive.

In other circumstances, Muslim students who normally wear the veil as a standard part of their school uniform are suddenly faced with having to explain why their uniform includes a scarf. Knowing the veil is viewed negatively, they have to decide whether to wear the scarf on the way to and from school or not (Kelly Spurles in this volume). Difficult for them to comprehend is the considerable tolerance that the wider society appears to demonstrate toward what they perceive as extreme nonconformist clothing choices on the part of, say, "punks." Muslim parents have difficulty explaining to their children why veiled Muslim girls are expelled from school and why passionate debate about veiling takes place on the front pages of newspapers (Lenk 2000).

Many young Diaspora Muslims have difficulty harmonizing their belonging to a religious (and often visible) minority with their citizenship in countries that harbour residual colonial ideas even while they try to make sense of the rise of political Islams in the Muslim world. Yet, such harmonization is essential to making informed choices concerning their needs as Muslims, as members of their communities and as citizens of their countries. Unfortunately, although there is no dearth of English-language material available on Islam, on the status of woman in Islam or on women's legal rights and the abuse of these rights through customary law and regional cultural norms, there is little that addresses the concerns of Diaspora Muslim communities. Most written material caters to the interests of non-Muslims. The continuing current in research and publication on women and Islam gives little space to Muslims themselves to voice their issues and priorities. The Muslim community is exhausted by being the subject of so much research about them rather than for them.

In this context we hope that the present volume will not only be informative to the general interested public, especially in Europe and North America, and to university students, but that above all, it will respond to the needs of young women and others in the Muslim world who are curious about dress code controversies among Diaspora Muslims. We hope to see a growing literature addressed to Muslims as well as to the community at large.

The Story Behind This Volume

This edited volume is the result of several somewhat independent projects. Homa Hoodfar, an Iranian anthropologist teaching at Montreal's McGill and Concordia Universities at the time, was approached by many young Muslim students during and after the Gulf War to air their grievances and stories of harassment both on and off university campuses. Gradually this led to a loosely formed Muslim Women's Study Group to look at the question of Muslim women's rights and status, particularly controversies surrounding veiling from a Muslim perspective. By the end of 1992, Hoodfar, with a small grant from Concordia University and the support of twelve Muslim women from diverse backgrounds, all of them students in the social sciences, embarked on a Canada-wide anthropological study of the veil among young Muslim women. The project took four years to complete. Chapter 1 contains the partial results of this project.

Patricia Kelly Spurles, who at the time of the Gulf War was a student of political science and Middle East studies (and would have then described herself as a secular Muslim), joined the Muslim Women's Study Group and became a research co-coordinator for the Hoodfar project. She went on to complete her MA program in Islamic Studies and carried out her anthropological field research at the Muslim School in Montreal before joining the Anthropology Department at the University of Montreal (Kelly 1997). Although she was more interested in the education and socialization of children in an Islamic school, she found that the question of dress codes remained central to the way the school and its students interacted with the general public. Her chapter in this volume is a detailed account of her participant observations over the course of a year in the school.

By 1995, with a noticeable increase in the presence of veiled Muslim women at universities and colleges and with the media's preoccupation with veiling, the veil had become a focal concern for Muslim women themselves, who expressed a need to know more about the veiling movement, particularly in the Diaspora context. The Canadian Council of Muslim Women (CCMW), a national organization with chapters in all major Canadian cities, had at this point held several conferences and workshops on the subject.[4] The CCMW felt that understanding the views of a cross-section of young Muslim women in universities would be helpful in advancing the debate. To that end, in 1996, they approached Sajida S. Alvi at the Institute of Islamic Studies to conduct research on the subject. Two graduate students, Reem Meshal, working initially under Alvi's supervision, and Paula Jolin conducted a survey of female Muslim university students. They presented their results at several public lectures and scholarly conferences, generating much debate both within and outside the Muslim community. Reem Meshal has summarized the findings of this research in Chapter 3 of this volume.

While we often hear about conservative and radical Islamic movements, we hear less often about alternative social and intellectual developments in the Muslim world. One important movement in this area is the demand for a rereading of Islamic texts from women's points of view, and for revisiting those claims about women's position that render them lesser members of the community. The debate concerning the *ḥijāb* and dress codes are a significant part of this inquiry.[5] While radical Muslim traditionalists have done their best to curb these debates by denouncing those involved, Western audiences and the scholarly community have not been receptive either. This has meant fewer opportunities to bring these debates into the public sphere. Nonetheless, many Muslim women are now entering theological and Islamic Studies, and are directing their scholarly research to these areas. Soraya Hajjaji-Jarrah, a Ph.D. candidate in McGill's Islamic Studies program who is working on early Qur'anic commentary, is an example of this new direction in scholarship. She had shared some of her findings with the Muslim community on several occasions, and a paper she presented to the annual conference of the CCMW generated much discussion. It was suggested that the CCMW make her research findings and others of a similar nature available to Muslim women and thus promote informed debate in the community. The CCMW once again approached Sajida S. Alvi, who in turn invited several colleagues to help provide a more comprehensive reader on Islamic dress codes. After several meetings, this book project was conceived of. Sheila McDonough, at the time professor of religious studies at Concordia University — who writes here on the reactions of non-Muslim Canadians to the veil — joined Alvi as co-editor along with Homa Hoodfar. The team then invited L. Clarke, professor of religion and Islamic Studies at Concordia, to write a chapter on her research on the *Ḥadīth* (sayings of the Prophet) concerning *ḥijāb* to complement the chapter by Soraya Hajjaji. To contextualize these investigations of the sources, Sajida S. Alvi has provided an historical overview of the subject.

The Organization of the Contents

The book is divided into two parts. Part I: Veiling Practices in Everyday Life in Canada covers the sociological and anthropological analyses of current ideas and practices of the *ḥijāb* among Muslim women. The primary focus of the first three chapters in this section is how the *ḥijāb* is perceived, particularly among Muslim school, college and university students and on how they understand the wider non-Muslim public perceptions of the veil, particularly their fantasies and colonial images. Hoodfar (Chapter 1) argues that clothing, including the veil, remains a powerful symbol and effective tool of non-verbal communication. While the veil and its meaning has, from the perspective of Western cultures, largely remained static — a sign of the inferiority of Muslim culture — in Muslim cultures its function and significance have varied tremendously, particularly during periods of rapid social change. Veiling is a lived experience full of contradiction and multiple meanings. In some contexts, it has been used as a means of controlling and regulating women's lives. However, women have frequently also used the veil to empower themselves and bring about structural changes in their societies. In the context of Canada, many women have adopted the veil, and have acquired religious knowledge, in order to challenge some of the cultural and traditional patriarchal practices that have historically denied women mobility, access to education, participation in the labour market and their own choice of husband.

Kelly Spurles's year-long ethnographic study of the Muslim day school in Montreal (Chapter 2) reveals veiling as a complex social and symbolic practice in which individuals exercise considerable personal freedom within the bounds framed by the community. While veiling was a formal part of the school dress code, the community recognized the legitimacy of each woman's choice to wear *ḥijāb* or not outside the school. Meshal's survey (Chapter 3) was primarily concerned with factors that influence young women in deciding whether or not to wear the veil. The population of this study, Muslim university students, was very similar to that of Homa Hoodfar, although it included a wider geographical space in Canada. Interestingly, this survey study, launched and analyzed independently of Hoodfar's study, has given a very similar picture in many respects, but also deals with some issues that Hoodfar's anthropological study did not address. The results of this survey indicate that socioeconomic background and access to religious information do play a role in deciding to veil. However, issues of identity and resistance to assimilation were also of concern to many of her respondents. Furthermore, research shows that, despite considerable awareness of the diversity of Muslim cultures, there is a tendency among Muslims in the Diaspora to construct a monolithic form of Islam, particularly among preachers in mosques, who also promote, if not construct, the modern version of the *ḥijāb* as an important site and symbol of shared Muslim identity.

In Chapter 4, Sheila McDonough, who has for years acted as a resource person for the Muslim community, frames and analyzes the views and statements of seven Canadian Muslim women on the *ḥijāb*. Like Hoodfar and Kelly, she concludes that the diversity of their perspectives illustrates their different realities, their individual interpretations and their agency in determining what best suits their needs. Several interviewees indicate that wearing the *ḥijāb* has been empowering and has given them a sense of dignity and self-worth, a message that the Canadian public needs to hear and reflect upon. In contrast, some Muslim women felt empowered when they removed the veil, which they saw as a public symbol of piety. The chapter argues that both choices are valid, readily understandable and work best for certain individuals. In Chapter 5, McDonough explores some responses of non-Muslim Canadians to the *ḥijāb*. She argues that negative reactions tend to be triggered by anxieties about reversion to social structures in which males exercise more authority over females than is currently the case in Canada. Given the historical resistance Canadian women have experienced — for example, on the part of the church to recognizing and granting them basic rights (such as the right to vote) — there is a degree of distrust of male religious authority on issues pertaining to women's roles and abilities.

In Part II: Women Revisiting Texts and the Veiling Discourse, the focus is on the *ḥijāb* discourse and on the recent but increasingly widespread movement, particularly among Muslim women, to reread the Islamic texts and to interpret them from women's perspectives (Mernissi 1991a, 1992, 1996; Sisters in Islam 1991a, 1991b; Wadud 1999).

The *ḥijāb* debates are part of the rethinking of Islamic jurisprudence and the role of contextualization (that is, a taking into account of socio-political context). A concern with how the Qur'an should be interpreted has always engaged Muslim minds. However, it is only recently that discussions are occurring regarding the founding documents (Qur'an, *ḥadīth* and other established historical sources) on which Islam is based and how these were and are influenced by the social, political and economic realities of the eras in which they emerged. Some Muslim reformers argue that the Qur'an, as a living document, should constantly be reinterpreted as social conditions change (An-Na'im 1990; Engineer 1986, 1992, 1999; Vakili on Soroush 1996).[6] Slavery provides a good example of how context has always influenced the understanding of Islam, prior to any significant theoretical debates on contextualization. For centuries, in many cultural and political contexts, Muslims considered slavery acceptable according to Islam; this is no longer the case. Clearly the Qur'an says that justice is an imperative, but what justice might constitute varies over time. The meaning of justice, in practice, is influenced by the norms — which themselves are evolving — of a given society. It is in light of these hotly debated concerns and reflections that Alvi describes the historical context within which interest in revisiting the *ḥijāb* debates has been brewing, while Clarke and Hajjaji Jarrah provide two groundbreaking contributions to the discourse of Muslim dress code.

Alvi, an historian of South Asian Islamic culture and society, examines in Chapter 6 several issues of concern to Muslim women past and present. After a brief history of Islam and its Prophet, the foundations of Islamic tradition and the development of that tradition over time, Alvi reviews the processes of change and development in Islamic history and law. This chapter outlines the teachings of the Qur'an with respect to the rights and responsibilities of women, and then discusses some of the roles played by Muslim women historically, highlighting some of their contributions to Islamic civilization and culture. Against this broader background of the historical development of different Muslim civilisations, she focuses on the role and status of the early generations of Muslim women in society and their intellectual and artistic pursuits in the premodern and modern periods. Included in the discussion is the interpretation of the sources of Islamic law in the modern period and its adverse impact on the rights of Muslim women enshrined in the Qur'an. She concludes her discussion with a brief history of the Muslim community in Canada and the role of women therein.

In Chapter 7, Soraya Hajjaji-Jarrah considers the Qur'an, the classical commentaries on the Qur'an, and the actual language used with respect to veiling and women's clothes. She indicates that much of the present controversy over what constitutes the actual obligations of Muslim women regarding clothing originates not so much from the actual text of the Qur'an, but rather from the classical commentaries written between the tenth and thirteenth centuries CE. She also indicates why the social context of those centuries, a time when slavery was widespread, affected the attitudes of the commentators toward the question of female modesty.

In Chapter 8, L. Clarke, a historian of religion, discusses the *ḥadīth* (the sayings of the Prophet Muhammad) that refer to the obligation to cover the body, to women's space and other related issues. The vast literature of the *ḥadīth* serves as a major source of Islamic law, second only to the Qur'an. Clarke's essay represents the first critical survey in a Western language of the *ḥadīth* texts concerning *ḥijāb*. She also addresses the context in which the materials were written and the current debates over the role of *ḥadīth* in Islamic thought. Clarke's work points to a new direction in recent scholarship that emphasizes contextualizing the collection, inscription and interpretation involved in producing *ḥadīth*.

In sum, this unique collection of essays provides glimpses into Muslim women's lives over a period of fourteen centuries, as persons, women, daughters, wives, mothers, teachers and political leaders. The cultural, ethnic and linguistic diversity of today's Muslim community of over one billion, is spread all over the globe. In Canada, where this diversity of communities is manifest in much smaller numbers, the challenges for Muslim immigrants, who hail from every possible background, are formidable. Having in many instances little or no practical experience of Western culture and lifestyle, Muslim women are confronted with the challenges of adaptation, integration or assimilation in the host culture and are terrified at the thought of losing their religious and cultural identities.[7] In this context *ḥijāb* is promoted by many as one medium of unifying these ethnically diverse adherents of Islam. Others, however, are apprehensive about burdening women with this potent symbol and communalizing a choice they see as representing individual piety and spirituality. The words of Rahat Kurd, whose voice is heard in Chapter 4, reflect this sentiment:

> I've taken the evidence of my alleged piety out of the public realm. I do not say, "I've stopped covering" because I refuse to make any final pronouncements, and because frankly my ears get too cold to go scarfless for long. I no longer believe covering one's hair is a formally required act of worship. At the same time, I know that choosing to wear a scarf can have rich personal meaning, be it a source of comfort, strength, and good subversive fun, and for these

reasons I honour and defend the choice rigorously. In order to keep my own spirituality from exhaustion, to safeguard and nourish it in more substantive ways, I have taken my scarf out of the target range of public fear and desire.[8]

Notes

1 In fact, lively debates emerged at the turn of the twentieth century between conservatives and modernists throughout the Middle East — particularly in Egypt — over whether or not veiling and segregation were required by Islam. These debates resulted in various de-veiling movements (Badran 1995; Amīn 1899, 1900). In Iran and Turkey the modernist state intervened in the first half of the last century and made public veiling illegal; this moved the veiling debate from an issue of religion and piety to the political arena. Veiling has remained a contentious issue in the Middle East ever since (Hoodfar 2001).

2 Although fundamentalism is a problematic analytical concept, I use the term here to refer to those ideological beliefs that interpret text (in this case the Qur'an) without considering the context and spirit in which it was intended.

3 When a community or a society feels under threat, any dissent is viewed as betrayal. Thus Sunera Thobani's recent speech at a conference in Ottawa organized by women on the topic of violence against women, in which she held American foreign policies responsible for the Sept. 11 tragedy, created a national and parliamentary outcry. The story was covered by all national newspapers, as well as on the CBC, on October 3, 2001. The current War Measures Act and proposed anti-terrorist legislation with "a sunset clause" (the date on which the legislation expires) represent codified versions of the attitude that everyone must appear to support the official position in times of crisis.

4 The Canadian Council for Muslim Women (CCMW) was established in 1982 by a group of Muslim women who saw the need for an organization that would focus on the concerns of Muslim women in Canada. Its activities include organizing workshops and conferences, publishing books and article and encouraging more research on issues and concerns of Muslim women. For further information see www.ccmw.org, as well as McDonough and Alvi 2002.

5 For examples of writings in this area, see An-Naʿim 1990; Engineer 1999; Hassan 1994; Mernissi 1987.

6 Most of Abdolkarim Soroush's published works, although translated into Arabic, have not yet been published in English. For an overview of his work in English, see Vakili 1996. Similarly Asgar Ali Engineer's writings have been published mostly in India and by small alternative presses. He does, however, have a web page (www.asienhaus.org/islam/engineer.htm).

7 As a community, Muslims form just 1 per cent of the Canadian population (253,260 in total, according to the 1991 Canadian census, although unofficial estimates put

the present number at 500,000). Muslims are still in their infancy as far as articulating a vision of their place in Canadian society, and in terms of developing educational and community social welfare institutions. For more details, see Kelly 1998a.

8 See Chapter 4 in this volume for the full text of this quotation.

PART I:

Veiling Practices in Everyday Life in Canada

عالم الغيب والشهادة العزيز الحكيم

CHAPTER 1

More Than Clothing: Veiling as an Adaptive Strategy

Homa Hoodfar

Introduction: The Social and Political Dimensions of Clothing

While clothing fulfills a basic human need in most climates, what we wear also has significant social and political functions, serving as a non-verbal medium of ideological communication. However, until the recent surge of interest in popular culture (Barnes and Eicher 1992; Hendrickson 1996; Parkington 1992), few social scientists paid serious attention to this important aspect of clothing. But despite such scholarly neglect, the public, as well as those in power, have always recognized the significance of clothing as a vehicle of communication. Since most people easily and readily understand its non-verbal message, clothing has historically been a potent political tool for both rulers and ruled. A review of the somewhat scanty literature on the history of dress codes, particularly in Europe and the Middle East since the fourteenth century, makes this quite clear (Brewer and Porter 1993; Herald 1981; Perrot 1994; Sponsler 1992; Webb 1912).[1]

Clothing is probably the most silent of expressions used by human societies to demarcate social boundaries and to distinguish "self" from "other" at both the collective and individual levels (Barnes and Eicher

1992; Hendrickson 1996; Rugh 1986). Clothing indicates that the wearer shares certain cultural values with others similarly attired, while minor details may distinguish an individual from others in his or her social group. Thus clothing is a means of visually creating community, while simultaneously delineating individual features of the wearer such as gender, geographical origin, religion, ethnicity, profession, class orientation and life cycle (Abu-Lughod 1986; Rugh 1986). Indicating social hierarchy, unity and collectivity, as well as individuality, clothing's multilayered ability to communicate helps people at first glance to place those they meet within a context, be it class, religion, profession or even political rank, thus shaping subsequent communication.[2] It is this aspect of clothing as identity marker that has made it such a potent political tool for rulers since at least early Pharaonic times in Egypt (Brewer and Porter 1993; Payne 1965).

While a variety of dress codes emerged in Europe from the sixteenth to nineteenth centuries, both through state policy and in reaction to them in the form of popular resistance to such policy, it is perhaps the Ottoman Empire (1299–1922) — with its diverse religious and ethnic groups, and Islamic heritage — that provides the most compelling example of the social functions of clothing (Fandy 1998; Quataert 1997; Shahshahani 1995). The turban in the Ottoman Empire (and in many parts of the Middle East) distinguished social groups in various ways. For instance, certain colours were reserved for members of the court and certain ones for urban Muslims, while others distinguished Armenians from Greeks, just as the particulars of a turban also indicated civilian versus military status; this highly regulated social marker served to reinforce visibly the ranking of society (Quataert 1997, 406). Later, with the weakening of the Empire and increasing breakaway tendencies — particularly among the less privileged ethnic groups — the Ottoman rulers began advocating a unified style of clothing and headgear in order to minimize social divisions and create an illusion of oneness, hoping thus to reinforce loyalty to a unified state (Berkes 1964). Similarly Ataturk, despite considerable popular resistance, decreed European-style hats and clothing for all citizens in the name of

Turkish nationalism and modernity, a project later emulated by other countries, notably Iran and Afghanistan (Baker 1997; Fandy 1998).

While early dress codes were mostly concerned with male attire, the most controversial aspects of modern dress codes in Turkey and the Middle East have been those pertaining to women, and the debates over women's attire are particularly pertinent to the central focus of this chapter, i.e., the practice of veiling by Muslim women in North America and Europe. In this chapter, based on data collected during the period 1993–1996, I examine the social forces that encourage women outside Muslim societies to veil, and consider the implications of the "veiling movement" for Muslim communities, for the larger societies in which they are located and for gender relations among Muslims living in Canada and, by implication, in North America and Europe. By placing the debate over veiling into this broader context, I hope to avoid replicating methodological and epistemological problems present in many studies on veiling, which focus narrowly on the veil as a religious artifact but avoid analyzing it in its broader historical and social contexts. For this reason, I briefly review here the origins of the veil, and its emergence as an indisputable symbol of "Muslimness," before attempting to explore the meaning of the veil within the Canadian context.

The Veil and Colonial Discourse

In contrast to men's clothing, which was historically subject to legal rules in the Middle East, women's clothing was largely a concern of public mores. Historically, until the twentieth century there seems to have been little resistance to changes in women's dress or the adoption by women of diverse styles. One significant reason for this lack of concern with women's clothing may stem from the fact that, by the nineteenth century, women were largely excluded from formal political and public life. As well, even as women's clothing styles expanded, veiling became more encompassing. For instance, around the middle of the same century a thick black veil had come to replace the *yashmak*, the thin and filmy white veil worn by Turkish women. Similarly in Iran, the black *chador*, a long cloak that covers women from head to ankle, was becoming more widespread in most urban centres. The black veil/*chador* communicated to the public, particularly to men, that women's clothing was a private matter, not a public concern.[3]

With the expansion of European power and influence in Ottoman/Middle Eastern economies and politics, a huge body of "scholarly" and travel accounts of the people of the region emerged.[4] Considerable attention was paid by (mostly male) European writers to veiling practices (and, to a lesser degree, polygyny), and the alleged objectionable treatment of Muslim women by their male kin (Kabbani 1986; Mabro 1991). Implicitly or explicitly, the mission of these writings was to depict Muslim cultures as inferior/backward and in need of progress (Alloula 1986). It is important to note that modesty — particularly expressed through clothing and through varying degrees of gender segregation — has historically been practised by a wide variety of communities, including most Mediterranean peoples, regardless of religion. Indeed, prior to the nineteenth century, the veil was never viewed as a symbol of Muslim culture; the practice of the veiling and seclusion of women is in fact pre-Islamic and originates in non-Arab Middle Eastern and Mediterranean societies (Keddie and Beck 1978). The first reference to veiling dates to an Assyrian legal text of the thirteenth century BC, which restricted the practice to "respectable" women and forbade prostitutes from veiling (Keddie and Baron 1991, 3). Historically, veiling — especially when accompanied by seclusion — was a sign of status and was practised by the elite in the ancient Greco-Roman, pre-Islamic Iranian and Byzantine empires. Muslims subsequently adopted the veil and seclusion, and today it is widely recognized, by Muslims and non-Muslims, as an Islamic phenomenon, presumably sanctioned by the Qur'an.

However, despite belief to the contrary, veiling — particularly in the sense of covering one's hair — is nowhere specifically recommended or even discussed in the Qur'an (Hajjaji-Jarrah in this volume; Hassan 1994; Mernissi 1991a). At the heart of the Qur'anic position on the question of the veil is the interpretation of two verses (*Sūrat al-Nūr*, verses 30–31), which recommend that women cover their bosoms and adornments; this has been interpreted by some that women should cover themselves. Another verse recommends that the wives of the Prophet wrap their cloaks tightly around their bodies, so as to be recognized and not be bothered or molested in public (Sūrah al-Aḥzāb, verse 59). Soraya Hajjaji-Jarrah, in another contribution to this volume, has traced the development of the ideology of veiling and seclusion in early Islamic history. By reviewing the works of several scholars of the early Islamic period, she demonstrates that the idea of veiling and seclusion developed later as a consequence of the widespread phenomenon of slave women in the wealthy, urban centres of the Islamic empire. Nonetheless, it was not until the Ottoman Empire — which extended into most of the area that is today known as the Middle East and North Africa — and particularly until the reign of the Safavids (1501–1722) in Iran that the veil emerged as a widespread symbol of status among the Muslim ruling classes and urban elite. It is noteworthy that it is only since the nineteenth century, after the veil was promoted by the colonial occupiers as a prominent symbol of Muslim societies, especially in the travelogues and scholarly publications noted above, that Muslims have justified veiling as Islamic rather than as a cultural practice (Esposito 1988).[5]

Broadly speaking, one can recognize two different reactions on the part of Middle Eastern Muslims to these representations, though neither decried them as inaccurate. The first group, recognizing their pejorative nature, responded by advocating that the veil be abandoned. This constituency also advocated education for women, in part to increase their public participation. The second more conservative group claimed, on the other hand, that the veil was inherent to Muslim cultures and is a sign of their moral superiority. This group urged that veiling be preserved, insisting that any attempt to discard or modify veiling would push Muslim society toward immorality and decay. As well, they fundamentally opposed a higher public profile for women, and thus were hostile to girls' schools even when run and staffed exclusively by women, adopting — initially at least — a rigorous stance regarding veiling in Islamic educational institutions (Badran 1995;

Hoodfar 2000; Paidar 1995). Drawing on the popular perception of veiling as a religious practice, the conservatives galvanized some public opposition to unveiling and to the education of girls.[6] However, the issue of seclusion was difficult for the conservatives to justify or promote, in part because for all but the wealthiest segments of society, women's economic as well as reproductive labour was essential for the survival of their households. In reality, the majority of social classes, particularly in rural areas, practised segregation and sexual division of labour rather than seclusion. Thus, the goal of educating girls in all-girls schools was perfectly congruent with this practice.

Nonetheless, the veil, and to a lesser extent clothing in general, formed the symbolic battlefield on which the modernists and conservatives fought out their differences. After World War I, both women's education and unveiling gained increasing support among the urban populations of the Middle East, making it easier for the modernists, whose political presence was expanding, to press for de-veiling. In Egypt, women had become a visible political and intellectual force, participating in anti-colonial and democratic struggles. They organized themselves in both small and in larger, more formal groups to debate issues relating to the status of women. These issues included veiling, which most politicized women at the time viewed as a corruption of Islamic ideals instituted by men in the name of Islam to prevent women's advancement. In 1928, Egyptian women activists publicly removed their veils amid public debate.

In other countries, such as Afghanistan, Iran and Turkey, the state played a direct role in discouraging the veil.[7] Although national rhetoric championed de-veiling as a strategy to liberate women and involve them in modern nation building, in reality women's interests and position were incidental — if they mattered at all. The "women's question" was simply the arena where the political struggle for power between the secular modernists and the religious authorities took place. The struggle pitted modernist governments, eager to loosen the hold of the religious authorities who had historically shared the state's power, against the clergy, who opposed the trend toward secularization because it would divorce them from political power and, in particular, deny them the monopoly over education they had enjoyed for centuries.

Thus, de-veiling laws were significant on at least two levels: they alienated religious leaders from the political structure and, through legislation, confirmed European culture as the model to emulate, hence the insistence on Western clothing for men and women as well as on de-veiling. It was on this ground that women's attempts to adapt to the new requirements, while retaining a sense of comfort by wearing headscarves and modest local dress, were rejected. Clearly, unveiling was more than a simple clothing reform instituted to encourage women's participation in national economies and public affairs. As many argued, these goals were achievable without having to reproduce Western clothing styles — mobility and public participation for women was attainable through the modest attire that accommodated Muslim or local mores, as was the case in many Muslim cultures. It is, of course, very telling that in the drive toward modernization, the fledgling nations' goal of emulating European society engendered laws more concerned with clothing than with individual freedoms and the democratic rights of citizens, though the latter were viewed by these same democratic forces as the heart and soul of European civilization — and the very root of European dominance over the Middle East.

Given the continued absence of democratic participation and the omnipresence of censorship, it is not surprising that for the populace clothing remained an important vehicle for political expression and for contesting state ideology. For instance, both the socialists and those who favoured a particular brand of Islamist ideology wore a distinctive style of clothing that silently proclaimed their political positions and opposition to government policy. It was in this context that the world witnessed the arrests, during the 1980s, of male students attempting to enter Egyptian universities in traditional Egyptian clothing. Few Egyptians were surprised that they were charged with the political crime of subverting the state. Similarly, the ban against Turkish women wearing headscarves when attending university, taking official exams or sitting in Parliament stemmed from the recognition that their presence represents a rejection of the state ideology. Thus it is not surprising that the presence of veiled women — women clothed in long, loose dresses and head coverings — has attracted so much attention nationally and internationally. In the absence of democracy in most Middle Eastern countries, Islamist political groups promote the veil as a symbol of their public presence and their political will, both to the public and to the state.

Similarly, the black-veiled women who participated en masse in the 1978 Iranian revolution became the most powerful symbol of the revolution and its rejection of the previous government's gender ideology and Westernization. Iran's new Islamic regime, well aware of the symbolic power of the veil after more than a century of political struggle between secularists and Islamists, initially encouraged the practice. Later, however, it went so far as to enforce it through legislation and even violence, so important had the veil become as a symbol of its political triumph over secular forces. The draconian nature of compulsory veiling laws, with beatings, fines and imprisonment for non-compliance, is in principle no different from the compulsory de-veiling that had taken place some forty years earlier. This clearly indicates that, once again, neither woman's rights nor democratic rights were concerns of the Islamic state. These interventions have invested clothing with ever more political meaning. Iranian women have responded to the unwelcome state interference in their choice of attire by pursuing several initiatives. Fashion and makeup have become important vehicles for expressing resistance, which has meant ever-increasing employment opportunities in the ranks of the despised moral police who patrol the streets of urban centres in Iran (Hoodfar forthcoming[b]).

The political space and debate devoted in the Middle East to the issue of clothing, and in particular the veil, indicate that the latter is far more than just a head cover. In many ways the veil remains a most potent political and social tool. If it is true that a picture is worth a thousand words, the image of veiled women can account for literally hundreds of political speeches, whether as a symbol of opposition to the state, an expression of particular religious currents, a symbol of patriarchy and misogynist tradition, a declaration of Muslim identity in primarily non-Muslim society or a reassurance to one's family that one's respect for Muslim mores remains strong despite unconventional activities and circumstances. It is from this perspective that I examine the use of the veil in the daily lives of Muslim women generally, before turning to the politics of veiling in Canada.

The Veil in Practice

Although in Western literature veiling is often presented as a uniform and static practice going back over 1,000 years, the veil itself has had many variations and has been subject to changing fashion throughout history and in modern times. Moreover, like other articles of clothing, the veil may be worn for multiple reasons. It may be worn to beautify the wearer (Chatty 1996; Wikan 1982), much in the same way Western women wear makeup; to demonstrate respect for conventional values (Abu-Lughod 1986; Hoodfar 1991); or to hide the wearer's identity (Fernea 1965). Today, veiling typically consists of a long, loosely fitted dress of any colour combination worn with a scarf wrapped in various fashions so as to cover all the hair. Nonetheless, the imaginary veil that comes to the minds of most Westerners is an awkward black cloak that covers the whole body, including the face, and which is designed to prevent women's mobility (Dickey 1994).[8] Throughout history, however, except for among the elite, women's labour was vital to the household economy and women's clothing of necessity ensured freedom of movement. Even a cursory survey of clothing habits in rural and urban settings, both in the Middle East and in other Muslim cultures, indicates that women's costumes, though all considered Islamic, cover the body to widely varying degrees (Rugh 1986). The tendency of Western scholarly work and the colonial authorities to present a one-dimensional image of Islam, encompassing a seamless society of Muslims, precluded the exploration of the socio-economic significance of such variation, which is nevertheless widely evident, even in their own drawings and paintings.[9] Similarly, scholarly study of Islamic beliefs and culture has focused on Islamic texts, but generally overlooks the actual variations in the way Islam has been and is being practised.

The Research

Until the mid-1980s, when veiling began attracting attention in Europe and North America, debate and concerns regarding veiling seemed to be limited to the Middle East, particularly in relation to Iran, Egypt and the Gulf countries. Outside this region, what has made veiling so perplexing to many non-Muslims over the last fifteen years or so is the apparent fact that many of the young women in Europe and North America who have taken up the veil have been raised, if not in fact born, in the "West." The controversies surrounding the veil and the sometimes hostile attitude toward veiling and veiled women, combined with the insistence of the Diaspora Muslim community in presenting the veil as an Islamic symbol of Muslim identity, have given birth to a political battle where few combatants or onlookers have bothered to re-examine their assumptions about the veil or its implications for the women who wear it. The following data and discussion examine the politics of contemporary veiling from the perspective of Muslim women within the Canadian social and political context.

Given the intimate nature of the data this research required, and given the importance of age hierarchy in most Muslim cultures (Hoodfar 1995), anthropology by proxy was the most suitable research method. A research team was formed consisting of twelve Muslim women of different ages, both veiled and unveiled, with diverse cultural origins and trained in anthropology and other social sciences. Several workshops were also organized at McGill and Concordia universities in Montreal, as well as workshops in mosques in Ottawa and Toronto, to discuss the concerns of Muslim women. In light of these discussions, I prepared a guideline for interviews. Each of the research assistants then interviewed some ten young women from among their own friends and relatives. Each in-depth interview lasted two to eight hours, often extending over several sessions. We also carried out some interviews with the parents of our respondents.

The respondents ranged in age from fifteen to thirty-three, with the large majority between the ages of nineteen and twenty-three. In the tradition of anthropology, I rely in this paper on representative statements from the interviewees, or quote from my notes, where, as a rule, the informant's statements are recorded in the first person. At times, I have added explanatory phrases in order to situate the discussion, especially for non-Muslims readers who may be unfamiliar with the particular context to which the quotes are referring.

However, several important points must first be made. On examining the data it quickly became apparent that Somalis and Iranians occupy opposite poles with respect to their views on Muslim communities and Muslim women. The Iranians, who for the most part left Iran to escape the impositions of the Islamic Republic and in particular compulsory veiling, were very critical and skeptical of the veil and Islam (at least as interpreted by the Iranian regime) having anything to offer the Muslim community and in particular women. Interestingly, this group of Iranian women included a few supporters of the regime at the time studying in Canada — women who, while having a stronger religious inclination, nonetheless believe that Islam needs revision and reinterpretation if it is to survive and remain relevant to Muslims.

At the other extreme, the Somali women, many of whom had come to Canada as refugees escaping years of civil war and upheaval, turned to Islam and the Muslim community for support upon their arrival. As a symbolic gesture to confirm their allegiance to the Muslim community, the Somalis abandoned some traditional practices and especially traditional costumes in favour of modern "Muslim" clothing.[10] Since the Somali population is relatively small and new in Canada, without its own community centres or other formal organizations to support the newcomers in adjusting to their new home, for many Somalis emphasizing their membership and participating in the Muslim community is a means of coping with a new culture and social system. Mosques and the Muslim community provide support and a sense of belonging, crucial "for their mental health," as one Somali community worker put it. Given the ethnic divisions that exist among Muslims in Canada, absorption of newly arrived Muslim immigrants plays a critical role in the construction of a common, hybrid Muslim identity that transcends ethnic and cultural boundaries to assert a "Muslim" community and Islamic mores in Canadian society (Waardenburg 1988). Given this context, a detailed comparative analysis of these two Muslim cultural groups — Iranians and Somalis — deserves special consideration and historical conceptualization, a task that lies beyond the scope of this paper. Thus, except for highly pertinent and representative material, I have not focused greatly on this section of data.[11]

Veiling in Canada

The data revealed several compelling and very surprising results, some of which totally contradicted many commonly held assumptions, as well as some of my own preconceptions. The first of these to be disproven concerned the family backgrounds and cultural origins of the majority of young veiled university students and graduates. I had assumed that one major reason for the increase in the number of veiled Muslim women stemmed from changes in Canadian immigration policy. Until 1967 it would have been difficult for most people from Muslim countries, except those highly educated and wealthy (as well as "Westernized"), to emigrate to Canada (Kelly 1998a). In more recent decades, however, some discriminatory measures have been removed, and, more importantly, the needs of the labour market have changed from requiring highly educated professionals to skilled and semiskilled workers. This would, in theory, have allowed more people with religious backgrounds — including families who continued to observe veiling practices — to immigrate to Canada. With the second generation of these more recently arrived families now at university, we observed the presence of young veiled women at universities and in the labour force. The data, however, indicates that only seven out of sixty-nine of the mothers on whom we have data, wore the veil.

With the exception of two women, all Pakistani women wore their national clothing (the *shalvār qamīṣ*). Many of the others either wore the national long dresses (*jalābahs*) or opted for modest dresses, none of which necessarily incorporate the veil. These mothers may be described as being rather conventional. Neither the daughters, nor the mothers, nor the Muslim community consider such outfits to constitute veiling, except when a modern scarf is worn along with the traditional costume. Generally speaking, among our sample, considerable numbers of young, veiled women came from more conventional backgrounds, i.e., families that observed their heritage culture's norms and values — particularly as these related to male and female interactions — rather than from more religious families. The distinction, though perhaps a subtle one for North Americans whose understanding has been shaped by persistent colonial images of Muslims, is nonetheless considerable for Muslims. The data, as I shall demonstrate below, indicate that young Muslim women employ this distinction to reject those aspects of their parents' culture, which they see as incompatible with their view of Islam, rather than appearing to deny their ethnic roots or their parents' values.

In Canada, and particularly in Quebec, many feminists and Quebec nationalists who have advocated banning the veil in public schools claim that young women are forced by their families to wear the veil, and that banning it will free young women from such oppression. However, we did not find any evidence to support such claims among the participants in this study. Moreover, one very unexpected finding was that many young women had to fight with their parents — who in many cases had come to Canada to give their daughters "better opportunities" — for the right to wear the veil. Furthermore, while some mothers felt powerless to deny their daughters' decision to veil, they themselves did not associate veiling with Islam. Other parents reluctantly accepted their daughters' decision and continued to hope that the young women would "come to their senses" and give up the veil. Two fathers, after failing to convince their daughters not to veil, refused to talk to them for several months. Another father told me:

> I had to accept her choice; there was nothing I could do. I convinced myself that at least I did not have to fear that she is running around with unsuitable company, getting drunk or worse, coming home

> with the news of an out-of-wedlock pregnancy. But it was not easy. My father and his generation fought to remove the veil and free women and bring them into public life. Now how can I explain that my daughter, two generations later and in Montreal, chooses to take up the veil? Just as well that my father is not alive to see this.

I had also hypothesized that if women attended religious gatherings in mosques they might have been encouraged to take up the veil. However, many of the veiled women, particularly in Montreal, did not visit mosques for prayer or other religious activities. In fact, it emerged that weekend Qur'an lessons were not generally held in mosques. Some of the women said they had started attending mosque infrequently, but only some years *after* they began veiling. Many of the university students in the sample did frequent the university prayer room — where such a room existed — to rest, socialize with other Muslim women or to pray. Their reasons for not going to mosque varied: the Toronto women said the mosques were too far away; in Montreal the women claimed the mosques were not "real," that they were dirty or that the Imam knew only the Qur'an and old-fashioned *fiqh* (Islamic jurisprudence), but nothing about issues pertinent to Muslims living in North America. One young woman said:

> I understand why our grandmothers did not go to the mosques [in many Arab countries women did not traditionally go to mosque but prayed at home. This situation has been changing rapidly in most of the Arab world since the mid-1970s], if the mosques were as dirty and unwelcoming as they are here, with men standing at the door to tell you, "pull your scarf down and cover your hair" or something like that, just to reiterate their power over you as men. They forget that at the very least in the house of God they should obey the Qur'anic injunction and not look and examine a woman's physical appearance. You know, something worse about men in the mosque here is that so many women who go there get offers of marriage within a few minutes of their arrival. These places in

> Montreal are not real mosques. I have been in Egypt and Jordan. I know how a mosque is supposed to be. When there is a real mosque here, I will go all the time.

After further conversation, she smiled and said with a twinkle in her eye:

> Maybe me and a few other women will set up Montreal's first real mosque, just like we have set up our own Muslim women's group, which has worked well for the last two years. Why not? We will let men in only on Fridays and only in the back!

Our own and other more recent data indicate that young women are increasingly attending mosque (Haddad 2002, Meshal in this volume). There has also been an increase in the number of mosques and Islamic religious centres, discussion groups, youth camps and Internet sites where women can participate in discussion and debate, particularly younger women.[12] Some of the more established mosques organize talks, often in Arabic, on issues of interest to the various Muslim communities. Women also participate in social activities, including picnics and organized outings. As well, the Muslim community has become more politicized since the Gulf War and the conflict in Bosnia, from which Muslims were forced to flee for their lives. Montreal mosques, in particular, have become community centres as well as places of worship, as have many mosques in Toronto.

When we asked our veiled informants why they chose to veil, the majority said the veil was part of their religion and that they wanted to be good Muslim women. Only four out of fifty-nine veiled women claimed the veil to be part of their Arab or Muslim identity and not an Islamic requirement. Another woman said she was not really religious, and that she was not really sure if Islam required women to wear the veil, since neither of her grandmothers, both from very religious backgrounds, had ever taken up the practice. But she felt that in the context of North America the veil enables her to be a "person" rather than an object of male scrutiny. A closer reading of the interview transcripts regarding women's decisions to take up the veil reveals a somewhat different story, however. Beyond personal or religious convictions, there seem to be several overlapping reasons influencing them to adopt the custom. Some are individual in nature, while others stem from a communal impetus.

One common factor precipitating the decision to veil involved restrictive parents. Most girls said that once they reached the age of thirteen or fourteen, their parents were reluctant to let them visit their friends, particularly if the friends were not Muslim or were of a different cultural background. This was particularly objectionable to the young women, whose brothers by contrast enjoyed great freedom. Also frustrating was the disparity they observed between themselves and their Canadian or Québecoise friends, whose freedom and autonomy increased rather than diminished as they became teens. Increasing restrictions placed on Muslim girls as they entered the teenage years was common even among more educated and generally more "modernized" parents. Even when they were younger the women had recognized that their parents had their best interests and protection at heart, though they may not have agreed with their methods. Parental fears concerning drinking, sexual activity and possible pregnancy are even more pronounced among Muslim parents; the consequences of such actions for Muslim women, who must according to religious law marry Muslim men, and generally from within their own community, are inevitably disastrous. The interviewees noted that a woman whose reputation is questionable will have a difficult time finding a husband. Nevertheless, despite understanding their parents' concerns, many girls found themselves in conflict at home.

Under such circumstances the veil offers a means to mitigate parental and social concerns. Many of the women said that if they had realized how veiling could alleviate such parental fears, they would have taken it up even earlier. Reem, for instance, is seventeen and is very grateful for the peace and quiet that she has finally found in her heart and home since she began veiling:

I was two and my brother five when we came from Pakistan to Canada. We had other relatives here in Quebec, which was good, since it meant we were not lonely. My parents were both educated and professional and seemed to adjust to life here. We had friends of all sorts and played with them in the alley. The only thing different about us was that we had funny names, ate different food and my parents played different music, which sometimes became the subject of jokes among our friends, but nothing severe.

After I turned twelve my parents did not want me to visit my Canadian friends and more and more I had to stay home. I hated it because all my childhood friends had started to go to cinema and picnic with each other, but I had to stay home. Worse was that now I was expected to wear traditional clothing except when I was going to school, and God forbid if I wanted to try wearing a little makeup, because all hell would break loose in our house. If I was half an hour late from school, my mother would be out in the street looking for me, and then there was hell to pay for days.

This was very hurtful for me, because I didn't understand it. Even if my mother had lived that way in Pakistan, it didn't mean that I should live like this in Canada. After all, what was the point of coming to Canada if we were going to behave the same? What bothered me most and made it harder for me to put up with all these restrictions was that they did not apply to my brother because he was a boy. Of course, he was not as free as most of his friends, but the difference between my life and his was considerable. Sometimes he felt sorry for me and took me out. Other times, to hurt me, as siblings do, he would remind me that as a Muslim woman I have to be housebound and in my place. I had big fights with my parents and life was miserable. As news of my disagreement with my parents spread, other Pakistani families did not want to visit us, or if they did, they left their daughters at home for fear of being influenced by me. So my life became lonelier.

It was during this time that one of our relatives took up the veil.

> Like me she had had problems at home. She said that since she started wearing the veil, she feels so much happier and freer. It is as though she has suddenly matured in the eyes of her parents and everyone else. Now she is allowed to drive, to go to her friends or to have them come home. We talked and I spent more time with her. My parents were happy that I was spending time with a good Muslim girl. Then I decided to take the veil and my life has changed. It is true that I cannot have boyfriends and do some of the things my school girlfriends do. But I never wanted to do those things anyway. I know that I am a Muslim and I cannot have sexual relations before marriage. Now my parents respect me. I go to Qur'anic classes, I spend time with my friends, and not all of them are Muslim; some are Hindu and one is a Christian of Indian origin. I also have some Muslim-only get-togethers. Since I have my licence now, I can even have the car when I want it, something I never thought my parents would allow me. My brother respects me too. I do not know what happened. But I know that now that I wear the veil, no one in my family and community disrespects me. I wish I had taken it even earlier.

An articulate nineteen-year-old Palestinian woman told me:

> The veil has freed me from arguments and headaches. I always wanted to do many things that women normally do not do in my culture. I had thought living in Canada would give me that opportunity. But when I turned fourteen, my life changed. My parents started to limit my activities and even telephone conversations. My brothers were free to go and come as they pleased, but my sister and I were to be good Muslim girls. Even the books we read became subject to inspection. Life became intolerable for me. The weekends were hell.
>
> Then as a way out, I asked to go to Qur'anic classes on Saturdays. There I met with several veiled women of my age. They came from similar backgrounds. None of them seemed to face my

> problems. Some told me that since they took the veil, their parents know that they are not going to do anything that goes against Muslim morality. The more I hung around with them, the more convinced I was that the veil is the answer to all Muslim girls' problems here in North America. Because parents seem to be relieved and assured that you are not going to do stupid things, and your community knows that you are acting like a Muslim woman, you are much freer. Now I am happy, and since I go to Islamic study group, I have learnt a lot. From studying *true Islam* [emphasis added], and comparing notes with Muslims from other countries like Egypt and Syria, I have also realized that so much of what our parents impose on us in the name of Islam is not Islam but it is their cultural practice. So I can discuss with them and sometimes I succeed in changing their minds.

These narratives were typical of many young women who took up the veil toward the end of high school or upon entering university. In a sense, they had recognized the effectiveness of the veil in communicating certain values. By taking up the veil, they symbolically but clearly announce to their parents and their community that, despite their unconventional activities and involvement with non-Muslims, they retain their Islamic mores and values. They are modern Muslim women who want to be educated and publicly active, but not at the cost of their moral principles.

Some women said that since donning the veil, it has become easier to interact with men, both Muslim and non-Muslim:

> Previously, it was always the worry that maybe there would be a misunderstanding, that someone might think I was propositioning them [men], or that if someone sees me talking or walking with a man, they might think he is my boyfriend, and that of course is not good for one's reputation in the community. Since taking the veil these worries about talking with classmates or colleagues have disappeared.

Veiling also makes it clear to Muslim and non-Muslim men that the veiled women are not available for dating. The veil is a powerful means of communicating all these messages without uttering a word, and with this understanding, it is not surprising that women have discovered and adopted it.

There are other reasons behind the choice to veil or to adopt other perceived Islamic symbols, including religious language. In most Muslim cultures, parents have considerable influence in the choice of their child's spouse. This practice is usually justified with reference to Islam. While sons may have a voice in matters of marriage, in many contexts girls have limited opportunities to speak out, though passing on their wishes and feelings through close relatives is one of these. In the North American context, however, this channel is very limited because there are fewer aunts and uncles who can discreetly elicit a girl's views and advocate on her behalf in conversation with her parents. In their zeal to protect their daughters' reputations, some parents marry their daughters off against their wishes, sometimes at a young age when it is harder to resist. Islam, however, expressly gives all adult men and women the right to choose their spouse, though in some branches of Islam a first-time bride needs her father's consent as well. By increasing their Islamic knowledge of matters such as these, and through appearing to be serious and committed to Islam, many women have successfully resisted unwanted marriage arrangements without alienating their parents. Farida's story describes such a situation:

> When I was seventeen my father wanted to arrange a marriage for me to a guy from Pakistan. He had talked about this match before, but I had not taken it seriously. I knew that he worried I might fall in love and want to marry a person they wouldn't find acceptable. But since I had demonstrated my commitment as a student, and had taken the veil, I thought he was reassured. However, he went ahead with the marriage arrangements, and persisted despite my objections. I tried to get our relatives and friends here in Canada involved, but it did not work. It only made him more insistent. He

thought my objection was in itself proof that I was becoming too Canadian. He said for generations girls in his family had married whomever their fathers had chosen, and he was not about to allow a sixteen-year-old to break centuries of Islamic tradition.

So I went and studied Islamic books, sought knowledgeable people's views and prepared my arguments with references to Qu'ran and Islamic texts. I told my mother that I had talked to the Imam, who said that if I were married against my wishes, in the eyes of God the marriage would not be valid. I want to study, and if my father pushes me into marriage, according to Islam he has condemned me to a sinful life. I told her that a marriage without my consent, which is my Islamic right, is not an Islamic marriage. The same way as my marriage without my father's consent is also un-Islamic. I told my mother if he forces me into this marriage, he has to carry the sin as I do not give my consent.

I let all the friends and neighbours know my views; I also criticized their imposing outdated culture on us in the name of Islam. I told my parents and others that their mistake is that they have never bothered to read and learn Islam for themselves. Everyone was impressed by my knowledge of Islam and many young women became interested in having a discussion group. The marriage was called off on the pretense of me wanting to continue my education. My father, who saw that even in the heat of the debate I never denied his authority and rights as a father, did not hold this against me and I have heard him saying that he was proud of me. My using Islam as the basis of my rejection of the marriage, without reference to my right under Canadian law or the like, made it easier for my father to save face among his friends. After all, as you said earlier, Islam enjoys a much higher order of legitimacy than any laws and traditions. I have heard my mother pointing out to her friends, with some pleasure, that the world has turned upside down and they have ended up learning their religion from their Canadian children rather than from their Muslim parents back home.

Farida further explained that many young Muslim women increase their opportunities within their families and communities, and secure greater respect, by studying Islam and its diverse interpretations. In many ways, young Muslims in Canada view modernity and Islam as being fully compatible. Their education, along with their much broader contacts with Muslims of diverse ethnic backgrounds, has allowed them to separate cultural traditions and norms from what they view as religion and, more importantly, to privilege those interpretations of Islam that are more acceptable to them — a choice that their parents, having been brought up in a mono-Muslim culture and given only limited access to religious education, in most cases did not have.

It is important to note that many young women have witnessed unhappy marriages and sometimes divorce among Muslim friends and relatives who married against the wishes of their parents, and this has deterred them from discarding traditional practices and the support of their families and culture. We heard many second-hand stories of love marriages not blessed by parents, which turned out to be disastrous for the Muslim women involved. Our interviewees seemed to believe that using Islamic arguments to oppose certain restrictions or practices seems to be a much more effective and appropriate strategy than defiance. As one woman pointed out, veiling and learning about Islam has enabled young Muslim women to have their cake and eat it at the same time. They have the freedom to do much of what they want, and also have the support and protection of their families.

Fatemeh is a good illustration of this. Aged twenty-three and very happy with her life, she recently completed a degree in chemistry in Toronto and has worked for a few years, but is planning to pursue graduate studies. She told me:

> I wanted to go to university and there was no university in our area. In any case I wanted to go and live by myself and experience that kind of life as well. Everyone said I was crazy, that my parents would never let me do that. My older brother left for university in London, Ontario and there was no problem. Then it was my turn, but my father said it

> was out of the question, particularly because I wanted to go to Toronto, and not where my brother was. I stayed home for one year. During that year I took the veil and studied religious text and the more I read and thought about it, the more I felt I was suffering unjust discrimination that had no Islamic basis. In Islam parents are obliged to educate both their daughters and sons. I applied for university again and insisted on my Islamic rights and criticized my parents for misunderstanding Islam. Finally, they agreed. I guess they realized that I am so strong in my religious beliefs that, although in our little town it was not easy, I chose to wear the veil of my own free will. So they did not have to worry about my reputation or that I won't be able to find a good Muslim husband, or that I will fall in love with a non-Muslim, or start drinking or any of the things our Muslim parents are worried about. So my father came with me to Toronto, found me a place to live and I went to university. After my brother graduated, everyone moved to Toronto and I moved back home. Now I am my father's favourite child. I am a committed Muslim and a highly educated modern woman. I am very respectful of my parents as is my Islamic duty. Moreover, the Muslim community also thinks highly of me, because I am very active in community matters. To the community, I represent the best of Canada and Islam and modernity, so many urge their daughters to see me as a role model.

Some of the young women defend veiling, though they themselves do not veil. They suggest that much of the fuss in non-Muslim Canadian society over veiling, such as debates about banning veils from public schools, stems from anti-Muslim sentiment. They point out that wearing strange and unconventional clothing, tattooing, and piercing noses, lips and eyebrows — practices that many students engage in — go unremarked. Nahed, age sixteen, asked:

> Why is it that nobody is worried that these individuals, who are much more numerous in Canada than veiled women, might be

> oppressed? Or that they may be mutilating their bodies? We know that the fuss is all about their prejudices against Islam and the Muslim community. It makes me so angry that sometimes I feel like taking the veil to spite them.

In many ways Muslims themselves wish to deny the expressive power of the veil. I suggested therefore to Nahed that, while society may understand what is being communicated by radical hairdos and body-piercing, perhaps this same society does not quite understand or is worried about the message the Muslim community is sending through veiling. Nahed thought for a moment and said, "I don't think so. I do not see them trying to understand it. They are just using it as an excuse to vilify the Muslim community. Maybe you are philosophizing too much. I do not see much goodwill out there, just a lot of hypocrisy."

Many girls who don't veil, but have friends who do, recognize the benefits of hanging around with veiled friends. Afsaneh, a sixteen-year-old Iranian, complained about the restrictions her parents imposed when she turned thirteen, but said things had improved since she became friends with two Arab girls who wear the veil. Prior to this she couldn't go out with friends or even to a movie, while her three brothers had a fine time participating in sports clubs, travelling and staying with friends. Since meeting her two friends at school, she is allowed to go out with them, and they visit each other. I asked her why she thinks things have changed. She replied:

> It is obvious. Although my parents are not very strict Muslims and in fact came to Canada to escape the daily oppression of the Islamic regime of Iran, they don't approve of many things here in Canada. They worry about things that all parents, but particularly Muslim parents, worry about — that I will start drinking, that I will get a boyfriend or get into sexual relations. That would, in their minds, ruin my reputation and my future chances of marriage. But if I am hanging around with veiled women and go out with them to cinema

> or stay at their home, they know that I am not getting into trouble. More importantly, the community sees me with the veiled women, so they know that I am a virtuous young woman and not after finding a boyfriend and all things they consider evil.

I asked Afsaneh why she did not take the veil herself, since it would probably offer her even more freedom. She replied:

> Oh no. For one thing, though I defend the right of women to wear the veil, I don't see it as a necessary part of Islam. I know that at the time of the Prophet, people did not wear these kinds of clothes and these things are all made up to control women. Look at what is happening in Iran [referring to compulsory veiling and codification of *sharīʻah* laws that have rendered women second-class citizens]. Moreover, my parents would not want me to wear the veil because it probably would restrict the chances of me finding a husband in the Iranian community, something they desire for me. You know Iranians, having experienced the Islamic Republic that forced women to wear a veil instead of encouraging both men and women to avoid clothes that are seductive, this has turned a lot of people, including religious people like my parents, against the veil. But my parents wish me to hang around with good Muslim women.

It is clear from Afsaneh's statement, and other similar cases, that in the context of Canada, where women can choose whether or not to veil, veiling can be an indicator of a woman's commitment to Islamic mores. Despite her parents' ambivalence toward veiling, which they associate with the oppressive regime in Iran, they approve of Afsaneh's friendships with veiled women. This underscores the symbolic value of the veil as an effective vehicle for communicating a multiplicity of immediate visual messages.

There were other issues regarding identity and belonging that induced some of the younger women to begin veiling. Some felt isolated at school as they matured and their parents increasingly restricted their participation in various school activities, which invariably led to social exclusion. Activities such as gym class and swimming strained relations between the female Muslim students and their schoolmates. Parents sent letters excusing their daughters from swimming lessons on the basis that Muslim women should not reveal their bodies to unrelated men. This frequently made them the subject of discussion and occasionally of ridicule, even at times from teachers. The Muslim girls always wore tracksuits for gym. Though other students wore similar attire, some interviewees said it was only the Muslim girls who were the butt of jokes in this regard. They were made to feel like outsiders, not quite up to the standards of Canadian society. In this situation, taking up the veil was a means of turning the tables, actively asserting identity as opposed to being identified as different by exclusion or ostracism. By choosing to veil, they defined themselves, establishing their own collective to the exclusion of others. Seventeen-year-old Ziba from Pakistan explains:

> We came from Pakistan and since we had many friends and relatives, we lived near them. Financially we were not so badly off and that made it easier. Although we did not intermingle much with non-Indian-Canadians, I very much felt at home and part of the wider society. This, however, changed as I got older and clearly my life was different than many girls in my class. I did not talk about boyfriends and did not go out. I did not participate in extracurricular activities. Gradually, I began feeling isolated. Then my cousin and I decided together to wear the veil and made a pact to ignore people's comments, that no matter how much hardship we suffered at school, we would keep our veils on.
>
> One weekend we announced this to our surprised parents. They were perplexed that their fifteen- and sixteen-year-olds had decided to take such a drastic measure without consulting them. At that time, there were not very many Pakistani women in Montreal who wore the modern veil. Most women wear our traditional clothes. Our

> parents consented, though they did not think we would stick with it. But we did. At first it was difficult. At school people joked and asked stupid questions, but after three months they took us more seriously and there was even a little bit of respect. People no longer invited us to their parties, knowing we could not go, and we did not have to apologize or explain. The teachers did not try to convince our parents that swimming is compulsory. We even got a little more respect when we talked about Islam in our classes, while before our teacher dismissed what we said if it didn't agree with her casual perceptions. Now I have no problem wearing the veil, even though I do like to let my hair loose, but the trade-off is worth it.

In order to reduce their isolation at school or university, some of the women organized social groups and rotating parties, and actively involved themselves in community activities, a trend that has continued to increase since 1996. Others started Muslim clubs and societies in their educational institutions wherever none were already in place.

The interviewees with a postsecondary education, especially in the social sciences, as well as those who were more politically inclined, presented feminist arguments in support of the veil. They argued that Canadian society and the Occident as a whole have turned women into sexual objects, their half-naked bodies used to sell everything from toothbrushes to sports cars. In the West, a woman's breasts, waist, hips and clothing are supposed to conform to an ideal standard of beauty. Therefore, they argued, women preoccupy themselves with achieving these standards instead of improving their minds and becoming confident and useful members of society. The veil, according to these young women, even with all its problems, removes women to some degree from these preoccupations. It relieves the emphasis on their bodies, enabling them to participate in public life as people rather than as bodies.

Further discussion with this group of veiled women revealed that their arguments have developed following their decisions to veil and their need to defend their choice. In the process, they became more aware of feminist concerns and gender politics in the broader society as well as within the Muslim community. Tahera, for instance, a youngish-looking twenty-three-year-old trying to keep her slippery scarf on her head, explained:

> Perhaps the reasons I took the veil are not the same as the reasons I continue to wear it. Maybe I don't see it as much as a religious requirement. I will continue to wear the veil as a way of trying to cope and be what I want to be in this society. This scarf, that to so many appears such a big deal, at least has made others aware of Islam, and of my identity within the Canadian society, instead of looking at me and judging me for my figure and looks. This alone is sufficient reason to wear the veil, particularly since it reinforces my identity and that of Muslim community.

Questions of identity, and the demonization of Islam and Muslims in Canada and in the West in general, do play a role in the decision of some women to take up the veil. This was especially notable in Montreal following the Gulf War. Mona, always beautifully dressed in light, understated colours, including matching veil, was born in Montreal to an Egyptian family and was raised in that city. In 1994, almost two years after having adopted the veil, she told me:

> I would never have taken up the veil if I lived in Egypt. Not that I disagree with it, but I see it as part of the male imposition of rules. I believe that Muslims should try to bring order to their sexual urges and not be seductive, and not disrupt the social order. But the veil puts all the responsibility on women's shoulders. The double standard frustrates me. But since the Gulf War, seeing how my veiled friends were treated, I made a vow to wear the veil to make a point about my Muslimness and Arabness. I am delighted when people ask me about my veil and Islam, because it gives me a chance to point out their prejudices concerning Muslims.

I asked her what kinds of questions people ask her and how she responds. Mona replied:

> They ask all sorts of stupid questions and, of course, occasionally an intelligent one too. They ask me why I wear the veil since I live in Canada. I tell them I want to exercise my democratic rights, just like they do. I tell them that democratic rights are not enjoyed by everyone in other parts of the world. And I ask them if the governments of Quebec or Canada are so different from Khomeini's Iran, when they try to ban veiling in public schools or expel veiled students from schools. I ask them how many students would have to leave school if we were to expel all those who wore the cross, since that is also a religious symbol. Some ask whether I feel discrimination as a woman, since men don't have to wear the veil. I say yes, but I have yet to hear that people have raised a public outcry about Jewish men suffering discrimination or oppression because they have to wear Kippah and Jewish women do not. Or I tell them it can't be worse than seeing women's naked bodies at the sex shops and in all sorts of ads and maybe they should put their energies to solving those problems instead of worrying whether my veil is a form of oppression. Others ask me if the veil interferes with my hearing. I say yes it does, but I still manage to be at the top of the class and get A+ in all my courses, while many who don't wear the veil flunk. ... Every day something new happens. The other day some woman in the metro, after chatting with me a bit, said, "You with such beauty, how can you bring yourself to wear the veil?" I smiled and told her it is so people can see beyond my physical beauty and realize that I want to be a person.

Mona even suggested to me at this point that if I really wanted to instigate discussion about Islam, Muslim women and Arabs, I should go out veiled. This would generate all kinds of opportunities for me personally to experience people's perceptions and attitudes, and to get into arguments!

When I asked Mona if she didn't miss her sexuality, and whether she truly wanted to be considered exclusively in non-sexual terms, she admitted that while she would like to be admired for her beauty and femininity as well, the price in this society is too high:

> There is no in-between, at least when you are young. Our society forces you to be either a person or a woman and object of desire. So for now and as long as I have the courage, I would rather be a person.

When I pointed out that even with a veil she is, and is perceived to be, a woman, being that the veil is an exclusively female garment actually symbolizing femininity, Mona said:

> Right! Of course, I am a woman, but instead of people judging whether I have a nice body and whether my clothes are fashionable, they think of my veil. They discuss the veil. Similarly the men know that even though I am a woman, I am telling them [to] see me otherwise. Do not think of my body, but of me as a person, a colleague and so on.

Some of the veiled informants, who view the veil primarily as a political statement, use the veil specifically when they feel it important to reinforce their Arab or Muslim identities, and do not necessarily practise veiling regularly. The reception accorded to this type of "selective veiling," which is increasing within the Muslim community as well as within society at large, would be interesting to examine, though our attention was drawn to this practice only toward the end of our field research.

Among the women we interviewed was a group that recognized how veiling and other perceived religious practices had the potential to give them power over those normally exercising power over them. In a group discussion held at a mosque in Toronto, Samira, twenty-two, whose parents are of Indian and Syrian extraction, told me that her life had changed since she took the veil. As the eldest daughter in her family and her entire kin group in Canada, all her senior relatives felt they could tell her what to do and where to go. She explained:

> By the time I took notice of everyone's wishes, I was practically a prisoner. School was my only escape. Then I joined a group of women who had religious meetings and eventually I took the veil. Quite a revolution in the family despite their claim to being good Muslims. No one was veiled in my family and all were very lackadaisical about their prayers and fasting. Then it was my turn. I gave them lectures on Islam every time I got an opportunity and reminded them how they wanted me to be a good Muslim, and not do this and that. Now I have become one, and one of the duties of a good Muslim is to encourage others to practise their religion correctly and seriously. They really dislike that I, a young woman, do this. They never knew anything about Islam and just understood their cultural practices as Islam and forced them on us. Now they have to listen to me. The other day there was a big celebration in our house. Some thirty people in their best clothes were there and my mother had made a very nice dinner. She put the food on the table and announced that all should go to eat. I objected that we should not eat before praying, and that with the whole family together we all have to say a collective prayer. I knew that nobody wanted to do it. My mother was worried about her food being cold and tasteless. The girls and boys were worried about their clothes getting creased [because they had to kneel on the floor], but nobody dared object to such a legitimate religious request. We did the prayer. My father, who was the elder member, led the prayer and then we ate. Most people did not talk to me much after that, but what does it matter? They all had to do as I asked.

While historically unequal power relations have often been justified in the name of religion and Islam, women are now discovering that they too can use Islam to assert their will. Studying Islam, and in particular taking the veil (a public pronouncement of piety), subverts the veil as a symbol of patriarchal control and redefines it as a marker of status and as a tool of emancipation, empowerment and, in some cases, a means of exerting power over those generally considered to have ultimate control, as illustrated above in Samira's case. Many of the younger women we interviewed recognized this, and were able to demonstrate to their parents that cultural practices and values are not synonymous with Islam. According to our informants, it is not as easy for sons to use this strategy of introducing new views to their families based on the study of Islam. This reversal of influence in families, where traditionally males are significantly more influential than females, seems to stem from the power of the veil in the context of Canadian society, which publicly denotes women as religious. Many women are aware that the respect and power they gain in this way stem from the assumption that veiling in North America requires more courage and commitment than veiling in Cairo, Lahore or elsewhere in the Muslim world.

The data indicate other reasons as well underlying the decision to veil, particularly among those aged twenty-three to thirty, the most educated cohort in our sample. This segment included economists, accountants, computer scientists, fashion designers and social workers, who by conventional standards are successful professionals, fully integrated into Canadian society. However, despite this, many of them felt true contentment was to be found as homemakers and mothers, with time to enjoy their children. They were not interested in competitive struggles in the workplace, vying for insignificant promotions. They did not necessarily want to direct all their energies toward their careers, and felt that Islam allowed them this luxury by designating men as family providers, contrary to the Western feminist perspective, which sees the ideal of "man, the breadwinner" as one of the sources of Muslim women's oppression. Fatema explained in this connection how she rediscovered Islam and took the veil:

> Now I have a job with good money, but I see how much headache this job has, and while I was studying so hard to get here, I have

> lost many chances of a good marriage. Now men come and say you pay for this and that, or that I should keep working full-time after I have children. Well, these are not the kind of husbands I want. Not that I don't want to work, but for them to expect me to do so, it means they don't want to accept responsibility in life. I want a man who accepts his Islamic responsibility and provides for his family. Gradually I wised up and returned to my religion. The more I study the rights of women in Islam, the more I feel that as Muslim women, we are given the best opportunities. I wonder why we were so eager to throw this out for the vague feminist promise of equality. I have tried it, and I do not want to be a man, competing for a promotion and an increase of a $100 or so in my paycheque. I want to be a woman and enjoy my womanhood. As I became more aware of Islam and women's rights, I became more convinced of taking up the veil. Now that I am veiled, it is not a surprise when I tell a suitor I don't want to work outside home once I'm married, that I want to be a wife and a mother and devote myself to my family. I have studied and hold a good job, so men know that I am able to earn a good living, but I choose to be a homemaker. I think this is the nature of a woman as it has been said in Qu'ran. We [women] are kind and delicate and loving. Why should I want to change this state rather than enjoy it? Anyway, I don't see the point of fighting against nature.

By taking the veil, Fatema is publicly announcing her Islamic views pertaining to her expectations of a husband. This symbolic communication also indicates who may or may not be an appropriate suitor. Our informants were also aware that according to Islam, their husbands are bound to provide for them at the minimum level to which they are accustomed. This generally dissuades economically unsuitable men from presenting themselves as marriage candidates. Wearing the veil establishes basic values and expectations from the outset, and marriage negotiations take place within this framework of conventional values. This is not to say that all Muslims are in absolute agreement over these values, but the parameters of debate are set.

The return to Islamic values, which is communicated by many women through wearing the veil, may involve other motives too. Many Muslim women in North America, with advanced education and other credentials, have difficulty in finding a suitable husband. Muslim women can marry only Muslim men, while men can marry women of other faiths. Thus the Muslim community loses some potential husbands to other communities. As well, some men would rather go back to their countries of origin and marry *authentic* Muslim women (Aswad 1991; Cainkar 1991). This means that the pool of potential husbands becomes even smaller. On the other hand, many Muslim women raised in North America are not prepared to marry men from their parents' country of origin, because of the different expectations concerning the role of women and wives. Thus, many women past the age of thirty feel they may not get a chance to marry. This is unfortunate and even unacceptable from the point of view of both unmarried women and their communities, who consider marriage and raising a family an Islamic duty. Thus a few women in the sample chose to become second wives, justifying their decision on Islamic grounds.

Sherene, a university graduate who spent some time in the workforce, came to Canada when she was five years old. In retrospect she believes if she had followed a more Islamic path, her life would have been much better. She did finally return to Islam, as she recounts here in the story of her marriage:

> When I was young I had many suitors. I was rather beautiful. But I wanted to take full advantage of Canadian society, so I rejected them all. I went to university and then got myself a job. I was successful and had money and dressed very smartly. But I was lonely. There were no longer that many suitors and I could not accept non-Muslims. I had a couple of marriage offers from men from home, but I could not see myself marrying someone who had

> not lived in North America and does not know English, and probably only wants to marry me because he wants to come abroad. Otherwise such men would choose women from home who would not question their position as head of household. I knew I would be asking for trouble if I married that way. On the other hand, I wanted to have a home and children. Finally I met my husband, who is married and has three children. He proposed to me and I accepted. I think it is better to marry as a second wife of a good Muslim man than to marry a non-Muslim or not marry at all. Now I have a child and I am very happy with my husband.

Sherene's situation prompted a group discussion of polygyny, again a subject beyond the scope of this chapter. Of relevance to the issue of veiling is the consideration of how her family and her community would have reacted had she not been a veiled woman, well versed in religious reasoning and justifying her decisions within the framework of Islam. As far as Canadian law is concerned, she is an unmarried woman with a child; yet in the eyes of her community, she has fulfilled her Islamic duty in a prescribed fashion. Although many women did not approve of polygyny and did not quite feel it was fair for the first wife, nonetheless Sherene was not marginalized despite the fact that she moved within the same circle as her co-wife, a situation unthinkable within a secular Muslim community. Clearly, many women examine their Islamic rights in consideration of how to best serve their own particular situations.

Summary and Conclusion

In this paper, I have argued against a one-dimensional treatment of veiling as an unchanging practice symbolizing oppressive patriarchy in Muslim societies. I suggested we must examine veiling in a broader framework, situating the veil within the history of clothing as a vehicle for political and social expression and action. A cursory review of the history of clothing and dress codes of Europe and the Middle East since the Middle Ages disabuses any simple, functionalist or materialist perspective of clothing as a socially neutral response to biological and climatic needs. Historically, clothing has carried significant communicative power. Clothing frequently indicates age, gender, social class, ethnicity and religion. It can mark (or blur) social boundaries, forge or destroy alliances. Clothing is used by the powerful to reinforce power, while the underclasses, through the appropriation and manipulation of clothing, can shift the balance of power and challenge the status quo. In short, clothing has been and continues to be a potent vehicle of symbolic communication.

Framing the veiling debate in a context broader than the conventional, dichotomous one of religion/Islam/patriarchy versus individual freedom of choice provides a more comprehensive understanding of this practice. It cautions us, for instance, against transposing an Iranian or Saudi Arabian notion of the compulsory veil onto the Egyptian or European or Canadian context, where we must understand veiling as a voluntary act with a multiplicity of motives and meanings. This broadening of the discussion will help us view a veiled woman not as a passive subject, but as an active agent involved in redefining her position and options in the contemporary context of her life.

The veil in Canada plays a crucial role of mediation and adaptation for many young Muslim women, something the literature has totally overlooked. Often the veil has allowed Muslim women to participate in public life without compromising values and hard-won cultural and religious rights. In a North American context, adoption of the veil symbolizes women's religiosity and commitment to Islamic mores, while allowing them to resist patriarchal values and cultural practices imposed elsewhere in the name of Islam. In a similar fashion, veiled women can argue for their Islamic right to choose their spouse and resist arranged marriages without compromising family and community support. And veiling, along with a self-taught knowledge of Islamic practices, is used by some women to counter the control of male and senior family members and as a way of exercising considerable power themselves by preaching proper religious observance.

Wearing the veil has defused parents' resistance to their daughters' leaving home for university, entering the labour market and engaging in other activities in the public domain that are considered unconventional for Muslim women. The reason for this is that wearing the veil is a clear statement to parents and the wider Muslim community that these women are not relinquishing Islamic mores in favour of "Canadianness." Rather, they are publicly asserting their Muslim-Canadian identity. In effect, the veil has helped many Muslim women not only practise their religion, but also take advantage of what Canada, their new home, has to offer. The veil has thus been instrumental in helping Muslim women adapt to the wider Canadian society. Hence it is not the veil or Islam that has prevented the Muslim community from being fully integrated into Canadian society; rather, it is, to a significant degree, the colonial image of Muslims and the veil, along with the continuous demonizing of Islam, that has proved a major obstacle to such integration. As the data indicates, the continued negative portrayal of Islam and Muslims in the West has, in fact, motivated some women to take up the veil. They do so, not only because of their personal religious beliefs, but also out of a wish to assert openly the presence of the Muslim community.

Clearly, veiling means different things in different social contexts. While the veil was invented and perpetuated within a patriarchal framework as a means of controlling women, more often than not women have appropriated this same artifact to loosen the bonds of patriarchy. It is the lack of recognition of women's agency and the tendency to view women as passive victims that has flawed the current debate, distorted the image of veiled women and promoted the divide between those who do and those who do not wear the *ḥijāb*.

Notes

1 For a history of clothing since Egyptian times, see Crawley (1931) and Payne (1965). For a summary of definitions and categorization of dress, see Barnes and Eicher (1992), and Lindisfarne-Tapper and Ingham (1997).

2 Military uniform is perhaps one of the best examples of these functions. The uniform is designed to set its personnel apart from the public while creating an

impression of physical solidity, thus psychologically reinforcing the military physical presence and power. For example, it is reported that one reason the Ottoman military initially resisted a modern uniform was that its tight fit made soldiers less imposing (Wheatcroft 1993). Generally speaking, wearing a uniform creates a sense of belonging; however, the hierarchical nature of the military institution is maintained through creating subtle, and sometime not so subtle, details and differences to indicate and reinforce the rank of the wearer.

3 However, women's attempts to change the colour of the veil in Iran at the turn of the twentieth century created a public outcry, although no legal reaction (Bamdad 1977, Chapter 2).

4 One estimate puts the number of publications at 60,000 books — excluding articles and shorter writings — between 1800 and 1950 (Nader 1989).

5 Of course, this is not to say that historically there haven't been other attempts to control women's dress and clothing, but only that these attempts were not made in the name of Islam (see, for example, Ahmed 1992, 118).

6 Though Islam in fact supports education for both males and females; indeed, today many governments, including conservative ones such as those of Iran and Saudi Arabia, are promoting female education as Islamic. For example, since the revolution, the walls of all adult literacy classes in Iran are decorated with posters reiterating words of the Prophet, which advocate learning for all Muslims, especially his famous command to Muslim men and women to go even to China (which was, in the time of the Prophet, the farthest centre of intellectual activity) in search of knowledge.

7 Iran was, however, the only country that actually made veiling illegal and used the police to enforce the law.

8 In 1991, I conducted an informal survey among my Western acquaintances and students; they invariably described the veil as this all-enveloping black robe. Some added that it is designed to prevent or hamper women's mobility. Dickey's (1994) study yielded very similar results.

9 More recently, some of the Islamist political groups have adopted the same strategy of presenting one "Islam" and one transnational culture, each group championing its particular version of Islam and Islamic attire, which is claimed to be the only authentic version.

10 We can note that it was with some regret that most of these women made this change, feeling (and rightly so, I believe) that few other clothing styles in the world can match the beauty of Somali traditional clothing. Others continue to wear their traditional clothing under the cover of their "Muslim" costume.

11 I hope to examine in more detail the data collected from thirty-five interviews (of nineteen Iranian and sixteen Somali women) in a separate paper where I can do justice to the particular situations of these two Muslim ethnic groups.

12 We do not have comparable data on this particular trend for Ottawa, as this area was not in the interviews conducted there.

CHAPTER 2

Coding Dress:
Gender and the Articulation of Identity in a Canadian Muslim School

Patricia Kelly Spurles

Introduction

This chapter examines the role of gender in the construction of Muslim identity within a full-time Muslim school in Montreal. In 1996 and 1997, the school's combined elementary and secondary enrolment surpassed 225 students, of which girls made up 64 per cent. While only a fraction of the local Muslim school-age population attended the school, its location within a prominent Muslim community centre (which, though administratively distinct, provided some financial support) lent importance to the undercurrent of subtle debates on integration and particularly gender, which suffused policy and practice at the school. Gender roles and rules were important avenues of expressing an identity that was constructed from values and symbols chosen to reflect the community's diverse heritage and aspirations, and its situation in Canada as a minority community striving to maintain itself while managing its social and economic integration into broader society.

Muslim Families in Canada

As Muslim communities in the West grow through immigration and natural increase, they are rapidly surpassing longer-established religious minority groups (most notably Jews) as the primary focus of the dominant group's worried interest, often incorporating misconceptions and prejudices. In Canada, the 1991 census recorded 253,260 Muslims and 318,070 Jews; yet, because of continuing immigration and relatively large family size among Muslims, many anticipate that the 2001 census will indicate that Muslims have emerged as Canada's largest non-Christian religious community. While the Muslim population grew by 158 per cent between 1981 and 1991, the Jewish population grew by only 7 per cent over the same period. In some Canadian provinces, the community's growth was even more striking: Quebec's Muslim population, for instance, increased by 270 per cent between 1981 and 1991.[1]

Concurrent with this growth in numbers was an increase in institutionalization. Slow growth in the first half of the twentieth century produced the foundation for an explosion of institutional growth, while the loosening of immigration restrictions on non-Europeans in the 1960s allowed the settlement of young professionals who saw Canada as a permanent home. As the population grew dramatically and became more established, these new resources (both material and human) allowed the community to set up and maintain places of worship, community associations and social action groups. The late 1980s and 1990s were marked by the development of a political consciousness among ethnically and culturally diverse North American Muslims that they constitute a group, however tenuous, with shared interests in the social and economic integration, and in the welfare, of their children. A primary interest was the maintenance of Muslim identity, however varied its expression within this loosely knit multiethnic and multisectarian community.

Attitudes Toward Canadian Muslims

In the past twenty years, opposition groups of various shades in the Middle East have adopted Islamic symbols, challenging the role of the state as spokesperson for the imperturbable divine order. America's preoccupation with the "Islamic Threat" has increased internationally and, lately, domestically as well. As a result, prejudice toward Arabs and Muslims seems to be increasing, not decreasing. Farid Ohan and Ibrahim Hayani cite a survey of anglophone and francophone Canadians that showed that Arabs and East Indian-Canadians were perceived to be among the ethnic groups most dissimilar to them (Ohan and Hayani 1993, 5). Similarly, Muslim Arabs report more discrimination than do Christian Arabs (Ohan and Hayani 1993, 135–148).[2] A survey of 1,000 individuals from across Quebec (commissioned by the Quebec provincial government) supports these findings: not only is racism present, but in some cases it is apparently increasing rather than decreasing. In 1992, 21.3 per cent of respondents reported that they were "not at ease" in the presence of Arabs, whereas in 1996, 32.1 per cent responded that they had a similar sense of unease. The proportion of respondents who reported that they felt at ease, on the other hand, was slightly over half in both surveys, at 54 per cent in 1992 and 55.1 per cent in 1996. The survey indicated a similar dynamic of increasing racism toward Indo-Pakistanis. Those who reported feeling "not at ease" were 21 and 29.3 per cent in 1992 and 1996, respectively (Joly 1996, 69).

Community Responses to Prejudice

One consequence of increasing prejudice is that as the community perceives itself to be increasingly under threat, it adopts a defensive posture. Internal debate is thus marginalized relative to the effort to demonstrate united support for the community's tradition. This was the response, for instance, to the publication of *Femmes voilées, intégrismes démasqués*, in which Yolande Geadah (1996) argued that tolerance of the *ḥijāb* (headscarf) in public schools would lead to the implantation of less anodyne aspects of Muslim fundamentalism in Quebec. She concluded that while Quebec liberals favour allowing the *ḥijāb* to be worn in public schools, this constituted not an affirmation of individual freedom in the name of multiculturalism and anti-racism, but a concession to fundamentalist groups, which would sooner or later turn against Quebec society (Geadah 1996, 12). While she failed to show that Muslim women in Quebec actively, or even passively, support violent fundamentalist groups, the principal flaw in Geadah's logic was the assumption that outlawing the headscarf in public schools would improve the situation for Muslim women here. What seems to occur instead is that such periods of tension are marked by public pronouncements (usually, but not always, issued by male spokespersons) to the effect that a policy of this nature is unconstitutional and limits a Muslim woman's freedom of religion, *since Muslim women must wear* ḥijāb. This discourse in turn circumscribes the freedom of action of women who do not wear accepted forms of *ḥijāb* by effectively calling into question their morality and even their membership in the Muslim community. While in Canada, at least, the limitations on women's freedom initiated by such statements have never gained broad support within the Muslim community, neither have there been loud public pronouncements in the name of the Muslim community against these limitations. Democratic-minded women and men are often reluctant to draw public attention to coercive practices and situations, since these criticisms are immediately integrated into the larger Western social paradigm that reduces the richly diverse Muslim societies to a backward, malevolent and violent race. The vigorous debates in favour of equality and social change take place in other arenas, often in Arabic, where racism cannot intervene.

Concerns for Family Welfare and Community Survival

Prejudice against Muslims — but also against any form of social or racial difference — increases the pressure on them to assimilate. This is a problem that has often been expressed to audiences within the Muslim community as a distressing plea for survival, and to audiences outside the community as a failure of the Canadian social policy of multiculturalism aimed at removing such pressure from minority ethnic groups by structuring and defining their participation as subaltern groups within a society dominated by British and French ways and manners. A. Haleem, in the North American Muslim magazine *Islamic Horizons* (July 1987), writes:

> Welcome to the world where Muhammad is Mike and Fatima is Tina, Hasan is Sonny and Iman is Amy, Khalil is Cal and Alya is Ellen, and Hamdullah is Henry. The aliases seem an innocent linguistic compromise. But the double life led by most Muslim children here is serious business. Behind these socially acceptable names crouch an astonishingly broad repertoire of acceptable social behaviors to peers and teachers. When the doors of Muslim households across the continent are thrown open on school mornings, the children that march through them are headed for the front. It's heart-to-heart combat in the battle of values. The Muslim Community will take heavy casualties. Many will never make it back. (Quoted in Pulcini 1995, 181)

Zohra Husaini describes the dilemma of "fitting in" as a sociological question, stating:

> [How Muslims will continue to practice Islam in Canada] is an especially insistent question because, on the one hand, Canadian culture is increasingly secularized in the context of the modern industrial society, and on the other, for Canadians, ethnic and religious loyalties pull together against the demands of secular assimilation, often leaving one with an unwanted identity crisis. Hence, we need to examine how ethnic groups cope with the dual pressures of ethnicity on the one hand and secularization and assimilation on the other. (Husaini 1990, 10)

These issues involve children acutely: not only do young people experience the greatest part of their social learning within the new society and through its institutions, but they also represent the future of the family and the ethnic or religious community in the country of residence. Ahmad F. Yousif's study of Muslims in the Ottawa area revealed that for parents, raising their children according to their tradition, culture and religion was a source of anxiety (Yousif 1993, 57–59). Much writing about the Muslim community in North America expresses this concern, which, though located within the private realm of the family, is nevertheless a question of communal survival (e.g., B. Abu-Laban 1983; S. Abu-Laban 1991; Hashem 1991; Hogben 1983, 1991).

Muslim Schools in the West: One Solution to the Crisis of Integration

Since the 1970s, ad hoc groups of parents and concerned community members have struggled to set up Muslim day schools in Europe and North America as one response to the challenges of immigration and settling. While some schools, such as those in Quebec and in some European countries, receive government funding after demonstrating some degree of conformity to local standards, others have been refused such support, despite regular legal provisions (and precedents) for support to private confessional (i.e., religious) schools (Kelly 1999). In Britain, where Muslim groups have made a number of applications to receive funding for well-established and successful full-time confessional schools, opposition has been centred on questions of culture (Kelly 1999; Nielsen 1995; Parker-Jenkins 1992, 1995; Sarwar 1994). Children attending Muslim schools, opponents believe, are harmed by the lack of exposure to other cultural groups; furthermore, some argue that girls suffer in addition from the imposition of a traditional patriarchal culture by the school, which is normally perceived to be an agent of modernization. In North America, and Quebec in particular, such debates are beginning to emerge, as local authors such as Yolande Geadah (1996) link Muslim schools to the spread of political extremism. There is a pressing need for ethnographic and statistical data about these schools.

The development of Muslim schools in Britain, where at least fifty-four full-time Muslim schools now operate, highlights the social role of confessional schools for immigrant children. These schools were established under the leadership of intellectuals who believed that in order to preserve Muslim culture against Western dominance, modern educational institutions could embody an Islamic world view, incorporating research sciences without rejecting the existence of God. They challenged the disinclination of British school officials to accommodate the religious, cultural and educational needs of Muslim children, particularly those from low-income families whose educational and social needs were greatest. While laws allow for state funding of religious and other private schools, until 1998, applications had been refused on the basis of claims that schools lacked suitable facilities and would lead to the ghettoization of Muslim students. Muslim educators in turn accused state officials of acting out of prejudice, and pointed to several extremely successful Muslim schools to support their demands for recognition as a community with status and rights equal to Catholics, Jews and Presbyterians — all communities that received state funding for their schools. Within a field dominated largely by policy papers and theoretical or philosophical arguments from views both for and against Muslim schools as alternative educational institutions, several research studies have addressed the debate by investigating Muslim girls' schools. Marie Parker-Jenkins and Kaye Haw (1996) and Saeeda Khanum (1992) suggest that, despite school governors' patriarchal attitudes toward teachers as well as students, such schools provide a space in which girls advocate their own interpretations of Islam and attempt to sift out oppressive traditional practices from the egalitarian, revolutionary ethic that modernist Muslims believe underlies the Qur'an.[3] It is in this context that the existence of a well-established, full-time Canadian Muslim school gains importance as an arena where, collectively, identity is consciously articulated, i.e., expressed and negotiated, through the ongoing cumulation of statements and practices.

A Canadian Muslim School

The research on which this article is based was carried out in 1996 and 1997 (Kelly 1999). Over the course of a school year, I observed or took part in classes, meetings, breaks, lunch periods and special events; met with school and community officials, teachers, volunteers, parents and students; and discussed my observations with more than sixteen teachers, thirty-two parents and community members, and sixty students. It was immediately apparent that the school community was very ethnically diverse, with many children of mixed ethnic heritage. Nearly one in five students had a parent who was of European descent; a similar percentage had one or more parents of Iraqi background. Smaller numbers of students were of Lebanese, Algerian and other ethnic backgrounds. About a quarter of the students were Shī'ī, and the remainder Sunnī. Teachers were both male and female, and included both Sunnī Muslims (male and female immigrants and female converts) and a small number of non-Muslims (all women). The school was diverse ideologically as well, and despite common commitment to the basic tenets of Islam, interpretations of the details of how to be a good Muslim in the West abounded. While some families who supported the school were strictly traditional, others experimented much more with "modern" culture, and sought to incorporate and experience those aspects of Western culture that they judged beneficial, pleasant or at least harmless.

Integrating Islam: The School's Guiding Vision

Founded by a group of concerned Muslims who wished to create (according to a descriptive brochure) "institutions that function according to the Islamic code that are not insular nor detached from mainstream society," the school had an enrolment of twenty-five students in its first year. Although provincial subsidies and community support have allowed the school to maintain tuition fees at a reasonable level (they amounted to $1,500 per year in 1996–1997), the school was initially supported solely by tuition and donations from the local community. In 1987, the Quebec provincial government approved their application for partial funding on the basis that the school operated "in the public interest," a status given to private religious and non-religious schools that met the education ministry's criteria for curriculum and facilities. By 1990, the school was able to offer instruction for all primary grades, and by 1994 for all secondary grades as well. In 1997, the secondary grades were moved to a separate building, though the two levels continued to share some administrative and teaching personnel. Despite improvements to the building, the secondary school's application for government funding in 1997–1998 was rejected because its facilities were judged inadequate. Nonetheless, its students have performed very well on provincial standardized achievement tests, ranking eighteenth out of 141 public and private schools on the island of Montreal.

Curriculum and Language: Affirming Identity

Unlike entirely privately funded schools, those that receive partial government funding must follow education ministry curriculum guidelines, although they may incorporate additional classes. Hence, the Muslim school's curriculum was very similar to other Quebec schools. Additional classes in Arabic, the Qur'an and Islamic Studies were incorporated at both primary and secondary levels, adding up to five hours weekly to the timetable. These Islamic subjects constituted between 18 per cent (in Grade 2) and 9 per cent (in Grade 11) of the school week. English was another subject emphasized at the school, where the primary language of instruction was French. Usually reserved in most French-language public schools until Grade 5, English was taught at all levels in the Muslim school.

Although the mother tongue of most teachers and students was Arabic, the latter was not the dominant language at the school. Not only did the Arabic-speaking students come from many different countries whose spoken dialects were not mutually comprehensible, but they also joined the program at different ages and with different levels of language skill and were not equally (or easily) fluent.[4] In the classroom, teachers insisted that French was essential. In one Islamic Studies class, students had been asked to memorize a *ḥadīth* (a proverb attributed to the Prophet) and present it to the class, first in Arabic and then in French. One student was able to repeat the *ḥadīth* in Arabic, but not in French. The teacher asked him, "But do you understand it in Arabic?" "Yes," the student said. "Well, you still have to know it in French. What language is this class taught in? This is Quebec and we speak French here. It is important to me," the teacher answered. Through practices like this, teachers not only encouraged French language skills, but also asserted that the school was firmly anchored in Quebec society.

Creating Muslim Space

The school distinguished itself from non-Muslim Quebec schools not only through the inclusion of obligatory Islamic-content courses, but also through other formal and informal practices and structures that characterized the space as culturally Muslim. One informal structure was a mode of conversation favoured by some teachers and students that made liberal use of code-switching (Arabic phrases inserted into a conversation taking place in French or English) that was often religious in form. Such interjections had an Islamic structure, but, as in the Catholic school classrooms observed by Peter McLaren, served additional social purposes (McLaren 1993). Several children often tried to silence conversation in the classroom by clapping their hands and declaring "Allāhu akbar!" (God is greater). These mini-performances were mainly for my and the teachers' benefit, since they allowed the actor to participate in the classroom commotion while demonstrating conformity to the "quiet classroom" rule. While students weren't really able to effectively marshal religious legitimacy in this way and rarely succeeded in creating order by reminding the others that Muslims should be orderly, a few teachers used similar techniques.

Formal practices were spelled out in letter and law, and incorporated into the school's timetable, curriculum or calendar. These were important methods of asserting communal identity and affirming its strength, at least within the limited arena of the school community. Students attended class from 8:00 AM (secondary) or 8:15 AM (elementary) until 3:15 PM each day, with a fifteen-minute break in the morning and an hour at noon. After lunch, prayers took an additional twenty minutes; on Fridays, prayers and the sermon occupied at least thirty minutes in mid-afternoon and cut into the scheduled class (which was usually art in the primary grades). The schedule changed slightly during Ramadan, when the noon break was shortened to thirty minutes since many students and teachers were fasting. This also meant that the school day finished half an hour earlier, thus allowing parents and teachers more flexibility in picking up the children and rushing home to prepare the meal that would break the family's fast. The structural accommodation of fasting during Ramadan was highly symbolic, particularly in the elementary grades since most children began fasting only in Grade 5 or 6. In a sense, it represented the autonomy and power of the minority immigrant community, which was able to assert its own cultural norms over how time is publicly organized and marked, and to subvert the monopoly of dominant secular, White, European North American society over the public sphere.[5]

The school day was slightly longer than at most schools, which allowed time to be granted to Arabic, Islamic Studies and Qur'an classes without sacrificing other subjects. The schedule also incorporated both statutory holidays (state holidays that often correspond to Christian holy days) and Muslim religious holidays. In 1997, students and teachers received a three-day-long holiday for 'Īd al-Fiṭr ('Īd al-Ṣaghīr) in February at the end of Ramadan. The mid-winter break was scheduled to fall in mid-April during the week preceding 'Īd al-Aḍḥā ('Īd al-Kabīr), the Muslim holy day that commemorates Abraham's submission to God in preparing to sacrifice his son, and God's compassion in ordering him to sacrifice a ram instead. Several "Islamic Days," where children attended Islamic-themed movies and talks, played quiz games with

Islamic themes and did arts and crafts, also took place during the year, on one occasion after ʿĪd al-Fiṭr and on another during the statutory Easter holiday. This choice of dates reflects a widespread practice among North American Muslim community groups, which have begun a tradition of holding Islamic conferences for adults as well as children on Christian holidays (especially Christmas) with the intent of reinforcing Muslim identity, and perhaps also of reminding Muslims that they should not view Christian religious feasts as civic holidays to celebrate with parties, Christmas trees or Easter egg hunts.

Communal Prayer: Solidarity and Independence

Communal prayer was also integrated into the school's public life, as students were obliged to take part in afternoon prayer in the adjoining mosque each day. Several people I talked to recognized problems with the concept of "obligatory" worship, even though it has a long history in religious schools of all denominations. Students could be required to come to the mosque, and compelled to go through the motions of prayer, but if the actual intention to pray was missing, then from a religious standpoint their prayers would be invalid in any case. Hence, for some students, daily prayers were an obligatory school assembly far more than an exercise of faith. Moreover, one staff member told me that some of the older girls, who were excused from prayers during menstruation, attempted to prolong this absence as much as possible. And although teachers brought their students to the mosque, they were not obliged to attend prayers, and many didn't, perhaps because they weren't in the habit of praying regularly and wanted to avoid any pretense of appearing to do so publicly. This was not always the reason, however. Some teachers who didn't pray with the students prayed alone in the mosque at other times of the day. One teacher said she prayed regularly at home, but was simply "unable to do a good prayer" in the same room as the children, since she found it impossible to discard her role as teacher and supervisor in order to concentrate on her prayer, an essential requirement for its validity. In fact, although teachers and other adult women customarily prayed together in the back row, they also occasionally prayed in the girls' rows in order to supervise noisy or inattentive children, or sometimes to help younger children remember the sequence of the prayers. While teachers' praying habits were sometimes the subject of gossip among the parents, the fact that the women teachers were able to maintain their participation in group devotions despite periodic pressure was evidence of the school's general policy of tolerance and respect for individuals. On the other hand, almost all male employees attended communal prayers consistently. While women can adequately fulfill this religious duty at home, Friday's public prayer is considered a duty for men.[6]

Gender Roles as a Locus of Communal Identity

Muslim identity was constructed through formal and informal practices. While some of these were gender neutral (that is, they affected men and women in the same ways), other practices intervened in gendered relationships to produce effects that were positive or negative or ambiguous. The girls' attempts to exert their right to legitimately abstain from communal prayer was one positive outcome of their dissimilar rights and responsibilities. These gender rules also determined relations between people according to their gender in ways that were considered "Islamic."

One instance was the adoption of a form of address favoured by some Western religious groups and now employed by Muslim and Christian groups alike. Students thus addressed teachers and other adults as "Sister" or "Brother" (using the English words even when the language of conversation was French), sometimes coupled with the first name ("Sister Fatma") and sometimes without. While this form of address was also extended by the younger children to non-Muslim teachers (and consistently by all the students to one particularly well-liked Christian teacher), older children and staff members used the kinship terms

"Sister" and "Brother" to refer only to Muslims. Women teachers generally used the kinship term to address male staff members, while male staff members did the same. The use of fictive kinship terms legitimized inevitable interactions between non-related Muslim men and women by placing them in an Islamically acceptable context.

Other gendered norms of social relations operated as well. Men and women maintained a degree of informal, yet palpable, segregation at the school. Male employees rarely entered the teachers' preparation room, for instance, even though the door was virtually always half open and men sometimes stopped to talk from the doorway without entering. Male teachers kept to other areas of the school, partly because the teachers' preparation area was often terribly crowded, but also because they must have perceived it to be a women's space. This seemed very clear one day during Ramadan, when a teacher who was feeling tired took off her scarf and lay down to rest during the noon hour break, out of sight of the door. The door remained partially open, as usual, until one of the older women purposefully got up and closed the door. On other occasions, women removed or rearranged their headscarves in the preparation room, something that otherwise normally took place only in the segregated privacy of the washrooms.

The extent of gender segregation practised at the school was limited, and it created no apparent problems for the teachers. Female and male staff members interacted freely, though rarely with easy familiarity, a situation that many in this context would see as undesirable in any case, and even a hindrance to the maintenance of healthy working relationships. As a consequence of the unanimous respect shown for these proprieties in male-female professional relationships, staff members of opposite genders had little reticence about conducting work-related conversations alone in closed offices, despite the well-known *ḥadīth* to the effect that when a man and a woman are alone together, the third person in the room is the devil. In sharp contrast to what I observed in Montreal, Parker-Jenkins and Haw (1996) found that female Muslim head teachers in the United Kingdom were often excluded from participating in meetings with male board members on grounds of modesty.

Identity and Uniform(ity)

One aspect of the school's encouragement of an Islamic atmosphere was the dress code, which both students and teachers were formally and informally asked to respect. In contrast to other Muslim schools (e.g., described in Haddad and Lummis 1987, 80), however, this code did not distinguish between Islamic and un-Islamic clothing on the basis of ethnic tradition but rather according to what is covered and what is not. Thus, despite Jamal Badawi's statement in his book *The Muslim Woman's Dress* (a widely circulated text regarded as authoritative by many who consider the *ḥijāb* obligatory in Islam) that both men's and women's clothing must not resemble non-Muslims' clothing (Badawi n.d., 9), none of the mothers I talked with, even those who preferred to wear distinctive *jalābah*s or *jilbāb*s themselves, felt that it was un-Islamic for schoolgirls to dress in modest Western clothes. One staff member said that the uniforms were appropriate and Islamic:

> The girls are covered; the older ones wear cardigans to cover their bodies. The boys too are covered, the pants are loose. Not everyone remembers that it is just as important for boys to be modest as it is for girls. But I don't think they have to dress differently other than that. Muslims are not supposed to dress to attract attention.

The students wore standard uniforms purchased from a company that supplies clothing to other private schools in Montreal. Some parents bought second-hand uniforms, had them sewn privately or purchased similar styles elsewhere. Boys and girls were considered equally responsible for dressing in the style the school viewed as Islamic. Elementary schoolgirls wore navy jumpers and white blouses; older girls wore green-and-blue plaid skirts, long-sleeved white blouses and navy cardigans bearing the school crest. The skirts were to be no shorter than eight inches above the ankle, and very few skirts were any longer than that. The uniform of girls in Grade 4 and up included white headscarves. Boys wore grey or navy pants, long-sleeved white shirts with navy vests and ties. For physical education, students of both sexes wore loosely fitting tracksuits.

From time to time, teachers took several minutes after morning assembly or noon prayer to conduct a uniform review. Those wearing clothing other than the prescribed styles were admonished and told to wear the standard uniform the next day. This was a bone of contention: many students wore clothing that more or less closely resembled the assigned uniform while asserting individuality and personal taste in minor variations. In these uniform reviews, the boys' clothing was scrutinized as carefully as the girls', and their non-standard sweaters and shirts were picked out just as frequently. One particular criticism of boys' uniforms was that pants were judged to be too tight.

As a condition of employment, Muslim female teachers were required to wear headscarves at the school. In fact, until 1994, all female teachers (Muslim or not) were required to cover their hair.[7] While some questioned the implications of the rule or acknowledged that wearing a scarf part-time meant that it was difficult to grow accustomed to the reduced sense of hearing that it entails, none of the Muslim teachers and parents who did not wear *ḥijāb* outside the school considered the rule oppressive to the extent that the media did; many felt the media's interest in the school's dress regulations was an attempt to vilify Muslims and their beliefs. During the 1996–1997 school year, non-Muslim teachers dressed as they wished, in short-sleeved tops, scoop-neck blouses, tight leggings and knee-length skirts, or, as some did, in clothing that greatly resembled the modest Western outfits of Muslim teachers.

Muslim teachers for their part dressed in a variety of modest (and often fashionable) styles. A few wore the new-style *jalābah* (a floor-length loose dress worn over other clothing) usually purchased in the Middle East, where the garment is seen to convey the message that the wearer is educated and modern while still identifying with Islamic values.[8] Most, however, wore off-the-rack clothing: usually a long-sleeved top and jacket or sweater that fell below the hips, a calf-length skirt or pants (or jeans) and a scarf covering the hair. Details such as a few inches of hair showing at the crown or a loosely tied scarf rather than a tightly pinned one distinguished between those whose headscarf was religious and those whose headscarf was pragmatic and worn only at school. Male staff also wore Western clothing, although from time to time several wore a *jibbah* (a long, loose garment) over their usual occidental attire. Typical clothing consisted of a suit and tie, or other pants and a long- or short-sleeved shirt. In fall 1996, only three of the nine men employed full-time or part-time at the school wore beards.[9] Along with several of the male students, two or three wore traditional skullcaps on occasion, but not regularly.

*Ḥijāb*s and Headscarves

Section 12 of the students' code of conduct read: "*Ḥijāb* (Headscarves). All girls from grade four upward are expected to wear headscarves to cover their hair properly." The school leadership justified their headscarf requirement by reference to the Qur'anic verse, which tells "believing women" to cover themselves (for a broad discussion of this, see the article by Soraya Hajjaji-Jarrah in this volume). There is, however, some disagreement in the wider Muslim community about the legitimacy of the school's requirement that female Muslim teachers and female students in Grade 4 and above wear headscarves. Some people I talked with voiced their concerns in terms of customary practice. One woman, an observant Muslim, said, "We don't even force girls to wear headscarves in Egypt and of course we are Muslim there!" Others referred to *sūrah* 2 (al-Baqara), verse 258, which states "There is no compulsion in religion" in support of their view that even if the school can legitimately advocate "covering" (i.e., wearing a headscarf and clothing that covers the chest, body, arms and legs), it cannot enforce such a policy since this is a religious practice — a fact that the school has acknowledged in requiring this only of *Muslim* teachers. One individual said that the school should be particularly sensitive to any appearance of coercion since "we know they — the media and the rest of society — are watching us for the slightest proof that we are as bad as they think." The policy enunciated by the school's administrators was that each school is free to establish its own requirements and that the headscarf is one on which they insist. Several staff members, even though they told me that wearing the *ḥijāb* had to be a personal decision, said that parents have the responsibility to raise their daughters properly and can force them to wear the *ḥijāb* (just as they can oblige them to wear knee-length skirts rather than mini skirts) until they reach adulthood. Parents, however, delegate this authority to the school in the same way that they delegate the authority to discipline their children.

Muslims who believe that women should "cover," state that this is not required before they reach puberty, which in Muslim legal tradition is fixed as the onset of menstruation. However, a staff member told me that they had decided that girls would begin wearing the scarf at school in Grade 4: "There are girls in grade four who are beginning puberty, and it would be too embarrassing for them if we said that this one has to but this other one doesn't. So everyone does it together."

There was no pressure on younger girls to cover their hair, although partway through my fieldwork it was decided that they would, like the other girls and women, be required to cover their hair in the mosque. One staff member explained this decision to me: "If they are old enough to be praying, then they are old enough to be covering their hair." As this policy was being introduced, girls had difficulty remembering to bring scarves with them for prayer. The teachers displayed ingenuity and flexibility in finding a solution that would promote their wish that the girls perform their prayers and cover their heads while doing so: they collected knitted winter hats for the girls to wear in the mosque.

Some of the girls in grades 1, 2 and 3 regularly wore scarves, though they often showed considerable nonchalance about the practice. In contrast to the white scarves worn by older girls as part of their uniform, younger girls often wore patterned, brightly coloured or black scarves. Several girls wore their scarves so casually that they were usually half on and half off; others, when their scarves came untied, simply took them off and stored them in their desks. In the middle of class, these younger girls sometimes took off their scarves and asked a teacher to put it back on nicely. There was no embarrassment that they had become "uncovered," nor was there any indication of pressure on the girls to quickly put their scarves back on. What I observed at the school contrasted markedly with claims that kindergarten girls are forced to wear the *ḥijāb*, such as those made in the film *Au nom d'Allah* ("In the Name of God"), a Radio-Canada documentary that featured the same school.

Older girls were required to wear the scarf, although the distinction between the scarf as part of a dress code and the *ḥijāb* as personal religious commitment was retained. Several girls estimated that perhaps no more than a third of all girls in the school wore the *ḥijāb* "full-time." One girl mentioned the distinction between *ḥijāb* and headscarf, and recognized that for many of her classmates, the scarf had no ideological significance. She said, "At the school, it is just a part of our uniform. When teachers see a girl without her scarf, they don't say, 'Where is your *ḥijāb*?' They say, 'Where is your uniform?'"

Similarly, one mother said:

> You see it is just a part of the uniform because the girls who are not practising take it off as soon as they go out of the door. They are not harassed because of it, as soon as they leave the school they are free to do what they want. I know them, these girls. They take it off before they get to the bus stop![10]

Outside the school, the school cannot say anything. But inside the school, the *ḥijāb* is part of the uniform, just like the navy skirt and the white shirt.

I asked one student what she thought of the "*ḥijāb* rule," especially since most Muslims in Montreal believe it is a matter of personal choice. She said:

> Well, there are two answers. First, it is good because the girls get used to wearing the scarf and so it is not strange to them. And the girls who wear the scarf full-time aren't made to feel strange. If only those girls wore the scarf, then it would be like a public school and they might be teased by the other girls since most of the girls here only wear the scarf because they have to. And also it is part of the Islamic environment of the school. But on the other hand, it is not so good because the girls who are forced to wear the *ḥijāb* by their mothers aren't doing it because they want to. When girls wear the scarf because they want to, then they will keep it up; but no girl who is forced to wear the scarf will keep it up when she is older. So it is not really good for them.

This reality was reflected in the behaviour of these girls and in how they wore their scarves. Like the teachers, girls varied in how much hair they covered, and older girls had considerable leeway. While some girls wore the scarf folded in a dart at the temples to form what they called a "tent" covering the forehead (at least several inches and sometimes down to the eyebrows), others displayed a fair bit of their hairline. Many older girls arranged their scarves loosely, leaving them untied with the ends simply crossed under the chin and placed over the opposite shoulder. Sometimes the scarf was not wrapped at all, but draped over the head and pinned under the chin, with the ends hanging straight down. Girls and women whose scarves represented commitment to the religious idea of *ḥijāb* were usually meticulous about covering their hair and chose styles that stayed easily in place. Some wore sewn head coverings of one or two pieces devised to be comfortable and no-fuss, while others used a safety pin or straight pin to anchor their scarves first under the chin, and then secure one tightly pulled end above the opposite ear or at the back of the head.

During my fieldwork, none of the staff or students wore face veils (known as *niqāb* in the Middle East), although this practice is becoming more common in the wider Muslim community. I learned that some of the students' mothers dressed in this style. One opinion in favour of covering the face asserts it is necessary because of the corruption of modern society in which "even the face may attract sexual glances from men" (Muḥammad Nasīr al-Dīn al-Albānī, quoted in Doi 1989, 15; see also Khurshid Ahmad, quoted in Lemu and Heeren 1978, 50). Several women with whom I spoke considered this practice extreme and un-Islamic, saying that what is obligatory during prayer is the best dress for Muslim women. Since women may not veil their faces during prayer or pilgrimage, then this practice is not recommended (see, for example, Mutahhari 1989, 64ff).

Diversity in Muslim Identity

While the proportion of Canadian Muslim children attending full-time Muslim schools is very low (2 per cent in Montreal, for instance (Kelly 1999, 201), compared to 50 per cent of Jewish children in Montreal who attend full-time Jewish schools), the schools wield disproportionate influence in the formation of opinion, both within the Muslim community and in the larger community. One area where this is particularly evident is in the school's gender vision. Issues that were often resolved by tradition, consensus or legislation in the country of origin are addressed at the individual or family level in Canada. In the Muslim community at large, these questions often include the payment of the religiously mandated poor tax (Is paying taxes to the state sufficient?) and food purity (Is it permissible to eat food fried in fat of unknown origin?). However, in a context where ethnic identity is defined in important ways through the reputation, appearance or behaviour of women, the most intense debates focus on gender. This is so, particularly since conflicts between East and West have often focused on women and women's status as symbols of modernity.

Not the least marker of Muslim identity was the school's dress code, which required that older female students and all Muslim female teachers wear headscarves. Yet, while the headscarf policy was defended and legitimized as a dress code, it cannot be viewed without also acknowledging that the *ḥijāb* — which stands for modesty and the privacy of women's bodies — has ironically been appropriated as a public symbol of communal identity. One of the parents said, "It was not the school which asked that the girls be required to wear the scarf in the beginning, it was the parents who said that if they sent their children to the school, it was because they wanted them to really be Muslim."

Time and time again, students, parents and school employees linked the headscarf with communal identity, saying, "It is so they know we are Muslim." "They" referred alternately to the students themselves and to society at large. At the same time, however, many defended the legitimacy of some women's choice not to wear the *ḥijāb* outside the school grounds. As one mother said, "If the teachers are not observant Muslims, but they understand their role and they respect that the students have this faith, then they don't try to destroy it, then it is okay. It is not a problem at all." As members of a community that perceived itself to be under close scrutiny and threat of increased prejudice, women (and men) found subtle ways to express disagreement with institutionalized piety in the form of scheduled communal prayer and obligatory *ḥijāb*. Understated expressions of differentiation, such as praying privately instead of communally or wearing a "relaxed" headscarf, asserted solidarity with the group without giving in to the pressures of conformity.

While the school's policy on women's and men's clothing conformed to all but the most conservative opinions on Muslim dress,[11] adherence to this policy meant a fair number of women were required to put on special dress (i.e., at the very least a headscarf and long-sleeved blouse) for school. Although this situation indicates some ideological distance from the fundamentalist movements that seek to impose "correct" forms of dress and other aspects of gender roles, it confirms a hierarchy that has emerged within many conservative Muslim communities in the West in which some preserve their own freedom of action against fundamentalist dictates while substantiating their Islamic identity by imposing (formally or informally) these dictates on the women of their community. Other views of Muslim identity emphasize that *ḥijāb* is one possible personal choice linked to ethnic tradition, and one that is minimized relative to other aspects of

Islamic practice, such as prayer, payment of *zakāt* (poor tax) and good character. Thus, while some may prefer *ḥijāb* for themselves and for others as the proper dress for Muslim women, in this view they do not seek to impose it by force of law, regulation or violence on others.

The desire to enforce conformity emerges from the struggles that go on as Muslims in North America try to maintain the borders of a community whose members sometimes tend to syncretism, or forgetfulness, or compromises of convenience. Some of these issues, such as women's clothing and religious rituals, have until recently been characterized by views that varied according to region, social class and sect. In the Diaspora as well as in the Middle East and South Asia, there is increasing pressure to conform to models defined by various (often competing) groups as "Islamic." Community and autonomy emerged as major themes during the period of my own fieldwork. I began to see that a fine equilibrium was maintained between, on the one hand, a family's desire to retain and reproduce not just piety and religious feeling, but also the degree of conformity within the community that could be called Muslim social identity, and on the other, its autonomy in emphasizing aspects of that identity.

Prayer was one example of this. Even parents who did not themselves pray agreed that their children should learn how to pray "since it is their heritage" or "so that they will remember it for later." While all students were required to pray at school, the community generally recognized that teachers decided for themselves whether or not to participate. This was, however, influenced by the traditionally different discourses on men's and women's participation in public prayer. Whereas most female teachers opted not to pray at school, virtually all male teachers accepted the consensus on the preference of communal prayer for men and performed the early afternoon prayer in the mosque when they were at the school, although they never came in uniquely for noon prayers as did a number of other men from the community. While women's practice was coherent with the traditional beliefs of some Muslim societies that discourage women's mosque attendance, in this context it was used by women to increase their autonomy, and not by men to limit it.

The boundaries drawn by the community include Muslim women who do not wear *ḥijāb* and who at the same time often view this choice as a matter of public debate. Unlike prayer, which can be delayed and performed at home or in private, *ḥijāb* is material, visible and public. While headscarves were a required part of older girls' uniforms, the administration acknowledged that most did not wear it outside the school; similarly, while Muslim female teachers had to wear headscarves, religious and ideological commitment to wearing *ḥijāb* was not a condition of employment. Furthermore, one of the mothers who volunteered at the school wore *ḥijāb* only in the mosque. Her identity as a Muslim woman of modest values, however, was never questioned since she always dressed in traditional *shalvār qāmīṣ* (pants and calf-length tunic), with her *dupatta* (traditional Pakistani scarf) worn in the usual style, that is, around her shoulders and not over her head. She (and others) described this clothing as "what Muslim women wear in India and Pakistan." By contrast, the headscarves worn by the teachers and students whose normal attire did not include a *ḥijāb* were the only outward indications that they were Muslim.

Yet, while the Muslim community may be criticized for placing too much emphasis on headgear and not enough on more traditionally important aspects of Islam (notably the payment of zakāt, which is one of the Five Pillars of Islam),[12] the popular media has also exaggerated the oppression of women forced to endure the "veil." Furthermore, the fact that women and girls who don't normally wear *ḥijāb* were not excluded from the school might be looked upon as an indicator of the community's acknowledgment of diversity. The principal of a Muslim school in the United States told me quite bluntly, "If I found out one of the teachers was not wearing her *ḥijāb* after school, she would be out of here." All of his former female graduates, he said, still "wear their *ḥijāb*s." The parents I talked with had resolved the issue of community/conformity versus autonomy (though sometimes with difficulty) by asserting that it was important for them that teachers support the values of the community, even if they were not practising Muslims.

Muslim or Islamic?

In many ways, but most notably through obligatory *ḥijāb* and prayer, religious feeling is being divorced from practice, though perhaps this is the case in many instances around the world and is another aspect of this drive for conformity I have noted. By formally requiring women and girls to cover their heads and all students to participate in prayer regardless of intention, the school provided for a distinction between what is "Muslim" and what is "Islamic." Philip Lewis describes how, during the Gulf War, Muslim South Asian pupils in one British school showed a high level of support for the Iraqi government. This was interpreted by Lewis as evidence of strong ties to Muslim identity, characterized by a shared history and culture, which existed separately from piety or religious sentiment, a fact that he gauged by the low level of participation in public prayer:

> At the height of the Gulf crisis in a Bradford upper school with a largely Muslim intake it was evident that most youngsters were pro-Iraq. Yet, in this same school, throughout the crisis, no more than two or three prayed in the area set aside for prayer. This episode illustrates the distinction between Muslim and Islamic identity. The youngsters felt that, as with the demonization of Islam in the wake of the Rushdie affair, their Muslim communal identity was once again under attack from negative media coverage. This perception, however, did not translate into prayers. (Lewis 1994, 177–178)

Girls in Muslim Schooling

The distinction between cultural and religious obligations and practices is important in understanding the potential role of Muslim schools in shaping the upbringing of girls. Critics have expressed concern that Muslim schools, by definition, abdicate the role schools play in mediating the rights of the child against those of the family. This may be the case in schools where teachers and staff lack the authority — and most importantly, the knowledge — to challenge oppressive practices. Yet, in some instances that I observed, teachers and staff had a positive impact on encouraging the integration of students (and, by extension, of parents) while preserving Muslim identity. This was precisely because of their "authority" as Muslims as well as teachers. While parents can easily discount the advice of non-Muslim social workers or teachers as racist or immoral, it is much harder to ignore the counsel of a Muslim teacher who is well known and trusted within the community. While I was at the school I heard of numerous cases where staff had formally and informally intervened with parents to promote a child's welfare.[13]

Another way this occurred was by correcting misperceptions about Islam (as well as about Western society and Christianity), particularly by sorting out the cultural traditions of Muslim societies from what many scholars would argue is authentically Islamic (i.e., based on a holistic understanding of the Qur'an). For instance, teachers felt very strongly that girls and boys should be treated with equal attention. When this norm was violated — as in the case of a visiting speaker who spoke directly to the boys while ignoring the girls — teachers complained. Similarly, while some Muslim girls attending Quebec public schools have apparently refused to sit near boys (Geadah 1996, 235), girls and boys routinely sat next to each other at the Muslim school. While parents or children occasionally objected, these cases were dealt with as they arose by the classroom teacher. Overall, the school maintained a policy of coeducation that was effectively accepted and supported as appropriately Islamic, according to one explanation, since students were expected to be studying in class, not socializing.

Girls' participation in sports was also promoted by the school. Indeed, whereas in public schools there are instances of some parents requesting the withdrawal of their daughters from physical education classes (Geadah 1996, 235; Parker-Jenkins 1995), the Muslim school community distinguished between women's physical activity (which is permitted) and immodest dress (which is not). Consequently, female students at the Muslim school took part in physical education dressed in long-sleeved t-shirts and loose sweatpants.

Thus, it is unfair to suggest that Muslim schools are more harmful to women and girls (particularly immigrants) than secular schools within the same context. In fact, Muslim schools, including the one where I conducted my fieldwork, offer women an institutionalized place in the life of the community and provide a model for women's public roles in other arenas.

Integrating Sectarian Diversity

Another aspect of the tension between conformity and diversity within the community was periodic difficulties between the administration, dominated by Sunnī Muslims, and the large Iraqi Shī'ī minority. While the pressure to conform was less blatant than in the past — in the early 1990s, according to one student, Sunnī classmates had to be informed that Shī'īs are indeed Muslim — distinctively Shī'ī practices were discouraged by some staff members and recognized as legitimate by others. Tensions between Sunnīs and Shī'īs at the school were highlighted by emphasis on conformity during prayer. Shī'ī students said that these problems "come and go," and although some incidents have led to conflicts, others have been allowed to pass. To cite but one instance, the school's staff have sometimes discouraged the Shī'ī practice of using an object (normatively an object from nature and often a small tile made of earth from Karbala or Mecca, but in practice frequently a Kleenex tissue) on which the worshipper places his or her forehead during the prostration.[14]

These periodic incidents have marred what has been an otherwise successful experiment in cooperation, and an atmosphere that in other ways was open to differences in belief. As one Shī'ī parent told me, "It makes us feel second class." When I talked with several staff members, it became clear that these problems were situated within the construct of community and diversity. Several people seemed embarrassed to say that all Muslims do not recognize identical traditions and authorities. When I asked about the different religious beliefs families had, one teacher said in a low voice, "Well, there are the Sunnīs and the others ..." I asked who the others were, thinking she was referring to a secretive and blasphemous sect. Another woman answered, "She means the Shi'ites." She began to tell me that she recognized the legitimacy of Shī'ī beliefs and practices, but that not all families do, and that in some cases, Sunnī students had begun to imitate the Shī'īs — whom many regarded as models of devotion — by praying with a *turbah*. "What happens," she said, "is that now the Shi'ite girls pray as they wish, but do it so that you do not see."

This was the same attitude displayed by and toward women and girls who disputed the *ḥijāb* rule. A comment from one informant highlights the school's tolerance of diversity and its practical basis. "They can't just put all the people who are different out. There would be no one left," she said. Relying for its yearly budget on donations from the mosque, parents' tuition fees and government per-student subsidies, the school depended on a broad coalition of support for its continued existence. Other schools, particularly in Britain where the student roll is often drawn from the sectarian and ethnically homogeneous mosque associated with the school (Parker-Jenkins 1995, 48–49), may provide less room for diversity in ideology and practice. In fact, in cases I heard of where students were withdrawn by parents following a disagreement with the administration, complaints about religious "strictness" (or lack thereof) were seldom behind the decision, whereas disputes over other matters — such as grades or behavioural problems — were.

Funding and ideology (expressed through curriculum and other policies) are strongly linked. While some American and British schools are rigidly conservative and receive financial support from conservative Muslim states, the Canadian school was locally funded through tuition, donations and provincial government subsidies. The necessity of maintaining a coalition large enough to support the school brought about policies that were flexible and inclusive.

Conclusion

This chapter examined the construction of gender within a full-time Canadian Muslim school. The school community was diverse. Its students and teachers came from different ethnic and religious tendencies, and explored their relation to modern Western society in different ways. Individuals engaged in strategies of differentiation that promoted their own gender visions while maintaining group solidarity. Processes of gender construction within the school community were linked to changes within the Muslim community at large, as well as Canadian society as a whole.

Attire represented, in this context, the school community's identification with the general themes of contemporary Western society, which they moulded to fit their vision of Islam. The adoption of Western uniforms was essential to this vision. While some members of the community advocated a radically reformed modernist interpretation of Islam critical of blind adherence, and especially critical of ethnic traditions, which place patriarchal customs above fairness and justice, other members were much more conservative and reluctant to question their heritage. Flexible interpretation of the headscarf rule reflected the compromise between these two groups.

Notes

1 See Kelly (1998a) for a brief history of Muslim immigration, as well as a socio-demographic portrait of Muslims in Canada. The history of Arab and Muslim immigration to Canada is also documented in: Abu-Laban (1983, 1995); Haddad (1978); Jabbra and Jabbra (1987); Ohan and Hayani (1993).

2 Many studies reveal the attitudes and perceptions of Westerners toward Islam and Muslims. Aziz Azmeh (1993, 122–145), Rana Kabbani (1986) and Edward Said (1978) look at how fantasies and biases about Muslims are entrenched and formalized by Western specialists. Earl H. Waugh (1991) discusses discrimination against Muslims in North America. Gerald Darren Gowlett (1995) shows how coverage of Islam in the Canadian media has focused on violence and extremism. The anthologies edited by Kamal Rostom (1989) and Joanna Kadi (1994) document how these attitudes are experienced psychologically and socially.

3 On British Muslim schools, particularly the effects of single-sex schools on Muslim girls, see: Halstead (1991, 1993); Haw (1994); Khanum (1992); Parker-Jenkins (1992, 1995); Parker-Jenkins and Haw (1996). On American schools, see: Durkee (1987); Selby (1992).

4 On the other hand, all Arabic-speaking teachers were North Africans who had immigrated as adults. Although linguistic differences between Moroccans, Algerians and Tunisians meant much accommodation was necessary, informal social conversation between the teachers took place in Arabic. This meant that non-Arabic-speaking teachers (both converts and non-Muslims) often felt somewhat or even significantly excluded, despite attempts by both groups to bridge the linguistic and social gaps (Kelly 1998b).

5 On the significance of social hierarchies in regulating social time and space, see Metcalf (1996).

6 As in the *ḥadīth* that states, "A person [man] who leaves three Friday prayers consecutively, Allah puts a seal on his heart" (Saqib 1986, 64). Thus, even though prayer can be performed privately, mosque attendance is sometimes used to judge the number of practising Muslims in a locality, as in Kelley (1994). Similarly, an extensive study of assimilation among Muslims in the U.S. , conducted by Yvonne Yazbeck Haddad and Adair Lummis, used a mosque-based sampling frame to recruit interview subjects. Haddad and Lummis believe that the attachment to Islam felt by unmosqued Muslims (Muslims who do not regularly attend a mosque) depends primarily on "confessional allegiance," rather than practice or belief (Haddad and Lummis 1987, 9). In contrast, during my fieldwork I heard of many men and women who were very observant yet rarely attended the mosque. A similar view was expressed in Haddad's earlier work (Haddad 1978, 86).

7 When Muslims denounced the ban on *ḥijāb* in a public Montreal Catholic school, the Muslim school's own *ḥijāb* policy was criticized by the press. The Muslim school responded by excusing non-Muslim teachers from the headscarf requirement.

8 For more discussion of veiling in the Middle East, see: Hoodfar (1991, 1997b); MacLeod (1991).

9 None of the students wore beards. In Britain this is a more common practice, however, and cases have been reported of Muslim boys attending public schools who have been told to stay home unless they shaved their beards. See Parker-Jenkins (1995, 66).

10 This practice is not unique. A park in one northern Indian town is called "Purdah Bagh," a place for young girls to take off their *burqa* (cloak-like garments covering the body head to toe, including hair and face) as they leave the traditional neighbourhoods and put them on again before entering (Anjum 1992, 114). Older girls from the Montreal school often spent several minutes in the bathroom before leaving the school in the afternoon, carefully layering their street clothes under their uniforms. Once out the door, they might remove the outer layer — the uniform — in the street or parking lot, or wait until boarding the bus.

11 Men's attire has also become a visual statement of a religious and political vision in some Muslim societies. See Gaffney (1994) and Raza (1993).

12 See Haddad (1978) for a discussion of variations in *zakāt* payment and other forms of religious practice among Muslim Canadians, and Haddad and Lummis (1987) for a discussion of religious attitudes among Muslim-Americans.

13 It is a mistake to believe that only girls suffer from "patriarchal" authority in the family; sons seemed to be dealt with more violently by abusive fathers, some of whom sadly had lower academic expectations of their daughters.

14 Arabic-speaking Shī'īs call this tile a *turbah*, meaning "soil" in Arabic. The importance for Shī'īs of the object from nature is underlined in Ayatollah Khomeini's *Risālah Tawẓīh al-Masā'il* (1984), which contains fourteen questions on this subject. The practice is not optional, although Ayatollah Khomeini's opinion is that it may be foregone "where one must conceal his faith" (Khomeini 1984, 145).

CHAPTER 3

Banners of Faith and Identities in Construct: The *Ḥijāb* in Canada

Reem A. Meshal

Introduction

Like their counterparts the world over, Muslim women are well aware of the significance of dress as a vehicle of gender expression. This awareness grows only more acute as the question of female dress in Islam is increasingly and more hotly debated. Far from being confined to the Muslim world, this debate spills over into the Western discourse on women's rights, feminism in Islam and Muslim immigration. For many Muslims in Canada the issue is closely linked to questions of cultural assertion and assimilation, and is part of an inter-Muslim dialogue on the interpretation of public symbols of Islam and "Muslimness." These exchanges within and across cultures place Muslim women at the centre of an increasingly intrusive debate in which men and women, both Muslim and non-Muslim, define the "correct" attire for a Muslim woman. The following research was conducted in an effort to engage Muslim women in a frank discussion of the issues, and to identify the factors that prompt a young Muslim-Canadian woman to adopt or decline the *ḥijāb*.[1]

While it is important to contextualize any discussion of the *ḥijāb* within broader, global, Islamic trends that women in Muslim countries either support or oppose, it must be remembered that the North American setting engenders a unique host of variables not shared with the Muslim world proper. Paramount here are questions of identity and assimilation. The past two decades have witnessed a rise in the number of Muslims immigrating to Canada, a situation that compels both the adoptive society and the new minority to grapple with difficult questions of cultural exclusivity, assimilation, discrimination and identity. Under the Canadian multicultural umbrella, the generic "Muslim community" stands as a mosaic within a mosaic. From West to East, this community encompasses immigrants from the edge of the Moroccan Atlantic coast to the Indian subcontinent; from North to South it spans the European Balkans down to the southernmost tip of the sub-Saharan belt. As one might expect, this expansive geographic bloc defies singular depictions. Islam is far from monolithic as the plethora of linguistic, racial and cultural groups to which Muslims belong attests. This difference is also reflected in the interpretation and practice of Islam worldwide.

Nowhere is this more apparent than in what is deemed "modest" — particularly for women — in terms of dress. As demonstrated by Homa Hoodfar (in this volume), the modesty threshold rises and falls from one Muslim society to the next, and sometimes even from one village to the next. In certain Muslim societies, particularly Iran and parts of the Arab world, the veil has, in the modern contours of the *ḥijāb*, carried over into the present age. But for most South Asian Muslims, the modern equivalent has not emerged in the same manner, though veiling is gaining popularity among young women in Indonesia. In Canada the *ḥijāb* seems to be increasing in popularity, not just among women from countries where the *ḥijāb* is widespread, but also among those for whom the garment is culturally alien, at least in their twentieth-century urban history. While one expects to find high disparities in the incidence of *ḥijāb* depending on ethnic or national origins, its use among all ethnic groups suggests that cultural origins play a diminishing role in shaping attitudes toward this practice.

However, there seemed to be a lack of a systematic data on how young Muslim women, whether or not they have adopted the veil, view debates over the question of female dress. It was in an effort to bring their views to the fore that the Canadian Council of Muslim Women approached Sajida S. Alvi to supervise this research.

The Research

This chapter is based on the results of a survey of young Muslim women between the ages of eighteen and thirty, most of whom were university students, conducted during the academic year 1997–1998. An eleven-page questionnaire was distributed to Muslim women in ten Canadian cities (Vancouver, Edmonton, Saskatoon, Toronto, Oakville, Mississauga, Kingston, London, Halifax and Montreal). There were 129 respondents — sixty-two of whom wore the *ḥijāb* and sixty-seven who did not — and they came from a variety of backgrounds: South Asian (57 per cent), Arab (34 per cent), European (5 per cent), Iranian (2 per cent), African (2 per cent), Turkish (1 per cent) and Others (4 per cent). While we strove to garner a representative sample of young Muslim-Canadian women, our sample includes a large proportion of university students, as a considerable number of Muslim-Canadian women between the ages of eighteen and thirty attend university. Nonetheless, we are aware that our sample is self-selected since only women interested in the topic chose to participate in the survey. However, the data is indicative of the interest that this issue ignites both within the Muslim communities and within the wider Canadian context, and will, I hope, serve as a springboard to further research and debate.[2] The study itself is directed more specifically to the ideas and practices of young Muslim women in Canada and tries to identify the factors that prompt a young Muslim woman to adopt or decline the *ḥijāb*. The questionnaire included several sections addressing different parts of the inquiry, though it primarily sought to derive information on: family, including levels of parental education, socio-economic status and attitudes toward the *ḥijāb*; attitudes within the Muslim and mainstream communities; scriptural knowledge and the process by which it is acquired. The questionnaires were distributed to female Muslim students through university Muslim societies and Muslim community centres as well as Muslim women's organizations, including the Canadian Council of Muslim Women.

Findings and Discussion

In this study 52 per cent of the Arab women surveyed wear the *ḥijāb*, compared with 40 per cent of Pakistani/Indian women; most of the other groups were evenly split, except for European (converts) Muslim women, where five out of six claim to wear it. These figures are remarkable when contrasted with the incidence of *ḥijāb* in the culture of origin. Arab women's use of *ḥijāb*, depending on the country of origin, more or less coincides with the incidence of *ḥijāb* in much of the Arab world. But to what can we attribute the rising incidence of *ḥijāb* among Canadian women of South Asian, European and Turkish descent? To suggest that this phenomenon is the product of a heightened awareness of the spiritual and material requirements of the faith is to imply that, in their country of origin, this awareness was lacking. Our research has shown that wearing *ḥijāb* is not, however, simply a question of "true" versus "nominal" faith; to what then can we attribute a Muslim woman's decision to adopt this practice? Is choosing the veil part of a dialectical process whereby the construction of identity occurs through contrast with the majority "other"?

TABLE 3.1: ETHNICITY

South Asian	Arab	European	Iranian	African	Turkish	Other
57%	34%	5%	2%	2%	1%	4%

It is important to note that, like other communities in Canada who are latecomers on the immigrant stage, Muslims are still grappling with rudimentary questions of cultural assertion and assimilation. How do Muslims conceive of their place within Canadian society? By virtue of their formidable diversity, Muslims constitute a mosaic of their own within the larger Canadian mosaic. As such, the encounters between Arab, African, South Asian, Iranian, Turkish and European Muslims are as significant for the immigrant as the encounters between Muslims and their adoptive Western, predominantly Christian society.[3] Many scholars theorize that this Muslim mosaic will assume more and more the contours of a Muslim melting pot. This argument may help explain why women of vastly different cultural and ethnic backgrounds are opting for a standardized "Islamic" mode of dress as opposed to traditional costumes, which are often just as modest. Certainly, the question of female dress in Islam reveals a growing parity in religious interpretation between Muslim-Canadians of various backgrounds, as is evidenced by the ranks of women from diverse national backgrounds wearing the *ḥijāb*. This is further supported by the fact that every convert in the survey wore the *ḥijāb*.[4] Metcalf (1996, 10) notes that this idea of a standardized Islam has been the goal, indeed the expectation, of some Muslim leaders, who have hoped that in a new setting, particularly when Muslims from different areas were joined together, individuals would examine their practices in light of scriptural norms and focus on what was sanctioned and could be common to all.

To whom, or to what, is a Muslim woman subscribing when she decides to don or decline the *ḥijāb*? Whose interpretation of Islam directs her? Her family's, her community's, her own, that of her mosque or of the larger Canadian society? One avenue to investigate the forces that motivate a Muslim woman's decision to shroud herself or, conversely, to go bareheaded is by probing her religious knowledge, including her familiarity with Islamic scripture, and inquiring into the means by which this knowledge was acquired (for example, whether through direct reading of the Qur'an or *ḥadīth*; through secondary literature; or through oral transmission, etc.). A complementary approach is to try to determine the role that the donning of the *ḥijāb* plays in the construction of Muslim identity in a specifically North American environment. Thus for our study we not only investigate the transmission and acquisition of religious knowledge, but also measure levels of integration against a number of indicators that include:

the number of non-Muslim friends a woman has; the labels she uses to identify herself; and the opinions she holds on questions of feminism, gender relations and her place in Canadian society.

Veiling and Socio-economic Background

As may be seen from Table 3.1, the respondents in this survey are proportionately representative of the ethnicities that comprise the Muslim population of Canada.[5] Because the survey was directed primarily at university students, it does reflect a limited population of upwardly mobile and highly educated women. Nonetheless, two very discernible patterns emerged in this section of the survey: (a) women born in Canada are less likely to wear *ḥijāb* (37 per cent) than immigrant Muslims (54 per cent); and (b) women whose families belong to higher socio-economic brackets are also less likely to do so. Thus, without overemphasizing the point, class does appear to play a role.[6] Women who do not wear the *ḥijāb* generally come from more educated families in higher income brackets. Fifty-nine per cent of those who do not wear the *ḥijāb* had mothers who had completed university or postgraduate work, while among their veiled counterparts only about half that proportion (31 per cent) had educated mothers. Seventy-seven per cent of those who do not wear the *ḥijāb* had fathers who had completed university or postgraduate work, as compared to 58 per cent of those wearing it. It may be tempting to interpret this data to mean that better educated families are less likely to raise their daughters to wear the *ḥijāb*. It is important to recognize, however, that other factors may contribute to these statistics. For example, the families of women who do not wear the *ḥijāb* may have been in Canada longer and, therefore, exhibit signs of acculturation; or, they may originally come from the more privileged social strata in Muslim countries, where the upper classes have remained fairly immune to the appeals of Islamic revivalism and are relatively Westernized. Lest we overstate the significance of class as a factor in the incidence of *ḥijāb*, it should be recognized that the majority of all the women we surveyed come from educated families; over 80 per cent of the parents of these women had at least completed high school. That said, the statistics do indicate that the education levels of parents are linked with young women's use of *ḥijāb*. Parental occupations reflect the same schisms. An overwhelming percentage (83 per cent) of fathers of those declining to wear the *ḥijāb* are professionals, compared with 53 per cent of fathers of young women who do wear the *ḥijāb*. Even more significant, twice as many women who do not wear the *ḥijāb* have mothers who are employed outside the home.

The final section of our background check divided the women into four age groups, ranging from eighteen to thirty, and into two groups denoting their status as single or married. We found no correlation between age and the incidence of *ḥijāb*; there were, however, striking correlations between the incidence of *ḥijāb* and a woman's marital status. Most of the women who wore the *ḥijāb* (63 per cent) were married. Moreover, many of the women who do not presently wear the *ḥijāb* (47 per cent) say that they are open to the possibility of doing so at a future date. Almost a third of them (28 per cent) said they would consider adopting it if urged to do so by a future spouse. This finding demonstrates, in the first instance, a readiness on the part of almost half the women currently declining *ḥijāb* to accept it at a later date; and, in the second, a willingness to accommodate the opinions of a future spouse on the issue. As some of the women said, they are "open to suggestion."

Our research also sought to determine whether a Muslim education plays a role in the rising visibility of the *ḥijāb* in Canada. Muslim summer camps and weekend Muslim schools, for example, were attended equally by both categories of women as they approached adulthood. Thus, the likelihood that these extracurricular associations are vehicles for the promotion of *ḥijāb* seems — at least for the young women who filled out the questionnaire — to be unfounded. Just over half (52 per cent) of the women who went to summer camp and just under half (46 per cent) of the women who went to weekend school wear the *ḥijāb*. We must conclude, therefore, that these schools and camps are having a negligible impact on a woman's decision regarding *ḥijāb*. There is, admittedly, a larger gap between women who attended Muslim schools and those who did not — 31 per cent of the former wear *ḥijāb*, as opposed to only 18 per cent of the latter.[7] These figures, however, may be explained by the fact that immigrants from Muslim countries are more likely to have gone to Muslim schools and that more immigrants wear *ḥijāb*. This is not to suggest that "Islamic" schools are not propagating an orthodox message with respect to the *ḥijāb*, but it is important to restate that judging from the data, weekend schools and camps are as yet peripheral to the debate.

Veiling and Practising Islam

In this section I ask the following questions: To what extent are the women who do and who do not wear the *ḥijāb* practising Muslims? From where do they derive their knowledge of Islam? Most importantly, on what do they base their conviction, if any, that the *ḥijāb* is an Islamic prescription? And finally, how do they acquire an understanding of the tenets of the Islamic faith?

Without assuming that there is a definitive way of "being Muslim," one may still separate those who adhere to Islam as culture from those who adhere to it as spiritual ethos and, yet again, from those who adhere to Islam as an orthodox, ritual-based faith. In this context, "practise" signifies those aspects of *'ibādat*, or worship, common to both Sunnism and Shi'ism, the two prominent sects of Islam. These include the five daily prayers and fasting in the month of Ramadan. As the reader will find, the statistical contrast between Muslim women who do and do not wear the *ḥijāb* is striking in the area of practice.

TABLE 3.2: INDICES OF RELIGIOUS PRACTICE

	Veiled			**Unveiled**		
	Woman	Mother	Father	Woman	Mother	Father
Fast Ramadan	98%	79%	64%	51%	79%	64%
Pray daily	79%	87%	87%	10%	84%	66%

Referring to Table 3.2, we see that a majority of the women wearing *ḥijāb* claim to fulfill their daily prayer and fasting requirements. By contrast, only 13 per cent of those who do not practice *ḥijāb* reported fasting during at least a portion of Ramadan, while over a third (36 per cent) never fasted. Even fewer of those who do not cover their heads pray on a daily basis, while the remaining 90 per cent of women who do not observe the *ḥijāb* indicated that they prayed during holidays only, or not at all.

The above reflects a schism in adherence to ritual between Muslim women who veil and those who do not, as well as indicating that Muslim women adhere to different sets of beliefs. At first glance, the claim that women who wear the *ḥijāb* do so "for purely spiritual and religious motives," as some of our respondents stated, seems to be substantiated. This brings us to a vital question: From whom or where does a woman derive her religious understanding of *ḥijāb*? Whose interpretation of Islam is she availing herself of? To help us answer these questions, we chart the consistency with which Islamic ritual is maintained within the families of women wearing *ḥijāb*.

A significant majority of parents seem to adhere to both prayer and fasting rituals, including parents of women who do not wear the *ḥijāb*, who are almost equally diligent about ritual observance. The distinction Hoodfar draws between "conventional" and "orthodox" Muslims, whereby one group participates in the rituals of their faith as an extension of their "conventional" culture and the other seeks to align its practices with "orthodox" tenets, is important here. A high proportion of parents, regardless of whether their daughters wear the *ḥijāb*, are practising Islam in either a conventional or more orthodox sense.

One-third (34 per cent) of the women who chose not to veil themselves had mothers who were veiled. By contrast, most (82 per cent) women who wear *ḥijāb* also had mothers who covered their heads. Additionally, 73 per cent of the grandmothers of women who don the *ḥijāb* also cover their heads, often because they opt for a traditional style of dress that entails a modest scarf or veil. Many of the women who characterized their grandmothers as *ḥijāb*-wearing tended to regard tradi-

per cent, felt that it did not prejudice their families or diminish their trust or respect.

TABLE 3.4: SUPPORT FOR *ḤIJĀB* AMONG FAMILIES OF RESPONDENTS WHO DO NOT WEAR *ḤIJĀB*

Spouses	Mothers	Fathers	Sisters	Other Relatives
9%	35%	31%	19%	31%

The data given below in Table 3.5 indicates that Muslim women who do not wear the *ḥijāb* feel considerably more censure from community as opposed to family. A direct correlation between the absence of family pressure and the absence of the *ḥijāb* is also apparent.

Muslim women of all persuasions are highly attuned to family and community expectations; some, as Hoodfar argues in this volume, even appropriate symbols of orthodoxy, such as the veil, as a strategy to negotiate for greater personal freedoms. The line between subtle persuasion and coercion can often be ambiguous. The demarcation is an important one, however, in that it separates acceptable forms of persuasion or encouragement from those that transgress an individual's freedom to choose. Mild community disapproval, as alienating as it might be, is a far cry from coercive censure.

TABLE 3.5: PERCENTAGE OF WOMEN WHO REPORT THAT THE *ḤIJĀB* EVOKES THE RESPECT OF THEIR FAMILIES AND COMMUNITIES

	Veiled	Unveiled
Family	74%	60%
Community	72%	61%

A majority of the women we surveyed have not faced "overt coercion" or "pressure" from any corner. Among women who do not wear the *ḥijāb,* only 25 per cent reported overt coercion or pressure to don the *ḥijāb*. One respondent stated, "My father refused to come to my graduation ceremony if I did not wear it," while a second woman said that when living in Saudi Arabia and Pakistan, "my father made me wear the *ḥijāb* without any explanation as to [its] purpose."

Among women who wear the *ḥijāb*, 27 per cent reported feeling coerced or pressured to remove it. As one woman said, "my family thinks it's backward and can't understand why I would do this. They do not hide their disappointment." Our statistics clearly document that a sizable minority of both those who wear the *ḥijāb* and those who do not will endure some form of direct, applied pressure to "reform" their dress code.

The *ḥijāb*, as a bone of contention in Canadian society at large and specifically within the Muslim community, subjects Muslim women to a fair degree of acrimony. But to infer from this that the women facing this daily pressure are its helpless victims would be a mistake. In response to the question, "Would you agree to reverse your position on the *ḥijāb* if urged to by a spouse or family member?" the great majority of veiled women (87 per cent) responded with a resounding "never." On the other hand, only just over half (58 per cent) of the unveiled women insisted that they would "never" reverse their position. This second lower ratio may be explained by the fact that a high proportion of those who do not wear the *ḥijāb* (47 per cent) profess an interest in wearing it at some future date.

Whether or not women in the latter category are responding to family/community pressure or other factors, including increasing devoutness, cannot be determined until we have answered three questions: First, where do such pressures come from and how do Muslim women encounter them? Second, how do Muslim women from either side of the veil view each other? And lastly, how do they interpret and internalize the mainstream attitudes they encounter in Canadian society?

While both groups of women expressed the belief that mosques and national Muslim organizations are almost universally pro-*ḥijāb*, this perception appears to be stronger among women who do not cover their heads. Those who wear the *ḥijāb* have a fairly positive view of the Muslim community's perception of them; however, one-third of the entire survey reported "mixed reactions" from their Muslim counterparts. As one woman put it, "women who wear it like it, and women who don't wear it, don't like it."

Those not wearing the *ḥijāb* had a more ambivalent view of the Muslim community's opinion of them. Most reported a neutral reaction from other Muslims — this includes the 25 per cent of unveiled women who say they've felt pressure to wear the *ḥijāb*. Nearly half, however, believed that wearing *ḥijāb* does (would) inspire the respect and trust of their Muslim community. Women wearing the *ḥijāb*, on the other hand, felt more ambivalence from the greater Canadian society, reporting a broad spectrum of reactions ranging from tolerant, respectful and highly supportive, to rude, disdainful and even insulting. Many felt that non-Muslims were fixated on the *ḥijāb* as a mark of "Islam's oppression of women." As well, a substantial number (27 per cent) reported that they had experienced overt pressure from society at large to remove the *ḥijāb*. As one woman said:

> Most non-Muslims think [Muslim] women are putting themselves down and are backward. Rarely, [do they] respect a woman for wearing it. There is a lack of understanding about the *ḥijāb*.

These figures suggest that Muslim women are torn, both by internal dissension from within their communities and by negative reactions from without. What impact these pressures have on a woman's final decision is difficult to gauge. We venture to suggest that in view of the family's prominent role in shaping attitudes to the veil, this decision depends as much on its members' responses to these pressures as on the individual woman's.

Let us now return to a question posed earlier: To whom or to what source do women and their families subscribe for religious views? Despite the fact that historically, Muslim societies have responded to Qur'anic injunctions for modesty in very different ways — ranging from face veils in the Middle

East to virtual seclusion in parts of the Indian subcontinent, to far more liberal interpretations in Malaysia and Indonesia, where women have only recently begun to cover their hair — a new consensus has emerged. In the last century, mainstream orthodox attitudes have been in agreement that a woman is required to wear *ḥijāb* — covering her entire body except for her face and her hands — in the presence of males, save for immediate and some extended male family members.

Canadian mosques, our respondents confirmed, appear to accept and promote the *ḥijāb* as the ideal for a Muslim woman. A third of those surveyed reported that sermons on the *ḥijāb* are delivered on a regular basis at mosques. Overwhelmingly, both groups of women (74 per cent of those who do not and 79 per cent of those who do wear the *ḥijāb)* concurred that the mosques are "in favour" of *ḥijāb*. One woman noted that the subject is often alluded to as part of an overall sermon on a topic such as "Conduct in Islam" or "What is a Muslim?": "I feel that at the mosque, they [Muslim men] give women who wear the *ḥijāb* more respect."

It should be recalled that most of the women did not report attending mosque services themselves, but said that their male relatives did. It may be reasonably assumed that some or all family members are attuned to the prevailing climate in the mosques. The probability that mosques are setting the tone in the local communities cannot be discounted. According to Metcalf, "mosques increasingly represent Islam in the West to Muslims and non-Muslims alike" (Metcalf 1996, 18). To test this, our study compared the information that we acquired on the prevailing climate in mosques (with respect to the *ḥijāb* alone) with the climate in national and campus Muslim organizations.

The message that our informants claim is being propagated by mosques has also found its mark in national and campus organizations, which are also largely pro-*ḥijāb*. Sixty-eight per cent of women reported that campus organizations are "in favour" or "strongly in favour" of the *ḥijāb*. One Edmonton woman reported the following incident during "Islam Awareness Week" at her campus: " [T]he women in our [Muslim campus] association were informed by the male students that any woman not wearing the *ḥijāb* was not welcome to sit at the [information] table." However, the pro-*ḥijāb* policy of some campus associations is not yet having an impact on their female membership. Although slightly more women wearing the *ḥijāb* belong to national Muslim organizations (35 per cent as opposed to only 27 per cent of those not wearing the *ḥijāb*), women who do not wear *ḥijāb* are, by contrast, more likely to belong to campus organizations. Judging by these statistics, women who participate in Muslim national or campus associations do not, in most instances, uniformly reflect an organization's pro-*ḥijāb* stance. In the face of pressures from the organizations to which they belong, these women often demonstrate resistance and autonomy. Just under half of the women from both groups say the issue of *ḥijāb* is debated on their campuses, an indication that for many of them, the issue is unresolved.

The prevalent pro-*ḥijāb* sentiment of most Muslim associations in Canada does appear to mirror the climate in the mosques. This strongly suggests that the dissemination of a single, hegemonic doctrine on the *ḥijāb* has been successful. The mosque, as the lynchpin of Muslim associations and the site of religious instruction, is highly active in any process that determines how Muslim women appear — or are hidden. The role of the mosque is further explored in the next section, where respondents identify the sources of Islamic knowledge to which they subscribe.

Imbibing Islam

Any discussion on Muslim women and *ḥijāb* in Canada would be incomplete without an analysis of the women's understanding of Islamic scripture and religious tenets. When asked to characterize their knowledge of Islam, 81 per cent of the women who wear the *ḥijāb* and 79 per cent of those who do not rated their knowledge from "good" to "very strong." The remainder characterized their knowledge as "weak" or "fair." To test their claims, we solicited answers to the following questions: "From where do you derive your knowledge of Islam?" and, "What scriptural support can you give for your position on *ḥijāb*?"

Prior to embarking on this study, I had hypothesized that the increasing visibility of the *ḥijāb* may be linked directly to the mosques, or to Muslim associations and *da'wah* groups. However, the findings of this study show that mosques and Muslim associations play only an indirect role in many instances, in contrast with the direct role of the family. Less than one-third (32 per cent) of those wearing the *ḥijāb* cited the mosque as a primary source of instruction or learning, while over half (55 per cent) cited the family as primary. Along parallel lines, only a quarter (25 per cent) of the women who do not wear the *ḥijāb* rate the mosque as a primary site of their Islamic education, while far more (64 per cent) indicated that the family was responsible for this. The emphasis on learning within the family suggests that knowledge of Islamic teachings is most often being communicated or transmitted orally. Nevertheless, both groups of women rated the Qur'an and *ḥadīth*, and not their families, as the principal sources of their knowledge. When asked what sources most influenced their position on *ḥijāb* in particular, again an overwhelming number cited the Qur'an and *ḥadīth*. In this instance, the family came in second (see Table 3.6).

TABLE 3.6: SOURCES OF ISLAMIC KNOWLEDGE

	Veiled	Unveiled
Qur'an and *ḥadīth*	82%	44%
Family	35%	18%

It should be noted that almost half of the women who do not wear the *ḥijāb* did not answer the second of these questions. Their reticence may suggest that their understanding of the *ḥijāb* as an Islamic prescription is rather vague. Of those who answered, many said they were certain that the Qur'an enjoined the wearing of the *ḥijāb*, though very few were actually able to identify specific Qur'anic *sūrahs* or *ḥadīths* as sources for this prescription. Recalling the high number of women from this group who were contemplating donning *ḥijāb* in the future, their lack of scriptural knowledge on the issue suggests that their convictions on the *ḥijāb* cannot be reconciled with their claims to first-hand knowledge of the sources. For the women who do wear *ḥijāb*, most regarded the practice as mandatory, while 5 per cent described it as a "preferred state" and 15 per cent did not respond. Yet when asked to give scriptural support for their beliefs, only 37 per cent of the women who answered "Yes, *ḥijāb* is an Islamic prescription" were able to provide supporting Qur'anic or *ḥadīth*-based references.

TABLE 3.7: IS *ḤIJĀB* PRESCRIBED BY ISLAM?

	Veiled	Unveiled
% claiming knowledge from Qu'ran and *ḥadīth*	94%	73%
% who believe *ḥijāb* is prescribed in Qur'an	79%	32%
% who could identify relevant verses of Qur'an or *ḥadīth*	37%	3%

While Muslim women who wear the *ḥijāb* appear to be more familiar with the scriptural texts than their counterparts (see Table 3.7), overall acquaintance with the scriptures is minimal for both groups. The claim made by the overwhelming majority to having a "good" to "very strong" knowledge of Islam and to formulating independent views concerning *ḥijāb,* based on primary Islamic scripture, must, therefore, be discounted. Despite protestations to the contrary, the women in our survey had only a vague grasp of the Qur'anic verses that have been interpreted as prescribing the *ḥijāb*. Here are a few sample remarks made by them concerning Islamic scriptural references to *ḥijāb*:

> I know it's in the Qur'an, but I don't know where.
> In the verses that everyone talks about.
> Ask an *ālim*! [a Muslim scholar].

The respondents' evidently shallow familiarity with Islamic texts reinforces the idea that religious knowledge is primarily acquired as a result of oral transmission and the filtration of religious knowledge through family and mosque.

Through Women's Eyes

What are the motives that prompt women to wear the *ḥijāb*? When asked if their reasons for wearing *ḥijāb* were purely religious, social or political, an overwhelming majority (81 per cent) cited religious motives alone, 5 per cent cited additional political motives and 8 per cent cited all three. These figures will be cross-referenced with other factors when we come to consider Islam and identity, and explore how Muslim women see themselves within Canadian society.

Much depends on the personal encounters that transpire between members of Canada's Muslim communities. Such encounters can be sites of empowerment and support as well as censure and admonition; both groups of women reported a range of positive and negative reactions to their dress code. Women wearing the *ḥijāb* were far more likely to report positive feedback. Most (61 per cent) felt that Muslim men saw them in a positive light, while half (52 per cent) got the same feeling from other Muslim women. Only a small minority (4 per cent and 5 per cent, respectively) felt that other Muslim men and women regarded them negatively.[8] Only 4 per cent could report that their fellow Muslims regarded them with neutrality.

On the other hand, Muslim women who do not wear the *ḥijāb* reported predominantly neutral reactions: 39 per cent said Muslim males reacted with indifference, while a third (27 per cent) said the same for female Muslim reaction. Six per cent reported mixed reactions from Muslim women while 10 per cent said the responses had all been negative. Only 3 per cent described positive reactions from other Muslim women. Nine per cent reported mixed reactions from Muslim men, 4 per cent reported positive reaction and 3 per cent reported negative reactions on the part of men to women who do not wear the *ḥijāb*.

We also explored the opinions that our respondents had of other Muslim women. Of those who wear *ḥijāb,* under half (38 per cent) made negative comments about Muslim women who do not, while almost half (47 per cent) expressed neutrality. Only 3 per cent made a positive comment while many more were of the opinion that their co-religionists were, as one respondent put it, "wrong," that they were "harming themselves."

By contrast, just over a quarter (28 per cent) of the women not wearing *ḥijāb* voiced a positive opinion of those who choose to wear it. This high figure makes sense when we reflect on the proportion of women in our survey who foresee a day when they might themselves adopt the veil. We can speculate that approval rate would be much lower in an exclusive sample of Muslim women who would "never" consider *ḥijāb* for themselves. However, whether or not they disapproved of it, the women in our sample who do not wear the *ḥijāb* consistently supported the rights of their co-religionists to do so.

The sense of alienation, if not siege, with which many Muslim communities live in the West may also explain why so many women who do not wear the *ḥijāb* defend its presence. For such, it serves as a symbol of their community. One unveiled woman wrote:

> What is the debate here? I fear it is not the superficiality of the veil, it is rather the fear of Islam itself. We do not, for example, fear nuns in their habits nor do we want to rescue them from the male oppression of the church.

Tension between Muslim women over this issue certainly does exist. This is evidenced by the perception and treatment of women who have abandoned the *ḥijāb*. Women from this group elicited the greatest number of negative comments from both groups. Over half (58 per cent) of those wearing the *ḥijāb* questioned the spiritual integrity and moral fibre of Muslim women who had ceased the practice. They were joined in their condemnation by 15 per cent of those who themselves wore no veil. According to one woman, "They are weak and have low self-esteem. No faith."

However, among those who do not wear *ḥijāb* an almost equal margin, 12 per cent, rated its removal as, in the words of one woman, "enlightened." A scant majority, 51 per cent, were neutral.

Clearly, the figures cited above reveal Muslim women themselves as protagonists in the discourse on *ḥijāb*. This is not to shift the weight of blame for any social or community pressure onto the shoulders of Muslim women, but rather, to identify them as active and responsible agents in this debate.

It is apparent from our data that Muslim women who do not wear the *ḥijāb* are conscious of a stronger reaction from both Muslim men and women than are their veiled counterparts. The data also suggests that Muslim women are more inclined than Muslim men to pass judgment on the choices of their co-religionists in this matter. This is perhaps not surprising in view of the fact that the question of dress is, in this case, gender exclusive, and because it raises a moral flag as well. Just under 25 per cent of the women surveyed who wear the *ḥijāb* used words such as "impious" and "immoral," and phrases like "badly brought up" to refer to bare-headed Muslim women. One woman said:

> The debate in our Muslim community is around [this question] ... is a Muslim woman a good Muslim if she doesn't wear *ḥijāb*? Some of the Muslim hijabee [*sic*] women sometimes look down upon other non-hijabee women in the mosque and outside too. It sometimes feels that the issue will never be resolved because of people always judging others.

Almost a third of the women who decline the *ḥijāb* reacted with a mixture of neutrality and negativity to women who do wear it. Many of them described their *ḥijāb*-wearing co-religionists as "backward." One of the latter replied:

> [T]he women who themselves do not wear the *ḥijāb*, but know that it is obligatory, respect and admire me. As for those who dismiss the *ḥijāb* altogether, well they hate me and consider me a fundamentalist.

Implicit here are notions of modernity, progress and feminism to which, in the minds of this woman's critics, the *ḥijāb* does not conform. What the women who do not wear the *ḥijāb*, and the Canadian community at large, fail to appreciate are the decidedly modern contours of the *ḥijāb* as a twentieth-century adaptation of traditional modest dress. For some women in *ḥijāb*, their bare-headed counterparts are blind imitators of Western society. These opposing perspectives hold true for both men and women; however, they do not illuminate the factors that compel Muslim women to judge one another more harshly than Muslim men do. It may be enough to point out that the issue is ultimately gender exclusive, and, by virtue of its personal and controversial nature, cannot but evoke strong sentiment from those whom it most affects. From the internal dynamics of the debate over *ḥijāb*, we now turn to an examination of the attitudes of the mainstream Canadian community.

The Mainstream Gaze

The act of donning the *ḥijāb* renders its wearer more visible even as it covers her form. Veiled, she is marked and identifiable, not just to the Muslim community, but also to the wider Canadian society. The *ḥijāb* "is a flag," said one woman. Indeed, when in the generally tolerant Canadian social climate controversies over immigration and multiculturalism bring intolerance to the fore, women in *ḥijāb* become targets, identified as "other." This is not to suggest that all non-Muslim Canadians are averse to the sight of a veiled woman, since 35 per cent of women in *ḥijāb* reported that they had never experienced discrimination at work, 27 per cent had never met with prejudice from their non-Muslim peers and 39 per cent had never had problems with their professors. However, an equally high, and in some areas significantly higher, ratio of women reported incidents of overt discrimination related to the *ḥijāb*: 34 per cent at work, 63 per cent with their non-Muslim peers and 39 per cent from professors.

While it is possible that the instances of discriminatory behaviour, cited in Table 3.8, may be related to other factors such as race, ethnicity,

TABLE 3.8: INCIDENTS OF DISCRIMINATION REPORTED BY WOMEN WEARING THE *ḤIJĀB*

	Yes	No
Work	34%	35%
Peers	63%	27%
Professors	39%	39%

accent, etc., as opposed to the *ḥijāb* per se, nearly half the women (47 per cent) reporting harassment said discrimination rose significantly upon their adoption of the *ḥijāb*. This seems to be substantiated by the converts to Islam in our sample, all of whom reported experiencing prejudice after taking up the practice. While non-converts described neutral or mixed reactions,[9] almost 30 per cent said that non-Muslim men had negative responses and another 32 per cent that non-Muslim women reacted badly. Consider the words of these three women:

> The reactions are different. Some of them have this stereotype — that all of us are ignorant, submissive fools and this is apparent in their treatment of us.

> Aside from [people] trying to prove my insanity for converting to Islam and wearing the *ḥijāb*, either they felt it wasn't necessary or they thought I was trying to imitate "someone from one of those countries." But to me it was a step forward.

> They don't understand why I wear it. They think that I'm oppressed.

It is difficult to ascertain any clear connection between reported discrimination based solely on wearing the *ḥijāb* when almost half (49 per cent) of the women who do not wear it also report incidences of racial or ethnic discrimination; we can only conclude that at least some of the negative responses the *ḥijāb* evokes find their origin in age-old religio-racial prejudices, and there is no denying that the sight of the *ḥijāb* can stoke such bigotry.

In summary, women who adopt the *ḥijāb* encounter little in the way of positive feedback from the wider mainstream society. Whatever support or encouragement for the *ḥijāb* exists is to be found at home, or in the Muslim community; the wider Canadian society reacts at best with tolerance, manifested as indifference, and at worst with discrimination.

Identities in Construct

Who am I? For the overwhelming majority of the 129 women we surveyed, the answer seems to be Muslim-Canadian. Only a quarter of the women who do not wear the *ḥijāb* identified themselves by national origin — e.g., Iranian-Canadian — while an even smaller number of the women who wear *ḥijāb* did so. No woman in *ḥijāb* identified herself as merely "Canadian," although a small number of unveiled women did.

The significance of the results (Table 3.9) cannot be overstated. They tell us that for the linguistically, racially and culturally diverse group of women who filled out the survey, being "Muslim" signified an ethnicity; only a quarter of the women who do not wear the *ḥijāb* identified themselves by making reference to their former nationality, while 52 per cent of them identified themselves as Muslim-Canadian.

TABLE 3.9: FORMS OF SELF-IDENTIFICATION

	Veiled	Unveiled
Muslim-Canadian	76%	52%
Canadian	0%	10%
Ethnic-Canadian (e.g., Arab-Can.)	19%	25%
Other	15%	13%

The process of assimilation and amalgamation underway within the Muslim mosaic in particular has already occurred at a fundamental level.

Diverse groups are beginning to identify with one another as members of a single community; second-generation Iranians, Pakistanis, Palestinians, etc., are no longer identifying with their country of origin, but are indistinguishable from their co-religionists under the common label of Muslim. To what extent is this process a reaction against an alien, and often alienating, dominant culture? Are Arabs, Bosnians and Somalis "one," by virtue of being Muslims, in the face of the "other"? The answer seems to be affirmative, as Muslims, because of their status as a religious minority, rally around their common faith as a platform of identity.[10] Diop and Michalak argue, "almost all Latin American migrants to the U.S. in recent years have been 'Christian,' but religion plays no part ... in the American discourse on [their] migration. ... If migrants speak as 'Muslims,' finding such an identity natural and effective in the new context where they live, we must see that in part as a label thrust upon them" (Diop and Michalak 1996, 74).

Do the contours of this new Muslim identity fit into the Canadian mainstream? Indeed, are they intended to? Metcalf asserts that Muslims are drawing attention to the differences between Islam and the West as a way of expressing dissatisfaction with the "totalizing culture of the nation-state" (Metcalf 1996, 16). What we are concerned with here are the ways in which the answers to the questions posed above touch on a woman's motive in deciding to wear the *ḥijāb*. Does a woman's sense of integration, or lack thereof, in Canadian society, influence her decision? We are better positioned to answer this after a perusal of the patterns of integration into which the women we surveyed fall.

As expected, women who did not wear the *ḥijāb* reported feeling more integrated into Canadian society. Almost a quarter (29 per cent) of this group called themselves "very integrated," while the remainder considered themselves "integrated to some degree."[11] Only 4 per cent described themselves as "not integrated at all." Conversely, a substantially lower percentage (10 per cent) of women who wear the *ḥijāb* felt "very integrated," while a substantially higher percentage claimed they were not integrated at all (21 per cent). The number of non-Muslim friends the women counted was also taken as an indicator of levels of integration. The same patterns reveal themselves here. Women who do not wear the *ḥijāb* are twice as likely to have over ten non-Muslim friends. Over a third (35 per cent) of those wearing it said they had only one to three non-Muslim friends.

That women who wear the *ḥijāb* feel less integrated into Canadian society is perhaps self-evident. To extrapolate further from this information we must consider another indicator: the gender roles to which the women subscribe and the cultural references that these entail.

When questioned about their professional or domestic aspirations, fully 40 per cent of those who wear the *ḥijāb* cited domestic ambitions alone, compared to just 7 per cent of women who do not. This staggering discrepancy cries out for explanation. It points to the gulf that separates women in *ḥijāb* from their non-veiled co-religionists. The former perceive their role and place in society to be that of wives and mothers, while the latter express an almost unanimous interest in a career beyond the home. Note, however, that over half (60 per cent) of the women wearing the *ḥijāb* also described themselves as career-oriented. Having said this, we must still ask why so many more of these women prioritize their lives differently. We use the word "prioritize" here in view of the fact that fully three-quarters (75 per cent) of women wearing *ḥijāb* reported having been employed, while only 60 per cent claimed to be interested in working outside the home. Obviously the remainder were forced, by economic imperatives, to work. Why is this the case?

Clearly, any answer to the above question must touch on the issue of gender identity. In view of the fact that more recent immigrant women are wearing the *ḥijāb*, it may be a reflection of conventional gender roles in the country of origin. This is borne out by the fact that the respondents born in Canada, who wore the *ḥijāb* in fewer numbers and exhibited a career-minded outlook, appear to have imbibed the feminist values of the local culture to a greater degree. This explanation may be true for some women, but not for all. The feminist movement in Muslim countries can, after all, boast of a century-long pedigree in places like Egypt and Turkey. Furthermore, of the respondents not born in Canada, exactly half refuse to subscribe to so-called "traditional" gender roles or wear the *ḥijāb*. It is telling to note that of the Egyptian, Iranian and North African (Algerian, Moroccan) immigrants — all from countries weathering strong Islamic revivalist movements — only a fraction wear the *ḥijāb*. Second-generation Canadian respondents coming from these backgrounds were far more likely to wear the *ḥijāb* than those born in these particular countries. South Asian immigrants usually adopt the *ḥijāb* upon arrival in Canada, and not prior. Thus, we must assume that the forces that shape this new, North American Muslim identity are to be located in Canada itself.

From the foregoing, we may deduce that Muslim women, like all women, are defining their sense of self in reaction to, or against, societal currents. What are these currents? In the Muslim East, women are contending with two trends: one, a process of Islamic revivalism that often entails certain gender roles; the other, a process of westernization, often packaged as modernization, which espouses Western feminist values. In Canada, the latter are ensconced as a feature of the dominant culture. The relatively smaller number of women in *ḥijāb* who saw their futures in terms of career and work are sending us a message with respect to that dominant culture: "Its [Western feminism] objectives and values do not represent me!" This should hardly come as a surprise given the criticism to which feminist theory is subject even within Western society, especially from women occupying low-income brackets and members of visible minorities (Aziz 1992; Harding 1992). Thus, it may be concluded that on a profound level, the answers of the women in *ḥijāb* are as significant for what they reveal of the values that are adopted in the Canadian context as they are for highlighting those that are rejected.

The final question in our survey, "Do you believe that men and women are equal?" evidenced support of the proposition that women who did not wear the *ḥijāb* were far more likely to employ feminist terms familiar to the Western ear. Nevertheless, caution should be exercised when interpreting the data provided in Table 3.10, since the answers do little to elucidate the women's views on the equality of the sexes, nor do they provide evidence of the strength of their feminist convictions.

TABLE 3.10: ARE MEN AND WOMEN EQUAL?

	Veiled	Unveiled
(a) In all respects	52%	79%
(b) In some respects	37%	21%

A number of women — from both sides of the veil — qualified answer (a), for instance, by adding, "Men and women are equal, but they have different duties and responsibilities." In other words, equal but different. Others marked "in some respects," but made sure we understood that "equal in some respects" alluded to anatomical differences.

The answers are significant, however, not for what they inform us of a woman's feminist convictions, but rather, for what they convey of her cultural and, by extension, political terms of reference. That women seem more likely to say "men and women are equal in all respects" suggests that they are comfortable with a key tenet of Western feminist thought, i.e., the deconstructionist argument that reduces all gender roles and traits to social and environmental conditioning. According to this line of reasoning, biological differences signify little and men and women are essentially the same. This argument boasts its fair share of critics and by no means represents the only line of feminist thought in the West. For many Muslim women, for whom the question is more a matter of perception than knowledge of the substantive content of feminist theory, the feminist slogans to which they are listening and the overt sexualization of women in the West to which they are spectators breed confusion. For many other Muslim women, who are highly informed with respect to the history and underpinnings of the feminist movement in the West, Western feminist theory betrays Eurocentric roots, emphasizing its local, as opposed to universal, character. We noted with great interest, for example, the number of women who defended the *ḥijāb* as a garb designed to desexualize a woman's presence in society and, thus, to promote her as a human being rather than as a sexual object:

> *Ḥijāb* gives me freedom to spend more time on development of my spiritual and intellectual self. That is more important to me than wasting time and money on my physical attraction. It protects me from being taken for my beauty rather than brains, making me a ... liberated feminist in the true sense of the word.

> I question the legitimacy of this so-called debate on the issue of *ḥijāb*. Why not debate instead the sexualized clothing of Western consumer culture. We should closely examine the fashions foisted upon women to entice men.

> Living in a Western world [I find] far too much emphasis on looks and size. I guess we all have to look like Cindy Crawford [a popular fashion model] to be accepted. How absurd these [Western] women are. And they claim to be feminists? I'd rather be judged for what and who I am.

From these and other direct statements made by the women, we may infer that two mutually antagonistic remedies to the "problem" of sexuality, feminism and public space have come to a head. Western society, for all its rhetoric over the "sameness" of the sexes, revels in the promotion of feminine sexuality (something many Western feminists abhor), while Eastern, Islamic culture moves in the other direction to quell its influence and excise it from the public realm.

A woman's options are not, of course, limited to either flaunting or shrouding her sexuality by the clothing she chooses to wear; nevertheless, in the debate over *ḥijāb* the perception is often that only these opposing paradigms exist. Thus, the side of the veil a woman chooses does, unwittingly, reveal the cultural references to which she subscribes. It follows that women who are less integrated into Canadian society and who have not imbibed the normative values of modern North American culture are more likely to decide in favour of the *ḥijāb*. This apparent rejection of Western culture, and indeed even values, does not preclude the potential for integration into the wider Canadian fold, but it does indicate that the terms and conditions by which cultural accommodation is achieved will be born of negotiation.

Conclusion

Is it religious conviction, resistance to the forces of assimilation or the assertion of identity (religious and cultural) that spurs Muslim women to don the *ḥijāb* in Canada? The process by which the "Muslim" ethnic identity is consolidated in Canada speaks of both a reaction to the "other" and a coalescing into the "we" at one and the same time.

Thus far, we have deduced that it is the views of her immediate family members that most influence a Muslim woman's outlook with respect to the *ḥijāb*. Whether a South Asian mother has adopted the *ḥijāb* in Canada, or whether *ḥijāb* represents traditional cultural norms — as is the case, for example, in parts of the Middle East — the outcome is the same: with remarkable consistency, young Muslim women are opting for the choices their mothers make. Additionally, they (81 per cent) claim to do so for purely religious motives; not one respondent cited purely social or political motives for wearing the *ḥijāb*.

Nonetheless, the results of the survey indicate that while objective measures of levels of assimilation — the language spoken at home, for example — reveal similar patterns for both groups of Muslim women, those who do not wear *ḥijāb* feel more integrated into Canadian society, are somewhat more inclined to call themselves simply Canadian and claim to have more non-Muslim friends. It is worth noting that all six of the converts in this study wore *ḥijāb* and several reported that they felt "somewhat integrated" into Canadian society, but "not by choice." Their responses reveal a greater sense of belonging to the Muslim community than to the Canadian community at large, and further support the contention that the *ḥijāb* as a "flag" is waved in common as a symbol of Muslim identity. This is neither a negation of women's claims to donning it as a simple act of faith, nor the attribution of political or social motives to their ends. Rather, it is an extrapolation from the fact that the *ḥijāb*, as a highly visible and ideological symbol of communion, gathers its adherents in an embracing, exclusive fold and, more often than not, extends to the individual a positive sense of belonging and a firm sense of identity.

We have also established that one of the results of the emphasis on family shows that most respondents rely on the oral transmission of religious knowledge. Only seventeen of the sixty-two respondents who wore *ḥijāb* could cite specific verses of the Qur'an relating to women's attire. None of the 32 per cent of those not wearing the *ḥijāb* — who nevertheless believe *ḥijāb* is mandatory according to Islam — could list such verses and only four could name relevant *sūrahs*. Findings such as these are telling, given the contentious nature of the modernist debate being waged over the interpretation of the Qur'anic verses in question. It would be fair to assume that, given the low number of women who were informed on the scriptural basis for *ḥijāb*, even fewer women would have an understanding of the intricacies of this debate where no consensus is currently to be found. This puts us in mind of the ways in which our respondents dismissed one other. Muslim women who did not wear the *ḥijāb* frequently described those who did as "backward," "old fashioned" or "out of touch with reality," while Muslim women who wore it called those who did not "shameful" or "weak in faith." Clearly the issue, even as it highlights a consolidation of Muslim-Canadian identity and practice, also betrays the community's deep divisions. In the mean time, negative backlash from the non-Muslim community at the sight of women in *ḥijāb* only exacerbates the issue. The larger Canadian community acts as a pressure point, often demanding, as the dominant culture, conformity with its own normative standards.

As we have seen, it is impossible to separate the issue of *ḥijāb* in the Canadian context from larger questions of gender and cultural identity, assimilation and discrimination. If Muslim women are to represent an effective interest group, entitled to assert their legal and moral rights within the local and larger communities, more nuanced discussion with respect to the nature of the debate on *ḥijāb* and their role within it is surely needed. Without, for example, gaining some insight into the traditional and modern methods of Qur'anic exegesis and interpretation, the debate and issues remain obscure to Muslim women themselves. Muslim women in Canada as a group are under the dual pressures of an ambivalent, larger society that would target the attire of a Muslim woman as a subject for legislation, and of communities that would enforce a standard of dress through censure. As such, their interests can only be served by further, subtler engagement with the issues at hand.

Notes

1 Given the debates on dress code among Muslim women, the Canadian Council of Muslim Women felt the need to provide more systematic data on how young Muslim women in Canada feel about the veiling and dress code. They approached Sajida S. Alvi to help supervise such a project. Paula Jolin and I jointly conducted this research, and as Paula shared in the painstaking process of data entry, quantification and early public presentation of our data, I would like to credit her and acknowledge her contribution to this paper.

2 Each section of the questionnaire included a set of multiple choice questions as well as space for the respondent to elaborate on her answers. The multiple-choice responses were later quantified by percentage.

3 See J. Waardenburg, "The Institutionalization of Islam in the Netherlands, 1961–86," in *The New Islamic Presence in Europe,* edited by T. Gerholm and Y.G. Lithman (Stockholm: Centre for Research in International Migration and Ethnicity, 1988), 8–31. In this article, Waardenburg describes what he foresees as an "Islam without ethnicity," wherein the processes of communications and migration foster an increasingly homogenous Muslim identity in the West.

4 Converts, by virtue of their newcomer status, generally subscribe to mainstream interpretations of a faith, and thus provide a good indication of its normative patterns of belief and conduct.

5 Muslims in Canada include the following nationalities: Bengali, Indian, Pakistani, Egyptian, Syrian, Jordanian, Palestinian, Turkish, Iranian, Indonesian, East European, East African, Caribbean and Canadian-born. As well, this pluralistic "group" adheres to a number of sects within Islam: Sunnī, Shī'ī, Druze and Isma'īlī. Followers of the latter two sects do not acknowledge the *ḥijāb* or veil as an Islamic proscription. Most Muslims in Canada are of Asian descent, with Indo-Pakistanis comprising the largest group at 42.1 per cent. Arabs follow at 22.8 per cent.

6 For more on the socio-economic place of Muslims in Canada, see Zohra Husaini, *Muslims in the Canadian Mosaic* (Edmonton: Muslim Research Foundation, 1990), and A. Rashid, *The Muslim Canadians: A Profile* (Ottawa: Statistics Canada, 1985).

7 A Muslim school denotes an institution that teaches both secular and non-secular subjects. For more on this subject, see Sheila McDonough, "Muslims of Montreal," in *The Muslim Communities in North America,* edited by Y. Haddad and J.I. Smith (New York: State University of New York Press, 1994), 317–334.

8 However, 14 per cent reported mixed or neutral reactions from Muslim men, and a full 31 per cent described the reactions of Muslim women as mixed.

9 Ten per cent reported neutral reactions from non-Muslim women and 14 per cent from non-Muslim men, while 19 per cent reported mixed reaction from non-Muslim women and 6 per cent mixed reaction from non-Muslim men.

10 Remy Leveau draws parallels between the experiences of Jews and North African Muslims in France. See Remy Leveau and Gilles Kepel, *Culture islamique et attitudes politiques dans la population musulmane en France: Enquête effectuée pendant le mois du Ramadan* (Paris: Fondation National des Sciences Politiques, 1985).

11 Thirty-four per cent said they were "integrated," while 31 per cent described themselves as "somewhat integrated."

CHAPTER 4

Voices of Muslim Women

Sheila McDonough

One day, Sajida S. Alvi and I were discussing how to produce a book on the *ḥijāb* that would be enlightening, but also as non-controversial as possible. We had accepted a mandate from the Canadian Council for Muslim Women (CCMW) for just such a project, but we wanted to create something that would stimulate thought, rather than stir up hostility and divisiveness. Sajida's husband, Sabir Alvi, a social scientist, who had been listening to our conversation over the dinner table, intervened to suggest that we approach a number of Muslim women and ask them to speak directly for themselves. Thus it was that the voice of a Muslim male called for Muslim women to speak for themselves.

As a result, the leadership of the CCMW contacted several Muslim women to see if they would be willing to make short statements on this subject. Sajida S. Alvi asked each of the women who responded to highlight the factors that had led to her decision either to wear or not to wear the *ḥijāb*. Each was asked to discuss this decision with respect to its impact on her understanding of her own spirituality.

What follows are seven brief statements by Canadian Muslim women made in response to the request. The diversity of their answers should come as no surprise. I myself was once present at a meeting in Montreal sponsored by the Ecumenical Network of Roman Catholic and Protestant Women (Réseau écuménique des femmes du Québec) at which five different Muslim women spoke to their Christian hosts. I overheard one Christian woman saying at the end, "Well, if you asked five Christian women, you would also get five different answers."

The seven women presented below have thus given a variety of different responses. That variety in itself is illustrative of the reality faced by Muslim women in Canada. Furthermore, each one of them is clearly thinking, and thinking for herself. Several of them indicate that, for each, the decision to wear the *ḥijāb* has been empowering. This is a message that the wider Canadian society needs to hear, namely, that for some women the *ḥijāb* serves to increase a woman's sense of her own dignity. Some Muslim women, on the other hand, have felt more empowered by giving up the veil. Both situations exist; both are valid for the individual.

In the Canadian context, many Muslim women are looking for ways to strengthen their sense of purposeful selfhood. They realize that there are many possibilities before them, and they are trying to make wise and informed decisions. They know that Canada makes available to them many avenues of education and employment, and many are availing themselves of these opportunities. Yet some of them are troubled by certain aspects of the wider culture. Some feel that society at large does not accord women as much dignity as it should.

Several of the women state that it was going on pilgrimage to Mecca (*ḥajj*) that encouraged them to make the decision to wear the *ḥijāb*. In my view, this is a significant finding. The Muslim pilgrimage is a duty, along with daily prayer, fasting, giving alms and witnessing to the reality of God, which is an obligation for all adult Muslims. In none of these basic obligations is there any distinction made between the duties of males and females. For members of both sexes, their performance amounts to stepping out of the everyday world to be alone before God, and then coming back into the world to serve God better.

The word "Islam" is a verbal noun in Arabic, derived from the root verb *aslama*, meaning to give oneself, to serve. A correct English translation of Islam would therefore be something like "serving God." It would help a great deal in facilitating understanding if non-Muslims mentally translated Islam in this way every time it is encountered. The word "Muslim" derives, moreover, from the same root, and means "the one who serves God." All Muslims think of themselves as serving God. Some of the women quoted below think they do this best by wearing the *ḥijāb*, while others feel that it is not essential to this purpose.

A woman going on pilgrimage does the same thing as a man. The clothes worn on the pilgrimage remove any distinctions of power or status. In a sense, this is something like standing alone before God on the Day of Judgment. The Qur'an teaches that nothing or no one mediates between the individual believer and God. Each is directly responsible in terms of what her or his conscience dictates. Each will have to answer for what she or he does in this world.

The women who felt that going on pilgrimage helped them decide to wear the *ḥijāb* were clearly making personal decisions based on their personal awareness of how best to witness to their faith in the reality and goodness of God. As one trained in the academic discipline of religious studies, I recognize that this is a very complex and awesome matter. The historian of religion Mircea Eliade uses the phrase "in illo tempore" to indicate that serious religious ritual in all traditions involves a sense of removing oneself from the concerns of everyday time, and entering into a state of awareness of the timeless. Religious experience is best characterized as increased awareness, deepened consciousness and greater focusing on the transcendent good. Pilgrimage rituals, such as the *ḥajj*, often involve a journey back to the sources of the community's life. Such journeys are undertaken partly for the sake of spiritual refreshment and renewal of purpose.

Statement 1: Mihad Fahmy

At the age of fourteen, I was unaware of the multiplicity of meanings embodied in the *ḥijāb*. However, I did understand that modesty in one's behaviour and dress was required of all believers, and I was convinced in my heart that part of a believing women's modesty included wearing loose clothing and covering one's hair. The question in my mind at that point was not whether I would wear the *ḥijāb*, but rather, when would I muster enough strength to do so. Since that first day in my teens when I showed up at school wearing the *ḥijāb* until today, my understanding of what it represents has developed considerably. It is hard to deny that the *ḥijāb* has many layers of meaning, and, in this way, it is often difficult to explain to those who are continually in awe of those of us who find peace, respect and strength in wearing it.

For me, it has come to symbolize my identity as a Muslim woman whose faith and ideals are often fundamentally different than those she studies and works with. Setting oneself apart from the rest can be both challenging and quite useful. For example, confronting and encountering the perpetual stereotype of the timid and subservient Muslim woman can be exhausting, as we tire of the need to continually explain and justify our choices. This is particularly frustrating when I am among professionals and academics who think of themselves as open-minded and progressive. However, adopting a distinctive mode of dress can also be useful in alerting others to our distinctive beliefs and practices. While my colleagues may not automatically understand the *ḥijāb* fully, most will realize that my values and standards of behaviour differ in some respects from the mainstream. As a result, they are not shocked to learn that I will not go to a bar after work, or that I need to take time out of the day to perform my prayers.

The *ḥijāb* also symbolizes a rejection of what every inch of society's fabric tells us should be important to women. It is this message that I wish had been conveyed to me as a young fourteen-year-old. Young Muslim women can derive a great amount of strength and dignity from the *ḥijāb*. After all, it cannot but help serve as a reminder that our worth lies not in whether a man finds us attractive, but rather in what we are doing in order to serve Islam. A great deal can be said of the empowering facet of the *ḥijāb*. However, when all is said and done, adopting this

Islamic mode of dress is an attempt to please and become closer to God, as this is the objective of all forms of worship. Those who continue to raise their eyebrows at the notion of a professional Canadian woman in the year 2000 choosing to wear the *ḥijāb* — in whatever form it may take — clearly underestimate the power of such an objective.

Statement 2: Shabnam Dhalla

I was born and raised in Tanzania. I got married in 1969 and immigrated to Canada in 1976. Since my arrival, I have worked for a major bank, the government of Alberta and the city of Edmonton. I have upgraded my skills by taking computer and other relevant courses.

All the years that I lived in Tanzania, I did not wear the *ḥijāb*, probably because there was no awareness of its importance. After and during the Iranian revolution, the *ḥijāb* received a lot of negative publicity in the West, and, ironically, brought about tremendous awareness of its importance and the dignity that it brings to women at large. In spite of this newly aroused turmoil within myself, I was still not ready for the *ḥijāb*.

However, when I returned from the *ḥajj* in 1989, I seriously started thinking about the *ḥijāb* and the dignity that it can bring to me. I struggled within myself and began to analyze the impact that it might have on things like my social life, my sports activities and my friends. Wow! I was not sure if my friends and perhaps even my family would accept me if I were to wear the *ḥijāb*. Without the *ḥijāb*, I was happy, had enjoyed my life, had travelled half the world. But something appeared to be missing.

During this period of turmoil, I met and befriended a lady lecturer who enlightened me on the merits of the *ḥijāb*. In December 1990, I went to visit her in Minnesota. After a lot of discussions and soul searching, I found out that it was the *ḥijāb* that was missing from my life. I got off the plane in Edmonton proudly wearing the *ḥijāb* and feeling extremely dignified. Somehow I felt good and proud and found the courage within myself to stand up for my beliefs. The next day I proudly went to work and did not feel any different.

Colleagues at work questioned me about my new attire. I responded in a positive manner and explained to them my beliefs. They soon realized that the *ḥijāb* does not change a person. I have had no discriminatory remarks about the *ḥijāb* and still have lots of friends. I know that I have been accepted as I am, and, if not, it is too bad for them. I still play my sports and go for my workout and continue my normal life, but in a more dignified manner.

I have found even better things to do with my time and now volunteer with five or six organizations; I find this work tremendously rewarding. The *ḥijāb* has given me inner strength and the spirituality that I was seeking. The *ḥijāb* is *wājib* [obligatory] in Islam. There are no ifs or buts about it. It is clearly stated in the Qur'an. Those who do not wear the *ḥijāb* should not be criticized, and such persons should not justify their actions by misquoting the Qur'an. No one has the right to judge others. I can only recommend the *ḥijāb* to those who are convinced of the dignity that it brings to women, and they should not wear it because of pressure from family or society. I have no regrets.

A woman is not a commodity or an object, but she is like [a] precious pearl. The oyster is the *ḥijāb* that covers and protects it from the dangers of the sea. The pearl remains pure and untouched by any corruption. But it is the brutal nature of mankind that strips this treasured gem from its covering and places it for display or sells it for a price.

Statement 3: Shaheen Ashraf

The head covering commonly known as "*ḥijāb*" literally means: modesty, curtain, veil, etc., and, through common usage, it has come to mean the headgear donned by Muslim women all over the world. Since time immemorial, women of all faiths have covered their heads in some form or another as a sign of modesty (since the hair forms an important part of a female's adornment, it has been considered worthy of concealment, forming a necessary component of a chaste woman's attire). This was the thought that triggered my intention to start covering my head.

With the passage of time and maturity of thought, at age forty I chose to cover my head/hair when I completed my *ḥajj* [pilgrimage to Mecca]. Spirituality, faith and religion guide you toward modesty, and a Christian nun's attire will definitely serve as a good example. Some people go to the extent of saying that the *ḥijāb* was adopted from the nuns as they were respected in the community. Hence every woman who wanted that kind of respect from the layman was better off dressing like that.

If one gives it a good thought and notices the paintings of the olden times, one will see clearly that every woman had some sort of a scarf or veil on her head. Over time and with the influence of different customs, a woman was expected to display her grace to please and attract the opposite sex, and slowly the modesty in dress started diminishing, along with the covering of the head.

The covering [*ḥijāb*] gives me a kind of self confidence that:

1 I am following one of God's orders.
2 I am able to pray wherever I may be.
3 I am protected from the eyes of certain kinds of men who look at women as an object of desire (I am asking to be judged for my intellect and not the way I dress).
4 Everywhere I go, people know that I am of a certain faith and I am greeted with good wishes from strangers of my own faith.

Of late, this subject of head covering has become quite a controversial subject and is being blown out of proportion. It should be understood as a matter of personal understanding and choice. In Canada, due to the lack of knowledge about different religions, women with *ḥijāb*s are sometimes misunderstood. I mean, I could go into a bank and the teller would think that I could not speak English or French and would start gesturing with her hands (until I would say something). This taught me a lesson, and from then onwards, I am the first one to greet people and start a conversation about something or the other so that they are put at ease that I am a normal human being and not some alien from outer space.

The *ḥijāb* does not affect my work environment as I am self-employed and the people who work with me are all mature individuals and strong followers of their own faiths. In fact my choice was appreciated. I consider myself lucky, as I have had very positive feedback from everyone that I have come across in my working life. I have attended banquets, business lunches, bank breakfasts, seminars, courses, etc., without any difficulty. I have travelled extensively all over the world for business and pleasure and have had no problems whatsoever. For me, the *ḥijāb* is a part of my dress — just like a blouse or a skirt or jacket; my outfits are incomplete without it.

Statement 4: Amira Elias

In the name of Allah, the most gracious, the most merciful.

As far back as I can remember, God was always very close to my heart. I not only felt His presence, but I delighted myself in conversing with Him every moment of my life. He is my eternal loving and reliable companion. From an early age in childhood, I started to pray, fast and read the Qur'an. Although my family were religious, in the way that almost all Iraqis were, none of the women wore the *ḥijāb* in the way that some people do now. Later I lived for some time with my husband and children in Canada and did not wear the *ḥijāb*. Then we moved to the United Arab Emirates.

The story of my *ḥijāb* began when I volunteered to teach Islam to a group of converts in the UAE. These women belonged to a group called Salafi. These women had accepted wearing the *ḥijāb* as soon as they converted. I was shown a video of a Kuwaiti Imam telling women a *ḥadīth* that related the Prophet saying that if a women who goes to the market has only a little of her ankle showing, then she will not be permitted to enter paradise, or smell its scent, which can be smelled 400 years away.

This made me feel "My God! I want to please God. If the *ḥijāb* pleases Him, I'll do it, and be proud of wearing it because of my love and faith in Him." So I completely changed my wardrobe, bought a black *abba* [covering] and many scarves, and transformed myself from a modern-looking Canadian woman to a completely shrouded woman. I was completely covered, including my feet, because the Salafis felt very strongly about covering the feet with socks.

The headmaster of the British private school where I was teaching was shocked by my transformation, but I persisted. He renewed my contract because he acknowledged that my professionalism had not been affected. For the next seven years, I devoted myself completely to *da'wah* — Islamic missionary activities. I studied and gave lectures to these Western women. We were bonded by our faith and love for God. They included American, British, German, Swedish, Japanese, Chinese, Indian and many Filipino women. We created our own family ties because some of them were cut off from their non-Muslim families.

Then my family moved back to Montreal, and problems began. I lost my *ḥijāb* clothes on the flight. When I got some more, and thought about walking around in Montreal dressed in this way, I was frightened of being looked at as strange. I hated being stared at. When I had lived formerly in Montreal, before I had adopted the *ḥijāb*, I used to go biking with my husband and children, play tennis, squash and swim. Formerly, I had worked as a real estate agent. Now, I secluded myself at home, and did not want to go out.

Some of my former friends had moved away, and others did not like the way I had changed my dress. My husband returned to work in the UAE and I was left alone to face the world in Canada. I became extremely depressed, and even got admitted to a hospital for a week because of depression.

Then I decided to make things easier for myself by modifying my dress. I started covering my head with a hat, or wearing my scarf in a fashionable style so that I would blend in, and not attract attention. I was still determined to obey God and not change the way I dressed. I worked as a fundraiser for the Muslim community of Quebec, and as a project director for them. Eventually I became principal of their high school.

Meanwhile, I had become divorced, and gone back to university where I got a graduate degree in comparative religion. This transition gradually opened my eyes to the reality of the misery I had put myself through. My God! How could I think that the compassionate and loving God could take pleasure from my misery? Through reading the history of women, I learned how the Assyrians kept their women segregated, and started to cover them up to increase their value. I discovered how a slave woman would have been punished by throwing asphalt on her head if she tried to dress like a free woman.

I understood that veiling had begun in ancient civilizations as a form of class distinction. I realized that the Qur'an was protecting women by recommending that the Prophet tell his wives and daughters to dress modestly. But I also learned that Omar bin al-Khatab actually scolded a Jariya woman for covering up or dressing like a free woman, which meant that class distinction was still alive at the time of the Prophet [*Pbuh*].

Still I did not take my *ḥijāb* off. I wanted to be sure. I studied the Qur'an and *ḥadīth* again thoroughly, and read all the commentaries I could get my hands on. Then I focused my attention on the two specific *ḥijāb* verses, and did not find any *ḥudūd* [warning of punishment] for not wearing *ḥijāb*. As a matter of fact, the reason for recommending it is "so that they will be known and not get hurt."

But here I was getting hurt to the core by wearing it. Some people could argue that *ḥijāb* protects a woman by keeping her from the harm of being molested or raped if dressed provocatively, but do they have to go to [the] other extreme? Can women not just dress respectfully in a dignified way without covering their heads? If there is no punishment mentioned in the Qur'an, it seems especially clear that this is not a compulsory duty.

Then I started to think that the promoters of the *ḥijāb* were none but the Wahabis and Salafis who emerged from Saudi Arabia, a country whose women are kept behind closed doors and prevented from driving their own cars, ignoring the fact that Ayesha, the Prophet's wife, may Allah be pleased with her, not only drove her camel, but led a whole army of men. For those who read my story, I want to say that my faith has not diminished nor my desire to please God in every way I can. The difference is I feel free to be a full contributing human being and not an ornament to be kept secluded.

Statement 5: Zia Afsar

I started wearing *ḥijāb* when I was in my forties. I was not influenced or pressured by my family to do so. It was my own independent decision, which I discussed with my family before starting to wear it. I am a religious person, and after the study of the available Islamic literature, I concluded that wearing *ḥijāb* is essential to portray my Muslim identity.

At that time we lived in a small town where most of the people knew me personally. My wearing of *ḥijāb* did not make any difference in my daily interaction with people. I was involved in many volunteer organizations and I continued doing so without any strange looks or remarks from anybody.

Shortly after that, we moved to a big city with a bigger Muslim community. I was received very well by the mosque community, especially by sisters with an Arab background. But the sisters of my own ethnic background (Indo-Pak subcontinent) were hesitant in welcoming me in their social circle. Perhaps they thought that either I was too religious or too backward. It took them awhile to invite me to their social and cultural gatherings. There were only a couple of ladies from my ethnic background who wore the *ḥijāb*.

As I had always done volunteering in community organizations, I wanted to get involved in this city too. That was an uphill battle. I had to struggle hard to make a place for me in the society at large. Communities where there are not many *ḥijāb*-wearing ladies, have the perception that *ḥijābī*s are not educated and that they are oppressed by the male members of their respective families, and that they wear *ḥijāb* because they are forced to. That was not the case with me. I have a Masters degree in physics from a Canadian university. I am an outgoing, outspoken person, and wearing a head covering did not change me as a person at all. I kept trying and proved that I am neither uneducated nor oppressed. Gradually

I changed the perception of people with whom I interacted as a neighbour, as a volunteer or as a citizen. I stayed in that city for six years and eventually I became a sought-for volunteer. I gained respect as an individual who believes in freedom of choice and respect for individuality.

We moved again to a small town where I am the only *ḥijāb*-wearing woman. Now I know how to handle the challenge. People talked to me slowly as if I did not understand English, or else they used hand gestures to make me understand the conversation. Once when I was standing in a checkout lineup, an Oriental man came up to me, who could speak English with much difficulty, and asked me if I could speak English. On my affirmation, he asked me a question, and was surprised to hear me replying in English.

Sometimes I laugh, other times I feel angry. Why is there so much emphasis on women's dress? If the dress does not fit the norms of society, then the woman is considered to be uneducated and oppressed. I have noticed that in big cosmopolitan cities, where the population is diverse in ethnicity, people accept *ḥijāb*-wearing women more easily than they do in smaller, less diverse towns. Now that the *ḥijāb* has become part of my personality, I usually forget that I am different from other women.

Statement 6: Naushaba Habib

I had never thought about the *ḥijāb* seriously until we went for *ḥajj* in 1988. We were an average Muslim family from an Islamic point of view. Neither I, nor my friends, who now wear the *ḥijāb*, used to take it seriously. We did cover our heads at Islamic gatherings, and I covered mine in the Islamic school where I was teaching. But it was only after going on *ḥajj* that I consciously decided to wear the *ḥijāb* regularly.

The pilgrimage convinced me that I should observe my Islamic duty of wearing the *ḥijāb*. My general idea was that a Muslim, especially one returning from *ḥajj*, should be as perfect as possible. I tried to accept this responsibility.

I did not face any problems related to my job. I had done my master's degree in political science. I remained a mother and wife until my children were grown up. I then started to manage the medical office of my husband, a job I still do. One day when I was walking downtown in Regina, a teenage boy struck me on the head with his hand. On another occasion, when I was walking in the neighbourhood, some children shouted "Hebrew lady." I stopped and told them I was Muslim and not Hebrew, and they ran away. I find that when I go shopping, or fill the car with gas by myself, people look at me curiously and whisper to one another.

I also had some good experiences. A lady patient of my husband remarked that I looked good, and looked different. She advised that I should not change. When I travel, especially in a long skirt, coat and *ḥijāb*, people seem to respect me. Perhaps this is a sign of better education and status among travellers.

I sympathize with Muslim sisters who have to work, and who feel inhibited about wearing the *ḥijāb*. This situation may be improved by educating the public at large to understand the religious concerns of Muslim women better. Some sisters may opt to wear the *ḥijāb* only in family and Muslim gatherings, and pray to God to make it easy for them.

Muslim men, who criticize Muslim sisters for not wearing the *ḥijāb*, should understand the problems faced by the women, and help ease the difficulties instead of just being critical.

Statement 7: Rahat Kurd

I was seventeen when I decided to start covering my hair every day. I acted from straightforward religious conviction; I was living away from home and could do as I liked. I was studying film, writing essays about *King Lear* and organizing "Palestine Awareness Week" on campus with my Muslim friends. I would soon read Malak Alalia's *The Colonial Harem* and experience a kind of angry epiphany, a synthesis of feminist politics and Islamic identity, which would sustain me, give a shape to much of my work and studies and social life, for a very long time. I don't think there was anything unique about my decision, except that I had deliberately waited until I was in a place, where, unlike the community I had grown up in, I felt welcomed and appreciated among Muslims as I was; my friend with whom I ate, prayed and studied Qur'an never pressured me to cover.

None of us had any idea how this issue would expand to fill our lives, what media darlings we would become. After several years of wearing a headscarf, of giving radio, TV and newspaper interviews to people about why I wore a scarf, of writing essays, poems and even making a documentary film about women who wear scarves, I began to notice its impact on my attitude toward, and expectations of, other people in general.

One afternoon, a woman sitting next to me on the train watched speculatively for several minutes. She clearly wanted to speak to me, and when I finished eating the lunch I had brought, she did.

"Excuse me," she began, "May I ask you a question?"

"Sure," I replied warmly, mentally gearing up for a lengthy explanation of Islam, my life as a Muslim and why I cover.

"Was that black bean soup you were eating? I'm trying to get more lentils into my diet and I can never think of good recipes to try."

I was dumbfounded for three seconds and then, somehow, delighted. For once, a total stranger was *not* interested in my scarf! I could have hugged the lady. I gave her the soup recipe instead.

I have realized that I want more requests for soup — to connect with people for real reasons. I don't want to be stopped on the street and congratulated for wearing something utterly banal any more than I want to be harassed or attacked for it. My exchange with the lady on the train was a rare, understated moment of civility. Such courtesy, grace, humour and generosity — the things I value far above the mere labels of Muslim or non-Muslim — are impossible when we overdetermine any symbol, when we say: only this can mean piety, piety can only be indicated by this; the absence of this means the unequivocal absence of piety for all time, without exception.

I have taken the evidence of my alleged piety out of the public realm. I do not say, "I have stopped covering" because I refuse to make any final pronouncements, and because, frankly, my ears get too cold to go scarf-less for long. I no longer believe that covering one's hair is a formally required act of worship. At the same time, I know that choosing to wear a scarf can have rich personal meaning, be a source of comfort, strength and good subversive fun, and for these reasons I honour and defend the choice rigorously. In order to keep my own spirituality from exhaustion, to safeguard and nourish it more substantive ways, I have taken my scarf out of the target range of public fear and desire.

Final Comment: Sheila McDonough

In opting to wear the *ḥijāb*, or not, Muslim women are deciding how to relate the values they perceive in their traditional heritage to the life situations in which they currently find themselves. The context in this case is contemporary Canada, yet it could apply anywhere, anytime. It is the same problem that the Muslim poet Muhammad Iqbal struggles with in his magnificent poem entitled "The Mosque of Cordoba," wherein he tries to relate the past to the present. Gazing upon the building itself — erected at a time when Muslim culture was flourishing in Spain — the poet recognizes that this outstanding piece of religious architecture testifies to the sense its builders had of the truth and beauty of God. Though living in a quite different age, he ponders the question of how to bear witness in his century as effectively as the builders of the mosque did in theirs.

The answer, it is implied, involves not doing the same thing exactly as it was done in the past, but seeking guidance from the wisdom of the past as how best to live creatively in the present. To seek inspiration from the past is not the same as seeking for absolute rules on how to do everything in life. The first option is more likely to make for creative spontaneity in the present as we move toward trying to create a better future for all.

These Canadian Muslim women are struggling with similar issues. Several of them note that they are professional women, committed to their professions, seeking to perform to the best of their abilities. Doubtless, they value having a vote in the political life of the society, and they expect to receive recognition for their contribution to Canadian society. They want to be respected by their fellow citizens. Among those who have adopted the *ḥijāb*, several indicate that they understand themselves to be affirming something significant in the context of contemporary Canada.

Nonetheless, some of them are aware that their head-covered presence sometimes elicits unfriendly responses. Some have experienced other Canadians behaving as if they think that the *ḥijāb* represents an inability to speak English. One author notes that wearing the *ḥijāb* can be a source of "good subversive fun." On one level, this suggests nothing more than the personal amusement that a *ḥijāb*-wearing woman may feel as she watches the responses she elicits. On a deeper level, however, and as several respondents suggested, they see their role in adopting the *ḥijāb* as a means of subverting the forces in Canadian society that tend to trivialize women or deny them dignity. Several say that the *ḥijāb* helps them feel that they are affirming their worth and their self-respect. Most of them agree, however, that having to explain themselves constantly is tiring. One said she became extremely depressed because of this burden, and was sure that she could not get a job wearing the *ḥijāb*. Most are careful to say that they have also encountered many good experiences of civility.

These seven women have chosen to respond as they have done, and thus represent a few Muslim women who wished to communicate what they felt. Even in this small sample, however, one can discern some of the divisiveness the issue creates among Muslim women themselves. We have a spectrum of opinion that ranges from those who think that only *ḥijāb*-wearing women are good Muslims, through to those who choose to wear the *ḥijāb* but are sympathetic to their sisters who make a different choice, to those who consciously decide not to wear it, and finally to those who think that piety and service to God can be expressed with or without covering the head.

CHAPTER 5

Perceptions of the *Ḥijāb* in Canada

Sheila McDonough

What are some of the typical ways in which non-Muslim Canadians respond when they see the *ḥijāb* on their streets? Why do some Canadians respond in these ways? Why are some responses negative and some positive? What are the issues of pluralism and justice raised by the disputes about the *ḥijāb* in Canada?

The reactions to the *ḥijāb* are a two-way street in that non-Muslims may wonder what the veiling means, and Muslims may wonder why the non-Muslims react in the diverse ways they do. In teaching courses on Women in Islam in Concordia University, I have learned that much mutual incomprehension exists between Muslim-Canadians and non-Muslims. The students have needed to spend time talking to each other, and learn to understand how and why others think and feel as they do.

Earlier I had taught in a Muslim women's university, Kinnaird College, in Lahore, Pakistan. In these teaching experiences in both Pakistan and Canada, I have learned that the issues of mutual comprehension between persons of different cultural backgrounds are complex (Said 1997, 36–68). One needs to be alert to recognize when a word or an example does not make sense to others. When necessary, people should go slowly and try to discover what lies behind the issues of mutual incomprehension. This has to be done in a step-by-step, careful way. The test as to whether or not mutual comprehension has occurred can only be done by consultation — "Does this mean what I think it means?" The *ḥijāb* question is one that requires careful unravelling precisely because Muslim-Canadians and non-Muslim-Canadians bring different backgrounds to the discussion. It is not easy to comprehend the reactions of others when words and actions have differing connotations for people.

As Edward Said has indicated, non-Muslims sometimes have a static image in their minds as to what "Islam" means. When this happens, non-Muslims tend to assume that all Muslims are the same and do things for the same reasons. Some of the reactions of non-Muslims in Canada to the *ḥijāb* may come from this kind of simplistic thinking, based on stereotypical images picked up from the media. However, there are also other reasons, some of them rooted in Canadian history, for the questioning attitudes some Canadians have to the *ḥijāb*.

In the Canadian past, changes in the status and roles of women were generally opposed by most of the male leadership of both Protestant and Roman Catholic Churches. This is one reason why Canadians might think that male religious leaders would oppose changes in the status and role of women. Experience has shown that male Christian leaders did oppose the nineteeth- and early twentieth-century movements to grant the vote and new social roles to women in Christian-dominated societies. Even though many women leaders of the struggle for the right to vote were active members of their churches, nevertheless resistance came from the male leaders of the churches. This opposition went on for over a century, and was strong and outspoken. Any Canadian woman who is aware of this long history has reason to be skeptical about male religious authorities of any kind pontificating about the nature and role of women in the family and in the world. Canadian distrust of the *ḥijāb* is linked with this memory of a long history of religious leaders opposing changes in the status of women. The sight of the *ḥijāb* in Canada sometimes triggers responses based on these memories.

The movements for changes in the status of women in Canada took place at more or less the same time and in the same ways as changes taking place in Europe and elsewhere in North America. Movements organized by women advocating changes in voting, property and legal rights began early in the nineteeth century in many parts of the world. The main religious forces behind these new ideas came from the left wing of the Protestant Reformation, as expressed through Quakers, Baptists and Methodists, and from the Enlightenment. The Enlightenment's emphasis on the "Rights of Man" were echoed in the seminal ideas of the English writer, Mary Wollstonecraft, author of *The Vindication of the Rights of Women*. She was writing at the time of the French Revolution.

Quaker women played a very significant role in the suffrage movement. Susan B. Anthony was the first woman to vote in the United States. She was arrested in upper New York State for doing so; she had five generations of Quaker women behind her. The Quaker movement, which had originated in England in the seventeenth century, had stressed the equality of male and females, and had permitted women to exercise leadership in the Church. Lucretia Mott, one of the leading Quaker suffragettes in the United States, kept a copy of the Bible, along with Mary Wollstonecraft's *Vindication of the Rights of Women,* on her hall table for her guests to read. The motivation for the Canadian struggle for women's rights is also a mixture of Protestant reforming ideas, particularly as expressed through Methodists, and Enlightenment ideals of equality, reason and justice. In Canada, as in the United States and in Europe, the struggle for a woman's right to vote and for equality under the law took a long time and was difficult. This is one reason why the sight of the *ḥijāb* may cause Canadians to fear regression to the attitudes and policies of an earlier age.

Recent Controversies

Recently, there have been several controversies about the *ḥijāb* in Quebec. One occurred in 1993 when a judge expelled a woman from a courtroom for wearing an *ḥijāb* (*The Montreal Gazette,* December 3,

1993, 1). After much controversy, the judge apologized. The president of the Quebec Municipal Judges Conference said that there was no rule against having the head covered in a courtroom. The attitudes of the judge who expelled the woman seem to represent an example of the prejudices of many ordinary people. The decision against him represents the importance of careful juristic reasoning on issues of this kind. Canada has traditions both of religious, racial and gender prejudices, and also of juristic reasoning against unreasonable prejudice.

In 1995, the CEQ, the federation of Quebec teachers, agreed by majority vote that no *"signe ostentaire"* should be permitted in Quebec schools. This meant, in effect, that the *ḥijāb* should not be permitted in schools. They also said that certain matters were non-negotiable, such as coeducation, curriculum and equality between the sexes. Further, they pronounced themselves against genital mutilation, and asked for a public discussion as to what degree of conduct was reasonable in terms of freedom or religion, liberty of conscience and equality between men and women. They stated that they were opposed to the wearing of the Islamic veil in public schools (CEQ 1995).

This phrase *"signe ostentaire"* is used also in the debates that have taken place in France about the wearing of the *ḥijāb* in public schools. The tradition of secular education is very strong in France because the French Revolution explicitly opposed the dominance of the clergy in relationship with the power of the monarchy. The Revolution executed the king and denied political power to the Church. Nowadays, the Muslims are the second largest religious community in France; they number about five million. France expects all its citizens to accept the principles established by the Revolution.

The opposition to the wearing of the *ḥijāb* in public schools in France uses rhetoric that claims that education must integrate children into society, and that this means that citizens must accept the equality of men and women as a principle of the state. The prohibition against the wearing of the *ḥijāb* is said to be based on the theory that "ostentatious religious symbols" represent a denial of the principle of the equality of men and women. Journalists and teachers unions in Quebec have used some of the same rhetorical symbols as those used in France in their protests against the *ḥijāb*.

The controversy about wearing headscarves in schools in Quebec began when a Muslim teenage girl was asked to leave school if she would not remove her *ḥijāb*. Both the parents and the school appealed to the Quebec Civil Rights Commission. The latter ruled in favour of the parents. An editorial written in 1995 by Marie Lavigne, president of the Council for the Status of Women, indicates recognition by the leadership of Quebec women of the complexity of the issue (Lavigne 1995). She indicates that it is well known in Quebec that the *ḥijāb* has been a controversial issue in France for many years. She notes that the *ḥijāb* is a complex symbol. As a religious symbol, it raises the question of freedom of religion in Quebec schools. As a cultural symbol, it forces the French-Canadian majority to consider their own capacity to assimilate people who are different. As a political symbol, it is associated in many minds with Islamic fundamentalism, and with opposition to democratic values.

Marie Lavigne says that one has to be careful not to allow one's critical conscience to lead to intolerance. Who, she says, will be penalized or threatened if some girls wear the *ḥijāb* in Quebec schools? Would these girls not be driven into a more restricted and isolated environment by such policies? She does not think that permitting the headscarf would necessarily go counter to the basic values of Quebec society. All women who live in Quebec have a fundamental right to equality. This is the law. Her arguments present the perspective that has influenced the decisions within Quebec society to tolerate the *ḥijāb*. The point is that wearing the *ḥijāb* does not of itself change the fact that equality between men and women is the law in modern-day Quebec as in the rest of Canada.

Populist Journalism

However, at the level of populist journalism, there sometimes still is a kind of inflamed rhetoric that perceives any person wearing the *ḥijāb* as an instrument of the threat of fundamentalist attack on the democratic values of Quebec and Canadian society. A recent example of such inflamed rhetoric is an article published in the French edition of *Chatelaine* in July 1997, which has upset many Quebec Muslim women (Turenne 1997, 27–33). The title *"Ce qui se cache,"* [She who hides herself] is very significant. The implicit and explicit connotations of this title are strong. One clear Canadian reaction to the sight of the veiled woman is "Why is she hiding?" This question carries deep historical resonances in terms of the last two centuries of the struggle of women in Western countries to come out of hiding, and to make their voices heard. The press and the television often carry images of veiled women in Muslim countries. That image conveys the implicit idea of oppressed and repressed women. In this respect, the *ḥijāb* suggests a situation in which women are not allowed to play any role in society outside their homes.

The Canadian women who react negatively to the image of "hidden women" often do so because the historical memory of the oppression and hiding of women in their own culture is fresh enough that a scar in the psyche is reopened by the sight of what appears to be another way of hiding women and silencing them. When something hurts, it is because the pain is real.

The fact that negative reaction to the *ḥijāb* may be strongest in Quebec may be linked to the fact that female suffrage and the legal guarantees of women's rights came later in that province than in the rest of the nation. The more recent the opening the doors of equal citizenship to women, the greater the fear lest those doors close again. This seems to be the reason for a greater level of anxiety on this subject in Quebec. The Quiet Revolution, which ended the hierarchical domination of the clergy in Quebec, took place in 1960, not very long ago. Quebec has come a very long way since then in terms of affirming the equality of women and men, in theory and in practice, but the memory of oppressive religious control is still strong. Perhaps many Quebecers, who were adults in 1960, still think of veiled nuns when they see the *ḥijāb*. This reaction triggers, consciously and unconsciously, anxieties about turning the clock back.

The Quebec intellectuals are aware of the conflicts in France on the *ḥijāb* issue. There are also a number of women and men immigrants to Quebec from North Africa who have bad memories of Muslim fundamentalist oppression in Algeria and elsewhere, and who fear that the *ḥijāb* in Quebec signals the possibility of similar developments here. This anxiety is also the major reason for objection to the *ḥijāb* in schools in France. The *ḥijāb* is particularly distrusted when it looks like a uniform, because the sight of uniformed young people awaken bad memories in European society of an association of youth in uniforms with fascist groups. The French Revolution had explicitly attempted to destroy the power of the Roman Catholic Church over law and education. Since the Revolution in the eighteenth century, schools in France have been central to the creation of a society free from domination by religious leaders.

However, where Quebec differs from France is that the revolt against clerical domination of society took place almost 200 years later in French Canada. After the persecution of priests and nuns in the French Revolution, many of these religious persons fled France and came to Quebec. They were permitted cultural autonomy by the Canadian system of government. For this reason, the authority of the Roman Catholic Church has remained very strong in this Canadian province until 1960. At that time, the elected government of Jean Lesage led what was called a Quiet Revolution against the domination of the Church over education and culture. This latter factor is more significant in explaining negative reactions in modern-day Quebec against the *ḥijāb*. The example of France is a partial explanation, but the recent memory of clerical domination is a deeper reason for the hostility in Quebec to the idea of patriarchal religious control. I also know of one Quebec woman who met antagonism at the American border when she attempted to cross into the United States wearing her *ḥijāb*. The hostility toward Islam that is characteristic of much contemporary American journalism is also a factor influencing the Quebec and Canadian press.

The article in *Chatelaine* suggests that the "hidden woman" belongs to a culture that hides her from the outside world, that does not permit her to interact openly with Canadian society, that may permit her to be beaten and oppressed behind the closed doors of the family and that does not allow her to defend herself. The Canadian readers of such an article can believe such things could be true because similar "hiding of women" happened within the recent past of their own culture. Wife-beating still goes on in the wider society, but its opponents have managed to do a lot to help women find shelter, to get the police to help them and to arouse sympathy from the culture. Most of this help has become available only in the fairly recent past. Thus, the sight the *ḥijāb* can trigger all sorts of anxieties in Canadian minds, including fear of returning to more brutality by men against women.

At its most extreme, the attitude exemplified in this article is that Muslims are dangerous for Canadian society because they may become a political force here and because, if they do become such a force, they will undo the liberation of women, which our mothers and grandmothers fought to create for us. The article also suggests that hidden political forces are at work among Muslims imposing the veil on women and seeking to reimpose male domination on the world. The author says that the veil sometimes symbolizes a Muslim attitude of moral superiority, revenge against Western society and pride. She argues that the kind of Islam being propagated through the insistence on the veil is one that insists on keeping women in the role of perpetual minors. She sees this as not only a personal family matter, but also as expression of a determination by many Muslim males to enforce their domination on the whole world through changing law and social practice.

She goes on to say that the condition of Muslim women is still second-class in the civil law of most contemporary Muslim countries. She quotes some teachers in Canadian schools who find Muslim boys characterized by male arrogance and unwillingness to treat females as equals. An example she gives of bad Muslim attitudes is boys washing their feet in a school bathroom in order to prepare to pray. She indicates that there is a lot of hate literature against the culture of Canada being spread among Muslims who live here. In general, she maintains, the Muslim immigrants to Canada are ignorant of and hostile to the values of the host country, and do not intend to integrate with Canadian society. The reader of this article is left with the impression that every *ḥijāb*-wearing woman on the streets of Montreal or any Canadian city is a symbol of hostility to Canadian society, and the agent of a political force determined to change Canadian culture back into one that silences, hides and restricts its women citizens.

The letters to the magazine following the publication of this article came mainly from local Muslims whom the author quotes or refers to. All these letter writers say that the author of the article used their words out of context and drew a malicious picture of Muslims that was unacceptable to the persons she had talked to. Certainly the article is poor journalism in that it is so unreservedly one-sided and dogmatic. There is no suggestion that the situation could be complex, not only in Canada, but in the wider Muslim world. There is a reiterated single, dominant theme portrayed in this article — that veiled Muslim women symbolize one thing only, the determination to defend male dominance over women and to keep women hidden, voiceless and controlled. The idea is expressed vividly. The Muslim women of Quebec were very upset by this article.

Another example of a similar approach is a book recently published in French in Quebec entitled *Femmes voilées, intégrismes démasquées* [Veiled Women: Fundamentalisms Unmasked] (Geadah 1996). As with the magazine article, the title is the significant key to the dominant theme. In both cases, the titles imply danger or threat. The veiled woman is shown as a symbol of a hidden and serious menace. The author, a non-Muslim woman immigrant from Egypt, discusses the attitudes and policies of Muslim fundamentalists in contemporary Egypt, and indicates that similar forces are at work among Muslims in Quebec. The veil is portrayed as symptomatic of fundamentalist intentions. Such fundamentalists perceive Western society as pagan, *jāhilīyah*, and tend to see themselves as ones who will reenact the original triumph of the followers of the Prophet Muhammad over the forces of paganism in seventh-century Arabia.

Yet another instance of negative journalism was indicated in an editorial in the newspaper *La Presse* on April 21, 1995. The Oklahoma bombing had just occurred. The editorialist, Claudette Tougas, admitted that no one yet knew who was responsible for the bombing, yet she goes on for the rest of the editorial to talk about the dangers of terrorists who oppose the civil values of democratic societies. A cartoon right beside the editorial shows a Muslim, with a mosque in the background, on his knees before a donkey, and agreeing with the donkey that the thinkers and the intelligentsia are the enemies of God. The implication of the editorial is that most probably it was Muslims who bombed the building in Oklahoma (Tougas 1995).

This cartoonist is a victim of the same dualistic thinking that characterizes the opponents of the *ḥijāb* in much of this populist journalism. The idea is that two realities are opposed to each other: on the one hand, there is reason, intelligence, democracy, equality of the sexes, and, on the other hand, religion, stupidity, violence and oppression. It is not surprising that Muslims feel very threatened by this stereotyping.

Historical Background in Canada

The instances given above are examples of extreme forms of negative Canadian responses to the *ḥijāb*. In order to understand why Canadians might respond to the idea that reactionary forces are out there to push Canadian society back several centuries, it may be helpful to look at the reasons for the actual changes that have taken place within Canada with respect to the role of women. As I have earlier suggested, the fear that women might become once again hidden and voiceless is a real fear because people remember that this repressed condition was once the situation here. The notion of menace linked with the symbol of a hidden woman is powerful because there is a memory of women being hidden and voiceless here not too long ago. In a way, the hidden woman feared by those who respond negatively to the *ḥijāb* is a woman hidden in the unconscious of those who fear the veil. The sight outside triggers a memory of experience within. It was not so very long ago that Canadian women fought their way out of isolation, so therefore the fear of being pushed back is real.

In order to explain something of the Canadian experience in changing ideas and practices about women, I will refer to the lives and thinking of Nellie McClung (1873–1951) and Thérèse Casgrain (1896–1981). When I was a little girl growing up in Calgary, my maternal grandmother sat on some committees with Nellie McClung, and my mother was a friend of Nellie's daughter, Florence. My grandmother and my mother were certainly aware of an ongoing effort in Canadian society to procure more rights for women. This struggle in Canada for political and social rights for women has been going on actively since the nineteenth century. Outside the room where the Senate meets in the Parliament Buildings in Ottawa, there is a plaque given by the business and professional women of Canada in memory of five women from Alberta, Nellie McClung and her friends, who succeeded in compelling the government of Canada to acknowledge that women were persons. This was necessary because the law said that only persons could be nominated to the Canadian Senate; some males were maintaining that this fact excluded females. The change in the law took place in 1930. Nellie McClung had been a leader of that battle, as she had been in many others.

When Nellie McClung was growing up at the end of the nineteenth century in a rural community in Manitoba, women did not have the vote, could not be ordained as ministers of the Church, could not work in the professions, except teaching and nursing, and were not officially persons before the law. She became a popular novelist and public speaker, as well as wife and mother. She was active in one of the earliest mass movements among North American women, the Women's Christian Temperance Union. The leaders of this group believed that the prevalent alcoholism among the men of their society was the main reason for the beatings of women and children by their drunken husbands and fathers, and for the general decadence of society. They believed that the absolute prohibition of alcohol would lead to many social reforms.

The voice of Nellie McClung spoke for the possibility of making the whole world a much better place. She believed that social institutions could and should be reformed, and that such reformation would make the world more just for everyone. She also believed in the use of reason to bring about the necessary changes. In one of her most dramatic presentations, she managed a debate in Winnipeg among women who were arguing the reasons why it would not be suitable to give the vote to men.

In January 1914, the premier of Manitoba had replied to a petition requesting the right of women to vote by a speech in which he used the traditional reasons for "why not." He said:

> My wife is bitterly opposed to woman suffrage. I have respect for my wife; ... Will anyone say that she would be better as a wife and mother because she could go and talk on the streets about local or dominion politics? I disagree. The mother that is worthy of the name and of the good affection of a good man has a hundredfold more influence on the molding and shaping [of] public opinion round her dinner table than would have in the market place, hurling her eloquent phrases to the multitude. It is in the home that her influence is exercised and felt. (Hallett and Davis 1994, 122)

Church leaders, businessmen and politicians in all Western countries actively opposed votes for women for more than 100 years on these and similar grounds. Nellie McClung's way of answering this was to hold a public debate, in which she imitated all the mannerisms of the same Manitoba premier, when she made a mock speech opposing giving the vote to men. In the satire, she argued: "The modesty of our men, which we reverence, forbids us giving them the vote. Man's place is on the farm" (Hallett and Davis 1994, 126).

Her audience was convulsed by laughter, and most of them got the point. She also wrote a poem ridiculing the typical stereotypes against women. In her version, the stereotypical male arguments were:

> The ladies — God bless them,
> Our troubles they share 'em
> So lock 'em away

> In the parlour or harem
> We give them ideas,
> We pay for their chains
> And what is more sweet
> Than a wife without brains?
> So here's to the angels
> We foster with elegance
> Bless their sweet eyebrows,
> But d—n their intelligence. (Hallett and Davis 1994, 123)

The ideas characteristic of Western males who opposed granting votes to women were, as indicated, that women belonged at home, that careful nurturance of children would suffer if women went out into politics and the workforce, that God had designed women to be mothers and to stay home, that society wanted women sweet but not intelligent, and that the stability of society required submissive wives and mothers, not political and business rivals of men. The women reformers rejected all these assumptions, and carried on until they got the social changes they wanted. Although the opponents of Nellie McClung were mainly Protestant, Roman Catholic leaders employed basically the same arguments later in Quebec against Thérèse Casgrain and the Quebec suffragettes.

Nelly McClung fought in many battles for social change; the first ones were for the abolition of alcoholism and the rights of women to vote. She was also active in the Methodist Church and subsequently in the United Church of Canada. She campaigned for the rights of women to be ordained as ministers. The first ordination took place in 1936. The Methodist tradition, which she came from, stressed the need to work in society on behalf of the oppressed; many Methodists and other Protestants had struggled for the abolition of slavery and for better working conditions in the new industrial age. Methodism became especially vigorous in the Western Prairies in which new cities had to be built and new ways of life designed in the context of an unsettled wilderness. In such a context, the fact that an idea was new, such as women voting or becoming ministers, was no reason to reject it. Just about everything was new.

The struggle to have the government acknowledge that women were persons arose because the founding document of Canada, the British North America Act, said that only persons could be elected to the Senate. When a woman wanted to become a senator, she was told this was impossible because she was not a person. Nelly McClung and her friends took this issue all the way to the British Privy Council, and finally got the ruling that women were indeed persons. The first woman was appointed to the Senate in 1930.

The ruling from the Privy Council reads as follows:

> Having regard finally to the provisions of the Interpretation Act of 1889 their lordships have come to the conclusion that the word "persons" includes members of the male and female sex and that therefore the questions propounded by the governor-general must be answered in the affirmative and that women are eligible to be summoned and become members of the Senate of Canada. (Hallett and Davis 1994, 212)

This decision was a landmark in Canadian history because it has become impossible since that date to argue for the exclusion of women from any aspect of government or business affairs. The process of women's entry into the professions has been a matter of one step at a time, but one by one, leadership positions in society have been opened to women. These changes have all taken place within the last three or four generations; therefore the present-day distrust of any efforts that appear to be setting the clock back is still strong.

The struggle for the right of women to vote in provincial elections in Quebec came a little later. I myself had a lengthy discussion with Thérèse Casgrain on the occasion on which my university, Concordia, in Montreal, gave her an honorary doctorate in recognition for her life-long struggles for greater social justice in Quebec.

Thérèse Casgrain (1896–1981) came from a well-educated and prosperous Quebec family; her husband served in the federal Parliament. In 1913, a Montreal Suffrage Association was formed to support the struggle for the vote for women. In 1918, women were granted the right across the country to vote in federal elections, but Quebec refused to allow them to vote in provincial elections. This did not change until 1941. Madame Casgrain and her friends had to fight for a long time.

In 1922, a letter from Cardinal Begin, archbishop of Quebec, indicated the attitudes of most of the Roman Catholic clergy toward votes for women:

> The entry of women into politics, even by merely voting, would be a misfortune for our province. Nothing justifies it, neither the natural law nor the good of society. The Roman authorities endorse our views, which are those of our entire episcopacy. (Casgrain 1972, 12)

Madame Casgrain and her friends were not intimidated by these views, although they were mainly Roman Catholics. As a matter of policy, the Quebec suffragettes decided to introduce a bill asking for the rights of Quebec women to vote at every session of the legislature. They did this every year from 1927 to 1941. She has written:

> As the mother of four children, I deprived anti-feminists of one of their favourite arguments: that most of the women who were seeking the right to vote were childless old harpies lacking any femininity. In this connection, I remember a conversation with Prime Minister Taschereau, when he said to me with a smile, "Of course now that you're campaigning for the woman's vote, there'll be no question of your having any more children. But if such a thing should occur, I'd like to be godfather. If it's a boy we'll make him a bishop." "And if it's a girl," I retorted "she'll be a suffragette." (Casgrain 1972, 56)

She adds that, in fact, she had been pregnant at the time. The child, a girl, did not need to be a suffragette because of the success of the work done by her mother and friends. That child became the mother of seven children.

The women in Quebec also campaigned for changes to the civil code to ensure fair wages for working women, and the protection of married women's property against husbands' arbitrary squandering of family assets. At the time, the husband alone had the right to administer all the family property. He could sell or in any way dispose of the property without consulting his wife.

Again, in 1938, the highest ecclesiastical authority in Quebec, Cardinal Villeneuve, published a statement opposing giving the vote to women. His statement reads:

> We are not in favour of female political suffrage;
> 1. Because it is contrary to the unity and authority structure of the family.
> 2. Because it exposes women to all the passions and intrigues of electoralism. ...
>
> We believe that We are here expressing the common sentiments of the Bishops of the province. (Casgrain 1972, 92)

In spite of this opposition from the clergy, the Legislative Assembly of Quebec in 1941 went ahead and granted the women of Quebec the right to vote and to stand in provincial elections. After the war, Thérèse Casgrain continued to take part in many struggles for social justice. She also understood her religion to mean that believers should work continually to create better social institutions. She, Nelly McClung and many like them were willing to combat the ecclesiastical authorities of their day when they considered that they had right and justice on the side of women. They did not accept the interpretations of their religious traditions given by the male Church authorities. Rather, they set out to change society and to change the views of the men. In this they were eventually largely successful.

This background may help explain something of the anxieties that the sight of the *ḥijāb* in Canada sometimes arouses. This image sometimes suggests, to the non-Muslims who see it, the possibility of society going backwards to the older structures in which women were hidden and had no effective role in the wider political life. However, there is debate within Quebec and the other provinces of Canada as to whether the *ḥijāb* really is such a serious threat. Those who do not fear the *ḥijāb* also have an effective voice.

The Tradition of Mutual Acceptance

Canada has an explicit acceptance of multiculturalism as a goal for Canadian society both at the federal and provincial level. The idea that Canada was formed by a co-operative joining together of French- and English-speaking people has developed an awareness that living together peacefully requires ongoing adjustments on all sides. The notion of two cultural heritages has been expanded since the end of World War II to include more recognition of the cultural rights of Native peoples and of other cultural groups that have become part of the wider society. There is a perspective that assumes that many forms of cultural difference are acceptable.

An example of this perspective is the Quebec Human Rights Commission, which ruled that girls could wear the *ḥijāb* to school if it was their free choice. Several months after a school banned the *ḥijāb* in 1994, a meeting was sponsored by an organization of Christian women, Protestant and Catholic, Le Réseau Ecumenique des Femmes du Québec. During this one-day meeting, five different Muslim women, some with the *ḥijāb* and some without, gave their views, answered questions and took part in a general discussion. Subsequently, the Quebec Human Rights Commission issued a report on the *ḥijāb* issue. This report says:

> It must be acknowledged that the veil is sometimes an instrumental part of a set of practices aimed at maintaining the subjugation of women, and that in some more extremist societies, women are actually forced to wear the veil. For example, we cannot but

> condemn in the strongest possible terms the terrorism to which some Algerian women are subjected. ... A major part of the public debate of recent months has been concerned with the interpretation of the Koran itself. ... We do not feel it is up to us to take a position on this particular question, which we believe should be considered first and foremost within the Muslim community itself.... In our view, it would be insulting to the girls and women who wear the veil to suppose that their choice is not an enlightened one,... In general terms, therefore, the veil should be seen as licit, to be prohibited or regulated only if it can be proved that public order or the equality of the sexes is threatened. (Commission des droits de la personne du Québec 1996, 17, 18)

A statement like this from the Human Rights Commission has the effect of enunciating a principle that, it is assumed, will influence future thought and action on this issue. The people in Quebec and in the rest of Canada who have been in favour of permitting the wearing of the *ḥijāb* have mainly been motivated by a concern for human rights.

Canada has a strong human rights tradition. In the beginning, English Canada was settled by both Church of England and Church of Scotland persons, as well as by other Protestants. Because of the active roles played by the Scots, the Church of England never became an established Church in Canada, as it was in England. Established means the official religion of the nation. Diversity resulted from the origins of the country because the Church of England was not permitted to become the official national Church. Quebec joined the new Canada with the understanding that Roman Catholics would have liberty as citizens. This was not the situation in England at the time, which means that the Roman Catholics had more freedom in Canada than their counterparts had in Britain. The traditional policy of acceptance of religious diversity thus has very strong roots in Canada because the people who decided to work together to build the new country realized that they would have to respect their diversity in order to achieve their common goals.

An interesting analysis of the characteristics of Canadian society by the distinguished novelist Hugh McLennan reads as follows:

> For not only was this country formed out of the flotsam and jetsam of three or four defeated racial and political groups; some of these groups had once been bitter enemies of one another. But they had to live here, and they had to live in peace with each other. (MacLennan 1971, 10)

Another author comments as follows about the origins of Canada in the context of distressed immigrants fleeing poverty and oppression in Europe:

> We were all poor, and we had no time for ideas. But we all did what we could, by and large, without vast economic resources and without the impulse of a revolutionary ideology. We worked with the moral and religious instincts (for we can hardly call them ideas) that we'd brought with us from 17th and 18th century England and France to lay the foundations of a civilized society. We began to build schools almost as soon as we pulled the last stumps from the clearings, and we quarreled over our rights to our religions and languages, without ever managing to bring to bear on the quarrels any great statement of principle. ...
>
> In this country, we never generated the psychology of a mass or a master race because there weren't enough of us, and we had too many cherished differences. ... It is the normal condition of Canadian politics that it should be a succession of shaky compromises and infirm assertions of the status quo. ...
>
> What we need to do is reject the mere moralism of our past — the censoriousness and exclusiveness and self-approval, the coldness of prudence and inertia of provincialism and colonialism — and, at the same time, preserve the real integrity of conscience that your best Canadian shows. (Hood 1971, 32–35)

As these comments indicate, Canadians are accustomed to compromises that have been imposed on them by their historical experience of religious and cultural diversity. Now they need to adapt to an even more culturally diverse nation. They seem to have the resources within their historical experience to enable them to do this if they will learn to exercise their moral imaginations and overcome their prejudices and inertia. The Charter of Human Rights set up by the United Nations at the end of World War II had the active support of Canada. A Canadian, John Humphreys, was involved in helping to draft the United Nations' Charter of Human Rights. The subsequent Quebec decision on the *ḥijāb* reflects these ideas, namely, that a religious and social practice that is freely chosen and that does no obvious harm should be accepted.

Conclusion

The issue between negative and positive responses to the *ḥijāb* hinges on this "doing harm" issue. Those who fear the *ḥijāb* think it "might" symbolize oppressive practices toward women, and it "might" create some kind of backlash against the rights that Canadian women have fought to establish over generations. The other response says that none of these negative effects can be proved. Justice requires non-interference unless actual harm can be demonstrated.

Another issue involves the recognition of social change as an ongoing and complex process. The *Chatelaine* article portrayed Muslim nations as backward, but the author was thinking of these cultures as static instead of recognizing the ongoing processes of change. In reality, shortly after the French Revolution, movements toward constitutional and democratic government began within the dominant Muslim power of the time, the Ottoman Empire (Berkes 1964). Both World Wars created havoc in the Muslim world and set back the processes of development. Nevertheless, all Muslim countries have been gradually developing their legal and political structures and practices. There have been active women's movements in most of the major Muslim nations campaigning for legal changes. Muslim women have the vote and access to education in most Muslim nations.

There are great numbers of well-educated professional Muslim women in the world, especially in the medical profession. Muslim women doctors are numerous. The history of Muslim women's movements in many parts of the world indicates that they have exercised considerable influence in their nations (Mumtaz and Shaheed 1987). It is true that many Muslim nations are not fully industrialized yet, but this is true also of many nations that have majority Christian populations. Simplistic popular journalism of the *Chatelaine* kind does a serious disservice to its readers by its failure to portray the realities of historical processes accurately, and by its crude stereotyping of what is a complex reality in the Muslim world of today.

Some issues, such as criticizing Muslim boys for wanting to wash their feet, indicate serious misunderstanding on the part of the Canadian schools in question. Muslims are expected to pray five times a day and to wash in a ritual fashion before doing so. One might think a courteous host nation would approve and help children who wish to pray. There may be difficulties for the schools in accommodating the needs of Muslims. However, it seems clear that the negative stereotyping of children who are seeking to be clean represents a form of unreasoning prejudice.

The positive responses to the *ḥijāb* recognize a practice that is not very intelligible to most Canadians, but that seems harmless. Canadians generally do not see covering the hair as an indication of modesty, although one or two generations ago, hats were commonly worn by women in churches. Clothing styles have changed enormously in Canada over the last three, four and five generations. The positive response is thus largely a matter of welcoming diversity of practice and culture, and affirming people's rights to clothing codes and other matters that do no demonstrable harm to the wider society.

Muslim-Canadian women have the same rights to equality under the law as all other Canadian women do. Given that Muslim-Canadian woman have access to education at all levels and the right to vote, the expectation is that they will be able to decide what dress codes they consider best for themselves. Although they may have to experience some instances of unreasoned prejudice, the human rights legislation protects their rights as citizens. As Canadians become more readily accustomed to the presence of Muslims in Canadian society, it is likely that prejudice will decrease. An editorial in *The Globe and Mail* of June 6, 1999, criticized the Turkish government for forbidding the wearing of the *ḥijāb* in Parliament. The editorialist's position was that governments should not fear their own citizens. This seems to be the consensus of Canadian opinion.

As indicated in our earlier quotation from Hugh Hood, Canadians in the past have managed to arrive at compromises in order to bridge their different cultural traditions and practices, and the nation has prospered because of this adaptability of spirit. There is good reason to hope that Muslim-Canadians will welcome, and will be welcomed by, many opportunities to participate in the ongoing national process of building cultural pluralism mixed with common goals and common enterprises. Adaptability of spirit on all sides is in our common interest.

PART II:

Women Revisiting Texts and the Veiling Discourse

سبح لله ما في السموات والارض وهو العزيز الحكيم

CHAPTER 6

Muslim Women and Islamic Religious Tradition:

A Historical Overview and Contemporary Issues

Sajida S. Alvi

This chapter provides basic historical background for chapters 7 and 8 on the Qur'an and *ḥadīth,* respectively. After a brief overview of Islam, its Prophet and the foundations of Islamic tradition, it outlines, in the first part, the development of that tradition over time, and particularly of Islamic law. The second part covers the role and status of women in society interspersed with glimpses of the early generations of Muslim women, their intellectual and artistic pursuits, and their participation in politics and society in the premodern and modern periods. In the third part, the focus is on interpretation of the sources of Islamic law in the modern period and its adverse impact on the rights of Muslim women enshrined in the Qur'an (the holy book of Muslims). The chapter concludes with an overview of Muslim women in Canada and their role in the building of Muslim community as a minority in this land.[1]

Islam, one of the fastest-growing world religions, remains a mysterious, exotic and strange religion for the majority of Canadians. In the media, distinction is rarely made between political/radical Islam (religion used for political ends) and spiritual Islam. The Muslims are frequently projected as a threat to the civil society and termed bigots and terrorists — the perception reaching new heights of frenzy and hysteria after the tragedy of September 11, 2001, in New York. Naturally, such perceptions are offensive and hurtful to the adherents of this universal religion. The label of terrorism is especially denigrating when Muslims are mindful of the Qur'anic depiction of them as a "justly balanced" and moderate community (Q. 2:143, 57).[2] "Ye are the best peoples, evolved for mankind, enjoining what is right, forbidding what is wrong and believing in [one] God" (Q. 3:110, 151).

The start of the Muslim calendar coincides with the year 622 CE, when the Prophet Muḥammad led his followers out of Mecca to establish a new form of community life in the city of Medina. The revelation of the Qur'an (the revealed "word of God," as Muslims believe) had proclaimed the foundation of a new path for human beings, one that would help them relate to their Creator and final Judge (Allāh). Allāh (the proper name of God in Arabic) is the only one with the power to reward or punish them for their deeds (Q. 90:4–20, 1737–1740; 53:39–42, 1449; 76:3–6, 1655–1656). For anyone seeking to achieve an integrated personality, remembrance of Allāh is important. It provides meaning and purpose in life (Q. 59:18–20, 1526–1527). The new community was open to all who would accept the one God as their Creator, and acknowledge Muḥammad as the last of the Prophets.

The new community developed distinctive characteristics such as a non-hierarchical framework that sanctified an individual's right to equal treatment before the law, freedom of conscience and the right to own property. Membership in the new community was based on belief in one God, acceptance of the Prophet Muḥammad as the final Prophet to humanity and accountability for one's deeds to God alone.

Muslims subsequently travelled to many parts of the globe, establishing several different forms of Islamic civilization in the process. They have generally been able to adapt to many diverse cultural contexts, and have shown great flexibility in developing patterns of existence to relate their values to different situations. At the same time, however, they have kept intact their firm belief in the reality of the one God, the significance of the Qur'an as a guide for humanity and the importance of the Prophet

Muḥammad as a moral exemplar. These were the most important factors providing constancy, continuity and unity within the Muslim universal community (*ummah*) through the centuries irrespective of their ethnic, linguistic and cultural orientation and geographical location.

The focal point of the message transmitted in the Qur'an, and the practical manifestation of that message in the Prophet's life, suggest a purpose to human creation in this world. As described in the Qur'an:

> We have not created the heaven and the earth and whatever is between them in sport. If We wished to take a sport, We could have done it by Ourselves [not through Our creation] — if We were to do that at all (Q. 21:16–17).[3] Do you then think that We have created you purposelessly and that you will not be returned to Us?[4]

Section I

Islamic Religious Tradition

Islam is an uncompromisingly monotheistic religion. Belief in the oneness of Allāh is its cardinal principle. There is a living God, the originator of everything. For Muslims, everything in the universe, including human beings, are signs of God. Muslims believe that "No vision can grasp Him, but His grasp is over all vision: He is above all comprehension, yet is acquainted with all things" (Q. 6:103, 319–320). An erudite jurist and mystic of the twelfth century, Imām al-Ghazālī (d. 1111), exclaimed that "Man's soul is like a mirror in which any one who looks sees God." Nonetheless, the yearning to feel, to know and to see the "Face"[5] of the invisible and yet so visible Allāh has found intense expression in philosophical discourses, mystical practices, literature in all genres, music and Islamic art and architecture.

Sulṭān Bāhū, the great Punjabi Sufi poet (d. 1691), for example, articulated his feelings in these verses:

> This body is a dwelling of the True Lord, and my heart like a
> garden in bloom.
> Within it are fountains, within it are prayer grounds, within it
> places to bow down in prayer.
> Within it is the Ka'ba, within it the *qibla*, within it the cries of
> "Only Allah!"
> I found the Perfect Guide, Bāhū, He alone will take care of me.
> (Bahu 1998, 42)

The term "Allāh" is mentioned in the Qur'an well over 2,500 times (Rahman 1980, 1). Among these descriptions of Allāh may be included the following:

> Allāh is the Light of heavens and the earth.
> The parable of His Light is as if there was a Niche and within it a Lamp:
> The Lamp enclosed in Glass: the glass as it were a brilliant star:
> Lit from a blessed Tree, an Olive, neither of the East nor of the West,
> Whose oil is well-nigh luminous, though fire scarce touched it:
> Light upon Light! Allāh doth guide whom He will to His Light:
> Allāh doth set forth Parables for men: and Allāh doth know all things.
> (Q. 24:35, 907–908)

The Qur'an, revealed to the Prophet Muḥammad, is also called the "Mother of Books." It unravels the mysteries of nature. It contains graphic description of heaven and hell among other things, but not the physical characterization of God. The imagery illuminates God's infinite majesty and power, but does not exhaust His infinite signs.

The Qur'an has inspired and guided this diverse and global community through all times and in all places. The Qur'an focuses on the guidance of humankind and is valid for all times, according to the Muslim belief. It is the primary source of Islamic law, not a legal code in itself. Its main objective, rightly pointed out by the acclaimed poet-philosopher of the twentieth century and the spiritual founder of Pakistan,

Muḥammad Iqbāl (d. 1938), is "to awaken in man the higher consciousness of his relation with God and the universe" (Iqbāl 1989, 131). The Muslims copied the Qur'anic text and perfected a variety of calligraphic styles to present the divine words. Islamic calligraphy developed into one of the most beautiful artistic forms representing the might, power and beauty of God as well as the souls of Muslims as it was transmuted by this divine and sacred text. It evolved into the most sublime non-religious "art of the book," synthesizing highly stylized calligraphy with miniature painting and beautiful illustrated borders in the same folio. It reached its epitome during premodern, highly cultured and powerful Muslim empires such as those of the Ottomans in Turkey and the Middle East, the Safavids in Iran and the Mughals in India.[6]

The transmitter of this text, the Prophet Muḥammad was born in Mecca in 569 or 570 as an orphan child, and after a remarkable career as a Prophet and statesman, he passed away in 632. The Prophet's sayings (*ḥadīth*) and his tradition (*sunnah*) are the major sources of Islamic law after the Qur'an. Over the centuries, writers, poets, jurists and Sufis have sought to preserve the Prophet's countenance by providing minute details and graphic descriptions of his habits, his preferences, his humility in particular and his compassion and affection for his wives. After all, he is the "beautiful role model" for Muslims.[7] The poetry written in the veneration of the Prophet in all dialects and languages of the Muslim peoples over a span of over 1,400 years transcends the barriers of time, space, race, colour and language. (For details, see Schimmel 1987).

One of the most popular Urdu poets of British India, Alṭāf Ḥusayn Ḥālī (d. 1914), wrote a magnificent long poem to lift the spirits of demoralized Muslims of the nineteenth century by outlining the "flow and ebb" of Islamic history and recounting the humanism of its founder, the messenger of Allāh, the "Seal of the Prophets":

> The one who received the title of "Mercy" among the prophets
> The one who fulfils the desires of the wretched
> The one who comes to the help of others in trouble

> The one who takes to his heart the sufferings of his own and other people
> The refuge of the poor, the asylum of the weak
> The guardian of orphans and the protector of slaves.
> (Ḥālī 1997, 111)

In expressing their devotion to the Prophet, the faithful attributed superhuman feats and qualities to him that he never claimed for himself. He was and wished to remain no more than the servant of God to whom the revelation came. In the Qur'an, there is a categorical statement to this effect:

> Say thou: "I am but a man like you: It is revealed to me by inspiration, that your God is One God: So stand true to Him, and ask for His forgiveness." And woe to those who join gods with God.
> (Q. 41:6, 1288)

Islam raises the Abrahamic ideal of human freedom to its climax (as Muslims believe). It liberates human spirit from all strangleholds and controls imposed by social and political powers. In order to give maximum liberty to humans, Allāh does not make decisions for humanity. Instead, He provides broad parameters for both men and women and gives them guidelines and full freedom to make decisions for themselves and be solely accountable for their actions. They are endowed with immense faculties and are encouraged to develop their potentialities to the maximum through choice and by developing their character and righteousness. In the words of the poet Iqbāl:

> The world is only to subdue,
> Its breast for the well-winged shaft.
> Its purpose is to enlarge the Muslim's soul,
> To challenge his potentialities.
> That, having won the mastery of powers of this world-order,
> Thou mayst consummate the perfecting of thy ingenious crafts.
> Man becomes the deputy of God on earth,

> And over the elements his rule is fixed.
> (Iqbal 1973, 141–143)[8]

Islamic Law

The *sharī'ah* — meaning the path leading to water (interpreted as ocean of Truth) — is the term used for Islamic law. The fourteenth-century jurist, Ibn Qayyim al-Jawzīyah (d. 1350), defined the essence of *sharī'ah* as

> God's justice among His servants, and His mercy among His creatures. It is God's shadow on earth. It is His wisdom which leads to Him in the most exact way and the most exact affirmation of the truthfulness of His Prophet. It is His light which enlightens the seekers and His guidance for the rightly guided. It is the absolute cure for all ills and the straight path which if followed will lead to righteousness. … It is life and nutrition, the medicine, the light, the cure and the safeguard. Every good in this life is derived from it and achieved through it, and every deficiency in existence results from its dissipation. If it had not been for the fact that some of its rules remain in [in this world] this world would become corrupted and the universe would be dissipated. … If God would wish to destroy the world and dissolve the existence, He would void whatever remains of its injunctions. For the *Sharī'ah* which was sent to the Prophet … is the pillar of existence and the key to success in this world and the Hereafter.[9]

Muslims worked out early on a method of deciding how to implement their values. While the Prophet Muḥammad was alive, he served as head of the community, and also as the final authority on the more controversial issues brought to him. He was therefore the primary interpreter of what the Qur'an really meant in the actual context of situations faced by believers in his day. After his death, the community chose various individuals to serve as caliphs (*khalīfahs*, or successors of the Prophet only in his role as leader of the community). Each subsequent caliph was the political head of the community, but did not exercise any exclusive authority to interpret the meaning of the Qur'an. In the first instance, those who had been members of the first generation of believers made such decisions. After 200 years, i.e., in about the middle of the ninth century, there began to be demands for more authoritative guidance to the community. The collections of *ḥadīth*, which had been preserved by oral tradition, were at last written down and collected. Once this was done, several devout believers worked out a logical system of jurisprudence (*fiqh*). This system became the framework within which the various schools of Islamic law developed. Abou El Fadl has succinctly discussed the dynamic role of Muslim jurists as mediators between social structures and political structures in the medieval period. They played an important role in the interpretation of the *sharī'ah* and gave juridical rulings, but these rulings did not necessarily shape state laws (Abou El Fadl 2001, 14–18).

The *sharī'ah,* according to Muslim belief, provides a comprehensive system for maintaining a balance in spiritual and temporal life. The five essential practices of Islam (belief in the unity of God and the prophethood of Muḥammad, praying five times day, fasting in Ramadan, paying religious tax (*zakāt*) to ensure fair distribution of wealth and making pilgrimage (*ḥajj)* once in one's lifetime, if circumstances permit) focusing on human-God relations are immutable for all times, all places and binding on all Muslims. Conversely, the interhuman relations (*mu'āmalāt*) are based on reason and subject to change and evolve according the dictates of locale and time. This dimension of the code of religious law has been elaborated through the intellectual processes outlined in the principles of jurisprudence.

In the Middle Ages, there emerged four major legal schools of *sharī'ah* law acknowledged by Sunnī Muslims, as well as separate schools of Shī'ī (a major sect of Islam) religious law. There is diversity in matters of detail among these various schools, but the underlying perspectives are similar. Medieval Muslim states also availed themselves of customary law (*'ādah)* in addition to the *sharī'ah* in the formulation of their ruling institutions.

Sufism and Islamic Law

Another equally important intellectual and religious tradition, complementing the *sharī'ah*, is mystical thought, known as *ḥaqīqah* (Reality), or perception of Reality (*ma'rifah*), commonly called mysticism (*taṣuwwuf).*

> Sufism is a form of free thought and is based on rationalism. It emphasizes integration of external behavior (*ẓāhir*) and inner thoughts (*bāṭin*) of an individual. And it has created an attitude of indifference and despise to all that applies to appearance and not to reality. (Iqbāl 1989, 119)

Sharīah and *ḥaqīqah* are supposed to be two integrated elements of one reality, but in the modern period, they are often identified as two parallel traditions. The Sufis believe that realization of the purpose of life and integration of character is not possible without spiritualism. The spiritual aspects of life can be revealed and felt by sensual images and Divine love. Even ritual duties can be interpreted beyond their external importance. Prayer, for example, is a loss of one's self for a short time in communion with the overpowering and most compassionate Allāh; fasting teaches one to live on less, to sacrifice, to care for others and to praise Allāh as do angels; and pilgrimage is a perpetual journey of the soul toward its fountainhead. Those who dutifully fulfill the prescribed rituals without looking for their deeper meaning feel that by doing so they have obeyed Allāh, and have thus prepared themselves for the way that leads to happiness in this world and the hereafter.

All major Sufi orders (*tarīqahs*) base their spiritual ascendancy on the solid foundation of *sharī'ah*. None of its cardinal principles are compromised in the name of spiritual sublimity. As an example of a Sufi-*'ālim*'s views on the subject, I cite below Shaykh Aḥmad Sirhindī's statements on *sharī'ah,* the form and essence of *sharī'ah* and the purpose of prayer. I chose Sirhindī (d. 1624) because of his special position in the history of Sufism in India, where Muslims were and still are a minority. He reformed the Naqshbandī Sufi order (of Central Asian origin) known as the Naqhbandī Mujadddidī order, of which he is regarded as its founder. His contemporaries honoured him with the title of Mujaddid Alf Thānī (Renewer of the Second Islamic Millennium). The Mujaddidī branch became popular in India and Central Asia during the life of Sirhindī, and in the Arab lands later on.

(1) *Sharī'ah* and *Ṭarīqah*:

> Sufi *ṭarīqah* and *ḥaqīqah* are subservient to the *Sharī'ah*: they are meant to produce sincerity *(ikhlāṣ)* which is one of the three parts of the *Sharī'ah*, the other two being faith *(imān)* and action *('amal)*. ... unless you fulfil the demands all these parts you do not obey the *sharī'ah.* ...The *ṭariqah* and the *ḥaqīqah* for which the Sufis are known, are subservient to the *Sharīah*, as they help to realize its third part, namely sincerity. ... The raptures and ecstasies which the Sufis experience ... are not the goals of Sufism. They are rather myths and fancies on which the children of Sufism are fed. ... The purpose of traversing the stages of *tarīqah* (path) and *haqīqah* is nothing than the realization of *ikhlāṣ* which involves the attainment of *riḍā* (satisfaction). (Ansari 1986, 221–222)[10]

(2) The application of *sharī'ah* in one's personal life:

> Let it be known that Sharī'ah is both form and a reality, the form is the outer Sharī'ah, and the reality is the inner Sharī'ah. Therefore the shell and the kernel are both parts of Sharī'ah, the truths which are clearly defined (*muḥkam*) and those which are put in symbolic language (*mutshābih*) are equally its parts. The scholars of the outer Sharī'ah (*'ulamā' ẓāhir)* attend to the shell; and the scholars

> who are well established (*'ulamā' rāsikhīn)* attend to the shell as well as kernel — they are grounded in the form as well as the essence. The Sharī'ah should be considered as a person made up of a form and reality. Some people mind only the form and deny the reality, they follow none other than *Hidāyah* and *Bazdawī*. They are the scholars of shell. (Ansari 1986, 226)[11]

(3) The purpose of worship:

> The service and [worship] (*'ibādat*) which the Sharī'ah of the Prophet speaks of (as the purpose of man's creation) is for the good of man and for the fulfillment of his life. It is not at all for the good of God. ... God does not need our obedience, yet He has bestowed on us a Code of Law which we absolutely need. (Ansari 1986, 230)[12]

The subject of *sharī'ah* and its interpretation in our times will be discussed further in the third section below.

Section II

Women and Society in Classical and Medieval Periods

According to Islamic tradition, the Prophet Muḥammad once said:

> "God has made dear to me from your world women and fragrance, and the joy of my eyes is prayer." (Schimmel 1987, 51)

About 600 years later, the master mystic poet, Jalāl al-Dīn Rūmī (d. 1273), sang of the special position of woman:

> She is a ray of God, she is not that (earthly) beloved:
> She is creative, you may say she is not created.
> (Schimmel 1997, 104)

These are not merely isolated expressions of love and affection for women in Islamic literature. The Qur'an gave dignity and respect to women. It is not only in the Qur'an but in the words and deeds of its transmitter — the most "beautiful role model" for Muslims, the Prophet Muḥammad — that woman is treated with affection and respect. In the collections of *ḥadīth* there are striking statements attributed to him concerning women, wives, mothers and daughters. The chronicles of early Islamic history in fact provide abundant material to construct a fairly detailed picture of the Prophet's interaction with women (Mernissi 1991, 49–140; Schimmel 1997, 26–68).

A Muslim woman who was brought up knowing Qur'anic teachings understood that she was worthy of respect. The first Muslim women believers — those who accepted the new teachings brought by the Qur'an to transform the older tribal society — understood themselves to be independent individuals, liberated from the shackles of pre-Islamic customs and a degrading social status. With the knowledge that she was accountable for her deeds, the Muslim woman was given responsibility to consent to her marriage, and to initiate divorce if it seemed necessary. She was entitled to a share of her own in any inheritance forthcoming from her parents, and was ultimately responsible to God for what she did with her life. She was free to develop her intellectual, personal and economic potential. This new-found role made it possible for Muslim women to become more sure about their personal dignity and status than had been the case in the pre-Islamic period. Some of these rights have survived 1,400 years of stormy and revolutionary twists and turns of political power, major disruptions in social order and the impact of modernity in recent times. Others, however, have been lost at the altar of culture and tradition.

In considering the status of women in Islam and their role in society, the logical starting point is the Prophet's own life and times. Among his wives, Khadījah and 'Ā'ishah are especially noteworthy, particularly because their engaging and vibrant lives manifested in the Prophet's own household the application of the status accorded to women by Islam.

Khadījah, the first wife of the Prophet, was a businesswoman, the first convert to Islam and an anchor for the Prophet during the most difficult period of early Islam in Mecca. She died in 619 when the Prophet was isolated and persecuted by his own powerful tribe because of his new religion. In her death he lost a companion, friend and supporter, as well as the mother of all his children who had come of age. The Prophet left for Medina three years later. 'Ā'ishah, the youngest of the Prophet's wives, was eighteen years old at the time of the Prophet's death. Known for her superior intellect, she was one of the most reliable transmitters of the Prophet's traditions, a politically active woman and a leading figure in some of the civil conflicts within the young Muslim community after the Prophet's death. She passed away in 678, forty-six years after the Prophet's death. Her life and activities represent a dynamic and diametrically different example from that of Khadījah in the service of the Muslim community.

The First Generation of Muslim Women and the Public Space

In view of the current debate on women's space in mosques in North America, we will indicate some of the background issues. In the Prophet's time, women were full and equal members of the mosque community. The Prophet and his companions in Medina built the first mosque, which was attached to the living quarters of the Prophet and served as a religious, political and residential centre for the Muslims and new arrivals. It was the public place where the community members, including women, prayed together, and discussed their religious, social and economic concerns.

> [T]he Prophet's architecture created a space in which the distance between private life and public life was nullified, where physical thresholds did not constitute obstacles. It was an architecture in which the living quarters opened easily onto the mosque, and which thus played a decisive role in the lives of women and their relationship to politics. (Mernissi 1991, 113)

Female participation in the Prophet's congregations was substantial and regular. Like 'Ā'ishah, many Muslim women were the transmitters of the Prophet's statements. Their meeting place was the mosque. In the biographical collections devoted to the Prophet's companions, roughly 10 to 15 per cent of the entries are devoted to women (Roded 1994, 19). Seven per cent of the material in the earliest *ḥadīth* collection — the *Muwaṭṭā'* of Mālik ibn Anas (d. 795) — were transmitted by twenty-five women who comprised 26 per cent of all the companions quoting directly from the Prophet. The *Musnad* of Ibn Ḥanbal (d. 855) includes traditions related in the first instance by 125 women from among the 700 companions (about 18 per cent). Thus, female participation in discourse with the Prophet in the early, formative period of Islamic history was far from insignificant (Roded 1994, 19, 65). The compilers of *ḥadīth* collections treated female transmitters in exactly the same way as they did male transmitters.

Even great religious scholars such as Imām Shāfi'ī and Ibn Ḥajar, the historian al-Safadī, and the biographer Ibn Khallikān all had female teachers (detailed below), which, of course, raises the question: Where was this teaching carried out? Was it in the mosques, the *madrasahs* (schools often attached to the mosques or located in independent buildings) or their homes? There is still no clear answer to this issue, which requires further investigation. But what is abundantly clear from the sources is that male students studied under erudite females. The question still remains whether female and male teachers of the late classical period instructed their male and female students together or separately. In Chapter 8, L. Clarke discusses the subject of women and public space in detail in the light of *ḥadīth* (section, "Disputes about Seclusion," in this volume; and Abou El Fadl 2001, 232–247).

Female Scholars, Teachers and Sufis

We come across numerous female attendants/companions (*ṣaḥābīyāt*) of the Prophet recorded in the histories and biographical dictionaries. Because of the close and extended contact with the Prophet, their accounts became significant sources as to the Prophet's interactions with women. In later centuries, the compilers of the biographical dictionaries cited the names of many learned female scholars who had been their teachers and certified them to transmit the knowledge they had acquired from them. Ibn Ḥajar (d. 1449), for example, studied with numerous women (Roded 1994, 68), while Imām Shāfi'ī, the renowned jurist (d. 820), was instructed in traditions by Nafisah, the daughter of al-Ḥasan who died in 824 (Ibid., 66). Al-Safadī, the historian (d. 1362), received teaching licences from at least eight female teachers (Ibid., 67). Then there was Zaynab, daughter of al-Sh'arī (d. 1218), who studied with a number of eminent scholars and received licences to transmit their teachings. Ibn Khallikān, the famous biographer, received a licence from her (Ibid.). Ruth Roded's research into biographical dictionaries has yielded examples of about a dozen learned women who specialized in Islamic law, though only four of them acted as jurisconsults. One of these women was the twelfth-century female jurist, Fāṭimah Samarqandī, who lived in Aleppo. There, she studied Ḥanafī law with her father, eventually marrying one of her father's students. She fully participated in legal decisions, and her name often appeared in legal rulings along with her father and husband's names (Ibid., 81). Roded's data shows that women jurists, though a few in number, were fully engaged in the teaching and practice of law.

Among Sufi women, Rābi'ah al-'Adawīyah or Rābi'ah of Basra (d. 801), a liberated slave girl, is renowned for having transformed asceticism into mysticism based on genuine love for the Divine. The story often repeated in the hagiographical literature is that the pious Rābi'ah ran through the lanes and alleys of Basra with a bucket of water in one hand and a burning torch in the other. When asked about the reason for her action, she replied, "I want to pour water into hell and set paradise on fire, so that these two veils disappear and nobody shall any longer worship God out of fear of hell or a hope of heaven, but solely for the sake of His eternal beauty. ..." In her human perfection she was "clearly superior to many men, and that's why she was also named 'the Crown of Men,' as Muḥammad Zihni wrote in his book about famous women

(*Meshahir al-Nisa*)" (Schimmel 1997, 34–35). In the chapter on Sufi women, Schimmel includes in her discussion the prominent women who made a mark in the circles of mystical Islam across the Muslim world, including the Indo-Pakistan subcontinent, during the classical and premodern eras (Ibid., 34–53).

Our discussion would not be complete without noting the women who belonged to the Prophet's family, particularly his daughter, Fāṭimah al-Zahrā' (married to 'Alī, the Prophet's cousin and the first Imām of the Shī'ī sect), and her pedigree. The female descendants of Fāṭimah are remembered with a particular reverence and hold a prominent place in the Shī'ī devotional literature. Prominent among them are Sakīnah (the daughter of Imām Ḥusayn, himself the Prophet's grandson and the third Imām of the Shī'īs), and Zaynab and Umm Kulthūm (Imām Ḥusayn's sisters), who are associated in one way or the other with the "Tragedy of Karbala," the death of Imām Ḥusayn at the battle of Karbala in 680 fighting against the despotic rule of Yazīd (d. 683), son and successor of Mu'āwiyah (d. 680). This event, according to Shī'ī belief, is pivotal in the history of Islam, if not in world history, and is widely commemorated even today. These female figures have a special place in the history of Shī'ī Islam and in the psyche of Shī'īs. It is interesting to note how female figures from Shī'ī sacred history were resurrected in 1978 before the revolution in Iran. Zaynab was projected as a symbol of assertiveness and defiance in the overthrow of Muḥammad Reza Shah Pahlavi in 1979 (Pinault 1998, 69–98).

The Queens and Princesses: Classical and Premodern Periods

Women's participation in political life during Islam's formative period is well documented. Based on historical chronicles and biographical and religious sources, Mernissi shows that Muslim women boldly entered the male domain and seized political power. She calls into question the objectivity of classical Islamic historians who used history as a political weapon to advance their particular point of view on women taking up political leadership by citing the same historical sources. By juxtaposing the past and the present and using the relevant historical data at hand, Mernissi demonstrates that the traditional position of men today with respect to veiling women and discouraging them from going to mosques and taking part in discussions is a distorted representation of the original Islamic intent and practice.

During the classical period, in the political sphere, considerable power was wielded by women such as Khayzuran, mother of the Abbasid caliph Hārūn al-Rashīd (d. 809), by Zubaydah, wife of the same caliph, and by Buran, wife of the caliph al-Ma'mūn (d. 833). Fatima Mernissi brings to life these and many other female role models from Islamic history who wielded political power. Of particular interest to us are fifteen queens of varying stature in such regions as Egypt, Iran, the Maldives, Indonesia and Yemen who became rulers. Some of them enjoyed all the symbols of sovereignty such as having coins minted in their names and having their names read in the sermon during Friday congregational prayers (*khuṭbah*). Mernissi has skilfully pieced together their rise to power and their fall, their manipulations and ambitions, their sense of justice and vengeance, and their contributions to their respective states, small or large. We cannot discuss all of them individually in detail for lack of space.

However, to illustrate the point, we may mention one such queen, Sulṭāna Raḍīyah (daughter of the freed slave, Sultan Iltutmish; reigned 1211–1236), the first woman to rule India (1236–1240). The rationale for selecting Raḍīyah here is to show a unique situation in Islamic history — Muslim rule in India over a non-Muslim majority population. By the time of Raḍīyah's accession to the throne, all four schools of Islamic law as well as the ruling institutions were fully developed. It was also a time when Baghdad, which had been a symbolic centre of spiritual and political power of Islamic empire, was crumbling, while the Mongols were overrunning the world of Islam. Yet the nobility and the religious elite in India, partners in the nascent and fledgling rule of a small Muslim minority, had no qualms in having a woman as their ruler. Iltutmish thus rationalized his nomination of Raḍīyah to take his place: "My sons are incapable of leading, and for that reason I have decided that it is my daughter who should reign after me." She was a powerful, absolute and successful ruler. Unveiled and dressed like a man, Raḍīyah mounted a horse like a man, armed with bow and quiver (Mernissi 1993, 95–96). The coin she had minted after her ascent to the throne had the inscription "*Pillar of Women, Queen of the Times, Sultana Radiyya Bint Shams al-Din Iltutmish*" (Ibid., 89). Ironically, she lost her power because of her love for an Ethiopian slave, Jamāl al-Dīn Yāqūt, who rose rapidly in the ranks because of his remarkable ability. In the extremely hierarchical socio-political order established by the Turkish ruling slaves, such folly by their competent queen was unforgivable. There was a revolt against her and she fought back, but she was defeated and murdered in the end (Ibid., 97).[13]

During the premodern period, Islamic civilization reached its apogee under the rule of Amir Timur (reigned 1366–1405) and three great successor empires: the Ottomans in Turkey and the Arab lands (1280–1918); the Safavids in Iran (1501–1722); and the Mughals in India (1526–1748). Throughout this period there were many accomplished and learned women who shaped, enriched and expanded the common Islamic heritage in the vast territories controlled by these great empires. They embodied the high culture and patronized and created art and literature, music and fashion; they built exquisite mosques, *madrasah*s and other monuments; and, above all, they participated in the political domain. Due to their astute political acumen, they often served as power brokers, advisers and counsellors to the sultans and emperors. Many of them are brought to life in a recent collection of essays (Hambly 1998).[14] Not included here is a long list of litterateurs, artists, musicians, businesswomen, warriors, rulers, queens and princesses who shaped and enriched Islamic civilization.

Daughters of the Queens of Islam: The Modern Period

Over the last fourteen centuries, Muslim women's roles in their respective societies have been determined and shaped by regional, ethnic and cultural norms. It is true that they came mostly from the ruling elites whose socio-political, religious, artistic and intellectual activities were recorded in the historical chronicles and biographical dictionaries from the classical, medieval and premodern periods. The traditions these women established, however, continued even when the Muslim power was crumbling in the face of the Western colonial powers' onslaught. Because of the printing press and widespread education from the late eighteenth century to the present, we are better informed about the participation of women in the social, political, artistic and educational spheres of this period. The majority of them came from the upper-middle, middle and lower-middle classes. Their daughters and granddaughters fought alongside their male counterparts to win freedom from colonial rule in India and Algeria, and to bring about a revolution in Iran in 1979, for example. The challenges of modernity transformed the traditional Islamic societies and impacted on women's lives. However, the traditions established by the women of previous generations of Islam continue. Today, we have Muslim women serving as heads of governments, judges, cabinet ministers, vice-chancellors of universities, hospital directors, surgeons, journalists and engineers, not to mention many other fields.

Why then is it that, against the backdrop of their impressive achievements and contributions in the past and present, the general perception today is that the Muslim woman is an oppressed, male-dominated individual? The roots of such perceptions can probably be traced back to the thirteenth century, to the time of the Crusaders who convinced themselves and others that Muslims were the enemies of Christians, as well as violent, sensuous, polygamous and abusive of women (Alvi and McDonough 1994, 13). Later on, the imperialist nations who came to dominate the Muslim world in the nineteenth century typically attempted to justify their power by asserting that Islam was a crude and dying religion, stressing alleged mistreatment of women as part of their anti-Muslim rhetoric (Ahmed 1992, 13). Such perceptions were reinforced and amplified in the Western nations, and have remained in the public consciousness ever since.[15]

Section III

Women and the Qur'an

The Qur'anic spirit of equity and justice is frequently noted in some chapters of this collection. Here, we cite some Qur'anic verses for those readers who have had little exposure to Islam and the Qur'an. These verses have been widely discussed in works on the status of women in Islam representing various schools of thought, many of which are included in the composite bibliography at the end of this volume.

The Qur'anic declaration of the equality of men and women is unequivocal:[16]

> It is He [God] Who created you from a single person [self/source] and made his mate of the like nature, in order that he might dwell with her [in love]. (Q. 7:189, 398)

Men and women are formed of a single reality, but are distinct and different in their physiological and biological characteristics. They are interdependent in worldly affairs, but equal in their rights and responsibilities. In religion, they are both equal and independent individuals, as the Qur'an categorically states:

> The Believers, men and women, are protectors, one of another: they enjoin what is just, and forbid what is evil: they observe regular prayers, practise regular charity, and obey God and His apostle. On them will God pour His mercy: for God is Exalted in power, Wise. (Q. 9:71, 461)

As believers, men and women are equally obliged to live morally and await the Final Judgment; the additional obligations of bearing witness (believing in one God, and accepting the Prophet Muḥammad as the final

Prophet to humanity), prayer, fasting, giving alms and going on pilgrimage to Mecca once in their lifetime are the same for men and women.

Family

The Qur'an does not recommend any social pattern from which family and children are excluded. In the Qur'anic text, there are many beautiful depictions of spousal relations and the very special stature of this relationship. Quoted below is one verse among the many on this theme:

> And among His Signs is this, that He created for you mates from among yourselves, that ye may dwell in tranquillity with them, and He has put love and mercy between your [hearts]: Verily in that are Signs for those who reflect. (Q. 30:21, 1056)

This frequently cited verse reveals that marriage brings out the best in men and women. A harmonious marital relationship furthermore nurtures the beauty of each, and enhances their inherent qualities:

> They [wives] are your garments and ye are their garments. (Q. 2:187, 73–74)

The metaphor of garment extends to covering one another's weaknesses, providing mutual support, mutual comfort and mutual protection and adorning each other's self-respect and dignity. Scholars and exegetes of the Qur'anic text have interpreted the metaphor of clothing for spousal relations in varying ways. Annemarie Schimmel and Abū al-A'lā' Mawdūdī (d. 1979) are cited here as examples of such interpretations. Schimmel, for her part, explains this verse in terms of the phenomenology of religion:

> [W]hen the Qur'an (Sura 2:187) says to the man: "Women are a raiment for you and you are raiment for them," the phenomenology of religion interprets it to mean that the one is always technically the *alter ego* of the other, simply because a garment (being a

> portion or an aspect of a person) is frequently used *pars pro toto* to represent the whole person. (Schimmel 1997, 18)

Mawdūdī, a widely read exegete of the Qur'ān, interprets it thus:

> Just as there cannot be any veil (*purdah*) between the body and clothing, as is the connection and close unity (*ittiṣāl)* between body and dress inseparable (*ghair-munfakk)*, should the relationship be between you and your wives. (Mawdūdī 1973, 145)

Society and Justice

If we broaden our view to include society at large, it becomes clear that the central objective of the Qur'an is to establish a just and ethical social order. Especially apparent is the severe denunciation it makes of economic disparities and social inequities:

> And those in whose wealth is a recognised right for the [needy] who asks and him who is prevented [for some reason from asking]. (Q. 70:24–25,1608; 51:19, 1422)

There is an equal emphasis in the Qur'an on *raḥmah* (tenderness and affection), justice and the sanctity of an individual's personal, intellectual and religious freedom. In the Islamic framework, an individual's rights are intertwined with collective rights. An individual's behaviour is expected to conform to the limits set by society, and he or she is responsible for maintaining equilibrium in the social, economic and political order according to the norms of a given time and place.

"Woman, Half-the-Man?"[17] The Interpreters of Islamic Law

Since the nineteenth century, religious reformers and intellectuals have bemoaned the significant decline in women's rights and status in Muslim countries, as well as the violation of categorical and clear statements in the Qur'an. Controversy over interpretation of the Qur'an and implementation of the *sharī'ah,* especially the provisions on women's status, and debates between various schools of thought continue to rage even in the present day.[18] Citing examples from Islamic history, Mernissi argues that whenever there is a crisis in a Muslim state, the state resorts to an approach she derisively refers to as "box women in and ban wine," for in the view of men in authority, these are the two elements that destabilize society and create strife (Mernissi 1992, 155). Imposing dress codes, killing unveiled women or burning the houses of feminists and dissenters sometimes become the crisis-management strategies to save a given social order from perceived moral corruption.[19]

A major threat to Muslim women's rights comes from those traditionalists who are semiliterate in the Islamic sciences and who, in the name of *sharī'ah,* turn Muslim women into scapegoats; they fear that changes in the status of women will undermine the faith. Their understanding of the *sharī'ah* in many cases is limited to chopping off the hand of a helpless poor person convicted of theft, or stoning to death women convicted of adultery. Hundreds, if not thousands, of women are killed across the Muslim world every year by their own brothers, fathers and husbands in the name of familial honour or to uphold what some of the perpetrators (mis)represent as Islam (Jehl 1999, 6–7).[20]

In several Muslim countries — including Algeria, Afghanistan, Iran and Pakistan, for example — Islamic law, as a set of rules, is very much alive today, but its application is selective and arbitrary. *Sharī'ah* is sometimes used to oppress the poor, to promulgate blasphemy laws and to declare fellow Muslims as non-Muslims. It is used to restrict women's movement and to impose a dress code on them — all this is done in the name of God and to please Him. It is obvious that the interpretation and application of *sharī'ah* today is very different from Ibn Qayyim's in the fourteenth century (quoted above). He defined *sharī'ah* to be "God's shadow on earth." For him it embodied the sanctity of human dignity and rights, and a cure for all social ills.

Today's media has further reinforced misinterpretations of the *sharī'ah* (until November 2001) by showing pictures of Afghani women in *burqa*'s being denied an education, suspended from employment and banished from the public space in the name of the *sharī'ah,* or of Algerian women killed by Muslim zealots for appearing in public without the veil, or of Iranian women subjected to a dress code imposed by the Iranian government after the revolution of 1979, all in the name of Islam.

This brings us to the root cause of the problem — deterioration in the quality of Islamic education and need for reform in the curriculum of the *madrasah*s (religious seminaries and institutions).

Problems of Islamic Education

The impact of colonization and modernization, even after the establishment of independent modern Muslim national states, has posed a considerable challenge to Muslim religious law because new modes of political, economic and social life have come into being along with new modes of legal reasoning. Each new Muslim nation has tended to develop its own modes of reconciling traditional and modern ways of handling legal codes and legal practices. This matter is further complicated because the new modes of education developed by universities and the traditional modes of training of the *'ulamā'* have seldom meshed together well. In his discussion, Abou El Fadl enumerates many factors contributing to the demise of the epistemology and structure of classical Islamic law, as well as the failing dynamism of the natural and continuous evolution of law in the newly constituted structures of modern, centralized, Muslim national states. Most notable among these factors have been the nationalization of endowments *(awqāf),* the depriving of the *'ulamā'* of their economic base (and their and the law guilds' consequential loss of autonomy) and the new challenges posed by state-financed secular law schools. This has led to the collapse of the jurists' mediating role between the cultural and social structures and the political structures of modern Muslim states (Abou El Fadl 2001, 16–18).

It should be noted, however, that efforts have been made in some countries, such as Egypt, Iran and Indonesia, to adapt the curricula of the *madrasah*s to changing needs. However, in many Muslim countries, the curriculum for training the *'ulamā'* has changed little over the centuries. A prospective Islamic scholar trained in a typical *madrasah* is generally not introduced to Islamic history, the language and literature of his region, Sufism, logic and philosophy. The curriculum of the *madrasah*s is a key issue because it shapes the outlook of these *'ulamā'* and how they perceive problems in our rapidly developing world. The other detrimental factor is that even the policy-makers and bureaucrats, trained in the Western system of education, have little appreciation of their own culture and heritage, and the economic disparity between the ruler and the ruled have created a big gulf between the ruling elite and the masses. Another issue is lack of interaction between learned scholars and religious leaders who control the pulpits in the mosques. The modernists and the traditionalists live in two solitudes (discussed further in the next section). In almost every Muslim country, there has been an ongoing debate on economic and political issues, personal and family laws, and women's dress codes. Views on human rights expressed by the jurists, the judiciary, policy-makers, liberals and human rights activists often run contrary to the traditionalists, fundamentalists or radicals.

Issues of interpretation of the Qur'an and *ḥadīth* in the specific context of *ḥijāb* are discussed and analyzed in detail in chapters 7 and 8 of this volume. In the second part of Chapter 8, the author has divided the interpreters of *ḥadīth* into conservative and liberal groups and spelled out their approaches to interpretation. The other controversial and much-debated topics concerning the status of women in Islam — such as men's superiority over women, wife-chastisement, inheritance, polygamy and law of evidence — are equally important but beyond the scope of this collection.[21]

Two Solitudes: The Modernists/Liberals and the Traditionalists/Conservatives

In search of a typology for Islamic ideology, social scientists and humanists have coined various terms and labels such as "secularism," "Islamic modernism," "fundamentalism," "radical Islamism," "Islamic totalism," "traditionalism," "neo-traditionalism" and more currently using the term "Islamism."[22] I have, however, used the terms "modernists/liberals" and "traditionalists/conservatives" loosely to be consistent with their use in Chapter 8. The reformers (sometimes called modernists), sensing the need to change how basic Muslim values were being interpreted in their countries, argued that the role of traditional scholarship was becoming problematic. However, the influence they enjoyed during the colonial period has been on the decline since the 1970s. The traditional *'ulamā'*, on the other hand, have gained power and control over the disenfranchised masses suffering from the failed economic and social policies of their respective governments. For more than two decades, modernists and traditionalists have lived in two solitudes.

It must be recognized, however, that new strategies are constantly being developed to regain the ground that modernists/liberals have lost to the traditionalists. Among the numerous jurists and thinkers of the present age, we see that Ḥasan Ḥanafī (of Egypt), 'Abdolkarīm Soroush (of Iran), Rachid Ghannoushi[23] (of Tunisia, an activist in exile) and Abdullahi an-Na'im (of Sudan) are making noteworthy contributions by taking a fresh look at the *sharī'ah*. These reformist Muslim thinkers, philosophers and jurists aim to revise Muslim jurisprudence and legal systems to make them compatible with the exigencies of today's global realities, especially in the areas of human rights, Islamic values and Muslim family law (an-Na'im 1990).[24]

It is noteworthy that interest in the area of Qur'anic studies is growing rapidly. Solid studies on the themes, style, literary structure and interpretation of the Qur'an have recently been published.[25] A comprehensive encyclopedia of the Qur'an is, furthermore, in progress. Among the scholars of

Islam who have suggested interesting approaches to the interpretation of the Qur'an and whose works are available in the West, one can cite Fazlur Rahman (of Pakistan, d. 1988), Asghar Ali Engineer (of India; though not a scholar of the Qur'an, he has studied it in the context of Muslim women's issues) and Naṣr Ḥāmid Abū Zayd (of Egypt, an activist in exile) .

Fazlur Rahman sees the "Qur'an as a divine response, through the Prophet's mind, to the moral-social situation of the Prophet's Arabia."[26] Some of the Qur'an's moral, religious and social injunctions are general laws, while others are responses to specific situations arising from a concrete historical context. Therefore, Fazlur Rahman goes on to suggest that Qur'anic content should be studied as a whole and that its interpretation be undertaken in two steps: the first is to identify specific principles and values, and then move to general and long-range objectives and systemize them, while the second and more important step is to apply them, keeping in mind the present socio-historical context. This approach thus requires a careful analysis of current exigencies, a clear determination of priorities and a fresh implementation of Qur'anic values. The goal of making Qur'anic imperatives alive and relevant for the present can only be achieved by the teamwork of a historian, a social scientist and an ethicist.[27]

Asghar Ali Engineer, like Fazlur Rahman, holds the view that the overwhelming emphasis of the Qur'an is on monotheism and social justice, particularly the rights and welfare of the indigent and weaker members of society — orphans, women and slaves. Engineer uses the terms "normative" and "contextual" in his interpretation of the Qur'anic text. By "normative" he means fundamental and universal principles applicable in all situations and times while "contextual" principles are specific and limited to a given situation that arose during the Prophet's time.[28] The controversial Naṣr ḤāmidAbū Zayd has for his part developed a hermeneutical theory whose guiding principle in the interpretation of Qur'anic verses affecting women is that, overall, the Qur'an advocates gender equality. He acknowledges that some verses appear to discriminate against women, but insists that such verses should be read and interpreted in light of the social and moral context of pre-Islamic Arabia.[29]

Muḥammad Shaḥrūr, a contemporary Syrian author, has also the "unique" approach of exploring "universal" meaning in his interpretation of Qur'anic verses, as Soraya Hajjaji-Jarrah has noted in the conclusion to her chapter in this volume on the Qur'anic commentaries (for details, see p. 209).

The major task facing today's liberal thinkers is how to make their new interpretations and approaches known to the students studying in *madrasahs* and to the masses living in Muslim countries, as they are lagging far behind in their influence in comparison with religious scholars such as Abū al-A'lā' Mawdūdī (1903–1979), recognized as one of the most influential Islamic ideologues. His Qur'anic exegesis, *Tafhīm al-Qur'ān* (six volumes), written in Urdu and translated into various Islamic languages, is the most widely read exegesis. Traditional in orientation, it has significantly influenced Muslim activists in many countries.

Muslim Women in Canada: Their Role in Community Building

Our discussion will not be complete without recognizing the role Muslim women have played in building institutions for their young communities in the Canadian landscape. In today's global village, Muslim women living as a minority group in Canada and the U.S. are not isolated from the larger Muslim world. They share the same hopes, aspirations and agonies in the social, intellectual and religious spheres. However, the growth of Muslim minority communities in North America and Europe and their integration into these societies have posed many challenges peculiar to them that have also been addressed in chapters comprising Part I of this volume.

The Muslim communities in Canada, like any other religious and ethnic group migrating to another country, developed their roots in their adopted home by building mosques, social, political and religious organizations for preserving their identity as a group and their religious and cultural heritage.

When pioneer Muslim families established roots in the Edmonton area in the 1930s, they felt an urgent need to establish a mosque where Muslims could pray and socialize. These pioneer Muslim men and women arrived in the provinces of Saskatchewan and Alberta in Western Canada around the same time as the first known Muslim family arrived in Ottawa in 1903. The experiences of the founding men and women of the first mosque, known as al-Rashid Mosque in Edmonton, Alberta, have been recorded by their children and grandchildren in a recent collection of seven narratives, *At My Mother's Feet: Stories of Muslim Women*.[30]

In Canada's largely secular society, there are many challenges faced by Muslim immigrants. Many have had little or no practical experience of the Western culture and lifestyle. Muslim men and women have to deal with the challenges of adaptation, integration or assimilation in the host culture, and are terrified of losing their religious and cultural identity. Approximately 650,000 in number, Muslims are just about 2 per cent of the Canadian population. They are still in search of their place in Canadian society, and the development of their educational, community-welfare and social institutions has just begun.

One such institution represents perhaps the most remarkable achievement of the third generation of Muslim women in Canada: this is the Canadian Council of Muslim Women (CCMW), established in 1982.[31]

I have watched the remarkable development of CCMW from its inception. Over the years, this organization has grown into a dynamic, highly organized and widely respected truly national organization. It has chapters in all major cities across Canada. At its annual national meetings, CCMW provides a forum for serious, well-informed and scholarly discourse on the most pressing issues confronting Muslim women and families. In addition to symposia and lectures to sensitize its membership to the main issues and their rights, CCMW publishes credible resource materials for general readership, but particularly for Muslim women.

This organization set out: (1) to assist new immigrant women in bonding with the larger Muslim community in Canada; (2) to help integrate them into Canadian society; (3) to sensitize the larger non-Muslim majority of Canadians about Islam and Islamic culture; (4) to build bridges between CCMW and other Canadian women's organizations; (5) to develop connections with international women's organizations to promote peace and awareness of human rights; and (6) above all to enhance the voice of reason and moderation.

Another important reality that has enriched the lives of Muslims is the Canadian government's official policy of multiculturalism. It was on October 8, 1971 that the late Pierre Elliott Trudeau (d. September 28, 2000), the prime minister of Canada, announced this policy, which over the last thirty-one years has brought about significant changes in the lives of Canadians. By it, Canada's character as a multicultural society is recognized and promoted. New immigrants are supported in their efforts to maintain their language, culture and heritage under this policy. They are made to feel at home in their adopted country. Various government programs are offered to help immigrants integrate into the culture of the host society, but without having to sacrifice their many different identities. One of the best features of this policy is the support of the provincial and federal governments for the instruction of children in their heritage languages. Thousands of children are thus being taught Arabic, Persian and Urdu and other lesser-spoken languages by Muslims and non-Muslims on the weekends through their own school boards. This, by the way, provides an opportunity for educated Muslim and non-Muslim immigrant women to get involved with the boards to teach their own mother tongues.

Concluding Remarks

In this chapter, we have given the reader a glimpse of the ebb and flow of Islam, and the rise and decline of the civilization that developed around this faith. Women played an active and central role in the affairs of the community right from the inception of Islam, when Khadīja became the first to accept the message of Islam brought home by her husband around 610 CE. They were warriors, Sufis, artists, scholars, teachers and freedom fighters. It is tragic to note how Muslim women lost many of their rights and the status given to them by Islam. The main reason for "the present epistemological crisis in Muslim jurisprudence over women's issues is the blatant absence of female voice in Islamic legal discourse."[32] Nevertheless, today they are trying to regain their lost status through their intellectual vigour and activism. It is an uphill task to reverse centuries-old, male-dominated epistemology and its attendant social and cultural attitudes. Here, we are talking about a small number of educated women who must provide leadership to millions of disenfranchised, uneducated and impoverished women living on the fringes of Muslim societies. However, we have also seen progress in making women aware of their rights. Women's rights groups are playing a positive and active role across the Muslim world. Solid scholarship is being produced both by men and women on women's issues, social inequities in Muslim countries, human rights and abuses of law by the custodians of religious authority in the name of Islam.

The task facing a Muslim woman today is precisely how such misinterpretations of *sharī'ah* should be questioned. While she is trying to maintain her traditional role in the family, she must also rethink her own religious tradition. In so doing she needs to examine the sources of Islamic law in order to understand it from her own perspective. She ought to seek restoration of the status that the Qur'an originally gave her, a status that has been robbed from her by Muslim male interpreters and implementers of Islamic law. The loudest protest against the so-called "honour killings" has been voiced by women's rights groups, which are forcing governments to bring the killers before courts of law. As Muslim women in contemporary society begin to study the meaning of their own tradition for themselves, they find themselves moving in directions quite similar to those taken by women in other traditions. They are beginning to write their own commentaries on Muslim scriptures (Wadud 1999), reopen questions of Islamic law and its application (Mernissi 1987, 1991a, 1991b, 1992, for example) and take on the role of theological experts, judges and political activists themselves (Alvi and McDonough 1994, 14–15). Muslim women, however, are not like those feminists in the West who reject men; they do not wage a war against Muslim men. They are simply becoming more aware of their rights and are learning to be more assertive. They have allies in many male reformers and modernists who have fought for the education and rights of women in the past.

Returning to the Canadian scene, we notice that, among the leaders (*imāms*) of the mosques across Canada, there are a few scholars of Islam, trained theologians and jurists, who are pursuing research, writing and publishing with a sensitivity to Western civilization and culture. Such an orientation exhibited by leadership in the mosques will greatly help young Muslim communities in Canada to integrate into the new society, while at the same time promoting their religious identity and practices. There is no reason for Muslims to develop a siege mentality as a religious minority. Indeed, as a community they are sufficiently matured to become actively involved in building social institutions and increase their participation in the social and political issues of the larger society.

Notes

1 I am grateful to the Canadian Council of Muslim Women for permission to use passages for this chapter from my "Foreword" to V.A. Behiery and A.M. Guenther, *Islam: Its Roots and Wings*; and to the editors of *Muslim World* for their permission to take some passages from the article jointly written with Sheila McDonough, "The Canadian Council of Muslim Women: A Chapter in the History of Muslim Women in Canada."

2 *The Holy Qur'an, Text, Translation and Commentary* by Abdullah Yusuf Ali (n.d.) 2:143, 57. All citations from the Qur'an are from this text with minor changes.

3 English translation is taken from Fazlur Rahman, *Major Themes of the Qur'an* (Chicago: Bibliotheca Islamica, 1980), 8.

4 Ibid., Q. 23:115.

5 "Send not away those who call on their Lord morning and evening, seeking His Face." (Q. 6:52, 302). For further discussion, see Abdel Haleem, *Understanding the Qur'an: Themes and Style* (London: I.B. Tauris, 1999), 107–122; and Andrew Rippin, "Desiring the Face of God: The Qur'anic Symbolism of Personal Responsibility," *Literary Structures of Religious Meaning in the Qur'an*, edited by Issa Boullata (Richmond, Surrey: Curzon Press, 2000), 117–124.

6 For specimens of calligraphy and miniature paintings, see *The Emperors' Album: Images of Mughal India*, compiled by Stuart C. Welch, Annemarie Schimmel, Marie L. Swietochowski, and Wheeler M. Thackston (New York: The

Metropolitan Museum of Art, 1987).

7 "Ye have indeed in the Apostle of God a beautiful pattern (of conduct)" (Q. 33:21, 1109).

8 English translation is taken from Bashir Ahmad Dar, *A Study in Iqbal's Philosophy* (Lahore: Shaikh Ghulam Ali and Sons, 1971), 120–121.

9 Ibn Qayyim al-Jawzīyah, *I'lam al-Muwaqqi'īn* (Cairo), 3:5, taken from Khaled Abou El Fadl, *Speaking in God's Name: Islamic Law, Authority and Women* (Oxford: Oneworld Publications, 2001), 14.

10 For the original text, see Shaykh Aḥmad Sirhindī, *Maktūbāt Imām Rabbānī*, Urdu translation by Qāẓi 'Ālim al-Dīn (Lahore, Maktabah-i Madanīyah, n.d.), 1:36, 91–92.

11 For the original text, see ibid,1:276, 571–575. The *al-Hidāyah* of Burhān al-Dīn 'Alī ibn Abī Bakr al-Marghīnānī (d. 1196), and the *Bazdawī* of Fakhr al-Islām al-Bazdawī (d. 1089) are two popular works of the Ḥanafī school of law on jurisprudence and the principles of jurisprudence, respectively. For details, see Ansari (1986, 226, note 56).

12 For the original text, see Sirhindī, *Maktūbāt*, 1:73, 159. On the subject of renewal and reform in the Indo-Pakistan subcontinent, see Alvi (1994).

13 For more details, see Peter Jackson, "Sultan Raḍiyya bint Iltutmish," in *Women in the Medieval Islamic World: Power, Patronage, and Piety*, edited by Gavin R.G. Hambly (New York: St. Martin's Press, 1998), 181–197.

14 Noteworthy chapters in this collection are: Geoffrey Lewis, "Heroines and Others in the Heroic Age of the Turks," 147–160; Priscilla P. Soucek, "Timurid Women: A Cultural Perspective," 199–226; Maria Szuppe, "The 'Jewels of Wonder': Learned Ladies and Princess Politicians in the Provinces of Early Safavid Iran," 325–347; Stephen P. Blake, "Contributors to the Urban Landscape: Women Builders in Safavid Isfahan and Mughal Shahjahanabad," 407–428; Gregory C. Kozlowski, "Private Lives and Public Piety: Women and the Practice of Islam in Mughal India," 469–488; and Richard Barnett, "Embattled Begams: Women as Power Brokers in Early Modern India," 521–536.

15 Nikki Keddie, in a recent article, reviews books on Muslim women published since 1990. The works reviewed for this article focus on women from Turkey, Iran, Egypt, the Arab World, Syria and Lebanon, Palestine and North Africa and are of interest especially to historians. See Nikki R. Keddie, "Women in the Limelight: Some Recent Books on Middle Eastern Women's History," *International Journal of Middle East Studies* 34, no. 3 (2002): 553–573.

16 Some more Qur'anic verses on the subject:

> Glory to God who created in pairs all things that the earth produces as well as their own (human) kind, and (other) things of which they have no knowledge. (Q. 36:36, 1178; also see 76:2–3, 1655)

> And God sets forth, as an example to those who believe, the wife of Pharaoh: Behold she said: 'O my Lord! build for me, in nearness to Thee, a mansion in the Garden, and save me from Pharaoh and his doings, and save me from those that do wrong.' And Mary the daughter of 'Imrān, who guarded her chastity; and we breathed into [her body] of our spirit; and she testified the truth of the words of her Lord and of his Revelations, and was one of the Devout [servants]. (Q. 66:11–12, 1573–1574, and notes 5550–5553)

The commentator remarks on this latter passage: "In Islamic tradition Āsiya is one of the four perfect women, the other three are, Mary, mother of Jesus, Khadīja, the wife of the Prophet and Faṭima, his daughter" (Q. note 5549, 1573).

[17] This part of the heading is inspired by Abdulaziz Sachedina's article, "Woman, Half-the-Man: The Crisis of Male Epistemology in Islamic Jurisprudence," in *Intellectual Traditions in Islam*, edited by Farhad Daftary (London: I.B. Tauris, 2000), 160–178. Another well-argued article on the subject is Mohammad Fadel, "Two Women, One Man: Knowledge, Power and Gender in Medieval Sunni Legal Thought," *International Journal of Middle East Studies* 29, no. 2 (1997): 185–204.

[18] It should be noted here that Sufis and the literati have not been historically favourable to the narrow-minded and traditional religious leaders. They have long bemoaned their legalistic and constricted interpretation of the sources of Islamic law. Some examples of their opinions are cited below for reference.

The eminent Punjabi Sufi poet, Sulṭān Bāhū (d. 1691), cited earlier in the first section of this chapter, frequently criticized his fellow religious elite's shaky scholarship and their use of it for worldly gain. In his words:

> Qur'an scholars read and aggrandize themselves, priests act sanctimonious.
> Like rain clouds in the monsoon, they wander heavy with books.
> They recite more wherever they see greater gain and plenty.
> Bahu, those who sell and eat up their earnings lose both worlds.
> (Bāhū 1998, 59)

Bāhū was not the first one to express his unhappiness with the scholars of Islam, the '*ulamā*.' He followed in the footsteps of his illustrious forerunners in Iran, such as the master mystic poets Rūmī and Ḥāfiẓ and scores of other poets in medieval Iran and India as well as in the modern period. One of the most eminent Iranian poets, Shams al-Dīn Muḥammad Ḥāfiẓ- i Shīrāzī (d. 1392), frequently expressed his disapproval of the self-proclaimed righteous. For example:

> The fire of deceit and hypocrisy will consume the barn of religion;
> Ḥāfiẓ, cast off this woolen cloak, and be gone.
> My heart is weary of hypocrisy and the drum under the blanket;
> O happy moment, when I hoist the standard at the wine-tavern.
> (Arberry 1970, 16, 18)

Among the many thinkers in the modern period who have expressed frustration over the misinterpretation of the Qur'anic text, we should mention the ideologue of modern, secular Turkish intellectual, Ziya Gökalp (d. 1924), as an example of one who was concerned about the decline of Muslim women's status in the modern period and who felt obliged to complain about the misinterpretation of the Qur'anic text in these words:

> There is the woman, my mother, my sister, or my daughter; it is she who calls up the most sacred emotions from the depths of my life! There is my beloved, my sun, my moon, and my star; it is she who makes me understand the poetry of life! How could the Holy Law of God regard these beautiful creatures as despicable beings?
>
> Surely there is an error in the interpretation of the Qur'an by the learned. (Iqbāl 1989, 128 and note 30)

[19] For an insightful analysis of the issues of "authoritative" and "authority," see Abou El Fadl, *Speaking in God's Name*, chapters 2–6, 9–208. I do hope that this challenging work generates public debate in mosques and Islamic centres in North

America and Europe, and helps Muslim communities to distinguish between obscurants and rationalists.

20 Under pressure from human rights activists, the government of Pakistan was compelled in April 2000 to pass a law declaring such killings to be no less than murder. In Jordan too there is candid discussion on the subject of honour killings: there the government under King Abdullah has promised to continue the fight against this cultural tradition, a fight that was started by the late King Hussein and Queen Noor.

21 Abou El Fadl, devotes one chapter to some of these controversial subjects in his provocative and scholarly work. The topics include: Prostrating to husbands, licking their ulcers while struggling with *ḥadīth* methodology; Keeping husbands and God happy, and making it to heaven; Bargaining with crooked-ribs, defective intellect, bad omens, dogs and women; Praying in closets, hugging the wall, and dangers of seduction; and Racism, sexism, and a sense of beauty. Abou El Fadl, *Speaking in God's Name*, 209–264.

22 See, for example, William E. Shepard, who defined and applied some of these terms on the constitutions and governments of some Muslim countries as well as on Islamic thinkers in "Islam and Ideology: Towards a Typology," *International Journal of Middle East Studies* 19 (1987): 307–336. Mahmood Monshipouri presents paradigms of continuity, deprivation, growth and agency in order to explain revivalism, secularism and human rights. Mahmood Monshipouri, *Islamism, Secularism and Human Rights in the Middle East* (Boulder: Lynne Rienner Publishers, 1998), 1–37. Robert D. Lee analyzes the thought of Muḥammad Iqbāl, Sayyid Quṭb, 'Alī Sharī'atī and Mohammed Arkoun through the categories of his theory of authenticity that includes "particularity, radicalism, autonomy, unicity, group action, institutionalization, etc." See his *Overcoming Tradition and Modernity: The Search for Islamic Authenticity* (Boulder: Westview Press, 1997).

23 For information on the background and activities of H. Hanafi, R. Ghannoushi, H. al-Turabi and A. Soroush, see John Esposito and John Voll, *Makers of Contemporary Islam* (New York: Oxford University Press, 2001).

24 In addition to his *Toward an Islamic Reformation*, Abdullahi an-Na'im has written numerous scholarly articles and edited three collections of essays. The recurring themes in his writings are human rights, civil liberties and Islamic law.

25 See, for example, Abdel Haleem, *Understanding the Qur'an*, a publication in the series entitled London Qur'an Studies, sponsored by the Center of Islamic Studies, School of Oriental and African Studies, University of London; Issa J. Boullata, ed., *Literary Structures of Religious Meaning in the Qur'an* ; Rahman, *Major Themes of Qur'an.*

26 Fazlur Rahman, *Islam and Modernity: Transformation of and Intellectual Tradition* (Chicago: University of Chicago Press, 1982), 5.

27 Ibid., 7.

28 Asghar Ali Engineer, *The Rights of Women in Islam* (Lahore: Vanguard Books, 1992), 6–17, 42.

29 Yusuf Rahman has recently completed an excellent Ph.D. dissertation, "The Hermeneutical Theory of Naṣr Ḥāmid Abū Zayd: An Analytical Study of His Method of Interpreting the Qur'ān" (Institute of Islamic Studies, McGill University, 2001). The main source that he used for women's issues is Abū Zayd's *Dawā'ir al-Khawf: Qirā'ah fī Khiṭāb al-Mar'ah* (Beirut: al-Markaz al-Thaqāfī al-'Arabī, 1999). Our discussion is based on Rahman's dissertation, 180–189.

[30] Sadia Zaman, ed., *At My Mother's Feet: Stories of Muslim Women* (Kingston: Quarry Women's Books, 1999).

[31] For details, see Sheila McDonough and Sajida S. Alvi, "The Canadian Council of Muslim Women: A Chapter in the History of Muslim Women in Canada," *The Muslim World* 92, nos. 1 and 2 (Spring 2002): 79–98.

[32] Sachedina, "Woman, Half-the-Man," 165.

CHAPTER 7

Women's Modesty in Qur'anic Commentaries:
The Founding Discourse

Soraya Hajjaji-Jarrah

The Qur'an is Islam's Great Code. It constitutes the divine revelations the Prophet Muḥammad received over a period of some twenty-three years. These revelations were the direct source from which he and the Muslim community then drew the prescriptions of their daily lives. They were also the pronouncements sent to deal with various issues that actually faced Muḥammad and his followers. This is in addition to the Qur'an's role as a guide to which Muslims now and then turn to find nourishment for their devotional life.

However, once the Prophet passed away in 632 CE, the Qur'anic revelations ceased to descend, and direct, authoritative, divine contact came to an abrupt end. Consequently, it became imperative for the Muslims of that age to collect and write down the Qur'anic revelation that had been received by Muḥammad.

With the passage of time and the spread of Islam to other parts of the world, various schools of Qur'anic interpretation gradually arose in the centres of learning of the Muslim empire. In time the task of supplying the Muslim believer with religious guidance was steadily taken over by Muslim scholars — including theologians, philologists, lexicographers and jurists — and, increasingly, by Qur'anic commentators. Indeed, by the middle of the tenth century a huge body of Qur'anic commentaries (*tafsīr*) had accumulated. Of these, al-Ṭabarī's (d. 923 CE) work constitutes the earliest, still fully extant example of this genre of writing.

Certain important characteristics of Qur'anic commentaries merit our attention. First of all is the fact that Qur'anic commentaries are not mere and simple interpretations of the Holy Text. Rather, the methodologies employed have a complex nature involving various sources. For in order to elucidate the meaning of Qur'anic words that were no longer familiar to later generations, the commentators quite often resorted to pre-Islamic Arabic poetry. Moreover, where the Qur'an makes no explicit prescriptions, Muslim scholars, in order to formulate them in harmony with the Qur'anic tenets, developed an ingenious method that claimed to produce an irrefutable link to the Prophet's sayings and actions. Additionally, for elaboration and explanation of the Biblical stories to which the Qur'an often refers (usually only by way of allusion), the commentators quite frequently consulted converts to Islam from Christianity and Judaism. Furthermore, and very importantly, a Qur'anic commentary not only demonstrates the commentator's religious devotion, intellectual skills and his doctrinal and sectarian allegiances, it also transmits the voice of the religious discourse of his time. In other words, in his work the interpreter is responding to the forces of his historical reality with the intention of either supporting or opposing them. For the Qur'anic commentators have been, without fail, an integral part in flesh and blood of the historical reality of their time; hence, their commentaries necessarily reflect their interactions with it.

This interaction constitutes the axis of the ensuing discussion. For as the literature of *tafsīr* became widespread, elaborated on, repeated, added to and taught in the various institutes of learning, the interpretations of its most esteemed authorities of the past came to be treated by some Muslim religious scholars as representative of eternal immutable truth. The interpretations of two Qur'anic verses that address women's modesty, i.e., verse 53 of Chapter 33 and verse 31 of Chapter 24, are a case in point.[1]

For centuries, these two verses have been held to mean that once a Muslim woman comes of age, she is required to conceal all her body except for the face and hands in the presence of a male who has come of age and who is lawful to her in marriage.

Focusing on the commentaries of two major Qur'anic interpreters of the tenth and thirteenth centuries, al-Ṭabarī and al-Rāzī respectively, I hope to demonstrate in the following pages that the persistent attitude with respect to the veiling of Muslim women has been the outcome exclusively of an affective relationship between the commentators and their social reality. The structure of this reality was characterized, among other things, by the widespread phenomenon of slave women (*jawārī*, sing. *jāriya*) and the particular social mores that grew with them. These special mores, as we shall see, led to a very different paradigm toward women than had existed during the lifetime of the Prophet.

Hence my argument is that the existence of a social structure in which female slavery was widespread influenced the members of that society who wrote commentaries on the Qur'an, and that they were unconsciously motivated to read their assumptions about the inferiority of females into their commentaries. As a result, assumptions of female inferiority in medieval Islamic societies derived more from scriptural commentaries than from the Qur'anic verses themselves. I hope to demonstrate in this paper that the later persistent attitude with respect to the veiling of Muslim women was the outcome of an affective relationship between the social reality during the ninth to thirteenth centuries in urban Islamic society, and of the assumptions of the scholars who were part of that society. It was the voices of religious scholars, who saw their own prejudices reflected in the Qur'an, that produced much of the fear of the female that dominated this society.

The Qur'anic *Ḥijāb*

Today both Muslims and non-Muslims are of the belief that the term *ḥijāb* refers to the style of clothing prescribed by the Qur'an for all adult

Muslim women. Thus, for our purposes, it is necessary to begin by investigating how the Qur'an actually uses the term *ḥijāb*. Verse 53 of Chapter 33 reads as follows: "And when you ask them [the Prophet's wives] for something, ask them from behind a veil (*ḥijāb*); that makes for greater purity for your hearts and for theirs."[2]

This represents the Qur'an's sole use of the term *ḥijāb* in relation to women. Its isolated appearance in this context is further confined within certain boundaries. *Ḥijāb* here refers exclusively to the Qur'anic prescriptive mode of communication between believing men and the wives of the Prophet. This segment of verse 53 falls neatly within the purpose of the entire verse. The relevant verse teaches Muḥammad's followers the niceties of social behaviour when entering his house, and continues the codification of the special status of the Prophet's wives mentioned earlier in verses 28–34 in the same chapter.[3] The Prophet's wives are — the Qur'an asserts in verse 32 — unlike any other women, and their extraordinary status requires that they comply with certain restrictive conditions.

Everywhere else in the Qur'an, the term *ḥijāb* — which, in its various derivatives, occurs seven times in all — retains the connotations of either a physical or a metaphorical barrier without any reference to women or their clothing. Verse 15 of Chapter 83, for example, reads: "Verily, from their God, that Day, they will be veiled." Likewise, verse 45 of Chapter 17 states: "When you recite the Qur'an. We have put between you and those who believe not in the Hereafter, an invisible veil."[4]

Thus, the Qur'anic usage of the term *ḥijāb* seems somewhat removed from the notion of dress or clothing of any kind. For this reason, we maintain that the early Muslims, Muḥammad's contemporaries, did not understand the Qur'anic term *ḥijāb* to mean what many people today think it means, namely, the near-total concealment of a Muslim woman's physical features.

Perhaps a journey back in time through the earliest extant Islamic biographical collection, Muḥammad ibn Sa'd's (d. 845) *Kitāb al-Ṭabaqāt al-Kubrá*, can give further evidence as to how the term *ḥijāb* was understood in relation to women at the time of the Prophet. Ibn Sa'd's work is a valuable compilation of biographical data about prominent Muslims in the first Islamic centuries. Not the least of its features is an entire volume dedicated to celebrating the lives of the most distinguished Muslim women from this period. It is an invaluable source for understanding the role of women in the early Muslim community.

In the chapter dealing with those women whose marriages to the Prophet were either annulled or unconsummated, a particular phenomenon is readily observable. One of the most important signs that confirmed the marriage of lesser-known women to Muḥammad was their concealment by a "veil" from the sight of equally marriageable men. This is in perfect accord with our above-quoted verse. Ibn Sa'd, for example, relates that when a certain Asmā' bint al-Nu'mān chose to marry soon after the Prophet passed away, 'Umar ibn al-Khaṭṭāb, the second caliph (d. 644), who believed that she was one of the Prophet's widows, decided to punish her and her husband. The Qur'an unequivocally prohibited men from marrying Muḥammad's widows, with verse 53 of Chapter 33 warning that this was a grave act in the eyes of God.[5] In order to ward off 'Umar's retribution, Asmā' had to furnish him with convincing evidence that she was never married to the Prophet. To achieve this, she resorted to emphatically disavowing the one mark of the Prophet's wives that visually separated them from all other believing women: the *ḥijāb*. Ibn Sa'd tells us that Asmā' told 'Umar "By God I was never put behind the veil." This was enough for 'Umar, who decided not to punish her or her husband (Ibn Sa'd 1990, 8:16).[6]

In the subsection entitled "Mention of the Messenger of God's Veiling of his Wives," Ibn Sa'd gives a clear definition of the *ḥijāb*, which was exclusively imposed on the Prophet's wives. He describes it as being a single curtain (*siṭran wāḥidan*) from behind which all the Prophet's wives communicated with men who were lawful to them in marriage (Ibid. 8:140–141).

The Modesty of Believing Women in Qur'anic Commentaries: Al-Ṭabarī's Interpretation

At the beginning of this article, we noted that the authority for the religious importance of the veiling of Muslim women was based more on later Qur'anic commentaries than on the Qur'an's own prescriptions. We will now discuss the interpretation of Q. 24:31 and Q. 33:59 by Abu Ja'far Muḥammad ibn Jarīr al-Ṭabarī as further evidence for our conclusion.

Al-Ṭabarī was born in Tabaristan in Iran in 839, and grew up in a household that had a great tradition of religious learning. He distinguished himself as a child by memorizing the entire Qur'an by the time he was seven years old. When he was only nine, he led prayers and began to record prophetic deeds and sayings (*ḥadīth*). As a young man, he travelled to the most important centres of learning of the Islamic world seeking knowledge from the Muslim community's best scholars. Eventually, he chose to settle in Baghdad, which was then the most important city in the Islamic Empire. Al-Ṭabarī was not only a Qur'anic commentator; he was also a traditionist, a jurist and a historian. Besides his thirty-volume Qur'anic commentary, known as *Jāmi' al-Bayān fī Tafsīr al-Qur'ān*, his voluminous annals *Tārīkh al-Rusul wa-al-Mulūk* stand as further testimony to his prolific output.[7] Al-Ṭabarī died in Baghdad in 923 (al-Dāwūdī 1972, 2:106–114; Ayāzī 1953, 406).[8]

Turning now to al-Ṭabarī's interpretation of the Qur'an with respect to Muslim women's code, we may begin with his commentary on the following key passage, Q. 24:31:

> And say to the believing women that they should avert their gaze and guard their modesty, and that they should not display their adornment (*zīnah*) except what is apparent (*ẓahara*) thereof, and that they should throw (*yaḍribna*) their head-scarves (*khumur*) over their bosoms/necklines (*juyūb*), and not display their adornment (*zīnah*) except to their husbands, or fathers.

After a brief explanation of the two Qur'anic injunctions about averting lustful gazes and covering private parts, with which the verse begins, al-Ṭabarī offers an opinion with respect to a dress code for believing women. He tersely states that, according to the Qur'an, a believing woman must not reveal her adornment except to those who are unlawful to her in marriage (*maḥārim*, sing. *maḥram*). He nevertheless immediately points out that the Qur'an is actually referring to, and differentiating between, two kinds of adornment: a hidden and concealed adornment, and a visible and apparent one. Since the Qur'an never defines either kind of adornment in any detail, al-Ṭabarī gives his own explanation. He holds that the concealed adornment includes anklets, bracelets, earrings and necklaces. But what appears to pose a problem for al-Ṭabarī is the meaning of the expression "apparent adornment" (al-Ṭabarī 1987, 18:91–92). For without defining the meaning of this expression, the Qur'an unequivocally permits the display of such "apparent adornment" to everyone, without exception (Q. 24:31): "[A]nd that they should not display their adornment except what is apparent."

Before delving any further into al-Ṭabarī's interpretation of this Qur'anic passage, it would be useful to explore the meaning of adornment (*zīnah*) in the Arabic language. In his widely acclaimed lexicon *Lisān al-'Arab*), Ibn Manẓūr (d. 1311) tells us that the term *zīnah* is a noun whose meaning encompasses everything used with the intention of beautifying or enhancing the appearance of a thing or a person. Furthermore, Ibn Manẓūr states that the verb form of *zīnah*, i.e., (*azyana*) means to counterbalance the monotony or plainness of someone or something as in "the ground is decorated or beautified by its grass." Finally, according to Ibn Manẓūr, *zīnah* refers also to the addition of something that contributes to the existing beauty or splendour and heightens its excellence (Ibn Manẓūr n.d. 13:202), much in the same sense as the English words "adornment" or "decoration."[9]

Clearly, therefore, we can safely take the Arabic term *zīnah* to mean, in general terms, a thing or an action intended to improve the aesthetic qualities of a person or a thing, in order to convey pleasure and appreciation of the beautiful. Nevertheless, in his attempt to define the characteristics of personal adornment that can be open to view, al-Ṭabarī tends to suggest that it would be better for believing women to avoid any adornment whatsoever. Since the Qur'an does not clearly explain what is meant by "permissible, apparent adornment," al-Ṭabarī exercises caution in giving his judgment. For although he indicates that he supports designating the face and hands of the female as coming under the Qur'anic category of "permitted-to-view adornment," he registers his uncertainty. He states clearly that his support for such an interpretation is based solely on the unanimous agreement of scholars (Ibid. 18:94).

In view of the shifts in speculation and the various definitions offered by interpreters over time, it is important to explore carefully how the Qur'an uses the term *zīnah*. In its various derivatives, the term is used in the Qur'an a total of forty-three times. Not unexpectedly, the idea of adding aesthetic or admirable qualities to a person, thing, or action in order to give pleasure or to generate esteem and appreciation is characteristic of the Qur'anic use of this key term. The most striking aspect of the Qur'anic use of this term is the fact that the word "adornment" invariably carries the connotation of being unessential and/or extraneous to the original.[10] "Apparent adornment" in the verse under discussion, therefore, cannot refer to women's hair, face, neck, arms or legs, as al-Ṭabarī speculates. These parts of the female body are neither unessential, nor extraneous, nor fundamentally intended to enhance the appearance of a woman. Rather, they are essential parts of the human anatomy. Consequently al-Ṭabarī's implicit definition of "apparent adornment" falls outside of the Qur'anic usage of the term. In other words, something natural, such as a nose, cannot be characterized as something unessential, or as added on for the purpose of eliciting admiration.

It is worth noting that al-Ṭabarī does not adhere to his interpretation of the term "adornment" when it occurs elsewhere in the Qur'an in situations unrelated to women's dress code. Rather, he interprets the expression as used in verses 31–32 of Chapter 7 within the boundaries of both the Qur'an's usage and Ibn Manẓūr's definitions of "adornment." The verses read as follows:

> O children of Adam wear your "adornment", beautiful apparel at every time and place of prayer, eat and drink, but waste not by excess, for God loves not the wasters. Say who has forbidden the "adornment" of all things beautiful which God has produced?

Al-Ṭabarī says that "adornment" in these two verses is unanimously agreed on by all authorities to mean everything that is intended to relieve the plainness of, and to beautify and embellish, the human body (al-Ṭabarī 1987, 8:214).

Continuing our exploration of al-Ṭabarī's commentary on Q. 24:33, we find that he reaffirms his definition of the "permitted-to-view adornment" in the course of interpreting the Qur'anic statement (in the same verse): "and that they should throw (*yaḍribna*) their headscarves (*khumur*) over their bosoms/necklines (*juyūb*)."

This Qur'anic phrase signifies, according to al-Ṭabarī, yet another instance of the divine command to the believing woman to cover and conceal her hair, neck and ears with her headscarf. Furthermore, despite the clear Qur'anic reference to the bosom/neckline area, al-Ṭabarī interprets it as referring to a part of the body above the "bosom/neckline" (Ibid. 18:94).

However, al-Ṭabarī's interpretation of the terms "headscarf" and "bosoms/necklines" does not correspond to their meanings as found in standard dictionaries of the classical language. In the first place, *khimār*, or headscarf, refers specifically to a woman's headscarf, and less frequently to the kind worn by a man (Ibn Manẓūr n.d. 4:254–259; 9:330–334). Second, when we come to explore the import of the Qur'anic term *juyūb* (sing. *jayb*), we find that it has two interrelated meanings. The first refers to the hollowed, rounded or inward-curving cut left for the head in a garment. The second meaning refers to the part of the human body between the neck and the breasts — the part which, depending on the curve of the neckline, is either overly exposed or completely concealed.

Now, looking carefully at the Qur'anic phrase under discussion, we find that its interpretation depends also on the verb *yaḍribna*, which in the context of the Qur'anic passage under discussion clearly means "to throw."[11] The divine ordinance "they should throw" should be taken to mean that the Qur'an is instructing the believing women to throw their already existing headscarves over their bosoms/necklines when these appear to have been overly exposed.[12] The Qur'an, therefore, is recommending a specific minor action, and not introducing a change to the style of clothing worn by believing women in the time of the Prophet.

When al-Ṭabarī arrives at the Qur'anic phrase "and [the believing women] should not display their adornment except to their husbands, fathers, etc.," he quite rightly understands the Qur'an to be referring to "adornments" that ought to be concealed from all except for particular categories of individuals enumerated by the Qur'an. However, instead of settling on "adornment" as applying only to certain private areas of the female body, al-Ṭabarī extends his definition to encompass the Qur'anic usage of the term, the lexicographical meanings and his own earlier definition. Consequently, from al-Ṭabarī's point of view, in this particular Qur'anic verse "adornment" refers to a woman's ornaments as well as to her entire body except for the face, hands and arms to the elbow (al-Ṭabarī 1987, 18:94). Clearly al-Ṭabarī's understanding of the meaning of "adornment" is strictly determined by whether the "adornment" is something that can be revealed or concealed.

In the section from verse 33 of Chapter 24 discussed above, the Qur'an seems to follow certain criteria when dealing with women's modesty, avoiding any reference to particular parts of the body, and introducing no major changes to the way Arab women dressed before and after they became Muslims. The women of Mecca and Medina who accepted the message of the Qur'an and became believers may have changed many things in their lives, but they did not change their normal way of dressing.

Q. 33:59, on the other hand, not only reflects this Qur'anic tradition; it is also linked to a historical context. It reads:

> O Prophet tell your wives, your daughters and the women of the believers that they should bring some of their cloaks (*jalābīb*)

> closer/nearer (*yudnīna*) to themselves, that is a minimum [measure] so that they would be recognized [as such] and hence not molested.

The context of this verse depends on the preceding verse (verse 58), and on the two verses that follow (verses 60, 61).[13] They all appear to have been revealed at the height of the power of the "Hypocrites" (the Prophet's covert enemies) in Medina. Verse 58 reads as follows:

> And those who annoy the believing men and women undeservedly, bear a calumny and a glaring sin.

Ibn Sa'd tells us that when the Hypocrites, who harassed Muslim women in the streets, were taken to task, they said "We took them for slaves." Consequently, according to Ibn Sa'd, distinguishing free, believing women from slave women became imperative. And so verse 33:59 was revealed commanding the Prophet to tell his wives, his daughters and the women of believing men to draw their *jalābīb*, or cloaks, closer to themselves in order that they might be recognized and not be attacked (Ibn Sa'd 1990, 8:141). The two verses that follow (60, 61) attest to the historical reality even further. They threaten the Hypocrites with grave consequences should they not refrain from attacking the Prophet and his followers:

> Certainly, if the Hypocrites and those in whose hearts is a disease and those who stir up sedition in al-Medina, we shall certainly stir you up against them, then will they not be able to stay in it as your neighbours except for a short time. They shall be cursed wherever they are found, they shall be seized and slain mercilessly.

In addition to the strong evidence suggesting that 33:59 was intended to deal with a specific situation facing the Prophet and his followers, the reference to a code of dress for women remains characteristic of the Qur'anic position on women's modesty. It introduces a minor action without adding any new piece of clothing, and does not insist on the continuation of any particular fashion of dress. The Qur'an in this verse not only tells the believing women to draw the cloaks they are already wearing closer to themselves, it also gives the rationale behind such a divine ordinance. In a few, very concise words, the Qur'an explains that it is the very least measure they may take to be recognized. Equally important is the implication in the verse that the line of distinction — the drawing of the cloaks — is intended to differentiate between those who belong to Muḥammad's camp and those who are against him, to distinguish the believing female from the unbeliever.

However, despite the clarity of the divine decree and the mutually corroborative nature of the four verses that lends weight to their historical context, al-Ṭabarī focuses on the concealment of the believing women even further. He says:

> God is telling His Prophet to tell his wives, daughters and the women of the believers that they should not dress themselves like slave women by revealing their hair and face. Rather they should bring their cloaks closer to themselves so that no dissolute person harasses them when he knows that they are free women. (al-Ṭabarī 1987, 21:33)

Al-Ṭabarī here understands the Qur'anic phrase "bring some of their cloaks closer/nearer to themselves" to mean the concealment of the hair and face of the free, believing woman.

This is a very good example of how al-Ṭabarī tends to assume that the social conditions of the earliest Muslim community must have been the same as those existing in his own time. Looking at the problem with the benefit of hindsight, he felt that it was urgent that Muslim women not be mistaken for slaves. He assumes that this was also the case in the Prophet's lifetime. But now we can see that the social conditions of the two historical periods were actually quite different. Al-Ṭabarī was assuming that the Qur'an had meant to say that believing women must cover their hair and face because, in his time, this was how men could recognize the difference between slaves and free women. Thus he transferred the anxieties caused by the social conditions of his age into his interpretation of the situation existing at the time of the Qur'an's revelation.

Women's Modesty and the Early Islamic Period

Perhaps we can see more clearly the difference between al-Ṭabarī's tenth-century commentary on the issue, and the original Qur'anic intent with respect to a dress code for Muslim women, by paying more attention to our sources of information about the first Muslim community. The first women believers and their male counterparts heard the Qur'an either directly from the Messenger of God or from his contemporaries. Gleaning data on these women's code of dress, however, is not an easy task. For in their biographical collections and books of history, the Muslims were hardly interested in the dress fashions of Islam's outstanding women. Rather, they were interested in stressing the contributions the women made to the new community. Muslims transmitted and recorded these women's deeds, their enthusiasm and commitment to the new religion, their inclusion in the public affairs of the newly founded state and community, their social independence and their stigma-free mingling with their fellow men. These women's proximity to the Prophet and their constant presence at the mosque in Medina — where Muḥammad dwelled, which was also the place of prayer, the Parliament, and the assembly house of the Muslim government — suggest a widespread phenomenon, rather than exceptional occurrences. The fact that the early historians emphasized these aspects of the life of women in the first Muslim community strongly suggests that women in early Islam were not in the least perceived as beings whose presence threatened social disorder. Rather, the women were regarded as full-fledged human beings, as principal partners and as indispensable as their male counterparts to the welfare of the community.

Since the early historians of the community did not concern themselves particularly with the matter of dress codes, we have to infer what the attitudes and practices might have been from such evidence as we do have. Three stories — each relating to a particular distinguished Muslim woman — seem to suggest that al-Ṭabarī's understanding of women's modesty was born out of his own social reality rather than that of the early Muslim community.

However, before exploring evidence for the code of dress adopted by believing women in early Islam, it is important to draw attention to a significant point at this juncture. Since the reliability of the sources is not beyond question, and since in many instances their authors reflect in their pages the ideologies of their own time, the selection of the three reports has been done with caution. None of them transmits any direct message in terms of time-bound social mores.

Our first heroine is Nusaybah bint Ka'b whose active participation in and strong commitment to the new faith and its messenger are recorded by many Muslim historians. She is spoken of by Ibn Hishām (d. 833) in his recension of Ibn Isḥāq's (d. ca 767) *al-Sīrah al-Nabawīyah*, the earliest extant biography of Muḥammad (Ibn Hishām 1987, 4:45). Ibn Sa'd includes her in his biographical collection, as does the medieval scholar Abū al-Fidā' ibn Kathīr (d. ca 1373) in his biography of the Prophet. In his entry on Nusaybah, Ibn Sa'd speaks about her in detail. He accords her more courage and steadfastness during the Battle of Uḥud — fought in 624 — than some of Muḥammad's most esteemed Companions. Her courage in combat, defending the Prophet and shielding him from his enemies is acknowledged to be one of the reasons the Quraysh failed to kill the Prophet during that battle (Ibn Sa'd 1990, 8:303–306). His teacher al-Wāqidī (d. 822) gives a more detailed account of her engagements in major wars fought against the rebellious Arab tribes immediately after the Prophet's death in 632. He reports that in the Battle of al-Yamama, Nusaybah lost one of her arms and received ten wounds (al-Wāqidī 1984, 1:268–273).[14]

These two early Muslim historians provide us also with further interesting details. They report that while Nusaybah was engaged in the fierce fighting undertaken in defence of the Prophet, she had lifted her garments and gathered them around her waist. She undoubtedly exposed her legs in the presence of a large number of men. Interestingly, both al-Wāqidī and Ibn Sa'd relate the scene without even hinting at any stigma against females exposing their legs.

Fāṭimah bint 'Alī ibn Abī Ṭālib and her sister Zaynab are our two remaining heroines. They were the granddaughters of the Prophet through his closest daughter, Fāṭimah, and the sisters of al-Ḥasan and al-Ḥusayn, Islam's most esteemed martyrs. While exploring the evidence for their code of dress, we must keep in mind the significance of their actions, for after all, the members of the House of the Prophet enjoyed privileged contact with him. They, more than any other believers, learned and comprehended the new or Islamic mode of behaviour by being an integral part of his private life. Ibn Sa'd relates the following story about Fāṭimah. He reports that a certain 'Urwah ibn 'Abd Allāh ibn Qushayr entered the house of Fāṭimah and watched as she donned two thick ivory bracelets on each wrist, a ring on her finger and a beaded thread around her neck. When 'Urwah questioned her (about this apparent excess of adornment), she answered in a brief retort that is a testimony to her pride in her femininity and her confidence that a woman's desire to beautify herself must not be contested: "Women are unlike men" (Ibn Sa'd 1990, 8:292). Furthermore the story, as we have seen, describes her in the presence of a non-*maḥram* male with a particular part of her body — her neck — visible, an adornment that al-Ṭabarī has stated must certainly be concealed. By revealing and adorning her neck, Fāṭimah — Muḥammad's own granddaughter — appears to have demonstrated a different regard for custom than al-Ṭabarī later thought proper.

The setting for our last story is the Battle of Karbalā' — fought in 680 — the paradigm of tragedy and disorder in Islam.[15] Occurring about fifty years after the death of the Prophet, this historical landmark represents, among other things, the last major event in early Islamic history in which Muslim women exercised free, full and profound participation in the public affairs of the *ummah*. They exhibited courage and a supreme sense of self-confidence and dignity even after the massacre of their men. In his valuable annals *Tārīkh al-Rusul wa-al-Mulūk*, al-Ṭabarī depicts Zaynab, the Prophet's granddaughter and heroine of Karbalā, as apparently oblivious to the same rules of modesty that al-Ṭabarī listed in his Qur'an commentary. She not only leaves her face, ears and neck revealed, she is also described as having torn, in a moment of despair and in public, the neckline of her garment (al-Ṭabarī 1997, 3:316–334). Obviously, Zaynab was not entirely concealed by a cloak as she did this. Interestingly enough, al-Ṭabarī relates this narrative without so much as implying that Zaynab bint 'Alī ibn Abī Ṭālib was breaking the Islamic rules of modesty. Nor does he feel the need to justify her unconcealed appearance or behaviour as an uncontrollable act born of grief and despair.

Undoubtedly, the discrepancies between al-Ṭabarī's explanations (al-Rāzī's will be discussed below) of the Islamic dress code for women and what appears to be our heroine's sense of modesty is bewildering. More importantly, the discrepancy between the views on this issue of a commentator of the status of al-Ṭabarī and the Qur'an itself seems to be even more puzzling. What could have been the underpinning of this discrepancy and dislocation? What could have motivated al-Ṭabarī to hold that a free Muslim woman must mask herself with a cloak and a headscarf as a sign of decency (Ibid. 1997, 12:58)? Let us leave behind for a moment the early decades of Islam and travel ahead in time to the commentators' social environment.

The Social Forces Behind the Commentaries

In the heartland of the Islamic Empire of the ninth century, we find a society that bears little resemblance to Muḥammad's Medina. Interestingly, women have not disappeared from public space. In fact we find them almost everywhere. They are unveiled and uninhibited, with many of them beautiful, eloquent, sophisticated and well educated! However, these women are not the heirs of the women of early Islam. Rather, they are slave women (*jawārī*), for due to the Islamic conquests and constant fighting on the frontiers of the empire, the Islamic cities had to absorb an unceasing flood of slave men and women who had been captured as the booty of war.

These slaves — mostly non-Arabs — were bought and sold as goods in the slave markets. They began their careers as domestic servants, although the females were often bought for sexual pleasure as well. For while a free Muslim male was not legally permitted to marry more than four freeborn Muslim women, the number of concubines he could have was legally unlimited. If, furthermore, a concubine became pregnant by her master and gave birth to a child, she became the mother of a legitimate child, and selling or buying her was rendered illegal. When the Abbasid caliph Hārūn al-Rashīd died in 809, it is reported that he left behind a great many concubines, among whom there were twenty who could not be bought or sold because they were mothers of his children.

Clearly, these legal rules were articulated on the basis of the slave girls' function, namely, as sexual partners. This, however, did not remain for long the full extent of their role. In order to make more profit, the merchants who sold slaves embarked on improving the quality of their goods. Great care and much effort were extended to giving the slave girls the highest level of education. The *jawārī* soon became knowledgeable in music, singing, poetry, literature, history, astrology, mathematics and calligraphy. They were also versed in the Qur'an, *ḥadīth* and jurisprudence. By the time they were sold or given away as gifts, they were a pleasure to the heart, eye and mind.[16]

Muslim society was clearly captivated by these extraordinary women. The Muslim male elite especially was dazzled by their beauty and knowledge. Men's fascination with the slave women, the ease with which they could be acquired and their constant availability on the market turned this trade into almost an unparalleled social phenomenon in the urban Muslim society of the time. The elite acquired slaves to entertain themselves and their guests. There were gatherings and parties at homes and palaces where all sorts of pleasures were offered, and where the slave women and singing girls occupied the central place. Important men fell in love with their slave women, such as the Umayyad caliph Yazīd ibn ʻAbd al-Malik (d. 724) with Habbaba, and Hārūn al-Rashīd with Dhāt al-Khal. Furthermore, these women were not confined to the private quarters of their masters; rather, they frequented urban public spaces in almost every city. They were on the streets, in the markets and in the taverns, and they travelled without a protector, a *maḥram*. They were also exhibited as showpieces in the caliph's palaces and accompanied their masters on their journeys and to the battlefield. The visibility of these slave girls was further perpetuated by their exhibition in the slave markets. A specific street in Baghdad was famous for this kind of goods and was called Shāriʻ Dār al-Raqīq, or the Slave Centre Street.

Certain important features of the lives of these slave girls interest us here. They were unveiled, they were masters of seduction and they were sexually promiscuous. For despite their education and sophistication, their sensuality and promiscuity were not simply part of their careers, they were the reasons for their existence. With these characteristics enhanced by physical unveiled beauty and refined education, the slave girls were not only the courtesans of the male Muslim elite, they also often played key roles in the lives of their masters.

Fortunately for our purposes, the prolific Muslim writer Abū ʻUthmān al-Jāḥiẓ (d. 868), gives us a remarkable picture of this social panorama. In a satirical attack on the institution of female slavery, its merchants and its customers, al-Jāḥiẓ describes and analyzes the mores and the lives of these women and the reasons behind their profound influence. He says:

> Love and passion for the singing girls is an epidemical bane despite their numerous excellences they offer a man a combination of pleasures such as nothing on the face of the earth does. (al-Jāḥiẓ 1980, 30)

However, the appearance of sensuality and lust for which these girls were famous had been imposed on them. They were raised in pimping houses whose customers were adulterers and where they were trained to suggest unbridled sexual desire. Lashing out at the institution of slave women, al-Jāḥiẓ warns that "in a man's consorting with a singing girl lies the greatest temptation and calamity" (Ibid. 30).

Countless stories, incidents and poems are related in Islamic literature of the period, and these attest to two phenomena: first, the slave girls' dominance of public space vis-à-vis free Muslim women was a fact of life; and second, the decadent relations between these tempestuous slave women and free Muslim men were an accepted social custom of the age. However, the epidemic of slave women did not escape condemnation on the part of the populace or the religious authorities, which occasionally took the form of public protest. An event that occurred in Baghdad in the eleventh century related by the Muslim historian Ibn al-Athīr (d. 1233) illustrates this well. When people displayed their indignation at the prevalence of slave women and alcohol, one of them, in a fit of anger, destroyed the lute of a singing girl owned by a soldier, who responded by striking the man. In despair, the common people, together with many religious leaders, appealed to the caliph al-Qā'im bi-Amr Allāh (d. 1075) and demanded the demolition of brothels and taverns. As if by coincidence, while they were awaiting a reply, Baghdad was drowned by a great flood. Ibn al-Athīr tells us that the natural disaster was perceived as a divine response to the widespread immoralities in the city (Ibn al-Athīr 1979, 10:90–91).[17]

The Manifestation of the Social Forces in al-Rāzī's Commentary

Fakhr al-Dīn al-Rāzī, our second commentator, reflects this social reality almost like a mirror in his interpretation of the Qur'anic verses under discussion. Al-Rāzī, who died in 1209/10, was one of Islam's most distinguished scholars, a most profound thinker. He was born in Rayy, Iran and received his early education from his father and from the most distinguished scholars of his time thereafter. He travelled widely in central Asia to such cities as Bukhara and Samarqand, preaching and lecturing in both Persian and Arabic. An extraordinary thinker, his works reflect his expertise in a wide range of fields. He mastered jurisprudence, philosophy, Iranian and Semitic scholarship, as well as Qur'anic studies, religious sciences, and Arabic literature, linguistics and grammar. His reputation as a distinguished scholar grew rapidly in his lifetime. It is reported that he attracted large numbers of students to his study circles from all over the Islamic world. His biographers also mention that about 300 students and jurists followed him wherever he travelled. So remarkable was al-Rāzī's knowledge that he has been called by some sources the renewer of Islam of the sixth century Hijrah.

His voluminous Qur'anic commentary *Mafātiḥ al-Ghayb*, also known as *al-Tafsīr al-Kabīr*, is his most important work. His unique method of interpreting the Qur'an embraces numerous branches of knowledge, and the complexity of his arguments takes his commentary far beyond the reach and comprehension of the general reader (Ibn Khallikān 1978, 4:249–251; al-Qifṭī 1326 AH/1908 CE, 190–191; al-Dāwūdī 1972, 2:214; Ayāzī 1993, 655–656).[18]

In his comments on the verses under discussion, al-Rāzī engages the reader in an exceptional web of complex arguments and subarguments. Through a prolonged and detailed treatment of Q. 24:31, al-Rāzī grounds his interpretation of modesty in Islam on three concepts. They are shameful nakedness, the lustful look and moral disorder. The first concept is based on the idea of shame, scandal and obscenity and is intended to refer to those parts of the human body whose exhibition is shameful and scandalous and hence prohibited. This prescription is intended to prevent the lustful look from gazing upon those parts. The lustful look is perceived as an act that has the potential of creating a state of moral sedition and disorder, in which the believer is seduced into committing the act of adultery (al-Rāzī 1976, 23:201–207). This terse summary, which represents a part of the foundations underlying al-Rāzī's explanation of the verse has an important dimension that bears careful examination.

From the outset of his commentary, one can observe that al-Rāzī's understanding of female modesty in Islam is fundamentally governed by a woman's social status. Clearly drawing upon the social reality around him, al-Rāzī divides the women of his world into three hierarchical classes and subclasses, each with its own moral prescriptions and particular definition of modesty. The first includes the woman who is lawfully marriageable to the free believing man; the second, the woman who is not lawfully marriageable (a relative by blood or marriage); and the third, the woman with whom a man may have sexual relations, such as a wife or a slave.

The three social classes of women are the justification for al-Rāzī's variable definition of what must be concealed or revealed of the female body. At the top of the pyramid of social hierarchy sits the legally marriageable, free Muslim woman. To her, al-Rāzī applies the ultimate restrictions in terms of modesty. In his view "a free woman's entire body is a shameful nakedness in itself" (al-Rāzī 1976, 23:202, 204). However, he goes on to echo al-Ṭabarī's position by enumerating the female body parts that may be left visible, i.e., her face and hands. Aware of the contradiction between considering the entire body of a free Muslim woman to be a shameful nakedness in itself, and the permission given to her to reveal her face and hands, al-Rāzī gives the following rationale. She needs to reveal her face when buying and selling; thus logic dictates that she must be able to use her hands to complete the transaction (Ibid. 23:203). Looking at the rest of the body of a lawfully free Muslim woman, however, is authorized, in al-Rāzī's view, only when necessary, such as for judicial or medical purposes.

How does al-Rāzī, then, square his restrictive prescriptions on the modesty of the free Muslim female with the Qur'anic verse (Q. 24:33), which clearly does not advocate the concealment of any particular part of the female body except for a rather ambiguous reference to the bosom? This is the verse that advocates the concealment of a particular kind of adornment, but does not define it, namely, the "hidden adornment." Al-Rāzī is aware of this. He initially acknowledges that the term "adornment" is held by some to refer exclusively to anything intended to beautify the human body, and is external to it. However, he quickly dismisses this view and outlines his conception of "adornment" stating:

"Most probably the human body is included in [the definition of] adornment. For many women are independently beautiful without any [external] adornment" (Ibid. 23:205).

This is a clear example of the way in which an interpreter can impose his own ideas on the actual text of the Qur'an. The next piece of evidence he furnishes for his conception of "adornment" stretches the Qur'anic pronouncement even further. Since the divine command requires that women cover their bosoms/necklines with their head-cover, he speculates: "It looks as though God is forbidding women from revealing their beauty" (Ibid. 23:205).

At the bottom of the social ladder, in al-Rāzī's scheme, is the slave woman. She is permitted, or, better still, is expected to transgress all the rules on female modesty laid down by the religious discourse of the time. Here the question for al-Rāzī is no longer how much a woman can reveal; rather, the discussion at this social level revolves around how much a woman can conceal. This difference is fundamentally based on whether a woman is free or without freedom. It is a consideration that is completely absent from Q. 24:33. This imposed criterion alters al-Rāzī's and his sources' definitions of shameful nakedness and the lustful look, now that the subject of investigation is a slave woman. He outlines the body parts of the latter that are not held to be shameful. These include the head, the arms, the legs, the top part of the chest and the bosom. Some religious authorities, according to al-Rāzī, go so far as to insist that shameful nakedness for a slave woman consists only in exposing the area of her body between the navel and the knee (Ibid. 23:204). The premise of his commentary is put very clearly before the reader by al-Rāzī. In his view, Q. 24:33 is exclusively addressing free women, for a slave woman, he says, "is property; consequently, precautions must be taken when selling and buying her, and that can only occur through an investigative and careful look at her" (Ibid. 23:206).

Al-Rāzī's commentary was not conceived in a vacuum. Rather, it was born of and nourished by a social reality that he lived and experienced. In this reality, the women of his world were divided visibly by the instrument of clothing. This instrument distinguished the slave woman, who was sold and bought publicly, from the free woman, who was hidden from public view by a piece of fabric. The sexually available woman was thus distinguished from the sexually unavailable one by a dress code.

In his commentary on Q. 33:59 al-Rāzī gives further evidence of the sexually oriented purposes of clothing. Like al-Ṭabarī, he ignores the verse's historical context, and suggests instead that concealment should apply as well to the sole body part of a free Muslim woman unanimously regarded as not constituting shameful nakedness, namely, her face. Having achieved utter anonymity, al-Rāzī explains, the woman sends a clear statement to the effect that she is not an adulteress, and has no intention of becoming one. Interestingly, al-Rāzī identifies the most likely beneficiaries of such conduct, i.e., her relatives, saying: "With a free woman's sexual misconduct her kin [understood here as men] are more dishonoured than her. When a man is bad-mouthed, he is harmed but his women are not" (Ibid. 25:230).

Immoral seduction through lustful gazing and shameful nakedness, the elements constituting the basis of al-Rāzī's view on women's style of clothing, represent but one part of the story. The other part is rooted in a third concept: lust itself. In his discussion of Q. 24:2 on adultery, al-Rāzī describes women as being naturally possessed by an insatiable sexual desire (Ibid. 23:136–137). To prevent them from committing adultery, women, he maintains, must always be accompanied by a *maḥram* (protector) when travelling.

Al-Rāzī's voice, however, was not an isolated one. The religious discourse of medieval Islam systematically reduced women to the lowest possible levels of sensuality and attributed to them a complete lack of moral discernment. 'Abd al-Raḥmān ibn al-Jawzī (d. 1200), a contemporary of al-Rāzī, echoes al-Rāzī's views and to some extent even builds on them.

A native of Baghdad, Ibn al-Jawzī was a lawyer whose literary activities covered all the branches of knowledge of his time, including Qur'an interpretation. Nevertheless, he is best known as a preacher whose moral and religious teachings were (and still are) widely read (al-Dāwūdī 1972, 2:270–274; Ibn al-Jawzī 1989, 4–5).[19] In his book *Kitāb Aḥkām al-Nisā'*, which discusses the Islamic ordinances on women, Ibn al-Jawzī upholds the tripartite definition of the female: immoral seduction, shameful nakedness and indiscriminate lust. This definition has "naturally" produced a specific kind of literature laden with the strictest religious decrees, for it is held that in order to attain her lustful ends, a woman, if she gets the opportunity, will trespass against all religious and moral boundaries. Consequently, to protect society from the most dreaded forms of moral disorder, Ibn al-Jawzī's religious zeal dictates that concealing a woman's entire body is not an adequate measure. Rather, he preaches, women must be placed behind the stone veils of their homes. His language has a strange intensity: "[I]mprison them in the homes … [for] like female snakes, women are expected to burrow themselves in their homes" (Ibn al-Jawzī 1989, passim).

In order to understand this contemptuous and obviously phobic attitude toward women as an element of disorder and an allurement to immorality, we need to understand the environment it reflected. Indeed, it is symptomatic of the social reality of late classical and early medieval Islam, by which time the meaning of woman had come to be redefined. The underpinning of this new reality was the disappearance of the vision that had dominated Medinan society in the time of the Prophet.

During Muḥammad's lifetime, Muslim women had been able to attain positions of high rank in the new community of believers. They were characterized as honourable and dignified Companions of the Prophet (*al-ṣaḥābīyāt al-jalīlāt*), putting them on a par with the Prophet's closest and most distinguished male Companions. Ibn al-Jawzī states that the Prophet used to attend the 'Eid celebration surrounded by dignified women together with Abū Bakr, 'Umar and 'Uthmān (Ibid. 72). Together with 'Alī ibn Abī Ṭālib, these men were Islam's first four caliphs and are held by Muslims in very high esteem. In Muḥammad's Medina, therefore, women occupied a prominent status in a public space free of anything resembling the notion that they were a threat to social order. In late classical and medieval Islam, women continued to occupy public space, but their rank and dignity had been profoundly altered.

Small wonder, then, that the religious discourse responded to its social reality the way it did in reference to women. Our commentators were speaking out of and in reaction to their own specific social environment. It was an environment where the lives and mores of slave women constituted the lens through which all unveiled women who mingled with men were seen. All the religious literature investigated for this survey propounds the idea that an unveiled woman is to be suspected of being unchaste and immoral. Al-Rāzī states this idea very clearly. In his commentary on Q. 33:59, he argues that the utter anonymity of a free Muslim woman (including the concealment of the face, which is not intrinsically a shameful nakedness) has a moral significance. It presents a clear statement by the woman indicating that she is not sexually promiscuous, hence adultery or fornication with her is forbidden (al-Rāzī, 1976, 25:198–199). Al-Ṭabarī before him put forward a similar idea in his commentary on the same verse (al-Ṭabarī, 1995, 12:58).

From the standpoint of this religious discourse, it is a given that all women are potentially licentious and susceptible to the same kind of behaviour as that expected of slave women when unveiled or mingling freely with men. For with the phenomenal prevalence of licentiousness that had accompanied the institution of female slavery, a certain image of all women became fixed not only in the religious discourse, but elsewhere as well.

An example of this attitude is expressed in the following story recorded in al-Aṣbahānī's *al-Aghānī*. It is reported that when a libertine poet who lived in the second half of the second century Hijrah asked two of his colleagues about the content of their conversation, they said that they were slandering chaste women. His response, "Is there a chaste woman left on earth who can be slandered?" (al-Aṣbahānī, 1983, 19:44), provides a good indication of the general perception of women prevailing in that day.

Consequently, it should come as no surprise that clothing should serve as the instrument of differentiation between the slave and the free woman, between the licentious and the chaste. Initially the veiling of elite (and therefore) chaste women was borrowed as a social custom from the nations that were conquered by the Muslim armies.[20] This explains why Muḥammad's great granddaughter, Sukaynah bint al-Ḥusayn, and Abū Bakr's granddaughter, 'Ā'ishah, had the choice of being unveiled without being condemned by the religious authorities (al-Qayrawānī 1953, 1:269).[21] But as the sexual mores of the Islamic urban societies became increasingly dominated by the presence of slave women, the social assimilation of the veiling of women acquired another function. It became sanctioned in religious terms.

The strong impact of institutionalized female slavery on the religious discourse was felt in another dimension. Since these women operated on the level of seduction and sensuality, the presence of women generally, in whatever style of clothing, came to be associated with moral disorder. A woman, even when veiled, came to be perceived as a source of distraction and temptation to the male believer. Thus the public visibility of chaste and veiled women was shunned; seclusion became an act of piety and dignity. Al-Ṭabarī relates that in the year 170 of the Hijrah, when al-Khayzurān, the mother of the Abbasid caliph al-Hādī (d. 786), resumed the active political involvement she had pursued during the reign of his father al-Mahdī (d. 785), al-Hādī reacted with indignation. He sent her a message that summed up the definition of a chaste, dignified woman at that time, and commanded his mother to abstain from the filth and vulgarity of degradation to which she had subjected herself when she abandoned the sanctuary of a woman's shyness and timidity. When al-Khayzurān refused to obey him, al-Hādī wondered disdainfully and impatiently why she was not confining herself to the role expected of her, namely, that of occupying herself with the spinning of yarn, reciting the Qur'an or remaining in her house, protected from worldly vulgarities (al-Ṭabarī 1997, 4:604).[22]

Under these social conditions and definitions, free Muslim women were made to recede into veiled-ness and seclusion. They were subjected to the most rigid restrictions. The chronological order employed by Muslim historians demonstrates the gradual disappearance of free Muslim women from public view. In their accounts of Muḥammad's Medina and of the empire several decades after his death, the Muslim historians document the visibility and prominence of Muslim women in public space. This in turn illustrates the early Muslims' understanding of the verses under discussion.

As we move chronologically into the second Islamic century, we see that the visibility of Muslim women is reduced. By the second half of the second century, their names are mentioned merely in connection with their status as mothers, wives or daughters of the male Muslim elite. Their disappearance from the history books reflects their gradual disappearance from public view, their seclusion and their adoption of the veil (al-Ṭabarī 1997, passim; Ibn al-Athīr 1979, passim).

The altered panorama of Muḥammad's Medina is also illustrated in the biographical collections. Whereas the collections that memorialize Islam's early prominent individuals dedicate hundreds of entries to women, similar collections of a later date are different. The entries on Muslim women in the latter are drastically reduced in number, while the women who do rate mention can hardly be described as visible or present. Take, for example, the biographical collection of early Muslims known as *Usd al-Ghābah*, by Ibn al-Athīr.[23] Out of 7,712 entries, as many as 1,022 of these entries are dedicated to Muslim women, contemporaries of the Prophet who occupied positions of prominence and visibility. By contrast, in his voluminous account of the history of Baghdad entitled *Tārīkh Baghdād*, al-Khaṭīb al-Baghdādī (d. 1071) dedicates no more than thirty entries to Muslim women out of a total of 7,831 biographies. The majority of the women included are transmitters of *ḥadīth*, which they heard from their male kin. Furthermore, if we take the time span that each author tried to cover, the numbers become even more telling. Ibn al-Athīr surveys a period of a few decades, while al-Baghdādī documents 200 years (Ibn al-Athīr 1979, passim; Ibn al-Athīr 1997; Ibn Sa'd 1990; al-Khaṭīb al-Baghdādī 1931).

The faith of Muslim historians and Qur'an commentators in the timeless truth of Islam must have mitigated any doubt they might have felt over these discrepancies in terms of women's status between their own time and that of Muḥammad's Medina. These discrepancies are sometimes evident in their own words. What is more, they sometimes even recognize the differences between their pronouncements and the Qur'anic injunctions, as well as between their reality and the ideal of Muḥammad's Medina. Major voices in past religious discourse such as Ibn Ḥanbal and Ibn al-Jawzī state this very clearly (Ibn Ḥanbal 1986, 46 and Ibn al-Jawzī 1989, 67).[24]

Al-Jāḥiẓ, our astute social observer, on the other hand, lashes out at the institutions of veiling and secluding free Muslim women. He calls for a reinstatement of the way of life practised by the Muslim women of early Islam. He criticizes the social mores of his own time and insists that the *ḥijāb* was imposed specifically on the Prophet's wives, while all other Muslim women continued to mingle freely with men without the imposition of *ḥijāb*. As he puts it: "Looking at each other [men and women] was neither scandalous in the pre-Islamic period (*al-jāhilīyah*) nor forbidden in Islam" (al-Jāḥiẓ 1980, 4–6).

Conclusion

Undoubtedly, it often happens that those who write commentaries on scripture unwittingly read the problems of their own social reality into the text. The late classical and medieval Muslim Qur'an commentators were certainly no exception to this rule. They tended to think that the problems of their age were the same as the problems of all ages. Thus they interpreted Qur'anic passages, such as the ones relating to the Prophet's female relatives and to other believers drawing their cloaks tighter, as applicable to the kind of social reality that the commentators in later centuries knew (Q. 33:59). These later commentators missed the point that the Qur'an did not introduce cloaks as a new piece of clothing, and failed to see that it did not imply that Muslim women must always wear cloaks (*jalābīb*). Thus these commentators, wittingly or unwittingly, tailored their definitions of the "visible ornamentation of a woman" and "the concealed adornment" to serve the needs and "ideology" of their own particular time and place.[25]

There may in fact be a good reason why the Qur'an leaves out the final definitions of these two crucial references to open and hidden "adornment" in Q. 24:31. The fact that the terms are not defined means that the interpretation of their implications can be expected to vary in accordance with differing social contexts. Their definitions are left vague so they can be interpreted according to the norms of conduct of a given community at a given time. This omission signals one of the important features of the Qur'an, namely, flexibility and dynamism. It is this feature that renders the Muslim Scripture valid for all nations, times and places.

Needless to say, the commentaries discussed above were composed in the spirit of *ijtihād*, or human endeavour, i.e., mortals' attempt to comprehend the wisdom of the eternal divine Word. However, the result is that these commentaries have come to substitute for the text of the Qur'an itself. Although their authors may well not have intended that their opinions should come to dominate Muslim social thought in this way, they have acquired an orthodox status in the collective Muslim mind, a status that has endured for more than a thousand years. Only a few voices contest the centuries-old prescriptions of women's style of clothing in Islam, and they do so in a timid manner marked by reservations and precautions.[26]

Some exceptions to this traditional approach can be found in the writings of the contemporary Syrian author, Muḥammad Shaḥrūr, and the contemporary Moroccan scholar Fatima Mernissi.[27] Each of them applies a unique approach, and both tackle the issues without being hindered by conservative voices. Mernissi analyzes what she calls "the descent of al-hijab" in terms of its being context-specific. She argues that the increased emphasis on secluding women brought a temporary halt to the ultimate goal and vision of Muḥammad's message, namely, the founding of an egalitarian society.

Shaḥrūr attempts to explore the universal meaning of the verses under discussion. He argues that the body of a woman, with the exception of certain parts, is in itself a "visible adornment" that, according to the Qur'an, need not be concealed. The exceptions include areas of the body that are not apparent by creation, such as the underarms. In presenting such an interesting interpretation, Shaḥrūr, however, stretches the meaning of two key Qur'anic terms almost beyond recognition. These are adornment (*zīnah*) and bosoms/necklines (*juyūb*). His initial point of reference is his view that since adornment can also refer to a location, a woman's body, therefore, is a spatial adornment. As for defining the Qur'an's unspecified references to both apparent and non-apparent adornment, Shaḥrūr forces his definitions by dividing the female body into two anatomical sections. The first consists of the parts of the nude body that are visible by creation, such as the limbs, the head, the back, etc. The second constitutes the areas of the female anatomy that are not visibly and immediately apparent by creation and divine design, such as the underarms. By virtue of their being hidden from view by folds of human skin resembling pockets, Shaḥrūr postulates, these areas are the *juyūb*, bosoms/necklines, referred to in the verse; consequently, they constitute the parts of the female body whose concealment is required by the Qur'an. Aware of the obvious implications of his interpretation, Shaḥrūr holds that ultimately the social norms of society always regulate how much a female can reveal of her body in public (Shaḥrūr 1993, 604–607).

However, more than 150 years before Shaḥrūr, the prominent Egyptian scholar Muḥammad 'Abduh (d. 1905) was already spearheading the progressive discourse in Islam. In an earnest attempt to improve the status of women in Muslim societies, he lashed out at the triple stigmatization of the Muslim female: a shameful nakedness, a dangerous temptation to immorality and an uncontrollable lust. In so doing 'Abduh put the cornerstone of the ideology of the *ḥijāb* into serious question. Arguing on the basis of reason, he writes:

> As for the fear of the temptation to immorality (*al-fitnah*), which we see roaming almost every line written about this issue [veiling], it is a matter that pertains to men whose hearts are phobic. And women

> are not required to assess it or to recognize it. Those men who fear the temptation (*al-fitnah*) must cast their gaze down. How odd! For what reason are men not commanded to veil and conceal their faces from women if they [men] are [truly] worried about the women being tempted? Is a man's willpower considered weaker than that of a woman, and is he considered less capable than a woman in controlling himself and restraining his passion? ('Abduh 1972, 2:112)[28]

And God knows best (wa Allāhu a'lam).

Notes

1 The numbering of the Qur'anic verses follows the Egyptian standard edition of 1952.

2 All translations of the meanings of the Qur'anic verses in this article are the author's modifications of A.Y. Ali's and N.J. Dawood's versions; see, Abdullah Yusuf Ali, *The Holy Qur'an: Text, Translation and Commentary* (Washington DC: American International Printing, 1946) and N.J. Dawood, *The Koran with a Parallel Arabic Text* (London: Penguin Books, 1995). On the issues raised by Q. 33:53 in particular, see the essay by L. Clarke in this volume, especially pages 228–230.

3 These exclusive verses read as follows: "O Prophet, say to your wives: 'If you desire the life of this world and its adornment then let me provide for your enjoyment and release you honourably. But if you seek God, His messenger and the abode of the Hereafter, verily God has prepared for the good-doers among you a great reward'. O wives of the Prophet, those of you who commit an evident sin shall be doubly punished. That is easy for God [to do]. But any of you who is devoted to God and His messenger and does righteous works, We shall doubly reward her; and for her We have prepared a generous provision. O wives of the Prophet, you are not like any other women. If you fear God, do not be tractable in speech, lest the lecherous-hearted should lust for you. And say what is commonly accepted as decent speech. And stay in your homes and do not make a seductive display [of yourselves] like that of the former times of the Jahiliya, attend to your prayers, give alms and obey God and His messenger. Members of the Household [of the Prophet], God only wishes to remove abomination from you and to purify you. And recite what is read in your homes of divine revelation and wisdom. Benignant is God and all-knowing."

4 See also Q. 7:46; 38:32; 41:5; 19:17.

5 The Qur'anic phrase prohibiting this reads as follows: "... and it is not allowable for you to annoy the messenger of God, nor is it permissible for you to wed his wives after him; this would be a grave offence in the sight of God."

6 Muḥammad ibn Sa'd, *al-Ṭabaqāt al-Kubrá*, edited by M. 'Aṭā, 8 vols. (Beirut: Dār al-Kutub al-'Ilmīyah, 1990).

7 Abū Ja'far Muḥammad ibn Jarīr al-Ṭabarī, *Jāmi' al-Bayān fī Tafsīr al-Qur'ān*, 30 vols. (Beirut: Dār al-Ma'rifah, 1987; idem, *Tārīkh al-Umam wa-al-Mulūk*, 30 vols. (Beirut: Dār al-Kutub al-'Ilmīyah, 1997).

8 Shams al-Dīn Muḥammad ibn 'Alī al-Dāwūdī, *Ṭabaqāt al-Mufassirīn*, edited by A. 'Umar, vol. 2 (Cairo: Maktabat al-Qāhirah, 1972); Muḥammad 'Alī Ayāzī, *al-Mufassirūn: Ḥayātuhum wa-Manhajuhum* (Tehran: Mu'assasat al-Ṭibā'ah wa-al-Nashr, 1373 AH).

9 Muḥammad ibn Manẓūr, *Lisān al-'Arab*, 20 vols. (Beirut: Dār Ṣādir, n.d.).

10 The Qur'an uses the term *zīnah* and its various derivatives forty-three times. See, for example, Q. 37:6; 41:12; 50:6; 10:24; 13:33.

11 The context is what decides the meaning of the extremely versatile verb *ḍaraba* — past tense of *yaḍrib* — in both the Arabic language and the Qur'an. Compare, for example, its meanings in Q. 47:4 and Q. 22:73. Note also the term's two different meanings in two different places in the verse under discussion. See also note 13 below.

12 Al-Ṭabarī himself relates, elsewhere in his commentary, that the pre-Islamic Arabs performed in the nude their circumambulation around the Ka'bah in Mecca. Al-Ṭabarī, *Tafsīr al-Qur'an*, 8:214.

13 The sole instance in which the Qur'an specifically refers to a particular part of a woman's body — the feet/legs — in the context of modesty is in another section of the verse under discussion. It reads "and that they should not [strike/stamp] (*yaḍribna*) their feet/legs in order to disclose their hidden [adornment] (*zīnah*). ..."

14 Muḥammad 'Abd al-Malik ibn Hishām, *al-Sirah al-Nabawīyah*, edited by 'U. Tadmurī, 4 vols. (Beirut: Dār al-Kitāb al-'Arabī, 1987); Abū al-Fidā' Ismā'il 'Umar ibn Kathīr, *al-Sīrah al-Nabawīyah*, edited by M. 'Abd al-Wāḥid, 4 vols. (Beirut: Dār al-Fikr, 1978); Muḥammad ibn 'Umar al-Wāqidī, *Kitāb al-Maghāzī,* edited by M. Jones, 3 vols. (Beirut: 'Ālam al-Kutub, 1984).

15 The Battle of Karbalā' was fought between the Prophet's grandson Ḥusayn ibn 'Alī and the forces of the second Umayyad caliph Yazīd ibn Mu'āwiyah (d. 683). Ḥusayn, who refused to recognize Yazīd's caliphate, was killed in the battle together with all the adult males that accompanied him. The women and children of Ḥusayn's family were taken initially as prisoners of war, but were freed soon afterwards. See several versions of detailed accounts of the battle in al-Ṭabarī's *Tārīkh*, 3:400–440.

16 For an interesting study of the rise of slave women in the political arena, see Fatima Mernissi, *The Forgotten Queens of Islam*, translated by M.J. Lakeland (Cambridge: Polity Press, 1990).

17 Fakhr al-Dīn al-Rāzī, *al-Tafsīr al-Kabīr* (Cairo: 'Abd al-Raḥmān Muḥammad, 1976) 23:201–210; Abū 'Uthmān 'Amr al-Jāḥiẓ, *Risālat al-Qiyān (The Epistle on Singing-Girls of Jahiz)*, edited with translation and commentary by A. Beeston (Warminster: Aris & Phillips Ltd., 1980), passim; 'Izz al-Dīn ibn al-Athīr, *al-Kāmil fī al-Tārīkh*, 20 vols. (Beirut: Dar Ṣādir, 1979), passim; Abū Bakr al-Khaṭib al-Baghdādī, *Tārīkh Baghdād*, 14 vols. (Cairo: Maktabat al-Khanjī, 1931), passim; Abū al-Faraj al-Aṣbahānī, *Kitāb al-Aghānī*, 20 vols. (Beirut: Dār al-Thaqāfah, 1983), passim; Abū al-Ḥasan 'Alī ibn al-Ḥusayn al-Mas'ūdī, *Murūj al-Dhahab wa-Ma'ādin al-Jawāhir*, 5 vols. (Beirut: Dār al-Kitāb al-Lubnānī, 1982), passim;

Jurjī Zaydān, *Tārīkh al-Tamaddun al-Islāmī*, edited and with commentary by H. Mu'nis (Cairo: Dār al-Hilāl, 1958), 4:58 ff; Ṭāhā Ḥusayn, *Min Tārīkh al-Adab al-'Arabī*, 2 vols. (Beirut: Dār al-'Ilm lil-Malāyīn, 1971), passim; Aḥmad Amīn, *Ḍuḥá al-Islām* (Cairo: Maktabat al-Nahḍah al-Miṣrīyah, 1964), passim.

18 Jamāl al-Dīn Abū al-Ḥasan 'Alī al-Qiftī, *Kitāb Akhbār al-'Ulamā' bi-Akhbār al-Ḥukamā'* (Cairo: Maṭba'at al-Sa'ādah, 1326 AH /1908 CE); Aḥmad ibn Muḥammad Ibn al-'Abbās Shams al-Dīn ibn Khallikān, *Wafayāt al-A'yān wa-Anbā' Abnā' al-Zamān*, edited by I. 'Abbās, 20 vols. (Beirut: Dār Ṣādir, 1978); Ayāzī, Muḥammad 'Alī. *Al-Mufassirūn: Ḥayātuhum wa-Manhājuhum*. (Tehran: Mu'assasat al-Ṭibā'ah wa-al-Nashr, 1414 AH /1993 CE).

19 Abū al-Faraj Jamāl al-Dīn 'Abd al-Raḥmān ibn 'Alī ibn al-Jawzī, *Kitāb Aḥkām al-Nisā'*, edited by Z. Ḥamdān (Beirut: Dār al-Fikr, 1989).

20 For a good study of the influence on Islam's social world view by the established civilizations of the Near East conquered by the Muslim Arabs, see Leila Ahmed, *Women and Gender in Islam: Historical Roots of a Modern Debate* (New Haven: Yale University Press, 1992).

21 Abū Isḥāq Ibrāhīm al-Ḥuṣarī ibn 'Alī al-Qayrawānī, *Ẓahr al-Ādāb wa-Thamr al-Albāb*, edited by Z. Mubārak and M. 'Abd al-Ḥamīd (Cairo: Maṭba'at al-Sa'ādah, 1953).

22 On the historical origins of the political inequality between men and women in Muslim societies, see Fatima Mernissi, "The Jariya and the Caliph: Thoughts on the Place of Women in Muslim Political Memory," Chapter Eight in her *Women's Rebellion & Islamic Memory* (London: Zed Books, 1996), 77–91.

23 'Izz al-Dīn ibn al-Athīr, *Usd al-Ghābah fī Ma'rifat al-Ṣaḥābah*, edited by K. Shīhah, 5 vols. (Beirut: Dār al-Ma'rifah, 1997).

24 Aḥmad ibn Muḥammad ibn Ḥanbal, *Aḥkām al-Nisā'*, edited by A. 'Aṭā' (Beirut: Dār al-Kutub al-'Ilmīyah, 1986).

25 For a good discussion on the mutually affective relationship between religious thought and social reality in Islam, see Barbara Stowasser, "Liberated Equal or Protected Dependent? Contemporary Religious Paradigms on Women's Status in Islam." *Arab Studies Quarterly* 9, no. 3 (1987):260–283, and idem, "Women's Issues in Modern Islamic Thought," in *Arab Women: Old Boundaries, New Frontiers*, edited by Judith E. Tucker (Bloomington: Indiana University Press, 1993), 3–28.

26 See, for example, Fazlur Rahman, "The Status of Women in Islam: A Modernist Interpretation," in *Separate Worlds: Slaves of Purdah in South East Asia*, edited by H. Papanek and G. Minault (Delhi: Chanakya, 1982), 285–310; Muḥammad Aḥmad Khalaf Allāh, *Dirāsāt fī al-Nuẓūm wa-al-Tashrī'āt al-Islāmīyah* (Cairo: Maktabat al-Anjlū al-Miṣrīyah, 1977); 'Ā'ishah 'Abd al-Raḥmān, *al-Mafhūm al-Islāmī li-Taḥrīr al-Mar'ah* (Cairo: Jāmi'at Umm Durmān al-Islāmīyah, 1967).

27 Fatima Mernissi, *The Veil and the Male Elite: A Feminist Interpretation of Women's Rights in Islam*, translated by M.J. Lakeland (Reading, Mass.: Addison-Wesley, 1991); Muḥammad Shaḥrūr, *al-Kitāb wa-al-Qur'ān: Qirā'ah Mu'āṣirah* (Beirut: Sharikat al-Maṭbū'āt, 1993).

28 Muḥammad 'Abduh, "Al-Kitābāt al-Ijtimā'īyah," in *al-A'māl al-Kāmilah lil-Imām Muḥammad 'Abduh* (Beirut: al-Mu'assasah al-'Arabīyah lil-Dirāsāt wa-al-Nashr, 1972).

CHAPTER 8

Ḥijāb According to the *Ḥadīth*: Text and Interpretation

L. Clarke

The *ḥadīth*s — the word means "tale" or "narration" — are brief reports of the sayings and doings of the Prophet Muhammad. After the death of the Prophet, *ḥadīth* reports continued to circulate orally, that is they were memorized and passed from one person to another. Very soon believers began also to note down *ḥadīth*s in writing. By the third Islamic century (corresponding to the ninth century of the Common Era), multivolume collections of *ḥadīth* material had appeared, carefully sifted by the compilers to exclude reports that might have been falsely attributed to Muhammad. The *ḥadīth* — as the entire corpus of Prophetic Reports is also called — became an important scriptural source; it is the second scripture of Islam after the Qur'an. The *ḥadīth* serves to establish the pattern (*Sunnah*) of the Prophet's life; for believers, this pattern is exemplary, guiding them in their behaviour and daily life. Traditional scholars use the *ḥadīth* together with the Qur'an to arrive at legal norms. Modern thinkers, both conservative and liberal,[1] also cite *ḥadīth*s in support of their arguments. It would be difficult to consider the question of *ḥijāb*, so hotly contested in our day, without taking into account the *ḥadīth*.

This essay on *ḥijāb* and the *ḥadīth* is divided into two parts. The first part describes the relevant texts, revealing a world of social norms and practice somewhat different, I think, from that imagined by either conservatives or liberals. The *ḥadīth* literature is vast; even using the searchable databases now available,[2] it has been possible here to take account of only a part of it. I have chosen to focus on the six canonical — canonical because they are believed to contain the most authentic texts — Sunnī collections, along with the *Musnad* collection of Ibn Ḥanbal (d. 855), the outstanding champion of faithful adherence to the *ḥadīth* and founder of the influential Ḥanbalī school of thought. These books are selected not because I hope to extract from them a social reality supposedly existing at the time of the Prophet (although I do argue at the end of the essay that the *ḥadīth* preserves at least a glimmer of historical truth). The aim of the essay is not this, but rather to provide insight into controversies and processes within Islam by describing the contents of a set of scriptures Muslims turn to in order to understand their religion. The canonical books are therefore chosen simply because they are — especially those of Bukhārī (d. 870) and Muslim (d. 875) — most revered by Sunnī Muslims. Thus for non-believers, the essay is merely a case study in the use of an important Islamic scripture, while the believer, I hope, will appreciate a complete and critical description that might help her to approach the *ḥadīth* and the issue of *ḥijāb* herself.

I do not discuss covering in prayer and during the *ḥajj* pilgrimage, as these concern limited ritual contexts that have not been so controversial,[3] although, as we shall see, they do enter into arguments concerning everyday *ḥijāb*. Nor have I treated the Shī'ī (meaning Twelver or "Ithna'asharī" Shī'ī) *ḥadīth*s. Their tone is similar to that of the Sunnī reports. The Shī'ī literature is, however, somewhat more detailed, specific and therefore more restrictive. This may be because the Shī'ī *ḥadīth*s are of a later date; nearly all are attributed to the charismatic founding figures of Shī'ism, the *imām*s, rather than directly to the Prophet. The Shī'ī *ḥadīth* canon[4] is also somewhat less well defined or less a focus of exclusive reverence, so that Shī'īs are more likely than Sunnīs to range outside the "canonical" books, routinely relying on even later and much larger collections such as al-Ḥurr al-'Āmilī's *Wasā'il al-Shī'ah* or "Teachings of the Shī'ah" and

Majlisī's *Bihār al-Anwār* or "Ocean of Lights" (both from the latter part of the seventeenth century). It is true that the Sunnī and Shī'ī collections do share some texts. In addition, some Shī'ī scholars in the past — such as the al-Ḥurr al-'Āmilī just named — worked with and collected Sunnī *ḥadīth*, while some modern Shī'ī scholars quote Sunnī *ḥadīth*s in their writings, giving the impression that they do consider them valid to some extent. Nevertheless, the Shī'ī *ḥadīth*s are a separate literature, with their own special authority for the Shī'ī faithful. *Ḥadīth* is also handled somewhat differently in the distinctive Shī'ī science of jurisprudence than among the Sunnīs (on this, see the second part of the essay). Shī'ī *ḥadīth* is therefore an independent subject, deserving of a separate study.

The second part of the paper outlines some of the trends in use and interpretation of this *ḥadīth* material in modern times. Here it will become apparent that the *ḥadīth* is not just a body of scripture; it is an issue in itself. Scholars and thinkers have disagreed about the proper way to approach the *ḥadīth*, about its authority or applicability, and even about its authenticity altogether. These controversies inevitably come to the fore when the matter of *ḥijāb*, or any sensitive matter, is discussed.

And that, of course, is the way with any scripture. The crux is not in the text, but in the interpretation; the essay by Soraya Hajjaji-Jarrah in this volume shows how this is also true for the Qur'an. In this case, I demonstrate how conservative understandings of *ḥadīth*s related to *ḥijāb* have grown out of certain attitudes present in the medieval literature, but also, without doubt, partly rooted in the *ḥadīth* itself. I also argue, on the basis of material introduced in the first section, that the *ḥadīth* can, with the application of skillful exegesis, be equally employed in liberal arguments concerning not only *ḥijāb*, but also other issues. This leads me to ask why the liberals have instead effectively abandoned *ḥadīth*, leaving their opponents to harvest the field uncontested.

Part 1: The *Ḥadīth* Texts

Ḥijāb as Covering

Clothing is an important topic of the *ḥadīth.* This is not surprising. For one thing, dress is a significant means of social communication, including the communication of religious values. For another, it was the goal of the narrators and gatherers of the *ḥadīth* to provide an account of the exemplary custom or *Sunnah* of the Prophet and early community. This would naturally have included dress, just as it did food and hygiene. Last but not least, the Qur'an itself addresses (though briefly) questions of clothing, modesty and space, and one of the functions of the *ḥadīth* is to clarify and supplement the Qur'an.

Thus the *ḥadīth* books contain whole chapters and even "Books" (*kitāb*) on dress (*libā*s) and finery or adornment (*zīnah*). *Ḥadīth* narrations regarding clothing discuss the kinds of cloth and decoration permitted or not permitted to believers (for instance, certain colours and precious metals), as well as clothing judged ideal simply because it was part of the practice of the Prophet (for instance, men wearing a single garment when praying).[5] Clothing *ḥadīth*s are addressed to both women and men,[6] including — as liberal and conservative authors both point out[7] — reports urging modesty for men. One very prominent theme of clothing *ḥadīth*s aimed at both sexes is avoidance of ostentatious dress.

The part of this extensive material that has to do with women's covering is, however, remarkably small. Not only that, but many *ḥadīth* references to covering are incidental, that is, they come up in texts in which the main subject is not covering. There is, in other words, no separate bundle of *ḥadīth*s (apart from a small one pertaining to ritual contexts) aimed at the subject of women covering their bodies. This holds true even though numerous *ḥadīth*s — in fact, whole books of the collections — speak, in the manner just described, of disapproved and approved styles of clothing and adornment.

There are, on the other hand, a large number of *ḥadīth*s relating to *men* covering their bodies, specifically the area from the knees upward, referred to as *fakhidh* or "thighs." This part of a man's body is termed in the texts *'awrah* – private or shameful parts;[8] the *ḥadīth*s give the impression that men were not in the habit of carefully covering their *'awrah* or that they did not always own enough cloth to properly do so.[9] In fact, despite the reference in the Qur'an to *'awrāt al-nisā'* — "women's private parts"[10] — and the popular tendency in our day to associate *'awrah* mainly with women (in Urdu, *'awrat* actually means "woman"), nearly all occurrences in the *ḥadīth* of the term where it refers to private or shameful parts relate to men's *'awrah* and not women's.[11]

To be more precise, women are mentioned in connection with *'awrah* in only a single report, which occurs only once in one of the canonical collections. The *ḥadīth* reads: "Woman is 'a shameful thing' [*'awrah*]. If she goes out, Satan attempts to control her."[12] Here *'awrah* is extended to mean the whole of woman's physical being, and thus, in effect, woman as woman, as she is by nature and constitution. It was this isolated but ideologically potent *ḥadīth* that gained currency in later Islamic texts and became popular among Muslims, for whom it has become a well-known saying, no doubt partly because of the neat encapsulation of the Arabic phrase "*al-mar'ah 'awrah*." Apart from legal rules governing the inspection of slaves in the marketplace, the concern with men's *'awrah* seems, on the other hand, to have dropped out of later Muslim discourse. Evidently, social attitudes have resulted in a very select use of *ḥadīth*.

Let us, in any case, examine the few reports that do mention women's covering. At least two *ḥadīth*s warn against wearing thin clothing. In one, the Prophet brings his Companion Diḥyah ibn Khalīfah al-Kalbī a "Qabāṭī" — according to the commentary, a thin, light-covered Egyptian robe — and tells him to tear it in two. Diḥyah was instructed to use one piece for a shirt and the other to "veil [*takhtamir*] your wife." As the Companion then turned to go, the Prophet added: "And order your wife also to put on a robe underneath that [is thicker and therefore] will not reveal her form."[13] In a second *ḥadīth*, the Prophet is reported as saying that one of the types of persons who would be "in the Fire" was "women who wear revealing clothes."[14]

Women's covering is not, however, the primary subject of either *ḥadīth*. The first is part of a group of reports concerning the Prophet's distribution of clothing (apparently obtained as booty) to the community. Often the garment was shared; the primary themes seem to be the scarcity of clothing in the early community along with instructions — to both women and men — to cover as they are able. The primary subject of the second *ḥadīth* is the strange and repugnant customs that would develop among Muslims of a future age or which they would encounter as they spread to foreign lands (the Prophet also describes the women he sees as arranging their hair on top of their heads "like the humps of camels"), as well as the ability of the Messenger of God to see into the future.[15] Flimsy or revealing women's clothing seems to be at most an incidental concern.

Curiously, considering the Qur'anic phrase that tells women to "throw their veils over their bosoms," the canonical *ḥadīth* is not at all concerned with necklines.[16] There are, however, two *ḥadīth*s that address hemlines. It is reported that the Prophet declared that "On the Day of Judgment, God shall not look upon those who trail their robes pridefully." His wife, Umm Salamah, then asked: "What then should the women do with their hems?" "They should," the Prophet replied, "let them down one span [*shibr*, which is some small amount such as the span of a hand]." "But what," asked Umm Salamah, "if their feet [*aqdām*] show?" (Some versions have "leg" — *sūq*, plural of *sāq*, also possibly meaning thigh — and one has *'awrah*, meaning "private or shameful parts.") "In that case," replied Umm Salamah, "they should let them down the measure of their forearm [*dhirā'*], but no more."[17] One version of this *ḥadīth* has Umm Salamah explain: "This gives permission for women to trail their garments, because that conceals them better."[18] The second hemline *ḥadīth* tells the story of how a woman went to Umm Salamah and asked her what she should do about her train dragging over impure ground and then over the pure ground of the interior of the mosque. The question implied is: May I pull up, or perhaps shorten, my skirt to avoid dragging it through filth? Umm Salamah indicated that neither was necessary, for the Prophet had said that "if she [a woman] passes through an impure place, and then through a pure place, that [i.e., her garment] is considered pure."[19]

These two reports are codicils to a "core" text, addressed to both men and women, which has simply to do with wearing a long, trailing robe out of pride — in short, showing off expensive and fashionable clothes. The core *ḥadīth* occurs in the collections many more times than the elaborated versions just cited. It is part of a very large bundle of reports having to do with ostentatious dress, an important subject of the *ḥadīth*. The questions of Umm Salamah are logical afterthoughts of the kind that so often give rise to elaboration of *ḥadīth* texts as they pass through different hands: If it is forbidden to wear long skirts — if, in fact, as the *ḥadīth*s say, doing so means that "God will not look at you on the day of Resurrection" — what should women do, since they need to hide their feet/legs? And if they *are* allowed to wear long skirts, how can they avoid dragging their skirts in the mud?[20] Once again, concern with women's clothing is limited to a few texts, to which it is also incidental.

Apart from these *ḥadīth*s, only one report in the canonical collections clearly refers to the requirements of women's covering. The *ḥadīth* tells how Abū Bakr's daughter, Asmā', came before the Prophet in thin clothes. He turned away and said: "Asmā', if a woman reaches the age of menstruation, it is not fit that anything be seen of her except this and this" — and, according to the *ḥadīth*, he pointed to his face and hands. The text is specific enough. A closer look at its status and placement, however, uncovers some complications.

First, the *ḥadīth* is found in only one place, in the collection of Abū Dāwūd (under the chapter heading "That of a woman's adornment that may [be allowed to] appear," a clear reference to Qur'an 24:31, "Tell the believing women not to let their adornment show, save that which is apparent").[21] It is attested nowhere else in the canonical collections or the *Musnad* of Ibn Ḥanbal. Second, it appears to have been the only viable text Abū Dāwūd was able to find that would support his preferred notion that women should cover themselves save for their hands and faces, for it is the single *ḥadīth* in the chapter, and is pronounced by Abū Dāwūd himself to be *mursal*, — that is, not supported by an unbroken chain going back to the guarantor.[22] Third, the *ḥadīth* seems to be actually indicative of a liberal trend. It is, in fact, a "protest *ḥadīth*," the purpose of which is not only to argue for women's covering but also *against* the necessity of including in that covering the hands and face.

The great exegete Ibn Jarīr al-Ṭabarī's (d. 923) interpretation of Qur'an 24:31 confirms the third point. Hajjaji has already treated this exegesis in Chapter Seven in this book, but since my reading is different — as I perceive it, far from laying down the founding discourse of *ḥijāb*, Ṭabarī's primary purpose is actually to argue for a *limitation* on covering — I will go through it here again.

The "apparent" adornment (*zīnah*) of the Qur'anic verse, says Ṭabarī, is explained by the early authorities in various ways. Some say it refers to the clothes (*thiyāb*), meaning the outer clothing, which would mean, of course, that no part of the woman could show except her form. Others say that it is her rings, bracelets and kohl applied to her eyes, or kohl and the face (meaning, apparently, the whole face and not just the eyes). Some say plainly "the face and hands," and in support of this position is cited the report — not, however, seen in the canonical collections — that the Prophet declared that a mature woman might licitly show only her face and the width of a hand above her palm. Having related these and other opinions, Ṭabarī concludes that the opinion "most likely to be correct" is that apparent adornment means the face and hands, since that would logically include the henna, kohl, rings and so forth with which they are decorated. In this way he both harmonizes different interpretations and — also important for his exegesis of the verse — makes the connection between the word *zīnah* (which clearly means, as can be seen in the *ḥadīth* books themselves, not any part of the body but rather added adornment) and hands and face.

Thus Ṭabarī chooses the most liberal interpretation of women's dress available to him, further reinforcing it by pointing out that, according to the consensus (*ijmā'*) of the scholars, a woman may expose during the prayer only that which is not ʻ*awrah*, while the Prophet has allowed that she may show her hands and face during the prayer; therefore (says Ṭabarī) these are not ʻ*awrah* and it is certainly not forbidden for her to show that which is not ʻ*awrah*, just as it is not forbidden for men.[23] The large number of statements of earlier authorities — from the ubiquitous Ibn ʻAbbās and others — Ṭabarī cites in support of his interpretation show that this opinion was already widely held in his time. Abū Dāwūd (who predeceased Ṭabarī by twenty-five years, in 889) certainly has this same relatively liberal argument in mind in connecting his *ḥadīth* through the chapter heading to the *zīnah* verse.

The lack of clear reference to women's covering in the canonical *ḥadīth*s is compounded by absence of any explicit reference to covering either the head or the hair.[24] There is no warning that stray hairs should not show, that those who expose their hair will be punished, or anything of this kind. There are, on the other hand, many reports involving both men's and women's hair from other points of view, e.g., the thickness, length and colour of the Prophet's hair; the undesirability of "binding back" (*kaff*) hair while praying; carefully washing hair during ablutions, especially after sexual activity; the right length and proper style of hair for men; the undesirability of braiding hair, or braiding it tightly so that it prevents proper ablution; permission not to unwind hair (apparently African-quality hair) in order to wash; styles of hair suitable for a woman's corpse; prohibitions on women's adding false hair to their own, and so on. One would think that, with so much attention paid to hair, if the covering of women's hair were of great importance, it would certainly be mentioned. Shouldn't we expect, in that case, not only explicit references to covering hair but even a discrete bundle of *ḥadīth*s on the subject, just as there are bundles of reports relating to, for instance, "altering God's creation" by tattooing, adding false hair and so on, wearing rich cloth, women wearing manly clothes (and men effeminate clothes) and other topics regarding the body and clothing? But there are none.

Instead, all we find is a slightly forced interpretation, again produced by Abū Dāwūd, of a report that recounts the "cupping" of the Prophet's wife Umm Salamah by a man. Muslim, Abū Dāwūd and Ibn Mājah each preserve a *ḥadīth* telling the story of how Umm Salamah asked permission to be cupped — that is, to have her blood let, a medical procedure indicating pressing need, but likely involving some exposure of the body. The Prophet, we are told, did give permission. Abū Dāwūd alone places the *ḥadīth* in the "Book of Clothing" (Muslim and Ibn Mājah think it has rather to do with Greeting, or with Medicine), and gives it a particular significance through his chapter heading: "Concerning the Slave *Looking at the Hair* of His Mistress." And indeed, there is some justification for this title, since the head was a common place for cupping; there are even a number of *ḥadīth*s about cupping on the head, including an entire chapter in Bukhārī. The text, however, has clearly been redirected by Abū Dāwūd's added heading. Originally, it is about permission for violation of seclusion in case of medical necessity, necessity being, as we shall see in our discussion of women's space, a powerful consideration in Islamic tradition and law. But it has been used here, for lack of other texts, as a *ḥadīth* specifically about hair.

In addition, the *ḥadīth* itself appears to have been doctored in order to completely remove the theme of "necessity" and thus exclusively spotlight the problem of "exposure." The text as Abū Dāwūd presents it has the guarantor add the comment that Umm Salamah was allowed to be cupped for the reason that — the guarantor here qualifies his words by saying "I think the Prophet must have said" or, in another version, "I assume it was because" — the man who was to perform the procedure was her foster brother, or a boy who had not yet experienced the nocturnal emission indicating the onset of sexual maturity. These are both males who would have been allowed to see Umm Salamah in any case; what we are thus to understand is that only a "non-prohibited" man (which would include the slave mentioned in Abū Dāwūd's title) may ever see a woman's hair, no matter what the circumstance.[25] The *ḥadīth* has been neatly transformed, as fits Abū Dāwūd's purpose, from a statement granting permission in case of necessity into one laying down a total, unconditional prohibition.

Those consulting Abū Dāwūd should, in any case, be aware of a peculiarity of his *Sunan*. His "Book of Clothing" is unusual among the Books of this name in the canonical collections as it contains nine consecutive chapters with headings relating to women's covering.[26] No other Book of Clothing or Ornament has even two titles of this kind.[27] Abū Dāwūd is, without doubt, unusually preoccupied with the covering of women. He fairly strains to present women's covering as an independent topic of the *ḥadīth* in its own right, with its own field of reports. To achieve this goal, he is sometimes compelled to resort to single or little-attested reports. We have already seen how, apart from using a chapter heading to inject hair into the discussion, he collects the sole *ḥadīth* referring clearly and specifically to the requirements of women's covering; and it is Abū Dāwūd alone, as we shall see shortly, who quotes an extra phrase ("cloaked as if there were on their heads ravens") in a *ḥadīth* to make a certain key verse of the Qur'an speak to covering. Similarly, the one *ḥadīth* in his so-called "Chapter on Veiling" (*Bāb al-ikhtimār*) does not contain, as one might have expected, an instruction to cover, but merely a warning to Umm Salamah not to fasten her headdress with two folds — apparently to avoid dressing like a man, this being a prominent concern of the *ḥadīth*s in general.[28]

There are, however, two groups of *ḥadīth*s that point indirectly but (in my opinion) quite clearly to the existence of some kind of rules about covering. One group treats problems arising from ambiguities in the boundaries between men and women; the other is aimed at explaining certain verses of the Qur'an. I will deal with each group in turn.

A number of *ḥadīth* reports discuss women's covering in relation to exceptional circumstances in which women interact with men with whom they would not usually be in contact, or where a man's legal status in relation to a woman is not entirely clear. (Abū Dāwūd seems to believe that the *ḥadīth* cited above concerning cupping is in this category.) What is permitted and what is not permitted in these marginal, sometimes ambiguous cases? One such report tells how the Prophet advised a certain Fāṭimah bint Qays — who had been widowed and was therefore obliged to observe the compulsory waiting period after the death of a husband — not to stay at the house of a woman who, though rich and generous, entertained so many guests that it would be impossible for her to remain secluded. "I would not," the Prophet commented, "like your veil (*khimār*) to fall [accidentally], or your robe to open and reveal your leg (*sāq*) so that people might see what you would not like them to see."[29] What if a strange man is blind? Does that remove the necessity of *ḥijāb*? It is reported that Ibn Umm Maktūm, a blind man of the Anṣār, entered the presence of the wives of the Prophet. The Prophet told them to cover or to place a dividing curtain, perhaps, between him and themselves, the verb used here being related to the word *ḥijāb*, which may mean either. They pointed out that the man could not see them. "Are *you* blind?" the Prophet retorted. "Do you not see *him*?"[30] It seems that the report has to do with space rather than clothing (and, in addition, with the attraction of women to men, rather than men to women). The canonical *ḥadīth* collector Abū Dāwūd, however, adds the comment: "This is special to the wives of the Prophet, for you will recall that Fāṭimah bint Qays observed the waiting period in the house of [this same] Ibn Umm Maktūm, [the Prophet] saying [in this case]: 'Observe the time in the house of Ibn Umm Maktūm, for he is a blind man, and you can take off your clothing/covering (*thiyāb*) there.'"[31]

Another exceptional case treated in the *ḥadīth* is that of the *mukhannath*, that is, a person of ambiguous sexuality or hermaphrodite. It is reported that a *mukhannath* used to visit the wives of the Prophet — apparently to entertain them — as they did not consider him to be "one of those possessed of desire" (*ulū al-irbah*, as in Qur'an 24:31, "Tell the believing women not to reveal their adornment except to ... male attendants not possessed of desire"). Since, however, the *mukhannath* had alluded to their charms in his poetry, the Prophet told the women not to let him in (literally, to "curtain him off," *ḥajjibūhu*).[32] A woman does not have to separate herself from her slave, due to his inferior social status. Apropos of this rule, it is reported that the Prophet once came to his daughter, Fāṭimah, with a slave he intended to give her. All she owned at that time was a garment not large enough to cover all of her at once. If she covered her head, part of her legs would show, and if she covered all her legs, her head would show. The Prophet, however, assured her that this would not matter, for "it is [just] your father and slave (*ghulām*)."[33] The rule about slaves gives rise to ambiguities. One slave relates how the Prophet's wife, 'Ā'ishah, used to sit and talk with him, even demonstrating how the Prophet used to perform the ablutions, which would certainly have involved some exposure of the body. But then he came and told her that he had been freed, "and she lowered the *hijāb* in front of me, and I never saw her after that day."[34] Another "slave" *ḥadīth* specifies that a woman must veil in front of a *mukātib*, that is, a slave who has agreed with his master that he may buy his freedom, as soon as he has gathered enough to do so and not later.[35] The case of a man wishing to see a woman because he is contemplating marrying her also involves some ambiguity, since he is not yet privy to her, but at the same time needs to inspect her. Here the *ḥadīth* rules that he may see her face and hands, some versions suggesting that permission depends on his suspicion of a defect.[36]

This group of reports makes sense only against the background of an established set of norms. That these *ḥadīth*s concentrate on marginal cases and ambiguities suggests that the basic rules of covering were well known at the time they were put into circulation. Conservatives could effectively argue that if rules about women's covering are scarce in the canonical *ḥadīth*, that is precisely because they were so well absorbed by society that they were self-evident and did not need to be restated.

There are, in any case, two references to articles of women's clothing in the Qur'an itself, and thus exegetical *ḥadīth*s that explain their meaning. The existence of this group of reports also points, as I suggested above, to some awareness in the *ḥadīth* of rules about dress. The number of reports of this kind in the canon is, however, very small, suggesting equally that the early generations who transmitted them were not overly concerned with the details of women's covering even when prompted by the Revelation. I have, in any case, added some material from the *ḥadīth* commentaries, both for the sake of the reader who might be interested in discussion of these controversial verses, and to show how the commentators tend to produce, no doubt in accord with the desires of their own age, restrictive interpretations.

Verse 31 of the Chapter of Light (*Sūrat al-Nūr*, Chapter 24), a passage commonly cited in connection with the *hijāb* controversy, reads:

> Tell the believing women to lower their gaze and guard their private parts, and to display of their adornment only that which is apparent, and to draw their veils over their bosoms, and not to reveal their adornment save to their own husbands or fathers. ... And let them not stamp their feet so as to reveal what they hide of their adornment. ...

The *ḥadīth* commonly linked to this verse is the saying of ʻĀ'ishah: "Blessings upon the women of the Emigrants [that is, those who came from Mecca to Medina with the Prophet on his Migration or Hijrah], for as soon as God sent down '[let them] draw their veils over their bosoms' (*wa-l-yaḍribna bi-khumurihinna ʻalá juyūbihinna*), they tore up their shawls (*murūṭ*) and veiled themselves with them (*fa-khtamarna bi-hā*)."[37] What ʻĀ'ishah's *ḥadīth* tells us here is that the Qur'anic word *khumur* or "veils" means that the women "veiled themselves" (using the related verb, *akhtamara*) with something called *murūṭ*.

This rather laconic explanation may have satisfied the earlier generations, but the extensive discussions in the *ḥadīth* commentaries show that it was not enough for those who followed. Perhaps as the ideal age of the Prophet receded, the community became ever more anxious to conform to the *exact* pattern of the life of that time and the commentators then set to meeting this need, or perhaps what inspired their work was a need to convince the community that the Qur'an and *ḥadīth* really did mean covering of a very specific and in fact extensive kind such as was already customary in their own time. Or perhaps the trends in the commentaries are indicative above all of the natural tendency of exegesis to reify the material it seeks to explain.

Whatever the case, the almost universal pattern of *ḥadīth* commentaries is to use elaboration of the text to limit women's dress. Thus Ibn Ḥajar al-'Asqalānī's (d. 1449) famous commentary on Bukhārī explains that the *murūṭ* were actually "wrappers," namely, *izār* , a word in fact used in a variant of the *ḥadīth. Izār*, a more common term than *murūṭ*, denotes a voluminous kind of cloak; according to another version of the *ḥadīth* uncovered by 'Asqalānī, the women "ripped" the *izārs* "along the hems [or borders, or seams]."[38] 'Asqalānī also informs us that *fa-khtamarna* — "they veiled themselves" — means "they covered their faces." "The way of it," he says, "is that they put the *khimār* on their heads and drew it from the right side onto the left shoulder." He reports that in the time before Islam, the women used to let down their veils behind them and let their faces show. Then they were commanded to cover, and the veil for women is like the turban for men (meaning, apparently, that it signals propriety and dignity).[39] Here the *ḥadīth* and *ḥadīth* commentary together suggest that the verse was aimed at a significant reform of a pre-Islamic style of dress, one that the women were so eager to obey that they sacrificed their garments — this in a time when people owned little clothing altogether! (Since 'Ā'ishah vividly remembers that the women hastened to tear up other garments to obtain the needed cloth, the *ḥadīth* does not support the assertion made by some liberals that the veiling referred to in the verse involved merely a readjustment of clothing already worn.[40]) 'Ā'ishah's blessing on the women recorded in the *ḥadīth*, backed by her authority as the Prophet's wife, effectively highlights the value of veiling as a religious act. The commentary then goes on to supply detail that, in attempting to make the injunction clear, also make it more restrictive, most notably by specifying covering the face.

Verse 59 of the Chapter of the Clans (*Sūrat al-Aḥzāb*, Chapter 33) also contains a reference to an article of women's dress. The verse reads:

> O Prophet! Tell your wives and daughters and the women of the believers to draw [a part] of their cloaks (*jalābībihinna*) close around them. That is more suitable, so that they will not be recognised and annoyed. And God is All-Forgiving, All-Merciful.[41]

One *ḥadīth* — which appears only in the collection of Abū Dāwūd — tells how after the verse came down, the women of the Anṣār who had enthusiastically received it went out clothed in garments "as if there were on their heads ravens."[42] This report, which seems to imitate 'Ā'ishah's *murūṭ ḥadīth* quoted above, suggests thorough covering, including the head, with a dark material. What the canon has to offer besides this one isolated text is a few reports that, though not linked explicitly to the verse, do at least employ the word "cloak" (the singular is *jilbāb*). One of these, given on the authority of 'Ā'ishah, implies that in the presence of men the *jilbāb* was draped over the head to cover the face.[43] Once again it is left to the *ḥadīth* commentaries to elaborate, which they do by specifiy-ing details that tend to be restrictive. Thus according to Muslim's commentator Nawawī (d. 1277), later scholars glossed *jilbāb* variously as "a garment (*thawb*) shorter and wider than the veil (*khimār*)," "a veil/face-veil (*miqna'ah*) with which the woman covers her head," "a wide voluminous garment underneath a cloak (*ridā'*), with which the woman covers the front and back of her upper body, that is a kind of wrapper (*malaffah*)," "an outer cloak (*ridā'*)" or simply "a veil (*khimār*)."[44]

Ḥijāb as Seclusion

The outstanding theme of the *ḥadīth* related to the concealing of women's physical being is not, however, clothing as such, but restriction of women's movements, that is, of their "space." This is a striking reversal of the dominant pattern of much current Islamic thought on *ḥijāb*, which places emphasis instead on clothing, partly with the aim of asserting that covering allows a woman to move freely.[45] I find very little trace of this view in the Prophetic Reports, in which space is an inseparable and in fact the central proposition of *ḥijāb*. That women should be confined to a certain space is, in my view, an uncontested rule of the *ḥadīth*. The titles of some of the chapters in the collections are indications of the entrenchment of this rule, for instance: "That which is related concerning the seclusion (*iḥtijāb*) of women from men" and "Prohibition against entering the presence of women except with the permission of their husbands" in the *Sunan* of Tirmidhī, "That no one should be alone with a woman except a man closely related to her *(dhū maḥram)*" in the *Ṣaḥīḥ* of Bukhārī, and so on.

Use of the term *ḥijāb* in relation to women is likely based on the famous verse 53 of the Chapter of the Clans (*Sūrat al-Aḥzāb*, Chapter 33); this is the only place in the Qur'an in which the word is used with reference to women.[46] In this verse, *ḥijāb* means not clothing but a "curtain" — that is, a divider of space — and the *ḥadīth*s also, as we shall see, interpret it in the same way. The verse reads:

> O you who believe! Do not enter the Prophet's dwellings to eat without observing the proper time, except if he gives you permission. And if you are invited, enter and disperse when the meal is finished, not lingering for conversation. For that would annoy the Prophet, and he would be shy [to ask you to go] — though God is not shy of [pronouncing] the truth. And if you ask them [female plural] for anything, ask them from behind a curtain (*ḥijāb*). That is purer for your hearts and for theirs. ...

The *ḥadīth* linked to the *ḥijāb* verse locates the "occasion" of its revelation in the Prophet's marriage to Zaynab bint Jahsh. Here is one version of the *ḥadīth* in full:

> 'Abd Allāh ibn Muḥammad told me that Ya'qūb ibn Ibrāhīm told him and others that his father had told him from Ṣāliḥ ibn Shihāb that Anas [ibn Mālik] said: "I am the most knowledgeable about the *ḥijāb*; [even] Ibn Ubayy ibn Ka'b used to ask me about it. The Apostle of God (may God's blessings and peace be upon him!) spent his wedding-night with Zaynab, daughter of Jahsh, having married her in Medina. He invited the people to a [celebration] meal as the day dawned, and the Apostle of God (may God's blessings and peace be upon him!) was seated and the men sat with him

> after the others had left. He got up and walked out, with me walking beside him, until he reached the door of 'Ā'ishah's chamber. Then, thinking that they must have left, [he returned, and] I returned with him — but they were still there. So he went out and I went with him another time until we [again] reached the door of 'Ā'ishah's chamber, and then he returned along with myself, and [we saw that this time] they had gotten up. So he placed a curtain between me and himself [that is, according to the commentary of Ibn Ḥajar, the Prophet hastily lowered a curtain over the door, before he even crossed the threshold], and the *ḥijāb* [verse or norm] was sent down.[47]

Anas ibn Mālik was, like Ubayy ibn Ka'b, a prolific relater of Prophetic Reports; according to his own account, told in some versions of the report,[48] he entered the service of the Prophet's household at the age of ten. Anas's pride in having related the incident that brought down the verse seems well justified. His anecdote was accepted as authentic and circulated widely. The *ḥadīth* is prominent in the collections; it is quoted in many more places in the canonical books than cited in the preceding notes. The verse to which the *ḥadīth* points was clearly considered to be of special importance, perhaps even to mark a turning point in the history of the community, and Anas's report attached to it is well known and cited by Muslims even today.

The conjunction of the verse and *ḥadīth* is therefore of considerable interest for the light it throws on at least one early understanding of *ḥijāb*. What emerges is that the text of the Qur'an prescribes both a general rule of family privacy ("Do not enter the Prophet's dwellings ... except if he gives you permission") and then a stricter rule of separation for the Prophet's wives ("ask them from behind a *ḥijāb*"). The famous report of Zaynab's wedding feast, however, locates the occasion of revelation in the first rule, not the second. Judging from the *ḥadīth*, the significance of Qur'an 33:53 was at one time felt to lie primarily in household privacy, and only secondarily in some kind of seclusion. This is borne out in the heading under which the *ḥadīth* commonly appears in the collections — *isti'dhān* or "asking permission to enter."

Several other *ḥadīths*, however, do focus on the Qur'anic phrase "ask them from behind a curtain" and point to a division of space stricter and more specific than mere family privacy. We read, for instance, in the *Ṣaḥīḥ* collection of Muslim how Jābir ibn 'Abd Allāh al-Anṣārī, having been invited by the Prophet to a meal, accompanied him to the room of one of his wives. The Prophet went in first and then gave permission to Jābir to enter. Jābir reports that he "entered the room through the *ḥijāb*" (*fa-dakhaltu al-ḥijāb 'alayhā*). The two were then served a meal, and there is no indication that it was served by the women, or that women were present.[49] The report suggests that the *ḥijāb* was a kind of door covering or dividing curtain behind which the women dwelt, and that in order for the stranger Jābir to enter beyond the *ḥijāb*, the women had to be sent away. It manages to connect the two injunctions (seeking permission to enter and "asking from behind a *ḥijāb*") of Qur'an 33:53. True to the first, the guest had to wait outside the women's quarters until permission was given, and in conformity with the second, they remained out of sight after he entered. We can imagine how, if he had come on his own, he would have been forced to state his request "from behind" — that is from outside — the curtain.

The *ḥadīth* tale of Muhammad's wedding with Ṣafiyah tells us more about the Muslim community's memory of the dividing curtain called *ḥijāb* (or *sitr*, a synonym for *ḥijāb* also sometimes appearing in the Prophetic Reports). It is reported that after the Jewish town of Khaybar was conquered and Ṣafiyah, an inhabitant of the town, was chosen by the Prophet as spoils after the massacre of the male population (all this in accordance with Semitic custom), he spent some time on the road from Khaybar to Medina consummating their union and celebrating with a hasty feast. Seeing this, the Muslims wondered if Ṣafiyah was to be one of the wives of the Prophet or simply a concubine. "If he confers on her the *ḥijāb* (*in ḥajabahā*)," they said, "she is one of the Mothers of the Believers, and if he does not, she is a concubine." As the Prophet set out again, he mounted Ṣafiyah on a horse behind him and, in the words of the report, "spread" or "extended" the *ḥijāb* (*madda al-ḥijāb*) about her.[50] Even when the woman is mobile, *ḥijāb* seems still to refer not to clothing but to a kind of curtain — perhaps in this case a draping over a booth on the riding animal — for it was not Ṣafiyah herself who donned the *ḥijāb*, but the Prophet who "spread" it in a way that was evident enough to allow the Muslims watching to draw the conclusion they did.[51] (This report also confirms that *ḥijāb* — again, in accord with long-standing Semitic custom — aided in distinguishing free women from slaves.)

The term *ḥijāb* in the Prophetic Reports finally acquires an abstract meaning. It becomes an institution rather than a thing. 'Ā'ishah uses "*ḥijāb*" in this way in a remark made apropos of the famous incident of the "Falsehood" (*Ifk*), that is, the false accusation of adultery against her after she was accidentally left behind by a caravan and rescued by a handsome young man. The young man, 'Ā'ishah later recalled, came upon her sleeping. He recognized her, she said, because "he used to see me before the *ḥijāb*." 'Ā'ishah also relates that as she woke up and saw him, she "drew her cloak (*jilbāb*) around her," since it was "after the *ḥijāb* came down."[52]

The institution of *ḥijāb* is portrayed in the *ḥadīth* as involving precise rules to which the wives of the Prophet adhered very conciously. Several *ḥadīth*s mention the careful observance of 'Ā'ishah in particular. 'Ā'ishah remembered that her paternal uncle through the relation established by fostership, that is, through nursing at the same breast, came and asked permission to enter into her presence. This, the *ḥadīth* notes, was "after the *ḥijāb* came down." 'Ā'ishah refused him entry. She told the Prophet of the incident, and he commented, "'Ā'ishah, [a relationship] licit through birth is also licit through fostership."[53] 'Ā'ishah's foster uncle knew that a strange man could not enter 'Ā'ishah's company and, being himself apparently unsure of whether he was in that category or not, cautiously left it to 'Ā'ishah to decide. 'Ā'ishah was in turn so scrupulous about observance of the *ḥijāb* that she mistakenly refused to let her legitimate uncle breach it. Another *ḥadīth* indicating a strict and precise institution of *ḥijāb* is preserved in which a petitioner who came to 'Ā'ishah to ask about an animal sent to the Ka'bah for sacrifice heard — apparently as a sign of her disapproval of his incorrect assumption concerning how the animal might be used — "the clapping of her hands from behind the *ḥijāb*."[54] 'Ā'ishah was a revered and prolific relater of *ḥadīth,* yet in this instance, while her words might be heard, the *ḥijāb* had to be maintained between her and her interlocutor.

Thus in material terms, *ḥijāb* denoted some kind of marker of space possibly intended to guard family privacy. It also, however, had or at some time acquired an extended, abstract meaning ("after the *ḥijāb* came down"). In this sense, it connoted a norm or institution that is the isolation of women — or perhaps the Prophet's wives in particular — from men's eyes, along with the restrictions that implied. The Indo-Persian concept of *Purdah* (also literally meaning "dividing curtain," an exact translation of *ḥijāb*) does accurately preserve the latter sense.

Disputes About Seclusion

There is evidence, however, in the canonical collections of some dispute about the extent of women's seclusion. Some of this dispute is expressed in what I call "protest *ḥadīth*s," that is, *ḥadīth*s contrived to express (sometimes quite strenuously) objections to restrictions. We are fortunate that the *ḥadīth* collectors, faithful to their task of carefully preserving all texts judged reliable by the standards of *ḥadīth* science, have also included these in their books. In what follows, I treat the texts that dispute restrictions on women's space in four groups: insistence that women may go to the mosque; permission to go out in case of necessity; resistance to seclusion imposed by the second caliph, 'Umar; and (much slenderer than the others) suggestion that *ḥijāb* means clothing and not seclusion. In each case we shall witness — not only in the *ḥadīth*s themselves but also in the commentaries and other *ḥadīth*-based literature — a struggle between texts expressing opposing views. There is, in addition, in the case of the mosque a striking instance of a single evidently original text in favour of women's attendance that has suffered later changes at the hands of those who opposed the practice. Mosque attendance, in any case, is the women's space issue that has inspired the most *ḥadīth*s, so I will begin with that.

Is it really necessary for a woman to go out to the mosque for the purpose of the ritual prayers or the 'Eid festivals? Is there any other legitimate reason for her to go out besides? What, in addition, are the precautions that must be taken if she does go out? These questions are the subject not only of numerous *ḥadīth*s but of whole chapters of the canonical collections.

The heart of the mosque attendance controversy and the text around which others revolve are the words of the Prophet: "Do not prevent your women from attending the mosque." This *ḥadīth* is reported in many places in the collections, with the usual variants such as "the handmaidens of God," "if they ask you," "in the night," "do not prevent them from their good fortune" and so on.[55] The Prophet's utterance "Do not prevent ..." is, however, opposed by other reports that attempt to limit its impact in various ways by adding to it, transmogrifying it or burying it under contrary reports. Thus one variant adds to the text the qualifying phrase: "but their houses are better for them."[56] A *ḥadīth* attributed to the wife of the Prophet, Umm Salamah, then actually separates this phrase from the original text and comes up with the saying: "The best mosque [or in a variant, 'the best prayer for women'] is the confines (*qa'r*) of her house."[57] The intention of the original *ḥadīth* has been completely reversed. It is no longer about "going out," but about a womanly ideal of confinement and isolation. Other reports then go on to elaborate on this reversed text; for instance: "The prayer of a woman in her house is better than her prayer in her courtyard, and her prayer in the storeroom is better than her prayer in her house."[58]

The powerful authority of 'Ā'ishah is also brought to bear on the problematic words of Muhammad. She is reported to have remarked that if the Prophet had seen women as they were in her day, he would have forbidden them to go out, "as the women of the Children of Israel were forbidden."[59] This *ḥadīth*, while it does not dare to cancel the Prophet's ruling, treats it by suggesting that it applied only in his time when, apparently, women were more virtuous or manageable than in later times.

Other *ḥadīths* nevertheless continue to insist on the unaltered meaning of "Do not prevent." One of these features the second caliph, 'Umar. It is reported that one of 'Umar's wives — the commentator identifies her as 'Ātiqah bint Zayd — used to offer her morning and evening prayers along with the congregation in the mosque. "Why," she was asked, "do you go out? Do you not know that 'Umar dislikes it and is jealous?" "[If this were so], what would prevent him from stopping me?" she said. "The words," her interlocutor replied, "of the Messenger of God, 'Do not prevent the handmaidens of God from the mosque.'"[60] It is also reported that a Companion recited to his son the Prophet's words, "Do not prevent your women from the mosques, if they ask permission to go." His son objected, saying, "We do forbid them!" or, according to a variant, "We forbid them, for fear of corruption." The father "cursed as he had never been heard to curse before" and said: "I relate to you words from the Messenger of God, and you say, 'We prevent them'?"[61]

Both these protest *ḥadīths* — for that is what they are — take the form of a reminder by a member of the first generation of an earlier, authentic practice that had been denied or forgotten. And this is, in fact, a common way of phrasing *ḥadīth* protest. In another example, Umm Salamah, the wife of the Prophet also featured in the anti-mosque *ḥadīth* cited above, remembers that "in the time of the Messenger of God" men and women used to make ablutions in the mosque together. Variants of this report take care to emphasize, apparently in the face of other views or of disbelief, that this was done "together," "together in one vessel" or "dipping our hands in the same vessel."[62] One version[63] has a man repeatedly question Umm Salamah — "In the time of the Prophet?" "Together?" — as if he could not digest these surprising facts.

A story featuring Ḥafṣah concerning going out to the mosque on the two 'Eids is constructed in the same way. Ḥafṣah was the daughter of 'Umar and one of the wives of Muhammad. She is reported as saying: "We forbid our girls who have reached puberty or are too close to it (*'awātiq*, explained both ways by the commentators) from going out on the two 'Eids." A woman visitor, however, informed Ḥafṣah that her sister, who had accompanied her husband on twelve campaigns with the Prophet, used to "treat wounds and take care of the sick." Her sister, the woman added, had directly asked the Prophet: "Is there a problem if one of us does not have a *jilbāb* [clothing being expensive and difficult to obtain], so that she should not go out?" The Prophet had answered: "Her friend should give her her cloak to wear,[64] and she should witness the good being done and the efforts of the believers for Islam." Apparently Ḥafṣah doubted what she had been told, for the *ḥadīth* goes on to say that she later asked Umm 'Aṭīyah, a Companion of the Prophet from the Anṣār, to confirm these words of the Prophet. Sure enough, Umm 'Aṭīyah swore that the Prophet had said: "Let the *'awātiq* and those who are behind [literally "possess"] curtains (*khudūr*, sing. *khidr*), and the menstruating women witness the good being done and the efforts of the believers for Islam. ..."[65] It is similarly reported that Umm 'Aṭīyah said: "The Messenger of God commanded us to go out on the Day of Breaking of the Fast and the Day of Sacrifice [the two 'Eids], and we said: 'What if one of us does not have a *jilbāb*?' He said: 'Let her sister clothe her with her *jilbāb*.'"[66]

Another kind of protest *ḥadīth* found in the Prophetic Reports paints a picture of a supposed actual practice of Muhammad or of the people in his time, implicitly setting it against different practices. In the case of the mosque, there are a number of *ḥadīth*s that pointedly mention the presence of women in the mosque while the Prophet was there. (These reports are significant because the Prophet's silence in the face of a practice he witnessed implies his assent (*iqrār*) to that practice and thus establishes a *Sunnah* norm.) 'Ā'ishah tells how "The Messenger of God used to pray in the darkness of early morning, and the believing women [attending the prayer] would leave indistinguishable in the dark," or according to a variant, "indistinguishable from one another."[67] The famous Companion of the Prophet, Ibn 'Abbās, recalls in another report how, after the Prophet gave a sermon, he would go to where the women were and exhort them.[68] We also hear, in a less well-attested report from Ibn ʿAbbās, that "the Prophet's daughters and wives used to go out" — one version even has the more pointed phrase "he used to order them to go out" — on the two ʿEids.[69]

We now turn to treatment of the women-mosque *ḥadīth*s by the eighth- and ninth-century authors of the canonical collections and by the later *ḥadīth* commentators. The dominant trend among these scholars, not only in the case of this group of *ḥadīth*s but also for reports in general concerning women's space, clothing (as we have seen above) and character, is to emphasize the most restrictive texts. There are, however, some exceptions to this trend; the pro-mosque-attendance argument, it seems, did not die out.

Earlier, I gave the titles of some chapters in the canonical books as evidence that seclusion is recommended by the *ḥadīth* scriptures. The reader is, however, already aware from the example of Abū Dāwūd's treatment of women's clothing that collectors are not necessarily neutral. Titles, the arrangement of *ḥadīth*s and added comments can and do communicate the authors' views. In the case of seclusion, Abū Dāwūd is again a prime example. In the Book of Prayer of his *Sunan*, one chapter is titled "Women's Going Out to the Mosques, *as Long as Sedition (fitnah) Does Not Result, and as Long as They Do Not Go Out Perfumed*." Abū Dāwūd has also arranged the *ḥadīth*s in the chapter with the more permissive first and the least permissive last, so that the last texts appear to be logical elaborations on the first, rather than contradictions of them. His own title completes this harmonization in favour of restriction.[70] The chapter in the "Book of Friday Prayer" on "The Going Out of Women on the ʿEids" in Tirmidhī's *Sunan* is a similar case. Tirmidhī opens his chapter with the *ḥadīth*, already cited above, reporting the Prophet's words that women should be allowed to attend the mosque "in order to witness the good being done and the efforts of the believers for Islam." But he does not allow that text to stand on its own. Instead, he follows it with the comment of ʿAbd Allāh ibn Mubārak (a Successor, that is, a member of the generation after the Companions, who died in the second century of Islam) in which he says: "These days, the going out of women on the two 'Eids is disapproved." If a woman insists on going out, Tirmidhī reports the Successor as saying, "her husband should allow her to do so, but in old, worn clothing and without adornments — and if she refuses that [condition], he should prevent her from going out [at all]." He then quotes, for good measure, the *ḥadīth* of 'Ā'ishah, "if the Prophet had seen. ..."[71]

The method of the *ḥadīth* commentators is to assemble material, including additional *ḥadīth*s, from other scholars, as well as offering their own opinions. The following are two examples of commentary on *ḥadīth*s concerning women and mosques.

Apropos of the words of the Prophet, "Let [the women] witness the good being done and the efforts of the believers for Islam," one of Tirmidhī's commentators of later times, Mubārakfūrī (d. 1866 or 1867), relates the verdicts of the different legal schools. The legal judgments he relates range from "disapproved" (*makrūh*) to "recommended" (*maḥbūb*). The first verdict is based on the argument — as in the *ḥadīth* of 'Ā'ishah — that deterioration of morals after the first generation has made necessary a much more restricted application. The second verdict, that women going out to the mosque to "witness good" is recommended, is based on the argument that one must adhere to the evident sense of the authentic words of the Prophet. The most extreme argument on the side of "disapproved" is that the *ḥadīth* is "abrogated" (*mansūkh*), meaning that, just as with certain verses of the Qur'an, God has cancelled the legal force of the text and replaced it with a new and different one (presumably, the more restrictive *ḥadīth*s). This argument demonstrates both the lengths to which those who wished to confine women absolutely were willing to go in diverting the texts, and the stubborn durability of the text itself.

Mubārakfūrī himself argues for the verdict of "recommended." To claim that women's going out to the mosque is disapproved is, he says, to oppose the clear sense of the text with "invalid opinions" (*arā' fāsidah*). That is to say, it amounts to allowing the workings of the human mind — which, according to strict revelationism, can never entirely compass the meanings of the scriptures — to interfere with faithful adherence to the literal reading of the holy text. Mubārakfūrī argues on somewhat the same principle against ʻĀ'ishah's *ḥadīth* concerning "the women of the Children of Israel." "This saying," he says, "does not change the rule (*ḥukm*, meaning legal ruling) [laid down in the first *ḥadīth*]," for ʻĀ'ishah made her words depend on an unreal condition — that is, she said, "if the Prophet had seen," which he could not have done, since he was deceased. In addition, God in his Omniscience surely knew what the women would do in the future — but He did not reveal to the Prophet that he should prevent them from going out to mosques.[72] Here is an example — not common, but also certainly not unique — of a commentator arguing for a more permissive interpretation.

Muslim's commentator Nawawī, however, goes in the opposite direction by favouring what he regards as a social imperative over the clear sense. Commenting on the *ḥadīth* "Do not prevent," he says:

> This and other similar [more permissive] *ḥadīth*s in the chapter may appear to mean that women should not be barred from the mosque. But that depends on the conditions the scholars have mentioned, which are [also] taken from the *ḥadīth*, those conditions being that she should not be perfumed, nor adorned, that she should not wear anklets that jingle, that she should not wear ostentatious clothing, that she should not mix with men or with young women, and other things of that kind that stir up sedition (*fitnah*), that there should be nothing on the way that might raise fears of corruption — and so on. ... If she fulfills the conditions named above, and if she has no husband or master, it is forbidden to prevent her — again, if she fulfils the conditions.[73]

Nawawī adds so many conditions of a moral kind to a woman's going to the mosque as to effectively cancel any such possibility. He makes it, in fact, a bad practice of bad women, so that (as other reports do say explicitly) prayer in isolation becomes infinitely better than prayer in the mosque.

We have just seen an apparently primitive permission — even a command — laid down in the Prophetic Reports that women should go to the mosque obscured and almost buried (despite protests that survive in the *ḥadīth* itself) by the stern thought that they should not venture forth under any circumstance. The *ḥadīth*s are, however, fairly amenable to allowing women mobility in case of necessity. The chief necessities addressed are travel, going to the baths and war. Each of these permissions is still a locus of controversy, and thus we also find some protest *ḥadīth*s; but the controversy is much less than in the case of the mosque. Necessity, it seems, it a powerful consideration.

As for travel, the *ḥadīth* does permit a woman to travel alone. The implicit reason for the permission is that the need to travel might arise at a time when there is no *maḥram*, that is, no accompanying male related in a degree that would prohibit marriage, such as husband, brother and so on. It is, of course, preferable that she be accompanied, if at all possible, so that, according to one well-attested report, a man's duty to accompany his wife on the *ḥajj* pilgrimage outweighs even his duty to fight.[74] But I find only one report, cited once, that actually forbids women to travel at all without a *maḥram*.[75] The chief concern of the travel *ḥadīth*s instead is how long a journey can be before a woman must take along a *maḥram*; the limit set by various reports ranges from one to three days, with the greatest number opting for the upper limit.[76] A commentary of Nawawī on Muslim's *Ṣaḥīḥ* enlarges further on the rule of necessity in travel. "Cases of necessity (*ḍarūrah*)," Nawawī says, "are excepted [from the rule that a woman cannot be with a stranger except if she is also accompanied by a *mahram*]. If a woman, for instance, finds herself stranded on the road, then a stranger is permitted to accompany her if he considers she would otherwise be in danger." There is, he claims, no dispute on this matter.[77]

As for the baths, there are numerous reports prescribing covering and other cautions when going to the public bath for both men and women; Abū Dāwūd's *Sunan* contains an entire "Book of the Bath" (although a short one), and chapters are also devoted to the bath in the other collections. The concern of most of the bath *ḥadīths* is modesty. Foreign places — "Syria," "Persia" — are mentioned, pointing to the anxiety of the Arabs as they came to terms with strange new customs. The key *ḥadīth* here concerning women's space comes from 'Ā'ishah. It is reported that a group of women from Syria — from Hama or Damascus — visited her, and she said: "Are you among those who let your women go the baths? — For I heard the Messenger of God say: 'Whenever a woman removes her clothing in a place other than her husband's house, the veil between her and Her Lord is rent!'"[78] Nevertheless, other *ḥadīths* do allow a woman to go to the bath if she is sick or has given birth or is pregnant (*nafsā'*).

Again we see that necessity rules. A woman is allowed to travel alone for a time apparently measured by various estimates of how long she might actually need to travel. Similarly, it is better that a woman not go to the baths, but illness and parturition are necessitous conditions that overcome that rule. The twelfth-century Ḥanbalī revivalist Ibn al-Jawzī, in whose time the bath had come to be considered indispensable and who is himself much preoccupied with women's cleanliness, appeals to the same principle as he argues that the *ḥadīths* against the baths were not for the women "of this time," but for the Arabs alone, for whom it [not bathing] was not a hardship![79] The report in which the Prophet tells a woman whose husband has died and who is being prevented by the overzealous from going out to maintain her date orchard that she is free to do so is also, in fact, about necessity. The *ḥadīth* addresses the exceptional case of a woman seeking permission to go out during the waiting period after divorce or death — when she would normally be strictly confined in order to establish paternity in case of a child[80] — because she needs to go out in order to earn a living.[81] The Prophet's final remark to the woman ("and you might [also] perhaps give alms or do some good deed") serves to further justify the exception to the rule by invoking pious intent (similar to the justification seen in the *ḥadīth* phrase quoted above concerning mosque attendance, "they should witness the good being done and the efforts of the believers for Islam"). Liberals sometimes use this report to argue for women's free movement. Such a reading is not, I think, justified, as the text is about something quite opposite, i.e., about a contingency that would allow a woman to interrupt her confinement.

The underlying rationale — the rationale of necessity — around which arguments in the *ḥadīth* about women's space revolve explains the remarkably permissive attitude toward women going to war. War, after all, is a greater necessity than the necessities of individuals.[82] In fact, the issue in many war *ḥadīth*s is not whether women should be present at battles, but whether or not they should receive a share in the booty! There are several chapters in the canonical collections devoted to women and war — in Bukhārī alone, "Women's *Jihād*," "Women's Attacking and Fighting Alongside Men," "Women's Treating the Wounded in War," "The Call to Battle and Martyrdom of Men and Women" and others. Umm 'Aṭīyah, whom we have already met, reports that she went to seven battles, cooking food and treating the sick and wounded.[83] One text (in addition to the *jilbāb* report given above that also speaks of war) again takes the typical form of a protest *ḥadīth*. There it is related that a certain Hashraj ibn Ziyād, a Successor, heard from his paternal grandmother Umm Ziyād, a Companion, how she had attended the battle at Khaybar with several other women. According to Umm Ziyād, this news reached the Messenger of God, who called for them. The women saw that he was angry. "Who did you go out with," he asked, "and by whose permission?" The women replied that they were spinning wool "to help in the Way of God" (apparently to make clothing or tents, or to sell so that they could contribute to the war effort), treating the wounded, giving out arrows and giving the fighters barley water to drink. "Then go to it," the Prophet said, "and if God should allow Khaybar to be conquered, I will give you the same share as the men [apparently, in booty, although the commentators resist this reading]!"[84] The *ḥadīth* dramatizes the principle that, even though one may rightly object to women going out without purpose or need, an urgent necessity or good purpose reverses the rule.

Protest *ḥadīth*s such as these indicate that even the limited permission afforded by necessity for women to go out was challenged. This is quite explicit in an incident in which the second caliph, 'Umar, plays a prominent role. Like the well-known report of the loitering guests at the Prophet's and Zaynab bint Jahsh's wedding feast, the incident is linked to Qur'an 33:53. It concerns Sawdah, another of the Prophet's wives. It is reported from 'Ā'ishah that 'Umar used to urge the Prophet to "seclude your wives" (*uḥjub nisā'aka*), but the Prophet chose not to do so. His wives, relates 'Ā'ishah, used to go out at night to the open area outside the town to defecate. Sawdah too went out for that purpose and, as she was unusually tall, 'Umar recognized her. He called out to her: "Sawdah, I recognize who you are!" That, says 'Ā'ishah, was because he wanted the *ḥijāb* to be revealed; then God revealed the verse.[85] Even though we are told in this version of the Sawdah story (the more common one) that the Prophet initially refused to institute seclusion, the point is not, I think, his reluctance, since the decisive revelation finally does come down. The report is rather meant to confirm or heighten 'Umar's prestige by crediting him with prompting the "occasion" for the revelation of an important verse, a theme of other tales relating to 'Umar and to other persons .[86] Another version, however, does use the story to defend necessity. The version places the incident of Sawdah "after the *ḥijāb* was prescribed for the Prophet's wives." According to this report, 'Umar called out to her: "You are not hidden to us. If you [have to] go out, be careful how you go!" Sawdah, apparently upset, went to the Prophet and told him what 'Umar had said to her. Even though he was busy eating the evening meal, the inspiration immediately came upon him — and so quickly did it come, or so absorbed was he in the experience, that as it finally lifted he still held in his hand the joint he had been eating. Then he said: "It has been permitted to you [feminine plural] that you go out for your needs."[87] The *ḥadīth* tells us that it is not true, as 'Umar here claims, that women must be absolutely confined; rather, they may go out if they need to. (Although Muslim's commentator Nawawī reports the "widespread" opinion — further evidence of challenge to necessity — that "it was for defecation, and not for any other need connected with other matters of daily life,"[88] the word "need" [*ḥājah*] has also been taken in the wider sense.)

This report is one of a number in which 'Umar's promotion of *ḥijāb* is resisted (our third category of *ḥadīth*s disputing seclusion). One such report begins with a group of women from the tribe of Quraysh in the Prophet's house speaking with the Prophet and pressing him in loud voices. 'Umar came, and as he was given permission to enter, they sprang up and hastened to put on their "*ḥijāb*" (here apparently clothing). The Prophet laughed and said to 'Umar: "I am amazed at these women who were with me [relaxed and not overly concerned about their *ḥijāb*] and who when they heard your voice, hastened to put it on." 'Umar reproached the women: "O enemies to your own selves! Do you respect me and not the Messenger of God?" "Yes," they replied, "for you are more rude and harsh than he!" The Prophet then commented — I think, from my reading, with a mixture of humour and reproach — "By Him in whose Hand is my soul, if Satan himself were to meet you on the road, he would take another way!"[89] In one report, Zaynab actually retorts as 'Umar orders the wives to seclude themselves: "So, Ibn Khaṭṭāb, you are against us [that is, you presume to reproach or give us orders], while the revelation comes down in *our* dwellings!"[90] 'Umar himself relates in another report that "one of the wives" (unnamed) came up to him as he tried to calm a group of them who were arguing jealously among themselves and said: "Can't the Prophet himself warn his wives, so that you have to warn them?"[91]

These stories may be the literary ghost of a real historical conflict between 'Umar and the women as he tried to impose restrictions on them. Or they may simply be the imaginative expression, in colourful anecdotes peopled by famous persons, of a more general dispute in early Islamic times about the nature and extent of *ḥijāb*. 'Umar, in any case, plays a role familiar from other Islamic lore. He is puritanic and severe, and nowhere more so than in matters concerning women. It is perhaps more than coincidence that it is 'Umar's daughter, Ḥafṣah, who is made to deny (in the report quoted above) that women are allowed to go out to the mosque on the 'Eids.

'Umar also figures in the fourth and last controversy we will examine in this section, that is, whether *ḥijāb* necessarily involves seclusion, or can mean merely covering. Bukhārī's commentator, Ibn Ḥajar, seems to take the side of Sawdah in her conflict with 'Umar related in the "joint of meat" *ḥadīth* quoted above. (His interpretation also allows him to explain how the action of the *ḥadīth* could have taken place "after the *ḥijāb* came down," yet still be linked with the revelation.) Ibn Ḥajar writes that:

> The *ḥijāb* referred to in the first instance is different from that referred to in the second. The import [of the first *ḥadīth*] is that 'Umar took a disliking to the familiarity of strangers with the Prophet's womenfolk (*ḥarīm*), so that he finally expressed his feelings in the words, "veil your wives." He insisted on this until the verse came down. Then [in the second *ḥadīth*, that is the "joint of meat" *ḥadīth*] he intended that not even their persons be seen, even if they were veiled (*mustatirāt*). *But he had overreached, and the Prophet refused him that*, instead permitting his wives to go out for their need in order to avoid undue hardship. ...[92]

Thus, according to Ibn Ḥajar's understanding, covering the body is enough; women can move about, if covered, on at least some occasions. His commentary on the *ḥadīth* concerning the marriage of Zaynab bint Jahsh makes the same point. He begins by indicating the legal necessity (*mashrū'īyah*) of *ḥijāb* for the Mothers of the Believers, that is, the wives of the Prophet. He then relates the opinion of 'Iyāḍ[93] to the effect that the duty (*farḍ*) of *ḥijāb* was one of the things that distinguished the Prophet's wives, that it was a duty for them that extended equally to the face and hands, and that it was not permitted for them to uncover any of that, either for witnessing or any other purpose. They were, Ibn Ḥajar further reports 'Iyāḍ as saying, not allowed to show their persons (*shakhṣ*) even if they were veiled (*mustatirāt*), except if they had to go out to defecate. Ibn Ḥajar himself, however, denies that the wives of the Prophet were forbidden to show their persons, for after the death of the Prophet, he says, they used to make the pilgrimage and circumambulate the Ka'bah, and the Companions and those who came after also used to hear *ḥadīth* from them. He concludes that their *bodies* must have been veiled, *but not their persons*; that is, they could be seen, but were seen veiled. He then briefly quotes an early Muslim who had witnessed 'Ā'ishah performing the circumambulation of the Ka'bah "after the *ḥijāb*."[94]

Ibn Ḥajar gives a hint of at least some small resistance to the tendency of the *ḥadīth* scholars to reify and maximize the *ḥijāb*. Muslim's commentator Nawawī, however, reports the same interpretation of 'Iyāḍ without objection, including the information that "when they [the Prophet's wives] used to sit [and converse] with people, they would do that from behind the *ḥijāb*, and if they went out, they used to put on the *ḥijāb* (*ḥajabna*) and veil (*satarna*) their persons ... and when Zaynab died, they placed a dome (*qubbah*) over her bier so that her person (*shakhṣahā*) would be covered."[95]

Thus, in conclusion, although there are disputes in the *ḥadīth* about a woman's "going out," these finally revolve merely around the few occasions when she might be released from confinement. We have also seen how strenuous is the argument, traceable in *ḥadīth*s expressing opposing views, over women's going to the mosque. This struggle over so little free space seems to me to be the strongest indication of the entrenchment and strictness of the rule of seclusion in the *ḥadīth*.

Part 2: Interpretation of the *Ḥadīth*s

Now we come to the decisive question — the question of interpretation. How have these *ḥadīth*s been applied by groups of various ideological tendencies, whether "conservative" or "liberal"? What other meanings might they yield for believers? And finally, what can they tell a historian of religion about processes of interpretation, or even about the historicity of the Prophetic Reports?

Before entering into this discussion, it should be acknowledged that many contemporary *ḥijāb* and other arguments do not take the *ḥadīth* into account, let alone base themselves upon it. For liberals, de-emphasis of the *ḥadīth* is part of a conscious strategy (discussed below). There is, however, a deeper current at work here, which sweeps a good deal of conservative discourse along in the same direction. The kinds of arguments most accessible to committed individuals and opinion leaders — the arguments most valued and best understood in today's marketplace of ideas — are not arguments from the text, but those related to morality, psychology (in the case of *ḥijāb*, the psychology of gender relations), personal experience and sentiment (for instance, "identity"), culture and politics. The use of texts is often secondary to these, a circumstance that may extend even to the Qur'an, but has an especially strong impact on the *ḥadīth*, since it is less known and more difficult of access in the first place. The tendency away from text argument is particularly pronounced in popular discourse; but it is not confined to it, as non-clerical spokespersons and even many clerics now exhibit a tendency to present Islam as a kind of generalized ideology. It was partly for this reason that the editors of this book made the decision to place the essays on the Qur'an and *ḥadīth* at the end of the volume. Much of the "real action" of modern debate, and certainly of popular opinion, is elsewhere.

Conservative Approaches and the Roots of Conservative Discourse

The group most likely to rely on the *ḥadīth*, including for the question of *ḥijāb*, are the conservatives. The overwhelming majority of the very large number of Arabic-language books published in the twentieth century that collect *ḥadīth*s having to do with women, or that use *ḥadīth*s to argue the questions of "the liberation of women" and "covering and uncovering" (*al-ḥijāb wa-al-sufūr*, a phrase appearing in the title of many such works) come from this camp. To be more precise, the group most devoted to the *ḥadīth* are conservatives of traditional education. This is because the *ḥadīth* has attached to it a special, intricate science that requires long training not only in a vast literature written in antique Arabic, but also knowledge of the form, terminology and standards of the *isnād*s or "chains of authorities" — such as the one illustrated in the *ḥadīth* of

Zaynab bint Jahsh in the first section — that authenticate the texts. The aim of this science is to establish the reliability of individual oral reports according to a graded scale, ranging from "attested by several trustworthy authorities" to "forged." (The reader should know that my presentation of the *ḥijāb ḥadīth*s, since it relies on text analysis rather than this traditional approach, would be regarded as invalid by many Muslims.)

The learned-conservative attention to *ḥadīth*s and *ḥadīth* science often extends, especially among adherents of the Ḥanbalī school of thought, to literalism, or more exactly, "fideism," that is, striving to ascertain that the text is authentically guaranteed, and then to receive that authentic text in its literal meaning without the intervention of the human mind implied by interpretation. Key to this attitude is the assumption that the human intellect is not equal to and never can completely fathom the divine wisdom handed down in the Revelation and Prophetic Reports.[96] This is not to say that fideist arguments do not rely on treatment of the text, for without treatment of the text, it is impossible to argue at all! Rather, the true fideist attempts to tie his argument closely to the text, and not stray from it. The rich material provided by the *ḥadīth*s is indispensable to this approach.

The argument of the well-known conservative scholar Shaykh Hindāwī against women's showing of the hands and face — an argument, in other words, for total *hijāb*, sometimes called *niqāb* — is a good example of contemporary *ḥadīth*-based fideism.[97] Hindāwī also presents some typical conservative contentions and favourite *ḥadīth*s. At the time he wrote his essay on this subject, Shaykh Hindāwī was a member of the "Bureau for the Redaction of the True Islamic Heritage" (al-Maktab al-Salafī li-Taḥqīq al-Turāth), an organization apparently based in Ḥanbalī-dominated Saudi Arabia.

The first part of the Shaykh's essay consists, in a style typical of traditional Islamic debate, of refutations of the "textual proofs" (*adillah*) of those who would argue that a woman's hands and face are not *'awrah*. He begins with the well-known *ḥadīth* of Abū Dāwūd featuring Asmā', the daughter of Abū Bakr, which says that a woman must cover all save her hands and face. In an effort to defeat this *ḥadīth*, Hindāwī points out (as does, in fact, Abū Dāwūd himself) that the *isnād* or chain of guarantors is missing a link. In addition, he says, another personality in the chain according to many experts is also "weak," or even worse, known to relate reports that "cannot be recognized" (*munkar*), that is, because of their dubious content. He rejects the argument of al-Shaykh al-Qaraḍāwī — a contemporary cleric known for his moderate views on many subjects — that the authority of the *ḥadīth* of Asmā', however weak, is strengthened by other, more sound *ḥadīths* that also allow uncovering of the hands and face where there is no danger of *fitnah* or "sedition." *Fitnah*, Hindāwī protests, is not limited by particular conditions such that one can say that this or that situation will produce it or not produce it. Hindāwī deploys similar arguments in the case of the equally well-known *ḥadīth*, also used by some to argue that the face and hands may be allowed to show, which tells how the Prophet after his sermon in the mosque encountered a woman with "darkish cheeks" (*saf'ā al-khadayn*),[98] and so on through a series of other texts and opinions.

All this is merely a prelude to a lengthy and erudite argument on the basis of the Qur'an and seventeen *ḥadīths* from the Prophet, as well as further reports from the Prophet's Companions and the Successors, that the face and hands must indeed be concealed. One of the Shaykh's contentions rests on the *ḥadīth* that prohibits women from wearing the *niqāb* or face mask and gloves during the *ḥajj* pilgrimage.[99] Noting the *ḥadīth* collector Tirmidhī's statement that the *ḥadīth* is "sound" (*ṣaḥīḥ*), he recounts the opinions of the great Ḥanbalī revivalists Ibn Taymīyah (d. 1328) and Ibn al-Jawzī (d. 1200) to the effect that the prohibition against the face mask and gloves itself indicates that these things were habitually worn by the women of the Prophet's time. Still following Ibn al-Jawzī, Hindāwī asserts that the *ḥajj* prohibition applies specifically to articles of clothing, which, like these, cover the hands and face in particular. It does not, he says, refer to covering hands and face per se, as indicated by other *ḥadīths* that also forbid specific articles of clothing to men but do not forbid them to cover the parts of their bodies that would be covered by that clothing, by the *ḥadīth* that describes how the female pilgrims "lowered their *jilbāb*s over their faces" as men passed by,[100] and finally the absence of any text telling women to uncover their faces on the pilgrimage apart from this one forbidding the *niqāb* in particular.[101]

Notice how the Shaykh, in fideist fashion, does not feel compelled to probe the rationale of a command that forbids the face mask, but nevertheless requires the covering of the face. The role of the believer is not to apply reason or to match the text to human norms and desires, but merely to extract, as faithfully and precisely as possible, the literal meaning (though that meaning may be embedded rather than immediately apparent).

As I see it, however, the ultimate rationale of the conservatives for seclusion and covering is not in the fine points of texts such as these. Rather, it rests in a notion of the danger to men and society of the temptations posed by women and by women's own nature and desires. The "dangerous feminine" has been central to the scholars' view of gender relations in the past, and it remains the heart and staple of conservative discourse today. Hindāwī's precise and very convincing textual arguments for total *ḥijāb* are founded, in the final analysis, on this assumption — as seen, for instance, in his remarks concerning *fitnah*.

The *ḥadīth*s have played a major role in the development of this foundation. The view of women as "*fitnah*" — as a "disturbing" element — is supported by the well-known report in which the Prophet says: "I will not leave after me anything more harmful for men than the sedition (*fitnah*) of women."[102] Another, lesser-known *ḥadīth* has the Prophet declare: "This world is a verdant chamber over which God has made you sovereign — so watch what you do, and beware of the world and of women!"[103] These *ḥadīth*s aimed at the "dangerous feminine" are complemented by reports that warn men against passions inadvertently stirred in their own volatile nature by contact with women whom they have not lawfully wed or owned. The temperaments of women and men together pose, the *ḥadīth* texts suggest, a double danger. "Every eye," it is said, "is a fornicator, so that if a woman applies perfume and passes by a gathering [of men], then she is [herself] a fornicator."[104] The Prophet is reported to have said: "A woman approaches in the form of Satan, and leaves in the form of Satan — so if one of you should happen to see a woman, he should go to his wife, and that will satisfy what he has inside him."[105]

So that men and women may avoid each other's temptation, the *ḥadīths* warn also against *khalwah* or "privacy." "When a man is alone with a woman," says one report, "Satan is the third."[106] "Do not sit in privacy with women whose husbands are not present," another warns, "for Satan will be flowing in one of you even as his/her own blood."[107] "Beware entering into the presence of women!" the Prophet warned. "Do you also mean," he was asked, "the husband's male relations (*ḥamw*)?" "The *ḥamw*," the Prophet replied, "are deadly."[108]

The scholars of medieval Islam make abundant use of such reports in the many fields of Islamic literature for which the Prophetic Reports provide the raw material, including exegesis of the Qur'an, legal writings, belles lettres and so on. Separate essays would be needed to describe the careers of the woman-negative *ḥadīths* (as well as the *ḥijāb ḥadīths*) in each of these fields. Two basic trends, however, can be distinguished and are briefly illustrated here.

The first trend is to accentuate and magnify woman-negative reports. Thus Tirmidhī's commentator, Mubārakfūrī, explains that "woman is *'awrah*" (referring to the exceptional *ḥadīth* described in the first section) because if she is conspicuous, one feels embarrassment or shame, just as one would with actual *' awrah*, that is, pudenda.[109] He also explains that women are *fitnah* "because [men's] natures incline much toward them, and thus fall on their account into that which is forbidden ... the least of which is encouraging them to turn to worldly things ... and what corruption is more harmful than that?"[110] The *ḥadīth* that has the Prophet declare Satan to be "the third" in the company of an unsupervised man and woman becomes a favourite text in medieval writings, where it is repeatedly cited and commented on, even though it appears in the canonical reports in only one place (the collection of Tirmidhī). This renown is, I think, a result of its gnomic encapsulation of beliefs concerning gender relations,[111] and the saying is still well known and popularly quoted today.

The second tendency is to fuse woman-negativity with confinement. *Ḥijāb* becomes, in effect, an antidote to the perils posed by women. The medieval genre of books of "*ḥadīth* on women"[112] reveals this trend clearly, especially as the authors openly employ the reports to express their own views rather than merely cataloguing the reports. The woman-*ḥadīth* books do include discussion of the mutual rights, duties and kindnesses between men and women, as well as generally edifying passages about religion that might well have been read and appreciated by literate women. They are finally best described, however, as handbooks for men seeking to relate to and oversee women. Women are, in short, presented as a "problem." This is evident in some (though not all) chapter titles: "Warning Women [against various things]" (*Taḥdhīr al-nisā'...*), "Deterring Women from Sins" (*Takhwīf al-nisā' min al-dhunūb*) and so on, as well as use of the provocative term *fitnah.*

The woman problem is to be managed chiefly through seclusion and covering; in these works, the struggle over space detectable in the original *ḥadīths* is finally lost. Thus one chapter heading in Ibn Ḥabīb's *Book of Etiquette in Matters Concerning Women* reads: "Why women's going out to mosques is disapproved," and another, "Why women's going out of their houses is disapproved, and the sin they incur thereby." Ibn al-Jawzī, the twelfth-century scholar we have already met above, does faithfully relate in his *Book of Rulings on Women* the reports that allow women to go to the mosque.[113] He is careful to add, however, that the Friday prayer is not obligatory for them,[114] finally concluding: "Therefore it is apparent that women's going out [on the 'Eids] is permitted [*mubāḥ*, that is in the legal category of "indifferent" rather than positively recommended or meritorious]. But if *fitnah* is feared, it is better to prevent them. For the women of the formative age and men too" — here apparently echoing 'Ā'ishah's "if the Prophet had seen" *ḥadīth* — "were better than what is seen from them today."[115] Subsequently, in this same chapter on "The Going Out of Women on the Day of 'Eid," Ibn al-Jawzī offers his own opinions as well as reporting the opinions of scholars of the early generations of Islam to the effect that women should not greet men,[116] that, like snakes, they are to "hole up in their houses" and so on.[117] Observations of this kind continue into the following chapters entitled "Warning Women Against Going Out," "The Virtue for Women of Staying in the House," and "If *Fitnah* Is Feared from a Woman, She Is Forbidden to Go Out."

The view of gender relations that combines *fitnah*-wariness with emphasis on covering and the rights and duties of the spouses is continued in the abundant modern literature on "Women's Rights in Islam." (The medieval books of woman-*ḥadīth*s appear, in fact, to be the ancestors of the modern women's-rights-*ḥijāb* genre, which is still penned almost exclusively by men, although, in accord with its new role as an apologetic, with a heightened emphasis on "rights" and a vision of the dimensions of the woman-problem as civilizational, rather than personal and familial.) The influential Pakistani thinker Mawdūdī's (d. 1979) book *Purdah and the Status of Women in Islam*, first published in the 1930s, is one example of a treatise of this kind, as well as of a different kind of conservative approach to the texts. Mawdūdī's approach to the *ḥadīth* as scripture is modernist. He does not favour literal reception of the text, but believes that the *ḥadīth*s must be judged in light of legal and moral principles, the ultimate witness being the "spirit" of Islam and of the primary scripture, the Qur'an, as subtly perceived by the trained mind of true Islamic intellectuals such as himself.[118] Nevertheless, his outlook is based solidly on the *ḥadīth* idea of the dangerous feminine, and is thus entirely conservative. His thesis in *Purdah* is that *fitnah* stirred by women, if not kept under control and channelled by the ideal system provided by Islam, will lead to the collapse of society. Mawdūdī's evidence for *fitnah* is not, however, drawn directly from the *ḥadīth*, but from Western moralistic and pseudo-scientific literature of the time expressing similar views, as well as statistics and anecdotes from American and European sources pointing to the imminent destruction of Western civilization by (here an echo of Freud) undisciplined sexual energy. He has apparently calculated that arguments from "science" will be better received by his audience than woman-negative reports.

Mawdūdī's argument for seclusion and covering, however, is still fastened ultimately to norms found in the *ḥadīth* and *ḥadīth*-based literature, although, since he does not believe in a strictly literal reading, this consists in simple citation rather than the close textual analysis of the learned *'ulamā'*. (Note how he reads the *ḥadīth* in each instance in the most restrictive way possible.) Thus, according to Mawdūdī, a woman has been "exempted from all outdoor religious obligations," including the Friday congregational prayer, other attendance at the mosque and *jihād*.[119] Mindful of the well-attested dictum of the Prophet that women should not be prevented from going out to prayer, he allows that "the Legislator does not prohibit [this], because it is not a sin to go to the mosques for offering prayer," but is careful to add that prayer in the mosque is "of less spiritual merit than the one of greater merit in the house."[120] Nor may a woman go on a journey, the various durations of unaccompanied travel mentioned in the reports as permissible actually pointing, according to Mawdūdī, to a principle that "a woman should not be given such freedom of moving alone as may land her in trouble."[121] A woman should go out of her house only "for genuine needs," and not for anything else, as suggested by the Prophet's words to Sawdah discussed in the first part of this essay. Mawdūdī now lays down the rules against exposure of a woman's body, citing some of the less numerous *ḥadīth*s that address clothing, while relying for more restrictive details on the commentary tradition attached to the *ḥadīth* and Qur'an. A good proportion of the *ḥadīth*s he cites is aimed at nakedness in general rather the exposure of women, but in the context of his argument, it is nevertheless clear that women are the target. All these texts are blended into Mawdūdī's own notions of biology, psychology and economics.

Another example of a contemporary conservative approach is Ayatollah Murtazá Muṭahharī's (d. 1979) *The Islamic Modest Dress in Islam* (in Persian, *Mas'alah-yi ḥijāb* or "The Question of *Ḥijāb*"). Muṭahharī — as evident, of course, from the title "Ayatollah" — is a Shī'ī scholar. I have introduced him here for the purpose of illustrating a conservative approach that begins to shade into liberalism. Muṭahharī follows exactly the same reasoning as Ṭabarī on women's covering, identifying the "apparent" *zīnah* or adornment of Qu'ran 24:31 with "collyrium, a ring ... [or] an anklet." That exegesis, along with additional Shī'ī and some Sunnī reports, brings him to the conclusion that the hands and face may be shown.[122]

Permission to show the hands and face is generally an indication of a relatively permissive spirit, and Muṭahharī does indeed go on to formulate, again on the basis of Shī'ī and some Sunnī *ḥadīths*, a somewhat relaxed ruling on women's space that, though it stresses the unique value of woman's endeavours in the home, also allows her (with the proviso that it is "not obligatory") to attend the mosque, congregational prayers, funerals and *jihād*.[123] Muṭahharī thus takes up the *ḥadīth* controversies over confinement and — moving in the opposite direction from Mawdūdī — settles them in favour of women. This opens the way for him to step even further away from the norms of the Prophetic Reports by — and here is the crucial turn — shifting the emphasis of *ḥijāb* from confinement to covering. *Ḥijāb*, for Muṭahharī, thus comes to mean essentially clothing, with limitation on space reduced from a divine command to a moral ideal (not fully attainable by all) of housewifery and modesty. He disposes of the phrase of Qur'an 33:53 often thought to dictate seclusion, "ask them from behind a curtain (*ḥijāb*)," by ruling that it refers only to "people who should not enter the House of the Holy Prophet," and thus "has nothing to do with our discussion." He means that it is one of that class of verses recognized by the exegetes as belonging to a particular historical situation and therefore does not lay down a universal command of *purdah*.[124] He also argues that even if covering the hands and face might seem preferable, since they are not less attractive than other parts of the body, uncovering them is nevertheless one of the "allowable expediencies." This is because God does not impose unreasonable hardship (*ḥaraj*) on believers, and a woman, in order to "fulfill her duties," must move about unencumbered in daily life, including driving and holding a job.[125] In this last statement, Muṭahharī neatly circumvents the traditional, *ḥadīth*-based rationale of female *fitnah* for confinement by attacking the problem of women's space obliquely through the hands-and-face argument. The statement is also an instance of the relatively free reasoning sometimes seen among Shī'ī *'ulamā'* in modern times.

The Ayatollah still accepts the *ḥadīth* idea that men are naturally and inevitably stirred to passion by even quite casual contact with women. But he turns away — and this is also crucial — from the companion *fitnah* proposition that women are compulsive temptresses. This allows him to consider women's covering *from men* sufficient to avert most dangers. To put it another way: women are, apart from the burden of their natural attraction, guiltless. They are even naturally pure and innocent, qualities they demonstrate through their covering. They can therefore be trusted to move in public space. Men, however, remain naturally volatile, and thus in order to protect themselves, women must carefully veil. This calculation completely reverses the gender psychology of the *ḥadīth* and *ḥadīth*-based literature, according to which women are the primary, if not exclusive, bearers of sexual guilt, and therefore obliged to stay out of sight.

The "modern" view of *ḥijāb* with its twin propositions that *ḥijāb* means defensive covering (not seclusion) and that the instincts primarily of men (not women) have to be managed, had already been widely absorbed by Muṭahharī's time as the perennial and authentic position of Islam.[126] He himself, of course, is aware of its novelty in relation to the Prophetic Reports. This is why he carefully deals with the *ḥadīth*s by passing in silence over the extremely problematic *fitnah* texts, and then balancing, rather like an inverted pyramid, an argument for free movement on the protest and necessity *ḥadīth*s. It seems to me, however, that most neo-conservative Muslims — a hazy category, but let us say those who would consider at least some free movement for women desirable, but do not view themselves as liberals — who hold and even passionately espouse the now nearly universal modern position are generally not so aware. The members of this neo-conservative majority, in the way natural to non-learned belief in any tradition, relate very strongly to the *ḥadīth* scriptures as a symbolic whole. But if they read the texts, they would, I imagine, be dismayed to find the *fitnah-purdah* complex very clearly outlined, with no overt support for their own ideals. If *ḥijāb* as conceived by the majority of Muslims in modern times is to prove intellectually defensible and durable, there will have to be a serious effort, I think, also on the part of neo-conservatives to delve into and reinterpret the *ḥadīth*.

Lack of Liberal Engagement with the *Ḥadīth*

Conservatives, especially learned conservatives, approach the issue of *ḥijāb* in the *ḥadīth* as they do the *ḥadīth* in general — as a project in which they expect success. The attitude of the liberals to *ḥadīth* seems to be based on the same premise. That is, they have come to regard the *ḥadīth* literature as the certain strength and preserve of the conservatives, so they have tried, in different ways, to downgrade or circumvent it.

Why the response of the liberal wing in modern times to the Prophetic Reports leaned in this direction is too long a tale to tell here in full.[127] Certainly, the quantity and thus relative specificity of the *ḥadīth*s, when compared with the text of the Qur'an, was one root cause of liberal reactions. Given this characteristic, restrictions unattractive to liberalism would be present and even well developed in the *ḥadīth*s, while absent or only distantly implied in the Revelation. Consequently, the *ḥadīth* came to be regarded by liberals as the font of medieval norms falsely attached to religion after the age of the Prophet and Revelation — norms that would have to be shed for Islam to renew itself and Muslims to rise up again among the nations.

This view of *ḥadīth* was readily absorbed by feminist hermeneutics. For feminist hermeneutics also asserts that religious texts have been interpreted in ahistorical, dogmatic terms (by men), for which the remedy is recovery (by feminists) of authentic text and original meaning. Most text-based writing on Islam by Muslim women now depends, consciously or unconsciously, on this assumption. The result is that *ḥadīth* has been viewed by liberal feminists not as a resource, but as a prime obstacle to construction of a positive and progressive view of women. Even when, as does happen, *ḥadīth* texts are cited by liberal feminists in support of their views, this is done only in a very piecemeal way by selecting a few apparently favourable texts. A defined, global approach to extracting positive content — that is, an applied theory of *ḥadīth* — is missing.[128]

The Orientalist critique of the authenticity of *ḥadīth* may also have served as a catalyst for formation of the negative liberal view.[129] The historicity of the texts having been called into question by what must have seemed at the time to be the overwhelming force of "modern science," many liberal apologists apparently decided that they would concur, and resorted to the strategy of building an alternate case for authenticity on the text of the Qur'an. The reactions of modernists to the perceived problem of authenticity were radical, ranging from a search for a *Sunnah* of the Prophet transmitted and defined by something other than the *ḥadīth* texts to the wholesale rejection of the *ḥadīth* literature not only on the premise that it is a largely false record, but also that the function of the Prophet Muhammad himself was limited to delivering the Revelation and ruling the Islamic community in his time, rather than setting an infallible example for all future generations.[130] All these approaches tended to disregard the partnership of the Qur'an and *ḥadīth-Sunnah* envisioned in classical legal theory.

Perhaps the most important factor, however, in liberal and feminist downgrading of the *ḥadīth* has been the simple matter of education. The *ḥadīth* texts are vast and, as I have said, "difficult of access." In addition, the traditional science of the *ḥadīth* with its reliance on testing of the *isnād* and other highly technical matters is a specialized knowledge requiring extensive training, and this long and specialized training is most readily (in fact, probably exclusively) available in traditional circles. Liberals are unlikely to have been formed in these circles; a liberal in these days can almost, in fact, be defined as someone who has not had a traditional education or any significant contact with it.[131] The Prophetic Reports have consequently been viewed as the strength and preserve of the *'ulamā'*, simply because it has been so in the past by virtue of background and education. In the meantime, the *'ulamā'*, not surprisingly, hold and promote the same perception, basing their claim to authority partly upon it, while liberal modernists counter that claim by turning aside from the *ḥadīth* itself.

By now, it is likely clear that I regard the lack of full engagement with *ḥadīth* on the part of contemporary liberals to be both a strategic and cultural mistake. The *ḥadīth* in the intellectual heritage of Islam is not less, after all, than one of the two scriptural supports on which the tradition stands. The liberal approach seems to me to be rather like amputating a limb without first inspecting it to see where the blood still flows and how it might be rehabilitated. The *ḥadīth* is also quite manipulable, since the science traditionally applied to it allows the ranking and cancelling of reports, on the basis of both reliability of the *isnād* and of the text. (In addition, such judgments of reliability are, in the final analysis, highly personal.) Most decisively, the *ḥadīth* is profoundly embedded in the piety of ordinary Muslims, so that their sensibilities are liable to be inspired by reference to the words of the Prophet, and this is ultimately the audience that needs to be captured.

The corpus of the Prophetic Reports contains — obviously — much material that is overtly positive; the mass of exhortatory *ḥadīth*s concerning personal and social ethics come readily to mind. This includes some material that is positive for women. There are, for instance, numerous reports that elaborate the anti-divorce ethic of the Qur'an,[132] almost all passages having to do with divorce in the Qur'an being already of this kind. There is also a significant bundle of *ḥadīth*s promising reward for the nurture and support of daughters[133] — again following on the Qur'an[134] — as well as on men's obligation and reward for providing sufficient and consistent maintenance (*nafaqah*) for their families.[135] Scriptural statements concerning rape and limiting purity restrictions surrounding menstruation can both be found in the *ḥadīth*.

I will describe here in detail just one instance of a relatively overt potential of the *ḥadīth*. This concerns the critical issue of physical violence. Apropos of the famous verse of the Qur'an (4:34) stating that the rebellion (*nushūz*) of women is to be punished, if other measures have failed, by hitting, the Prophet is made to say, in a dictum that has become famous among Muslims — "Strike them in a way that is not painful" (*ghayr mubarriḥ*).[136] There is a great deal of concern in the *ḥadīth* with moderating the Qur'an on this point; Bukhārī presents, in the *K. al-nikāḥ* (Book of Marriage), a whole chapter (*bāb*) on "That Which Is Abhorred in the Striking of Women, and God's Saying [in the Qur'an] 'Strike Them,' Meaning a Blow That Is Not Painful."

We do find the following contrary words attributed to the Prophet: "A man shall not be asked [that is, not reproached by God on the Day of Judgment] about his beating of his wife."[137] There is, however, a much better-attested report that accords with the general concern of the *ḥadīth* (and also of Islamic law) to limit violence inflicted on vulnerable persons. In this *ḥadīth* the Prophet's wife, 'Ā'ishah, says: "The Messenger of God, peace be upon him, absolutely never struck any of his wives or any servant, and he never raised his hand against anything except to fight in the way of God. ..."[138] Two views of hitting seem to have made their way here into the *ḥadīth*, and the dispute is again the subject of a drama — in fact, a protest *ḥadīth* — featuring 'Umar (on whose authority the "shall not be asked" *ḥadīth* cited above also rests). It is reported that the Prophet said: "Do not strike the maidservants (*imā'*) of God." But then 'Umar came to him and said: "The women have become impudent against their husbands!" Thus the Prophet permitted that they be hit. Subsequently, many women — according to one version, seventy women on that very day — came to the Prophet's wives complaining of their husbands. When the Prophet learned of this, he remarked, "Those [who hit] are not the best of you [men]."[139]

There is, in addition, a bundle of *ḥadīth*s that forbids damaging the face; this is a clear Islamic norm according to the *Sunnah* of the Prophet. The rule that one should avoid damaging the face is a general one.[140] The Prophetic Reports seem to be especially concerned, however, with persons in vulnerable positions. Thus it is "one of the rights of a wife over her husband" that he not strike her in the face.[141] In fact, it is forbidden according to numerous *ḥadīth*s to hurt the faces of not only women, but also slaves, those undergoing the *ḥudūd* punishments and even opponents in battle, as well as animals.[142] The face must not be mutilated, a *ḥadīth* says, because "God created Adam in His image."[143] Damaging the face is thus, according to the Prophet of Islam, an insult to the Creator Himself. These two complementary bundles of *ḥadīth*s might be useful in a scriptural appeal to counter the practice, apparently stemming from tribal and familial "honour" conflicts and recently the subject of campaigns by human rights groups in Pakistan, of mutilating the faces of women. [144]

The question of *ḥijāb*, from a liberal point of view, is not so overt. But this, of course, is exactly the kind of challenge for which feminist hermeneutics was made. Creative interpretation, including decisions about strategies and the measure of suspicion and imagination to be applied, are for those inside the tradition, and therefore outside the scope of this essay.[145] Since, however, I did not find any extensive liberal-feminist treatment of the *ḥijāb ḥadīth*s, or indeed of the *ḥadīth* as a whole, I have arranged the material in the first section to serve as a hypothetical illustration. (I could, of course, just as well have arranged it to support conservative views.) There it will be seen that even the simplest excavation of texts, digging through layers of *ḥadīth*-based belles lettres, commentary, collections and the *ḥadīth* texts themselves, reveals a struggle to be heard by other voices and the possible outline of a different set of norms than those most often communicated by the apparent sense.

Excavation is an initial technique that has its limitations. As another cautious illustration, one might compare the *ḥadīth* with the Qur'an. This would be one way of dealing with the highly problematic *fitnah* complex. It is evident, or at least seems so me, that the woman-*fitnah ḥadīth*s are a misogynist transmogrification of statements in the Revelation. The Qur'an exhorts the believers not to value wealth and worldly attachments more than God and His religion. It says, for instance: "If your fathers, sons, brothers, wives, tribes, wealth [and so on] are more dear to you than God ..." (9:24); "Know that your wealth and children are *fitnah*, while with God there is great reward" (8:28 and 64:15); "There are among your wives and children enemies to you; thus beware them ... [for] your wealth and offspring are *fitnah* ..." (44:14-15) and other similar verses. There is, to be sure, a large bundle of texts in the *ḥadīth* that legitimately continues the Qur'anic motif of attachment to wealth and family. This is an important theme of the Prophetic Reports. The much smaller number of female *fitnah ḥadīth*s, however, divert the exhortations of the Qur'an in a quite different direction by singling out women, and then, strangely, recasting *fitnah* — which in the Qur'an never means anything other than political upheaval, plot, test or punishment — as sexual mischief.[146]

In fact, the *ḥadīth*'s entire extravagant view of gender relations has but a slender basis in the Qur'an. The verses that define male relatives to whom women may "reveal their adornment" (24:31) and with whom they may "converse freely" (33:55) surely do imply some peril in the attractions of women. But the emphasis falls, nevertheless, on modesty and social propriety, not, as in the *ḥadīth*, on the character of woman or excitability of man. Other exhortations in the Qur'an to modest behaviour are — as is quite typical of the Qur'an in general — moderate and gender-neutral.

A holistic rather than atomistic treatment of the *ḥadīth* — that is, a search for basic norms that transcend the letter of particular texts — might also yield results. This method has already been applied to the Qur'an.[147] In the case of *ḥijāb*, the dominant and overarching themes of the Prophetic Reports relating to the body are surely ostentation, decoration and nakedness (in the true sense). As I have already remarked, almost all *ḥadīth*s regarding the body are of these kinds, while women's covering for the sake of modesty and sexual peace, including covering the hair, really owns no field of *ḥadīth*s of its own. In addition, most reports regarding ostentation, decoration and nakedness are aimed at men, not women. Men's dress, it seems, was at one time at least as problematic as women's. Thus it could be argued that the overall *ḥadīth* standard for clothing, a standard applicable to both sexes, consisted of nothing more than a kind of pragmatic moderation. The believers should, according to the Prophetic

Reports, try as much as they can to cover their nakedness, but they should not, at the same time, dress ostentatiously. The Qur'anic words telling women to draw their garments close while not publicly exhibiting their ornaments simply point (so it could be argued) to the same basic norm. A similar dress code emphasizing utilitarian moderation has been typical — to add a comparative dimension to the argument — of many religious and even political reforming movements.

These are a few arguments that might be made about clothing. The *ḥijāb* of confinement — the primary *ḥadīth* meaning, in my view, of *ḥijāb* — is more problematic. Confinement is much more deeply embedded in the texts. It also represents a real and inflexible restriction, unlike dress, which is a portable and flexible sign that may be construed as signifying any of a range of values. Liberals often assert that the rule of *ḥijāb* seclusion, along with the Qur'anic exhortation "Stay in your houses" (33:33), was meant to apply, as stated in the Qur'an where God says "You are not like any other women" (33: 32), only to the wives of the Prophet. This claim, I feel, is weakened by the fact that the example of the wives is featured throughout the *ḥadīth*, for the simple reason that their example is a model for women, just as the Prophet in gender-specific practice is a model for men.[148]

Some scriptural evidence, on the other hand, could be adduced in favour of the argument that the most severe limitations on women's space and covering were promoted by ʻUmar, somewhat against the inclinations of the Prophet and in the face of resistance by women, including the models for all women, the wives of the Prophet. To this may be added the texts from the genre of "protest *ḥadīth*s" — a literature of resistance in subtle form within the scriptures — that argue that the Prophet's own conception of women's space was more relaxed than imagined by later generations. The permission for mobility in case of necessity might also be employed to free women from confinement by arguing that the necessity to move about is much greater today than it used to be. Muṭahharī appeals to this argument, and *ḍarūrah* (necessity in the legal sense) is currently being invoked in innovative legal arguments of all kinds. There are also a few *ḥadīth*s that portray the wives interacting with men in situations in which they could not have been confined. These too seem to be traces left in the oral tradition of a suppressed gender norm, and the narrators or collectors are aware of the anomaly, as they add in each case: "This was before the *ḥijāb* came down."[149] The *ḥijāb* of seclusion, finally, rests in the Prophetic Reports largely on the idea of the "dangerous feminine," that is on *fitnah*. A blow at *fitnah* is in terms of the *ḥadīth* a blow at seclusion. Thus it may be argued that the luxuriant growth of *fitnah* in the commentaries, *ḥadīth* literature and modern conservative discourse is clearly out of proportion to the *fitnah* of the *ḥadīth* itself, while its roots in the *ḥadīth* are thrown into doubt in turn by the Qur'an.

The liberal position on women's clothing is, as I understand it, that covering (though perhaps not modesty) is a matter of personal choice — even that veiling is not a vital issue for women or Islam at all and has had the unfortunate consequence of diverting attention from the real systemic problems women face daily. The liberal position on freedom of movement takes cancellation of *purdah* as only a preliminary to a vision in which women play a full role in society, unhampered by any necessary division between male and female. This position depends, in the final analysis, on an ideal of voluntary restraint — of a society, in effect, free from sexual guilt. It would be difficult, I think, to extract this proposition from the Qur'an, the *ḥadīth*, or the law on the basis of strict textual criticism. (Freedom from sexual guilt is, in any case, a difficult proposition for humanity in general.) The potential for building a durable, rooted foundation for ideas such as these would appear to lie in hermeneutical procedures more radical than the "simple excavation" illustrated in this essay, so that the challenge for liberals becomes to develop and — most important — gain wide acceptance for those procedures, without skipping over or losing hold of the tradition. And this challenge, as it happens, is not for liberals alone, as the accent on *fitnah* and *purdah* evident in a literal reading of the *ḥadīth* also clashes (as I have argued) with the values and world view of the neo-conservative Muslim majority.

Conclusion

The author of this essay happens to believe that interpretation consists of the affective and creative interaction of the interpreter with the text, rather than the discovery of demonstrable truths. From this point of view (in my case, an outsider's view), all interpretations are valid on their own grounds and taken in their own terms. Thus conservatives, liberals and all shades between can produce viable exegeses if only they endeavour to do so. I believe I have adequately demonstrated that conservative understandings of at least one set of *ḥadīth* texts — the *ḥadīth*s concerning *ḥijāb* — are not inherently more plausible than others. Every exegesis, as it tries to build on a text that inevitably does not conform entirely to its desires, has to bridge or leap over certain gaps. And those gaps may, in turn, be tested by competing interpretations.

Such dialogical views of hermeneutics, which are currently popular in Western feminist circles, are not, however, likely to gain favour soon among Muslims. Current Islamic thought, including reforming and modernist thought, tends instead, quite different from the classical tradition,[150] to extract from the text exclusive "truths." Contemporary thought is, in addition, strongly biased toward historical positivism. This second characteristic seems to be a legitimate inheritance from the tradition, as the impulse of Islam has ever been to authenticate its truths historically — an impulse clearly displayed in both the content (carefully preserved anecdote) and form (concatenated chain of authorities) of the *ḥadīth*s themselves. While both conservatives and liberals focus on verities and verifiable history, they do so rather differently (here speaking quite generally, since approaches are sometimes mixed), and I will now attempt a broad characterization that might help to put the material in the last section in larger perspective.

Conservative, and certainly learned-conservative, approaches to the scriptures tend to be properly scriptural. The conservatives search in the text for the truths of command and prohibition, which are understood to be distillable — in the case of learned conservatives, distillable with the aid of the Qur'anic or *ḥadīth* sciences — rather than immediately accessible (though no less manifest for that). The liberals, on the other hand, treat the Qur'an not as a series of injunctions and prohibitions, but as a succession of fairly evident statements confirming basic values such as equality and modesty. Verses such as the *ḥijāb* passages are taken "at face value," so that, for instance, "draw your cloaks about you" will mean for liberals no more than what those words apparently communicate. This approach fits well with the liberal disposition to view *fiqh* and the other layers of exegesis as accretions.

As for historical positivism, liberals, feminists and conservatives alike believe in an ideal past and the recoverability of that past. The first two groups, however, are inclined to search the record for single and discrete examples of practices and personalities that might confirm their position. They do sometimes find these in the Prophetic Reports, although, as I have remarked in a few instances above, the examples adduced seem sometimes not to be apropos, a result, perhaps, of seizing on single instances rather than reading reports in the context of others with similar themes. The favourite texts, however, of this group are not *ḥadīth*s, but the rich heritage of Islamic biographies and histories. For it is here that early Islamic society and the lives of Muslim women within it are treated most expansively (such works being part of an attempt to set down a full record, rather than to establish, through anecdote, a narrower ideal). Thus the project of the liberals is to use the Qur'an and the historical record, including, where it fits, *ḥadīth* as history, to draw attention to past realities they believe to have been buried and obscured.

The conservatives, on the other hand, assume that the ideal historical example, as embodied in the original practice of the Prophet and Companions, is to be found mostly or exclusively in the *ḥadīth* and *Sunnah*, by delving into the fine points of the text and corpus. I have remarked on instances in which the spirit of certain *ḥadīth*s appears to differ from that of the Qur'an, or in which the *ḥadīth* appears to have been bent by successive generations of male scholars to their own purposes. I have also commented on the absence of canonical *ḥadīth* material having to do with widely accepted norms of *ḥijāb* such as covering the hair. The reader should, however, keep in mind that the Prophetic Reports, while they are certainly regarded by conservatives as a scripture laying down an ideal pattern of life, are also viewed as the remains of a historical record. They are not understood to be a series of certain edicts pronounced by the Prophet and the Muslims who lived in his age. It is thus considered necessary to infer norms, to piece together the evidence, as it were, much as a historian would do.

From this point of view, Abū Dāwūd's added chapter headings are not tendentious. They merely indicate his own perception, as a competent *ḥadīth* expert, of the subject the *ḥadīth* is aimed at — or one of the subjects, since several dicta may be extracted from a single text, for which reason, as one can see from the notes to this essay, a report may appear under several very different titles. (As far as Abū Dāwūd is concerned, it should also be appreciated that his collection is accompanied by critical notes on the degree of reliability of different reports. Like the *ḥadīth* experts in general, he does not claim equal and absolute authority for each report.) If, then, the challenge presented by the *ḥadīth* is, as conservatives think, one of extraction and reconstruction, one would have to say that they are able to present not only a very good case for limiting women's space, but also a good case for covering. The case for covering only requires more extensive piecing together, inferences, supplementary reports from the non-canonical collections and books of exegesis and (typical of traditional Islamic discourse, and illustrated several times in the first section) etymological arguments from the Arabic. One must also admit that covering the body when moving outside restricted space does seem a logical consequence of seclusion, as well as of limited contact between the sexes, a rule established in detail in the Qur'an itself (e.g., 24:31). One could say that the *'ulamā'* and modern conservatives are simply filling in the gaps — that they are engaged, in fact, in piecing together practices that were so completely natural to the social life of the early community that they left only faint traces in the record.

A study of *ḥadīth* through the *ḥijāb* issue also confirms — a circumstance any historian of religion will recognize — that norms regarded by believers as eternal truths directly dictated by their scriptures (in the case of *ḥijāb*, for instance, covering the hair and the sexual psychology currently favoured by neo-conservatives) often have quite a different background. Though religion must present itself, at least to the popular mind, as stable, like other social phenomena, it constantly changes and evolves. Thus the relation of some norms to the texts to which they are routinely attributed may actually be very tenuous. The loyalty of believers to the scriptures nevertheless remains strong, for scriptures function primarily as symbols and only secondarily as real textual inspiration. (This symbolic or emotive relation to scripture may be especially strong in a tradition such as Sunnī Islam, in which the gloss has very little prestige.) The basic task of interpretation is, in fact, as I have suggested above, to bridge the inevitable gap between accepted or desired norms and the all-important scriptural symbol. In the case of *ḥadīth*, the conservatives continue to undertake this task, while the liberals resort to the odd alternative of attempting to curtail or discard the symbol itself.

This investigation also suggests that the choice of scriptures on which to found a discourse may be dictated not so much by their content or potential as by prior, external factors. There is (in my view) no substantive reason why contemporary liberals should not use the *ḥadīth* to their advantage; that choice has been dictated by incidental factors such as education.

This essay has been about the dynamics of interpretation in relation to *ḥadīth*, and not about history; my aim, as I said at the beginning, is not to extract from the *ḥadīth* a social reality supposedly existing at the time of the Prophet, though this is, of course, the aim of believers. Nevertheless, the results of this study suggest that the *ḥadīth* texts may preserve some glimmer of history. It is in the nature of oral tradition, after all, not only to alter, elaborate and add to its stock of materials, but also to retain the core or trace of anything that comes to it, as a culturally valuable, even sacred artifact with the power to confer authority.

The case of *ḥijāb* clearly reveals this trait in the *ḥadīth*. Comparison of variant texts (which the collectors, fortunately, make it their business to preserve) uncovers layers of emendations. We can see that ideas of *ḥijāb* evolved and were sometimes controversial. Are we in any part of this on the trail of a primitive Islam, that is, an Islam reaching back to the first few generations (as the *isnād*s claim) or to the Prophet himself? Some material may, I think, preserve a memory of those early times. The texts that treat *isti'dhān* ("permission to enter") and relate the efforts of the early Muslims to clothe themselves while there was little cloth available seem to reflect the social realities of a society making the transition to a more settled, private and affluent life. This matches the circumstances of the first generations as the conquests gathered in sudden and unaccustomed wealth. That these anecdotes are of no real use for justifying the mores of the times when they were collected adds, I think, to the argument for their much greater age. They must have been well outdated when they were received, but they were nevertheless handed on and piously preserved. We have seen a very serious case of a disjunction between medieval Islamic mores and the content of the canonical *ḥadīth* in the case of covering. There is no real attention to women's covering and virtually no mention of their hair and *'awrah*, but much concern with the covering — or at least decency — of men.[151] It is a sign of some integrity of the canonical collections and of the critical apparatus that produced them that bundles of *ḥadīth*s supporting this axial norm were not gathered in, while the outdated texts on men's *'awrah* survived. Abū Dāwūd does manipulate his stock in several ways to make it appear (almost) as if covering is supported by the *Sunnah*, but far from allowing his evident desire for covering to substantially influence his selection, he introduces only one *ḥadīth* that might be decisive (the *ḥadīth* of Asmā'), being careful at the same time to note its weaknesses.[152] When one ranges, using a database, outside the canonical collections, hair and covering *ḥadīth*s multiply. The "soundness" of the *Ṣaḥīḥ* and *Sunan* collections seems to have some basis in fact, which can be detected from content without entering into the question of the reality of the *isnād*s.

Notes

1 By "conservative" and "liberal," I mean only a rough measure of either more or less attachment to traditional gender norms. Behind these convenient terms lies a whole range of responses to the issue of *ḥijāb* of varied content and not always easily categorized. A few of these responses are described in this essay, and more throughout the book.

2 The base used for this essay is Ṣakhr, *Mawsū'at al-ḥadīth al-sharīf*, 2nd ed. (2.0), 1 CD with commentaries on the same disk. I have identified *ḥadīths* by Book (*kitāb*) and *ḥadīth* number to help the reader find them in any edition, including (since I also translate the names of Books) in translations. There are, however, different numbering systems and some casting about might be needed. In order to save space, the chapter (*bāb*) is given, in Arabic and English, only when that might throw light on the context or meaning of a report. For Ibn Ḥanbal, which is not, like the six "sound" collections, arranged according to subject but rather transmitter, I have cited *ḥadīths* by *musnad* (that is "original transmitter," thus the title of the collection, "Musnad Ibn Ḥanbal").

3 For example, Umm Salamah was asked what clothes a woman was to pray in and she answered: "She should pray in the veil (*khimār*) and enveloping shirt (*dir' sābigh*) [of a length that] hides the tops of her feet" (Abū Dāwūd, *Sunan*, *K. al-ṣalāh* [Book of Prayer], *ḥadīths* 544 and 545). 'Ā'ishah remembered that once as the Prophet entered her quarters, a girl servant of hers tried to hide herself from him. "Has she menstruated?" he asked. 'Ā'ishah replied in the affirmative, and so the Prophet tore some cloth from his turban and said: "Veil yourself with this [when you pray]" or, according to some versions, he said: "The prayer of a menstruating woman is not accepted except with a veil (*khimār*)" (Ibn Mājah, *Sunan*, *K. al-ṭahārah* [Book of Ritual Purity], *ḥadīth* 646; Tirmidhī, *Sunan* (also known as *Jāmi'*), *K. al-ṣalāh* [Book of Prayer], *ḥadīths* 344, 346 and 547; Abū Dāwūd, *Sunan*, *K. al-ṣalāh*, *ḥadīth* 546; Ibn Ḥanbal, *Musnad*, *Bāqī musnad al-Anṣār*, *ḥadīths* 24,012, 24,649 and 25,028. A discussion of women's dress for prayer is found in Ibn Taymīyah's (d. 1328) *Ḥijāb al-mar'ah wa-libāsuhā fī al-ṣalāh* (Women's Covering and Her Clothing in Prayer), edited by Muḥammad Nāṣir al-Dīn al-Albānī (Beirut: al-Maktab al-Islāmī, 1405/1985).

4 Kulaynī's *al-Uṣūl al-kāfī*, Ibn Bābawayh's *Man lā yaḥduruhu al-faqīh* and Ṭūsī's *Tahdhīb al-aḥkām* and *Istibṣār* are reckoned as the four "canonical" works. The first two were collected in the tenth century, the last two in the eleventh.

5 Bukhārī, *Ṣaḥīḥ*, *K. al-ṣalāh* (Book of Prayer), *ḥadīth* 366.

6 *Ḥadīths* related to permitted, forbidden and ideal clothing for men and women are gathered in the last chapters of Abū Sar'ī Muḥammad, *Zīnat al-mar'ah wa-libāsuhā fī al-kitāb wa-al-sunnah* (Cairo: Maktabat al-Turāth al-Islāmī, 1985).

7 For example, the well-known conservative scholar Muhammad Nāṣir al-Dīn al-Albānī in his *Ḥijāb al-mar'ah al-muslimah fī al-kitāb wa-al-sunnah* (Beirut: Manshūrāt al-Maktab al-Islāmī, 1385/1965 or 1966), 2nd ed., revised, 16.

8 For example, Bukhārī, *Ṣaḥīḥ*, in the *K. al-ṣalāh* (Book of Prayer), see *Bāb mā yasturu min al-'awrah* (Chapter of That of the '*Awrah* Which Is to Be Covered) and *Bāb mā yudhkar fī al-fakhidh* (Chapter of That Which Is Mentioned Concerning the Thigh); Tirmidhī, *Sunan*, *K. al-adab* (Book of Etiquette), *ḥadīths*

2719–2722; Abū Dāwūd, *Sunan, K. al-ṣalāh* (Book of Prayer), *ḥadīth* 495; Ibn Mājah, *Sunan, K. mā ja'a fī al-janā'iz* (Book of That Which Has Been Transmitted Concerning Funerals), *ḥadīth* 1449; Ibn Ḥanbal, *Musnad, Musnad al-Makkīyīn, Ḥadīth Jarhad al-Aslamī, ḥadīth*s 15,361–15,368; ibid., *Bāqī musnad al-mukaththirīn, ḥadīth* 13,265 (how Moses was careful to cover his *'awrah*), and in many other places in this and the other collections. A secondary meaning of *'awrah* in the *ḥadīth* is "shameful moral fault," e.g., Tirmidhī, *Sunan, K. al-birr wa-al-ṣilah* (Book of Righteousness and Kindly Relations), *ḥadīth* 1955; Abū Dāwūd, *Sunan, K. al-adab* (Book of Etiquette), *ḥadīth* 4242; Ibn Ḥanbal, *Musnad, Musnad al-Anṣār, Ḥadīth Zayd ibn Thābit, ḥadīth* 20,678.

9 We will see below how the prophet tears up robes taken as booty in order to distribute the cloth to the Muslim men and their wives. Another *ḥadīth* tells how a new convert's garment did not cover him sufficiently while he prayed. A woman complained that she could see his *'awrah*, and thus he was given "an 'Umānī shirt." Ever after he remembered that he had never at any time after his conversion felt such joy as he did that day upon acquiring that garment (Abū Dāwūd, *Sunan, K. al-Ṣalāt* [Book of Prayer], *ḥadīth* 495).

10 Q. 24:33: "Tell the believing women ... not to reveal their adornment save to their own husbands (etc.) ... or children who are not aware of women's *'awrāt* (plural)."

11 This is leaving aside the much-cited *ḥadīth*, aimed at same-sex arousal, that warns men not to look on the *'awrah* of men, nor women on the *'awrah* of women. For example, Tirmidhī, *Sunan, K. al-adab* (Book of Etiquette), *ḥadīth* 2717; Ibn Mājah, *Sunan, K. al-ṭahārah* (Book of Ritual Purity), *ḥadīth* 653. A *ḥadīth* with a similar intent, also much-cited, forbids two men or women from lying together under the same covering.

12 Tirmidhī, *Sunan, K. al-riḍā'* (Book of Foster Relationship), *ḥadīth* 1093.

13 Abū Dāwūd, *Sunan, K. al-libās* (Book of Clothing), *ḥadīth* 3589; Ibn Ḥanbal, *Musnad, Musnad al-Anṣār, Ḥadīth Usāmah ibn Zayd, ḥadīth* 20,787.

14 Muslim, *Ṣaḥīḥ, K. al-jannah wa-ṣifat na'īmihā* (Book of Paradise and Description of Its Ease), *ḥadīth* 5098; ibid., *K. al-libās wa-al-zīnah* (Book of Clothing and Adornment), *ḥadīth* 3971; Ibn Ḥanbal, *Musnad, Bāqī musnad al-mukaththirīn, ḥadīth*s 8311 and 9303.

15 Muslim's commentator, Nawawī (d. 1277), says: "The *ḥadīth* is one of the miracles of prophethood, for these two types [of persons] have now appeared and do exist" (*Sharḥ Nawawī*, commentary on the *ḥadīth* cited in the previous note).

16 The large group of *ḥadīth*s prohibiting "ripping open garments at the neck" has to do not with necklines per se but with Islam's disapproval of self-mutilation and exhibition of sorrow, e.g., Muslim's chapter in his *K. al-īmān* (Book of Faith): "Prohibition against beating one's cheeks, rending one's garments at the neck (*juyūb*), and making supplication in the style of pre-Islamic times (*Jāhilīyah*)." Note that the chapter headings of Muslim's work are likely not his own, but have been added after him.

17 Tirmidhī, *Sunan, K. al-libās* (Book of Clothing), *ḥadīth* 1653; Nasā'ī, *Sunan, K. al-zīnah* (Book of Adornment), *ḥadīth*s 5241, 5242 and 5244; Abū Dāwūd, *Sunan, K. al-libās, ḥadīth*s 3590 and 3591; Ibn Mājah, *Sunan, K. al-libās, ḥadīth*s 3570 and 3573 ("legs"); Ibn Ḥanbal, *Musnad, Musnad al-mukaththirīn min al-ṣaḥābah, Musnad 'Abd Allāh ibn 'Umar ibn al-Khaṭṭāb, ḥadīth*s 4454, 4543 and 4926; ibid., *Musnad al-mukaththirīn min al-ṣaḥābah, ḥadīth* 5379 ("*'awrah*"); ibid., *Bāqī*

musnad al-Anṣār, Ḥadīth Sayyidah 'Ā'ishah, ḥadīths 23,329 and 23,771 ("legs," and on the authority of 'Ā'ishah instead of Umm Salamah); ibid., *Bāqī musnad al-Anṣār, Ḥadīth Umm Salamah zawj al-nabī, ḥadīths* 25,322, 25,418 and 25,459.

[18] Tirmidhī, *Sunan, K. al-libās* (Book of Clothing), *ḥadīth* 1654.

[19] Tirmidhī, *Sunan, K. al-ṭahārah* (Book of Ritual Purity), *ḥadīth* 133; Abū Dāwūd, *Sunan, K. al-ṭahārah, ḥadīth* 326; Ibn Mājah, *Sunan, K. al-ṭahārah, ḥadīth* 524; Ibn Ḥanbal, *Musnad, Bāqī musnad al-Anṣār, Ḥadīth Umm Salamah zawj al-nabī, ḥadīths* 25,283 and 25,464.

[20] Parallel to the question asked by Abū Bakr: "What if my hem drags down accidentally?" (Bukhārī, *Ṣaḥīḥ, K. al-manāqib* [Book of Outstanding Characteristics], *ḥadīth* 3392, and in a few other places in the collections). The Prophet's answer: "That does not count against you, since you do not do it out of pride."

[21] *Sunan, K. al-libās* (Book of Clothing), *ḥadīth* 3580.

[22] He points out that the link to 'Ā'ishah, Khālid ibn Durayk, was not born in her time (*lam yudrik*).

[23] Ṭabarī, *Kitāb jāmi' al-bayān fī tafsīr al-Qur'ān* (with the *Raghā'ib al-furqān* of Nīsābūrī on the margin), 30 vols. (Beirut: Dār al-Fikr, 1398/1978), VIII, 92–94.

[24] One can, however, find these outside the canonical collections.

[25] Muslim, *Ṣaḥīḥ, K. al-salām* (Book of Greeting), *ḥadīth* 4087; Abū Dāwūd, *Sunan, K. al-libās* (Book of Clothing), *ḥadīth* 3581; Ibn Mājah, *K. al-ṭibb* (Book of Medicine), *ḥadīth* 3471.

[26] Chapter on God's Saying "Draw Close Their *Jalābīb*"; Chapter on That Which May Show of a Woman's *Zīnah*; Chapter on the Slave Seeing the Hair of his Mistress; Chapter on God's Saying: "Those Who Are Not Possessed of Desire"; Chapter on God's Saying: "Say to the Female Believers, Lower Your Gaze'"; Chapter on Marrying a Male to a Female Slave [the Result Is That She Covers Herself from Her Master]; Chapter on Veiling (*ikhtimār*); Chapter on Women Wearing a Qabāṭī Garment; Chapter on the Length of the Hem. These follow the Chapter on Women's Clothing, which is, however, about both women and men dressing in clothes appropriate to the opposite sex.

[27] Three collections contain one each: Muslim on "Women who Wear Revealing Clothes" (containing the *ḥadīth* with that phrase, discussed above), and Nasā'ī and Ibn Mājah on the "hemline" *ḥadīth*, also discussed above. N.B: Clothing material in Nasā'ī is included in his *K. al-zīnah* (Book of Ornament). Ibn Ḥanbal does not arrange his material by Books and chapters, but according to the original transmitters.

[28] Abū Dāwūd does himself note in his added comment that the dictum has to do with avoiding dressing like a man: *Sunan, K. al-libās* (Book of Clothing), *ḥadīth* 3588. The *ḥadīth* is otherwise found only in Ibn Ḥanbal: *Musnad, Bāqī musnad al-Anṣār, ḥadīths* 25,313, 25,328 and 25,399.

[29] Muslim, *Ṣaḥīḥ, K. al-ṭalāq* (Book of Divorce), *ḥadīths* 2711–2715 and in other places in this book; ibid., *K. al-fitan wa-ashrāṭ al-sā'ah* (Book of Sedition and Signs of the Hour), *ḥadīth* 5235; Tirmidhī, *Sunan, K. al-nikāḥ* (Book of Marriage), *ḥadīth* 1054; Nasā'ī, *K. al-nikāḥ, ḥadīths* 3170, 3185 and others; ibid., *K. al-ṭalāq, ḥadīths* 3350–3352 and others; Ibn Ḥanbal, *Musnad, Bāqī musnad al-Anṣār, ḥadīth* 25,851 and in other places in this section; ibid., *Min musnad al-qabā'il, ḥadīth* 26,057 and in other places in this section. The Prophet himself had

suggested that she stay in the house of the woman, but then thought better of it — apparently because he planned to marry her to a favourite Companion.

30 Tirmidhī, *Sunan*, *K. al-adab* (Book of Etiquette), *ḥadīth* 2702; Ibn Ḥanbal, *Musnad*, *Bāqī musnad al-Anṣār*, *ḥadīth* 25,326.

31 Abū Dāwūd, *Sunan*, *K. al-libās* (Book of Clothing), *ḥadīth* 3585.

32 Abū Dāwūd, *Sunan*, *K. al-libās* (Book of Clothing), *ḥadīth* 3583; Ibn Ḥanbal, *Musnad*, *Bāqī musnad al-Anṣār*, *ḥadīth* 24,029.

33 Abū Dāwūd, *Sunan*, *K. al-libās* (Book of Clothing), *ḥadīth* 3582. This *ḥadīth* relies on the theme, often encountered in Islamic literature, of Fāṭimah's poverty.

34 Nasā'ī, *Sunan*, *K. al-ṭahārah* (Book of Ritual Purity), *ḥadīth* 99. The narrator's remark about his slave status, clearly designed to explain why he was in such close contact with 'Ā'ishah when he was not a relative but merely "hired" by her, is added by the collector in a statement separate from the *ḥadīth*. The subject of the *ḥadīth* itself is not covering, but the man's testimony as to the method of the ablutions.

35 Tirmidhī, *Sunan*, *K. al-buyū'* (Book of Transactions of Sale), *ḥadīth* 1182; Abū Dāwūd, *Sunan*, *K. al-'itq* (Book of Manumission), *ḥadīth* 3427; Ibn Mājah, *Sunan*, *K. al-aḥkām* (Book of Legal Rulings), *ḥadīth* 2511; Ibn Ḥanbal, *Musnad*, *Bāqī musnad al-Anṣār*, *ḥadīths* 25,268, 25,411 and 25,436.

36 Muslim, *Ṣaḥīḥ*, *K. al-nikāḥ* (Book of Marriage), *ḥadīths* 2552 and 2553; Nasā'ī, *K. al-nikāḥ*, *ḥadīth* 3182; Ibn Ḥanbal, *Musnad*, *Bāqī musnad al-mukaththirīn*, *ḥadīths* 7506 and 7638: The Prophet advises a man intending to marry a woman of the Anṣār to look at her before, since "they have something in their eyes" (probably meaning, according to the commentators, opacity). The Prophet looks at a woman who offers herself to him in marriage: Bukhārī, *K. faḍā'il al-Qur'ān* (Book of Excellences of the Qur'an), *ḥadīth* 4642 and in many other places in this and the other collections. A man is allowed by the Prophet to look at a woman he has proposed to, so that affection or attraction may begin to grow up between them: Tirmidhī, *Sunan*, *K. al-nikāḥ*, *ḥadīth* 1008.

37 Bukhārī, *Ṣaḥīḥ*, *K. tafsīr al-Qur'ān* (Book of Exegesis of the Qur'an), titled with this *ḥadīth*; Abū Dāwūd, *Sunan*, *K. al-libās* (Book of Clothing), *ḥadīths* 3579 and 3577 (praises directed instead at the women of the Anṣār).

38 Bukhārī, *Ṣaḥīḥ*, *K. tafsīr al-Qur'ān* (Book of Exegesis of the Qur'an), *ḥadīth* 4387. "Hems" = *ḥawāshī*.

39 *al-Fatḥ al-Bārī'*, commentary on the *ḥadīth* referred to in the previous note.

40 The exegetes of the Qur'an, on the other hand, do commonly say that the women used to let their necks and upper bosoms show, and that when this verse came, they were commanded to cover those parts, that is, to "throw" their veils forward and over those parts.

41 The story of the "occasion of revelation" of the verse, that is, the historical context in which it was sent down, does not seem to have made its way into the canonical books. However, Wāḥidī (d. 1075 or 76), author of a highly regarded book on Occasions, reports from a Companion of the Prophet that the Prophet's wives used to go out at night "for their needs," that is, apparently, to defecate. According to Wāḥidī, the Hypocrites, an opposition group in Medina, "used to interfere with and bother" the wives. It was for this reason, he says, that the verse came down. Wāḥidī further quotes al-Suddī, a Qur'an commentator who lived early in the second century of Islam, as saying that Medina had become crowded to the extent that when the

women used to go out for their needs at night, they would run into immoral persons who, if they were not wearing veils (*aqni'ah*, sing., *qinā'),* would try to accost them, whereas they would leave veiled women alone. It was because of this particular problem, says al-Suddī, that the verse was revealed; see al-Wāḥidī al-Nīsābūrī, *Asbāb al-nuzūl* (Riyad: Maktabat al-Riyāḍ al-Ḥadīthah, n.d., 245). Wāḥidī's account of the background of the verse, which is repeated in the work of other exegetes, tells us that the women veiled *to protect themselves from the immoral behaviour of others.* This emphasis is unusual in the *ḥadīth* literature, for the *ḥadīth*s point instead to the *danger posed by women* as the prime reason for *ḥijāb*.

42 *Sunan*, *K. al-libās* (Book of Clothing), *ḥadīth*s 3577 and 3578.

43 'Ā'ishah says: "The horsemen used to pass us by as we were with the Messenger of God in the state of consecration for the pilgrimage [and therefore with our faces uncovered], and as they hurried by, each of us would lower our *jilbāb*s from our heads over our faces — and when they had gone, we lifted them." Abū Dāwūd, *Sunan*, *K. al-manāsik* (Book of Rituals of the Pilgrimage), *ḥadīth* 1562; Ibn Mājah, *Sunan*, *K. al-manāsik*, *ḥadīth* 2926; Ibn Ḥanbal, *Musnad*, *Bāqī musnad al-Anṣār*, *ḥadīth* 22,894.

44 *Sharh al-Nawawī*, commentary on *K. Ṣalāt al-'īdayn* (Book of Prayer on the Two 'Eids), *ḥadīth* 1475.

45 See the essays in this volume by Kelly, Meshal and Hoodfar.

46 For a discussion of other meanings of *ḥijāb* in contexts not related to the question of covering, see *The Encyclopaedia of Islam,* 2nd ed., s.v. "*Hidjab*" by J. Chelhod.

47 Bukhārī, *Ṣaḥīḥ*, *K. al-aṭ'imah* (Book of Foods), *ḥadīth* 5044. Other versions in Bukhārī in *K. al-Isti'dhān* (Book of Asking Permission to Enter), in the *Bāb Āyat al-ḥijāb* (Chapter of the Verse of the *Ḥijāb*) and in other chapters in this same Book, as well as in the *K. al-tawḥīd* (Book of Unicity), *ḥadīth* 6871, the *K. al-nikāḥ* (Book of Marriage), *ḥadīth* 4768, and *K. al-wuḍū'* (Book of Ablution), *ḥadīth* 143.

48 For example, Muslim, *Ṣaḥīḥ*, *K. al-nikāḥ* (Book of Marriage), *ḥadīth* 2567 (along with other versions found under the heading *Bāb zawāj Zaynab bint Jaḥsh wa-nuzūl al-ḥijāb*); Ibn Ḥanbal, *Musnad*, *Bāqī musnad al-mukaththirīn, Musnad Anas ibn Mālik, ḥadīth* 11,585.

49 *K. al-ashribah* (Book of Drink), *ḥadīth* 3826.

50 Bukhārī, *Ṣaḥīḥ*, *K. al-maghāzī* (Book of Battles), *ḥadīth*s 3891 and 3890, and see also *K. al-nikāḥ* (Book of Marriage), *ḥadīth*s 4695 and 4762; Nasā'ī, *Sunan*, *K. al-nikāḥ*, *ḥadīth*s 3328 and 3329; Ibn Ḥanbal, *Musnad*, *Bāqī musnad al-mukaththirīn, ḥadīth* 13,286, and in many other places in Bukhārī, Muslim and the other canonical collections.

51 Another report has it that, as the journey came to an end and the animals were urged on toward Medina, the Prophet's mount stumbled so that both he and Ṣafiyah, who was behind him, fell. "No one," says Anas, the guarantor of the report, "looked at him or her until the Prophet of God got up and covered her (*satarahā*)." The report is found in many places in the canonical collections; this version (Ibn Ḥanbal, *Musnad*, *Bāqī musnad al-mukaththirīn*, *ḥadīth* 12,553), instead of using the word *ḥijāb*, says that Ṣafiyah was covered with a *qubbah*, apparently a kind of dome or booth (compare to note 94).

52 Bukhārī, *Ṣaḥīḥ*, *K. al-shahādāt* (Book of Testimonies), *ḥadīth* 2467. See also ibid., *K. al-maghāzī* (Book of Battles), *ḥadīth* 3826 and *K. Tafsīr al-Qur'ān* (Book of Exegesis of the Qur'an), *ḥadīth* 4381; Muslim, *Ṣaḥīḥ*, *K. al-tawbah* (Book of

Repentance), *ḥadīth* 4974; Ibn Ḥanbal, *Musnad, Bāqī musnad al-Anṣār, ḥadīth* 24,444. In addition, Anas ibn Mālik (who once served in the Prophet's household) tells how he was about to enter the Prophet's house as he was accustomed to doing, but this was just after the *ḥijāb* verse came down and the Prophet warned him: "Go back behind, my son!" (Ibn Ḥanbal, *Musnad, Bāqī musnad al-mukaththirīn, Musnad Anas ibn Mālik, ḥadīth* 11918, and other places in Ibn Ḥanbal).

53 Bukhārī, *Ṣaḥīḥ, K. al-nikāḥ* (Book of Marriage), *ḥadīth* 4838, and see also *ḥadīth* 4713; ibid., *K. al-adab* (Book of Etiquette), *ḥadīth* 5690; ibid., *K. tafsīr al-Qur'ān* (Book of Exegesis of the Qur'an), *ḥadīth* 4422; Nasā'ī, *Sunan, K. al-nikāḥ, ḥadīth* 3263 (and other versions under this chapter, the *Bāb laban al-faḥl* or Chapter of Suckling of Males); Ibn Mājah, *Sunan, K. al-nikāḥ, ḥadīth* 1938 (and again other versions under this chapter, the *Bāb laban al-faḥl*); Ibn Ḥanbal, *Musnad, K. Bāqī Musnad al-Anṣār, Ḥadīth al-Sayyidah 'Ā'ishah, ḥadīth* 22,956, and elsewhere in the collection.

54 Bukhārī, *Ṣaḥīḥ, K. al-aḍāḥī* (Book of Slaughter), *ḥadīth* 5140; Muslim, *Ṣaḥīḥ, K. al-ḥajj* (Book of Pilgrimage), *ḥadīth* 2341; Ibn Ḥanbal, *Musnad, Bāqī musnad al-Anṣār, Ḥadīth Sayyidah 'Ā'ishah, ḥadīth* 22,893 and *Bāqī musnad al-Anṣār, ḥadīth* 24,948. In addition, 'Ā'ishah is said in one *ḥadīth* to have given her brother, 'Abd al-Raḥmān, refuge from Mu'āwiyah's governor in her house, answering to his pursuers from "behind the *ḥijāb*" (Bukhārī, *Ṣaḥīḥ, K. tafsīr al-Qur'ān* [Book of Exegesis of the Qur'an], *ḥadīth* 4453). While on a journey, Umm Salamah also asks for water "from behind the veil" (*sitr*) — Bukhārī, *Ṣaḥīḥ, K. al-maghāzī* (Book of Battles), *ḥadīth* 3983; ibid., *K. al-wuḍū'* (Book of Ablution), *ḥadīth*s 181 and 189; Muslim, *Ṣaḥīḥ, K. al-ṣalāh* (Book of Prayer), *ḥadīth*s 777–779; Abū Dāwūd, *Sunan, K. al-ṣalāh, ḥadīth* 590.

55 Bukhārī, *Ṣaḥīḥ, K. al-adhān* (Book of the Call to Prayer), *ḥadīth*s 818 and 826; ibid., *K. al-jum'ah* (Book of the Friday Prayer), *ḥadīth* 848; ibid., *K. al-nikāḥ* (Book of Marriage), *ḥadīth* 4837; Muslim, *Ṣaḥīḥ, K. al-ṣalāh* (Book of Prayer), *ḥadīth*s 666–672; Tirmidhī, *Sunan, K. al-jum'ah, ḥadīth* 520; Nasā'ī, *Sunan, K. al-masājid* (Book of Mosques), *ḥadīth* 699; Abū Dāwūd, *Sunan, K. al-ṣalāh* (Book of Prayer), *ḥadīth* 481; Ibn Mājah, *Sunan, Muqaddimah* (Preface), *ḥadīth* 16; Ibn Ḥanbal, *Musnad, Musnad al-mukaththirīn min al-ṣaḥābah, ḥadīth* 4328, and in many other places in this collection.

56 Abū Dāwūd, *Sunan, K. al-ṣalāh* (Book of Prayer), *ḥadīth* 479; Ibn Ḥanbal, *Musnad, Musnad al-mukaththirīn min al-ṣaḥābah, ḥadīth*s 5211 and 5214.

57 Ibn Ḥanbal, *Musnad, Bāqī musnad al-Anṣār, Ḥadīth Umm Salamah zawj al-nabī, ḥadīth*s 25,331 and 25,358.

58 Abū Dāwūd, *Sunan, K. al-ṣalāh, ḥadīth* 483; Tirmidhī, *Sunan, K. al-riḍā'* (Book of Foster Relationship), *ḥadīth* 1093. According to the commentator, *ḥujrah* = *ṣaḥn al-dār*, courtyard, while *makhda'* = a small room where precious things are kept locked away.

59 Bukhārī, *Ṣaḥīḥ, K. al-adhān* (Book of the Call to Prayer), *ḥadīth* 822; Muslim, *Ṣaḥīḥ, K. al-ṣalāh* (Book of Prayer), *ḥadīth* 676; Abū Dāwūd, *Sunan, K. al-ṣalāh, ḥadīth* 482; Ibn Ḥanbal, *Musnad, Bāqī musnad al-Anṣār, ḥadīth* 23, 270, and in several other places in this collection. The report is one of a group of 'Ā'ishah traditions in which she uses the phrase "if the Prophet had ...," thus claiming, in effect, his authority.

60 Bukhārī, *Ṣaḥīḥ, K. al-jum'ah* (Book of the Friday Prayer), *ḥadīth* 849. The commentator Ibn Ḥajar al-'Asqalānī also relates a version in which 'Umar

reproaches 'Ātiqah directly, to which she replies: "I will not stop until you forbid me!"

61 Muslim, *Ṣaḥīḥ*, *K. al-ṣalāh* (Book of Prayer), *ḥadīth*s 667 and 670–672; Abū Dāwūd, *Sunan*, *K. al-ṣalāh*, *ḥadīth* 481, and in other places in the collections. As the father apparently wished to transmit the words of the Prophet to his son as a relater of *ḥadīth*, the report seems designed also to dramatize the general problem of social conventions distorting or blocking accurate transmission.

62 Bukhārī, *Ṣaḥīḥ*, *K. al-wuḍū'* (Book of Ablution), *ḥadīth* 186. Nasā'ī, *Sunan*, *K. al-ṭahārah* (Book of Ritual Purity), *ḥadīth* 70; Abū Dāwūd, *Sunan*, *K. al-ṭahārah*, *ḥadīth* 72; Ibn Mājah, *Sunan*, *K. al-ṭahārah*, *ḥadīth* 375; Ibn Ḥanbal, *Musnad*, *Musnad al-mukaththirīn min al-ṣaḥābah*, *ḥadīth*s 4251 and 5658 and in other places in this collection. The *ḥadīth* is also and perhaps primarily aimed at the question of whether men and women may wash from one vessel together, whether for prayer or otherwise. That question, judging from the *ḥadīth*s, has partly to do with the risk of contact with a menstruating woman, e.g., in the *Sunan* of Ibn Mājah, *K. al-ṭahārah*, chapters on "A Man and Woman Washing from One Vessel" and "A Man and Woman Performing Ablutions from One Vessel."

63 Ibn Ḥanbal, *ḥadīth* 5658 (as in the previous note).

64 The commentators disagree on whether this means a part of her cloak, the loan of another or the two wrapping themselves in a single one.

65 Bukhārī, *Ṣaḥīḥ*, *K. al-ḥayḍ* (Book of Menstruation), *ḥadīth* 313. The *ḥadīth* continues with discussion of the menstruating woman, which is the interest of the report for this particular Book. Also in ibid., *K. al-jum'ah* (Book of the Friday Prayer), *ḥadīth* 927 and *K. al-ḥajj* (Book of Pilgrimage), *ḥadīth* 1542, as well as Ibn Ḥanbal, *Musnad*, *Awwal musnad al-Baṣrīyīn*, *Ḥadīth Umm 'Aṭīyah*, *ḥadīth* 19,859.

66 Ibn Mājah, *Sunan*, *K. iqāmat al-ṣalāh wa-al-sunnah fīhā* (Book of Performance of the Prayer and the Approved Way of Doing It), *ḥadīth* 1297; Bukhāri, *Ṣaḥīḥ*, *K. al-ṣalāh* (Book of Prayer), *ḥadīth* 338; Muslim, *Ṣaḥīḥ*, *K. ṣalāt al-'īdayn* (Book of Prayer on the Two 'Eids), *ḥadīth* 1475; Tirmidhī, *Sunan*, *K. al-jum'ah* (Book of Friday Prayer), *ḥadīth* 495; Ibn Ḥanbal, *Musnad*, *Awwal musnad al-Baṣrīyīn*, *Ḥadīth Umm 'Aṭīyah*, *ḥadīth* 19,863.

67 Bukhārī, *Ṣaḥīḥ*, *K. al-adhān* (Book of the Call to Prayer), *ḥadīth* 820 and 825; ibid., *K. al-ṣalāh* (Book of Prayer), *ḥadīth* 359; ibid., *K. mawāqīt al-ṣalāh* (Book of Times of the Prayer), *ḥadīth* 544 — this version has "wrapped in their veils"; Muslim, *Ṣaḥīḥ*, *K. al-masājid* (Book of Mosques), *ḥadīth*s 1020–1022; Tirmidhī, *K. al-ṣalāh*, *ḥadīth* 141; Nasā'ī, *Sunan*, *K. al-mawāqīt*, *ḥadīth*s 542 and 543; Abū Dāwūd, *Sunan*, *K. al-ṣalāh*, *ḥadīth* 359; Ibn Mājah, *Sunan*, *K. al-ṣalāh*, *ḥadīth* 661; Ibn Ḥanbal, *Musnad*, *Musnad al-Anṣār*, *ḥadīth* 22,922, and in several other places in this collection. Fatimah Mernissi reads this report in a negative way, understanding it as a directive for women to slip away quickly and unseen after prayers. Slipping away decently in the dark may or may not be a significant element; it may, I think, be simply one of those lifelike details with which Prophetic Reports are often adorned. But the text, in any case, belongs (in my opinion) to the "positive" group of pro-mosque-attendance *ḥadīth*s.

68 Muslim, *Ṣaḥīḥ*, *K. Ṣalāt al-'īdayn* (Book of Prayer on the Two 'Eids), *ḥadīth*s 1464–1465, 1468–1469 and 1476, and in other places in the collections.

69 Ibn Mājah, *Sunan*, *K. iqāmat al-ṣalāh wa-al-sunnah fīhā* (Book of Performance of the Prayer and the Approved Way of Doing It), *ḥadīth* 1299; Ibn Ḥanbal,

Musnad, Musnad Banī Hāshim, Bidāyat musnad ʻAbd Allāh ibn ʻAbbās, ḥadīth 1950.

70 Compare to Muslim's chapter "Women's Going Out to the Mosques, as Long as Sedition Does Not Result" in the Book of Prayer of his *Ṣaḥīḥ* (though Muslim's chapter headings, as noted above, are likely added by a later hand).

71 *Ḥadīth* 495.

72 Mubārakfūrī, *Tuḥfat al-Aḥwadhī bi-sharḥ Jāmiʻ al-Tirmidhī*, commentary on *K. al-jumʻah* (Book of the Friday Prayer), *ḥadīth* 495.

73 *Sharh al-Nawawī*, commentary on *Bāb al-ṣalāh* (Chapter of Prayer), *ḥadīth* 668. Master = *sayyid*. I do not know whether this means the master of a slave girl, or any male in general who has authority over the woman, such as her father.

74 See the next note.

75 In Ibn Ḥanbal, *Musnad, Bāqī musnad al-mukaththirīn, Musnad Abī Saʻīd al-Khuḍrī, ḥadīth* 11,182.

76 Bukhārī, *Ṣaḥīḥ*, *K. al-ḥajj* (Book of the Pilgrimage), *ḥadīth* 1729; ibid., *K. al-jumʻah* (Book of the Friday Prayer), *ḥadīths* 1024, 1025 and 1122; ibid., *K. al-nikāḥ* (Book of Marriage), *ḥadīth* 4832; ibid., *K. al-jihād wa-al-sayr* (Book of War and Travel), *ḥadīth* 2784; Muslim, *Ṣaḥīḥ*, *K. al-ḥajj*, *ḥadīths* 2381, 2382 and 2391; Tirmidhī, *Sunan*, *K. al-riḍāʻ* (Book of Foster Relationship), *ḥadīths* 1089 and 1090 (Tirmidhī devotes a chapter to "Disapproval of a Women Travelling Alone"); Abū Dāwūd, *Sunan*, *K. al-manāsik* (Book of Rituals of the Pilgrimage), *ḥadīth* 1467; Ibn Mājah, *Sunan*, *K. al-manāsik*, *ḥadīths* 2889–2891; Ibn Ḥanbal, *Musnad, Musnad Banī Hāshim*, *ḥadīths* 1833 and 3062; ibid., *Musnad al-mukaththirīn min al-ṣaḥābah*, *ḥadīth* 4386, and in several other places in this collection.

77 Commentary on *ḥadīth* 2391, cited in the note above.

78 Tirmidhī, *Sunan*, *K. al-adab* (Book of Etiquette), *ḥadīth* 2727; Abū Dāwūd, *Sunan*, *K. al-ḥammām* (Book of the Bath), *ḥadīth* 3490; Ibn Mājah, *Sunan*, *K. al-adab*, *ḥadīth* 3740; Ibn Ḥanbal, *Musnad, Bāqī musnad al-Anṣār*, *ḥadīths* 24,238 and 25,100, with variations elsewhere in the collections.

79 *Kitāb Aḥkām al-nisāʼ*, edited by Ziyād Ḥamdān (Beirut: Dār al-Fikr, 1409/1989), 49. In the law, unusual hardship (*ḥaraj*) is taken into account in formulating a ruling; Ibn al-Jawzī may be appealing to this principle.

80 The first verse of *Sūrat al-Ṭalāq* — "The Chapter of Divorce" (Chapter XLV) — says: "Do not let them [women in the process of being divorced] go out, lest they do wrong. ..."

81 There are two occurrences of the *ḥadīth* in the canonical collections: Muslim, *Ṣaḥīḥ*, *K. al-ṭalāq* (Book of Divorce), *ḥadīth* 2727 (the title given the chapter in Muslim is "Permission for a Woman in the Waiting Period After an Irrevocable Divorce or the Death of Her Husband to Go Out in the Daytime for her Needs"); Ibn Mājah, *Sunan*, *K. al-ṭalāq*, *ḥadīth* 2024 (in the chapter, "Can a Woman Go Out During Her Waiting Period?"). Also cited in Ibn Ḥanbal, *Musnad, Bāqī musnad al-mukaththirīn, Musnad Jābir ibn ʻAbd Allāh, ḥadīth* 13,922.

82 Thus there is a legal rule that women and the elderly go on the *jihād* if the community is in danger.

83 Muslim, *Ṣaḥīḥ*, *K. al-jihād wa-al-sayr* (Book of War and Travel), *ḥadīth* 3380; Ibn Ḥanbal, *Musnad, Musnad Banī al-Hāshim, ḥadīth* 1866.

84 Abū Dāwūd, *Sunan*, *K. al-jihād* (Book of War), *ḥadīth* 2353; Ibn Ḥanbal, *Musnad, Bāqī musnad al-Anṣār*, *ḥadīth* 25,844.

85 Bukhārī, *K. al-isti'dhān* (Book of Asking Permission to Enter), *ḥadīth* 5771. See also ibid, *K. al-wuḍū'* (Book of Ablution), *ḥadīth* 143; Muslim, *Ṣaḥīḥ*, *K. al-salām* (Book of Greeting), *ḥadīth* 4035; Ibn Ḥanbal, *Musnad*, *Bāqī musnad al-Anṣār*, *ḥadīth* 24,682; ibid., *Bāqī musnad al-Anṣār*, *Ḥadīth Sayyidah 'Ā'ishah*, *ḥadīth*s 23,155 and 25,126.

86 It is reported that 'Umar proudly stated that he had "been in harmony with my Lord" — that is, his insistence had resulted in a revelation — three times. The first was when he proposed to the Prophet that the Station of Abraham should be established as a place of prayer; the second when he proposed that "your wives should be veiled, for not only the pious, but also the dissolute [try to] speak with them," which led to the *ḥijāb* verse; and the third when the Prophet's wives clashed in their jealousy over the Prophet. The first led to 2:125, "Take the Station of Abraham as a place of prayer," and the third to 66:5, "It might be that if he divorces you, his Lord would give him better wives than you." See Bukhārī, *Ṣaḥīḥ*, *K. al-ṣalāh* (Book of Prayer), *ḥadīth* 387, as well as *K. tafsīr al-Qur'ān* (Book of Exegesis of the Qur'an), *ḥadīth*s 4123, 4416 and 4535; Ibn Ḥanbal, *Musnad*, *Musnad al-'asharah al-mubashshirīn bi-al-jannah*, *Awwal musnad 'Umar ibn al-Khaṭṭāb*, *ḥadīth*s 152 and 155; see also Muslim, *Ṣaḥīḥ*, *K. Faḍā'il al-Ṣaḥābah* (Book of Virtues of the Companions), *ḥadīth* 4412 (in this version, instead of divorce, "the prisoners of Badr," referring to the revelation of Sūrah VIII, verses 67 ff., which agree with 'Umar's objection to the Prophet's holding hostage the prisoners of the Battle of Badr and his recommendation that they be killed instead). Ṣafiyah boasted over her co-wives that, because the *ḥijāb* verse was sent down concerning her, "God arranged my marriage from heaven" (*Allāh ... ankaḥanī min al-samā'*; see Nasā'ī, *Sunan*, *K. al-nikāḥ* [Book of Marriage], *ḥadīth* 3200).

87 Bukhārī, *Ṣaḥīḥ*, *K. tafsīr al-Qur'ān* (Book of Exegesis of the Qur'an), *ḥadīth* 4421; ibid., *K. al-wuḍū'* (Book of Ablution), *ḥadīth* 143; ibid., *K. al-nikāḥ* (Book of Marriage), *ḥadīth* 4836; ibid., *K. al-isti'dhān* (Book of Asking Permission to Enter), *ḥadīth* 5771; Muslim, *Ṣaḥīḥ*, *K. al-salām* (Book of Greeting), *ḥadīth* 4035; Ibn Ḥanbal, *Musnad*, *Bāqī musnad al-Anṣār*, *Ḥadīth Sayyidah 'Ā'ishah*, *ḥadīth* 23,155; *Sharḥ al-Nawawī*, commentary on *K. al-salām* (Book of Greeting), *ḥadīth* 4035.

88 Commentary on the *ḥadīth* from Muslim cited in the previous note.

89 Bukhārī, *Ṣaḥīḥ*, *K. bad' al-khalq* (Book of the Beginning of Creation), *ḥadīth* 3051. See also ibid., *K. al-adab* (Book of Etiquette), *ḥadīth* 5621; ibid., *K. al-manāqib* (Book of Outstanding Characteristics), *ḥadīth* 3407; Muslim, *Ṣaḥīḥ, K. faḍā'il al-ṣaḥābah* (Book of Virtues of the Companions), *ḥadīth* 4410; Ibn Ḥanbal, *Musnad*, *K. al-'asharah al-mubashshirīn bi-al-jannah*, *Musnad Abī Isḥāq Sa'd ibn Abī Waqqāṣ*, *ḥadīth*s 1392 and 1496.

90 Ibn Ḥanbal, *Musnad*, *Musnad al-mukaththirīn min al-ṣaḥābah*, *Musnad 'Abd Allāh ibn Mas'ūd*, *ḥadīth* 4132.

91 Ibn Ḥanbal, *Musnad*, *Musnad al-'asharah al-mubashshirīn bi-al-jannah*, *ḥadīth* 242.

92 The commentary goes on to explain that the sentence regarding the *ḥijāb* mentioned at the close of the report is therefore not different from that mentioned at the beginning; rather, "the second mention of *ḥijāb* refers to the basic subject (*aṣl*) of the *ḥadīth,* as sometimes does happen [in *ḥadīth*], but God knows best.

Al-Fatḥ al-bārī', commentary on *K. tafsīr al-Qur'ān* (Book of Exegesis of the Qur'an), *ḥadīth* 5795.

93 Likely the Malikite judge and *ḥadīth* commentator 'Iyāḍ (d. 1149).

94 *al-Fatḥ al-bārī'*, commentary on *K. al-tafsīr* (Book of Exegesis of the Qur'an), *ḥadīth* 4795. This same report concerning 'Ā'ishah's circumabulation discussed here in the commentary, from the same witness quoted by Ibn Ḥajar (i.e., 'Aṭā' ibn Abī Ribāh Aslam, d. near the beginning of the second century of Islam), is found in Bukhārī, *K. al-ḥajj* (Book of Pilgrimage), *Bāb ṭawāf al-nisā' ma'a al-rijāl* (Chapter of the Circumambulation of Women with Men), *ḥadīth* 1513. According to Bukhārī's report, however, while 'Ā'ishah did circumambulate, she and the others did not mix with the men. She entered only when they had left, and was covered by some kind of domed structure (*qubbah*), although 'Aṭā' also remembers that he could see her "flowered" (the meaning of *muwarrad*, according to the commentary of Ibn Ḥajar) blouse or garment.

95 *Sharḥ al-Nawawī*, commentary on *K. al-salām* (Book of Greeting), *ḥadīth* 4035.

96 For a description of the fideist method and world view, see Aziz al-Azmeh, "Hanbalite Fideism," *Arabica* 35 (November 1988):253–266.

97 Al-Shaykh 'Abd al-'Azīz ibn 'Abd Allāh Ibn Bāz et al., *al-Ḥijāb wa-al-sufūr fī al-Qur'ān wa-al-sunnah* (Beirut and Cairo: Dār Ibn Zaydūn and Dār al-Kutub al-Salafīyah, 1406/1986), 33–160. The essay itself is titled *al-Lubāb fī farīdat al-niqāb*, "The Essence of the Duty of Total Veiling."

98 Muslim, *Ṣaḥīḥ*, *K. ṣalāt al-'īdayn* (Book of Prayer on the Two 'Eids), *ḥadīth* 1467; Nasā'ī, *Sunan*, *K. ṣalāt al-'īdayn*, *ḥadīth* 1557; Ibn Ḥanbal, *Musnad*, *Bāqī musnad al-mukaththirīn*, *Musnad Jābir ibn 'Abd Allāh*, *ḥadīth* 13,900.

99 See Bukhārī, *Ṣaḥīḥ*, *K. al-'ilm* (Book of Knowledge), *ḥadīth* 131; Tirmidhī, *Sunan*, *K. al-ḥajj* (Book of the Pilgrimage), *ḥadīth* 763; Abū Dāwūd, *Sunan*, *K. al-manāsik* (Book of Rituals of the Pilgrimage), *ḥadīths* 1554–1556; Nasā'ī, *Sunan*, *K. al-manāsik*, *ḥadīth* 2625 and 2633; Ibn Ḥanbal, *Musnad*, *Musnad al-mukaththirīn min al-ṣaḥābah*, *ḥadīth* 5731.

100 'Ā'ishah says: "The horsemen used to pass by us as we were with the Messenger of God in the state of consecration for the pilgrimage [and therefore with our faces uncovered], and as they hurried by, each of us would lower our *jilbābs* from our heads over our faces — and when they had gone, we lifted them." Abū Dāwūd, *Sunan*, *K. al-manāsik* (Book of Rituals of the Pilgrimage), *ḥadīth* 1562; Ibn Mājah, *Sunan*, *K. al-manāsik*, *ḥadīth* 2926; Ibn Ḥanbal, *Musnad*, *Bāqī musnad al-Anṣār*, *ḥadīth* 22,894.

101 Ibn Bāz, *Ḥijāb*, 112–114.

102 Bukhārī, *Ṣaḥīḥ*, *K. al-nikāḥ* (Book of Marriage), *ḥadīth* 4706; Muslim, *Ṣaḥīḥ*, *K. al-dhikr wa-al-du'ā' wa-al-tawbah* (Book of Remembrance of God, Prayer and Repentance), *ḥadīths* 4923 and 4924; Tirmidhī, *Sunan*, *K. al-adab* (Book of Etiquette), *ḥadīth* 2704 ("I shall not leave anything more harmful *for my community* ..."); Ibn Mājah, *Sunan*, *K. al-fitan* (Book of Sedition), *ḥadīth* 3988; Ibn Ḥanbal, *Musnad*, *Musnad al-Anṣār*, *ḥadīths* 20,751 and 20,828.

103 Muslim, *Ṣaḥīḥ*, *K. al-dhikr wa-al-du'ā' wa-al-tawbah wa-al-istighfār* (Book of Remembrance of God, Supplication, Repentance and Asking Forgiveness), *ḥadīth* 4925; Tirmidhī, *Sunan*, *K. al-fitan* (Book of Sedition), *ḥadīth* 2117; Ibn Mājah, *Sunan*, *K. al-fitan*, *ḥadīth* 3990; Ibn Ḥanbal, *Musnad*, *Bāqī musnad al-mukaththirīn*, *ḥadīth* 10,716, and in other places in this collection. According to

Muslim's commentator, Nawawī, "verdant chamber" (*khalwah khaḍīrah*) refers either to the temptations of this world or to its ephemerality, since it is bound to wither as soon as it flourishes, as green things do. *Al-khalwah al-khaḍīrah*, I think, may also be an image of the world as a hermitage (*khalwah* also means hermitage or secluded space), with the blue sky imagined as the domed roof of that structure (green is thought of as the colour of the sky, *al-Khaḍrā'*, "The Green One," being one of its epithets.) This is a common image in Persian poetry. Thus: This world is in reality a place of prayer, meditation, and retreat; behave as you should in such a place, shunning the world and women! The *ḥadīth* is body-denying, as if it were of gnostic inspiration.

104 Tirmidhī, *Sunan, K. al-adab* (Book of Etiquette), *ḥadīth* 2710 (the only occurrence). The text actually reports a euphemism, apparently to avoid putting unclean language in the mouth of Muhammad: "she is such-and-such. "The guarantor adds the explanation, "fornicatress." Judging from this and other *ḥadīths*, "perfume" (*ṭīb*) involved, at least for women, coloured decoration of the skin.

105 Muslim, *Ṣaḥīḥ, K. al-nikāḥ* (Book of Marriage), *ḥadīths* 2491 and 2492; Tirmidhī, *Sunan, K. al-riḍā'* (Book of Foster Relationship), *ḥadīth* 1078 ("she has what the other has"); Abū Dāwūd, *Sunan, K. al-nikāḥ* (Book of Marriage), *ḥadīth* 1839; Ibn Ḥanbal, *Musnad, Bāqī musnad al-mukaththirīn, ḥadīth* 14,010, and in other places in this collection.

106 Tirmidhī, *Sunan, K. al-riḍā'* (Book of Foster Relationship), *ḥadīth* 1091.

107 Tirmidhī, *Sunan, K. al-riḍā'* (Book of Foster Relationship), *ḥadīth* 1092; Ibn Ḥanbal, *Musnad, Bāqī musnad al-mukaththirīn, ḥadīths* 13,804 and 14,740. Similarly, "A man shall not enter the presence of a woman whose husband is absent, except that he have with him another man, or two." See Muslim, *Ṣaḥīḥ, K. al-salām* (Book of Greeting), *ḥadīth* 4039; Tirmidhī, *Sunan, K. al-ṭahārah* (Book of Ritual Purity), *ḥadīth* 28; Ibn Ḥanbal, *Musnad, Musnad al-mukaththirīn min al-ṣaḥābah, ḥadīths* 6456 and 6700.

108 Bukhārī, *Ṣaḥīḥ, K. al-nikāḥ* (Book of Marriage), *ḥadīth* 4831; Muslim, *Ṣaḥīḥ, K. al-salām* (Book of Greeting), *ḥadīth* 4037; Tirmidhī, *Sunan, K. al-riḍā'* (Book of Foster Relationship), *ḥadīth* 1091; Ibn Ḥanbal, *Musnad, Musnad al-Shāmīyīn, ḥadīths* 16,708 and 16,755.

109 Commentary on *K. al-riḍā'* (Book of Foster Relationship), *ḥadīth* 1093.

110 *Tuḥfat al-Aḥwadhī*, commentary on *K. al-adab* (Book of Etiquette), *ḥadīth* 2704.

111 It appears in Ibn Ḥanbal in similar guise, in lists of moral imperatives (*Bāqī musnad al-mukaththirīn, Musnad Jābir ibn 'Abd Allāh, ḥadīth* 14,124; *Musnad al-Makkīyīn, Ḥadīth 'Āmir ibn Rabī'ah, ḥadīth* 15,140). The report is also cited as part of a sermon by 'Umar — the "usual suspect" in matters involving restrictions on women — in which he transmits some of the essential wisdom of the Prophet: Ibn Ḥanbal, *Musnad, Musnad al-mubashshirīn bi-al-jannah, Awwal musnad 'Umar ibn al-Khaṭṭāb, ḥadīths* 109 and 172.

112 For example (all titles published): 'Abd al-Malik ibn Ḥabīb's (d. 852 or 853) *Kitāb adab al-nisā'* (Book of Etiquette in Matters Concerning Women); Aḥmad ibn Ḥanbal's *Aḥkām al-nisā'* (Legal Rulings Pertaining to Women); the *Kitāb 'ishrat al-nisā'* (Book on How to Associate with Women) of Aḥmad ibn Shu'ayb al-Nasā'ī (d. 915, also author of one of the Sunnī canonical collections); Ibn 'Abd Rabbih's (d. 940) *Tabā'i al-nisā'* (The Natures of Women); and Ibn al-Jawzī's (d. 1200) *Aḥkām al-nisā'*.

[113] At one point, Ibn al-Jawzī even adds to the *ḥadīth* "Those who go to the Friday prayer should wash themselves" the clarification "both men and women" (*Aḥkām*, 65). (Although the editor places quotation marks outside the phrase, as if it belonged to the wording of the *ḥadīth*, this must be an error, given that the words are not found in any of the numerous occurrences in the canonical collections and that it is quoted by Ibn al-Jawzī apropos of women's ablutions, for which reason he would have added the words.)

[114] Ibn al-Jawzī, *Aḥkām*, 65. A common ruling, and not Ibn al-Jawzī's alone.

[115] Ibn al-Jawzī, *Aḥkām*, 67.

[116] The rule about greeting is presented as a *ḥadīth*, and the editor has located it in two other late — that is, fifteenth and seventeenth century — sources (*Aḥkām*, 67, n. 4). I have not found it in any of the canonical collections (although there is a rule there about shaking hands). The *ḥadīths* I have found on this subject are actually pro-greeting: Ibn Ḥanbal, *Musnad, Awwal musnad al-Kūfiyīn, Ḥadīth Jarīr ibn ʻAbd Allāh, ḥadīths* 18,365 and 18,417.

[117] Ibn al-Jawzī, *Aḥkām,* 67.

[118] Daniel W. Brown, *Rethinking Tradition in Modern Islamic Thought* (Cambridge: Cambridge University Press, 1996), 126–127. A fuller account of Mawdūdī's approach, including the aspect described in the text, in: Seyyed Vali Reza Nasr, *Mawdudi and the Making of Islamic Revivalism* (New York: Oxford University Press, 1996).

[119] *Purdah and the Status of Woman in Islam*, translated by "Al-Ashʻarī" (Lahore: Islamic Publications, 1972), 149–150.

[120] Mawdūdī, *Purdah*, 209.

[121] Mawdūdī, *Purdah*, 150–152.

[122] *The Islamic Modest Dress*, translated by Laleh Bakhtiyar, 2nd ed. (Albuquerque, NM: Abjad, 1989), 51–58.

[123] Muṭahharī, *Modest Dress*, 91–95. He also allows women to go to the ʻEid prayers, but adds, in an invalidating clause typical of older traditional thought, that "it is disapproved for women of great respect or beauty to participate in such prayers" (92).

[124] Muṭahharī, *Modest Dress*, 87. Muṭahharī deals with the *jilbāb* verse (Qur'an 33:59) using the same exegetical technique. He considers that the verse was sent down not as "a total ruling for all times," but is rather concerned with "particular events occurring at that time," that being the need of the women addressed to distinguish themselves from more sexually available slave women in order to avoid harrassment. Thus the verse according to Muṭahharī "adds nothing" to the *ḥijāb* argument; *ḥijāb* is instead established by the passage in Qur'an 31:24, which reads "display of their adornment only that which is apparent, and draw their veils over their bosoms" (89). This treatment of Qur'an 33:59 is apparently in answer to the assertion sometimes made, as in the previous essay in this book, that since the (unjust) distinction between free and slave women no longer exists, the verse cannot be taken as evidence that covering is obligatory.

[125] Muṭahharī, *Modest Dress*, 73–77.

[126] I am not certain when and where it first received full expression. This would be an interesting and important subject for research. According to the preface to the English translation, *Modest Dress* was first delivered as a series of lectures from 1966 to 1967.

127 For a clear and succinct discussion of not only liberal but the whole "prism" of modern responses to *ḥadīth*, see Brown's *Rethinking Tradition in Modern Islamic Thought*, already cited above; and for a brief description and critical view of modernist trends in the subcontinent, A.N.M. Wahidur Rahman, "Modernist Muslim's [*sic*] Approach *to Ḥadīth*: Aligarh School," *Hamdard Islamicus* 16, no. 4 (1993), 13–26.

128 Khaled Abou el-Fadl, in *Speaking in God's Name: Islamic Law, Authority, and Women* (Oxford: Oneworld, 2001), in the course of his critique of what he judges to be the unjustly woman-negative *fatwás* of certain Saudi-based organizations, does begin to construct such a theory, and that with great depth and skill. This essay was finished before I became aware of the book, but I will insert one comment: Abou el-Fadl considers some elements of the *fatwás* to be purely personal views surreptiously introduced by the *shaykhs*, but they do in fact have a basis in the texts, for example, the caution that women not misrepresent themselves to (marriageable) males, and the principle that a man has the right to enjoy any part of his wife's body. That is to say, the spirit of some of the *fatwás* criticized is (or seems to me to be) consistent with the apparent sense of *ḥadīths* and other literature, rather than simply "dishonest," as Abou el-Fadl charges. The task at hand would seem to be to systematically treat those texts and in general to promote different readings of the scriptures.

129 Brown, *Rethinking Tradition*, 35–36, 84–85.

130In Brown, *Rethinking Tradition*: For the first view, see the discussion of Fazlur Rahman on pp. 102–106 and Rahman's own "Sunna and Ḥadīth" in *Islamic Studies* 1, no. 2 (1962): 1–36; for the second view, pp. 38–42, and discussion, passim, of names found there, especially Ghulam Ahmad Parvez.

131 I am speaking here of Sunnism. In Iranian Shiism, there has been more contact and exchange between the two worlds.

132 A few examples: Abū Dāwūd, *Sunan*, *K. al-ṭalāq* (Book of Divorce), *ḥadīths* 1863 and 1863; Ibn Mājah, *Sunan*, *K. al-ṭalāq*, *ḥadīth* 2008.

133 For example, Bukhārī, *Ṣaḥīḥ*, *K. al-zakāt* (Book of Obligatory Alms), *ḥadīth* 1329 (whoever takes trouble for daughters, that shall be for him a shield from the Fire) and Ibn al-Jawzī, *Aḥkām*, chapter on "Reward for Providing for Daughters and Sisters."

134 Q.16:58–59 and 81:8 (and similarly 6:151 and 17:31).

135 Bukhārī devotes a whole Book (*Kitāb*) to Maintenance; for a Shī'ī example, see al-Ḥurr al-'Āmilī, *Wasā'il al-Shī'ah*, *K. al-nikāḥ*, *Abwāb al-nafaqāt* (Book of Marriage, Chapters on Maintenance).

136 For a similar limiting *ḥadīth*, see Tirmidhī, *Sunan*, *Kitāb al-riḍā'* (Book of Foster Relationship), *ḥadīth* 1083; here permission for striking is given in case of a "grievous offence" and is embedded in a lengthy statement emphasizing the rights of wives to kindness and maintenance, a common subject of *ḥadīths*.

137 Abū Dāwūd, *Sunan*, *K. al-nikāḥ* (Book of Marriage), *ḥadīths* 1835 and 2147.

138 The word "anything" (*shay'an*) suggests animals. The force of the wording in Arabic is not only did the Prophet never strike his wives, he would not strike a servant or even an animal. Muslim, *Ṣaḥīḥ*, *Kitāb al-faḍā'il* (Book of Virtues), *ḥadīths* 4294–4296, and in other places in Bukhārī and the other collections. On striking a slave, see Abū Dāwūd, *Sunan*, *K. al-adab*, *Bāb fī ḥaqq al-mamlūk* (Book of Etiquette, Chapter on the Rights of Slaves), *ḥadīth* 4500; he who strikes his slave has either to expiate (perform *kaffārah*) or manumit the victim. On striking

a servant, Tirmidhī, *Sunan*, *K. al-birr wa-al-ṣilah 'an Rasūl Allāh*, *Bāb mā jā'a fī adab al-khādim* (Book of Piety and Human Relations According to the Messenger of God, Chapter on How to Treat a Servant), *ḥadīth* 1873.

139 Abū Dāwūd, *Sunan*, *K. al-nikāḥ* (Book of Marriage), *ḥadīth* 1834; Ibn Mājah, *Sunan*, *K. al-nikāḥ*, *ḥadīth* 1975; also Dārimī, *Sunan* (not one of the canonical collections, but much respected), *K. al-nikāḥ*, *ḥadīth* 2122. (Does the *ḥadīth* suggest that 'Umar's complaint occasioned the revelation of 4:34?) In Ibn Mājah, *Sunan*, *K. al-nikāḥ* (Book of Marriage), *ḥadīth* 1976 and Ibn Ḥanbal, *Musnad*, *Sanad al-'asharah al-mubashshirīn bi-al-jannah*, *Awwal musnad 'Umar ibn al-Khaṭṭāb*, *ḥadīth* 117, in a further development of the 'Umar theme, he uses the words of the Prophet ("a man shall not be asked") to justify hitting his own wife!

140 For general statements, see Muslim, *Ṣaḥīh*, *K. al-birr wa-al-ṣilah wa-al-ādāb*, *Bāb al-nahī 'an ḍarb al-wajh* (Book of Piety, Kindly Relations and Etiquette, Chapter Forbidding Hitting the Face), *ḥadīth*s 4728–4730 and 4732; Ibn Ḥanbal, *Bāqī musnad al-mukaththirīn*, *ḥadīth* 7113, *Bāqī musnad al-mukaththirīn*, *Musnad Abī Sa'īd al-Khudarī*, *ḥadīth*s 10,902 and 11,452, and other places in Ibn Ḥanbal. Some versions have that one should not hit the face of "one's brother," a kind of limiting phrase.

141 Abū Dāwūd, *Sunan*, *K. al-nikāḥ* (Book of Marriage), *ḥadīth*s 1830–1832; Ibn Mājah, *Sunan*, *K. al-nikāḥ*, *ḥadīth* 1840; Ibn Ḥanbal, *Awwal Musnad al-Baṣriyīn*, *Ḥadīth Ḥākim ibn Mu'āwiyah 'an abīhi*, *ḥadīth* 19162 and *Ḥadīth Bihz (?) ibn Ḥākim*, *ḥadīth*s 19,171 and 19,174.

142 For slaves, see Bukhārī, *Ṣaḥīh*, *K. al-'itq*, *Bāb idhā ḍuriba al-'abd fa-lyajtanib al-wajh* (Book of Manumission, Chapter [establishing that] If a Slave Is Hit, One Should Avoid the Face), *ḥadīth* 2372. For lashing, see Abū Dāwūd, *K. al-ḥudūd*, *Bāb fī ḍarb al-wajh fī al-ḥadd* (Book of *Ḥudūd* Punishments, Chapter on Striking the Face in Carrying out the *Ḥudūd*), *ḥadīth* 3895; and similarly in *ḥadīth* 3854 of the same work in the same book, in the *Bāb al-mar'ah allatī amara al-nabī bi-rajmihā ...* (Chapter on the Woman Whom the Prophet Commanded Be Stoned), on avoiding the face in stoning. Abū Dāwūd also fits the *ḥadīth* that simply recommends avoiding hitting the face in general with the title *Bāb fī ḍarb al-wajh fī al-ḥadd* (Chapter Concerning Hitting the Face During [Execution of] of *Ḥudūd* Punishments); see *ḥadīth* 3895 of the Book of *Ḥudūd*. For not hitting the face in fighting, see Ibn Ḥanbal, *Bāqī musnad al-mukaththirīn*, *ḥadīth*s 7021, 7777, 7989, 8087, 8219 and 9423; here also some *ḥadīth*s limit the prohibition against fighting to "one's brother," which seems illogical but may be inspired by the *ḥadīth* prohibition against fighting one's brother in general (as in Muslim, *Ṣaḥīh*, *K. al-īmān*, *Bāb mā jā'a fī sibāb al-mu'min fusūq* (Book of Faith, Chapter [establishing that] Cursing a Believer Is Iniquity), *ḥadīth* 2558). One should neither brand nor hit an animal on its face: Bukhārī, *Ṣaḥīh*, *K. al-dhabā'iḥ wa-al-ṣayd*, *Bāb al-wasm wa-al-'alam fī al-ṣūrah* (Book of Slaughter and Hunting, Chapter on Branding and Marking on the Face), *ḥadīth* 5115; Muslim, *Ṣaḥīh*, *K. al-libās wa-al-zīnah*, *Bāb al-nahī 'an ḍarb al-ḥayawān fī wajhihi wa-wasmihi fīhi* (Book of Clothing and Ornament, Chapter Forbidding Hitting or Branding an Animal on Its Face), *ḥadīth* 3952; Tirmidhī, *Sunan*, *K. al-jihād* (Book of War), *ḥadīth* 1632; Abū Dāwūd, *Sunan*, *K. al-jihād*, *ḥadīth* 2201; Ibn Ḥanbal, *Bāqī musnad al-mukaththirīn*, *Musnad Jābir ibn 'Abd Allāh*, *ḥadīth*s 13,903, 13,935 and 14,516.

143 Muslim, *Ṣaḥīh*, *K. al-birr wa-al-ṣilah wa-al-ādāb*, *Bāb al-nahī 'an ḍarb al-wajh* (Book of Piety, Kindly Relations and Etiquette, Chapter Forbidding Hitting the

Face), *ḥadīth* 4731; Ibn Ḥanbal, *Musnad, Bāqī musnad al-mukaththirīn, Musnad Abī Hurayrah, ḥadīth*s 7021 and 7113 and *Bāqī musnad al-mukaththirīn, ḥadīth*s 9231, 9583 and 10,314.

[144] See the Web site of the International Network for the Rights of Female Victims of Violence in Pakistan, at www.inrfwp.org (30/03/2002), where updates are also provided.

[145] It should be kept in mind that approaches used for the Torah and the Bible in a Western context will not all necessarily suit Islam, for reasons not only of the different natures of the texts, but also possibility of reception by the audience.

[146] Some exegetes (e.g., Ṭabarsī in his *Majma' al-bayān*, in the sixth century of Islam, but not the earlier Ṭabarī) treat Q. 3:14 this way explicitly, apparently in an attempt to harmonize what they recognize to be the very different meanings of *fitnah* in the two scriptures. The verse, "Longing for women and offspring, stored-up heaps of gold, silver, branded horses, cattle, and land has been made to seem beautiful to people — but those are the goods of the life of this world" receives the comment: "God mentions women first because the *fitnah* in them is greatest; for the Prophet said: 'I have not left after me any *fitnah* more harmful for men than women,' and 'Women are Satan's snares' ... (and so on)." The woman-negative *ḥadīth*, "There is calamity (*shu'm*) in three things: horses, women, and habitations" (Bukhārī, *Ṣaḥīḥ, K. al-jihād wa-al-sayr* [Book of War and Travel], *ḥadīth* 2646, and elsewhere in the collections) seems to be a similar development of this verse of the Qur'an. 'Ā'ishah — see Ibn Ḥajar's commentary on Bukhārī — is said to have vehemently denied this report, though it is not exactly clear if this was because it denigrates women.

[147] Fazlur Rahman, *Major Themes of the Quran* (1980) and *Islamic Methodology in History* (1965); Amina Wadud Muhsin, *Qur'an and Women* (1992).

[148] Nevertheless, the liberationist *Encyclopédie de la femme en Islam: la femme dans les textes du Saint Coran et des Sahih d'al-Boukhari et Mouslim* manages to devote a whole section to this proposition (Abd al-Halim Abou Chouqqa, 6 vols., Paris: al-Qalam, 1998).

[149] For example, the *ḥadīth* quoted above in which 'Ā'ishah sits and talks with a man and teaches him the ablutions (Nasā'ī, *Sunan, K. al-ṭahārah* [Book of Ritual Purity], *ḥadīth* 99). The narrator also adds: "this was before the *ḥijāb*." Relating an incident that places the Prophet's wife Sawdah in the company of men, the relater of a *ḥadīth* comments: "That was before the *ḥijāb* was prescribed for them" (Abū Dāwūd, *Sunan, K. al-jihād* [Book of War], *ḥadīth* 2305).

[150] An irony, since classical exegesis and law (though not, of course, philosophy and theology, which are concerned with foundational principles) have not pretended to distinguish absolute truth. Through probably not actually dialogical, these Islamic disciplines are at least probabilistic.

[151] My colleague Ira Robinson points out that covering the head in Judaism similarly lacks a scriptural basis; for a summary, see Barbara Goldman Carrel, "Hasidic Women's Head-Coverings," in Linda B. Arthur, ed., *Religion, Dress, and the Body* (New York: Oxford, 1999), 177, n. 3. Covering is, of course, firmly entrenched in Judaic law, just as it is in Islamic law. The parts to be covered are also referred to in Hebrew as *ervah*. Comparison of the Judaic and Islamic cases may help to explain the development of this extra-scriptural norm. One wonders if the two communities developed it together.

152 I do not take the introduction of clothing texts as necessarily indicating a move from relative freedom to restriction. Increased preoccupation with clothing could point instead to anxiety inspired by changing circumstances of some kind, for instance, a need to regulate male-female relations in the close living space of rapidly expanding urban centres in which most women, practically speaking, could *not* be effectively secluded through means previously recommended in the received *ḥadīth* texts. Attention to clothing may then actually address — as it does in our day — problems of the entry of women into public space.

Bibliography

‘Abd al-Raḥmān, ‘Ā’ishah (Bint al-Shāṭi’). 1967. *al-Mafhūm al-Islāmī li-Taḥrīr al-Mar’ah*. Cairo: Jāmi‘at Umm Durmān al-Islāmīyah.

Abdel Haleem, Muhammad. 1999. *Understanding the Qur’an: Themes and Style*. London: I.B. Tauris.

‘Abduh, Muḥammad. 1972. *al-A‘māl al-Kāmilah lil-Imām Muḥammad ‘Abduh*. Vol. 2, *Al-Kitābāt al-Ijtimā‘īyah*. Beirut: al-Mu’assasah al-‘Arabīyah lil-Dirāsāt wa-al-Nashr.

Abou El Fadl, Khaled. 2001. *Speaking in God’s Name: Islamic Law, Authority and Women*. Oxford: Oneworld.

Abu-Laban, Baha. 1983. “The Canadian Muslim Community: The Need for a New Survival Strategy.” In *The Muslim Community in North America*, edited by Earle H. Waugh, Baha Abu-Laban and Regula Burckhardt Qureshi, 75–92. Edmonton: University of Alberta Press.

Abu-Laban, Sharon McIrvin. 1991. “Family and Religion among Muslim Immigrants and Their Descendants.” In *Muslim Families in North America*, edited by Earle H. Waugh, Sharon McIrvin Abu-Laban and Regula Burckhardt Qureshi, 6–31. Edmonton: University of Alberta Press.

______. 1995. “The Muslim Community in Canada.” In *Muslim Minorities in the West*, edited by Syed Z. Abedin and Ziauddin Sardar. London: Grey Seal.

Abu Lughod, Leila. 1986. *Veiled Sentiments: Honour and Poetry in a Bedouin Society*. Berkeley: University of California Press.

Adeney, Miriam, and Kathryn DeMaster. 1994. "Muslims of Seattle." In *Muslim Communities in North America*, edited by Yvonne Yazbeck Haddad and Jane Idleman Smith, 195–208. Albany: State University of New York Press.

Agius, Dionisius. 1997. "Fashions and Styles: Maltese Women's Headdress." In *Languages of Dress in the Middle East*, edited by Nancy Lindisfarne-Tapper and Bruce Ingham, 107–126. London: Curzon.

Ahmed, Leila. 1992. *Women and Gender in Islam: Historical Roots of a Modern Debate.* New Haven: Yale University Press.

Albānī, Muḥammad Naṣīr al-Dīn. 1965 or 1966. *Ḥijāb al-Mar'ah al-Muslimah fī al-Kitāb wa-al-Sunnah.* Beirut: Manshūrāt al-Maktab al-Islāmī.

Ali, Abdullah Yusuf. 1946. *The Holy Qur'an: Text, Translation and Commentary.* Washington, DC: American International Printing.

Alloula, Malek. 1986. *The Colonial Harem.* Translated by Myrna Godzich and Wlad Godzich. Minneapolis: University of Minnesota Press.

Alvi, Sajida S. 1994. "The *Mujaddid* and *Tajdīd* Traditions in the Indian Subcontinent: An Historical Overview." *Journal of Turkish Studies (Schimmel Festschrift)* 18:1–15.

______. 1996. "Polygamy"; "Evidence"; "Inheritance." In *International Conference on Islamic Laws and Women in the Modern World: Islamabad, December 22–23, 1996*, 78, 96–97, 129–132, 144, 147–149, 165. Islamabad: Giant Forum.

______. 1996. "Muslim Women and Society." In *An Anthology of Islamic Studies*, edited by Howard M. Federspiel, 235–285. Montreal: McGill Institute of Islamic Studies.

Alvi, Sajida S., and Sheila McDonough. 1994. "Unpacking the Symbolism of the Muslim Veil." *Ecumenism* 115 [special issue "Women of Faith in the World's Religions"]:13–17.

Alvi, Sajida S., and Sabir A. Alvi. 2002. "Career Development of Women in Indonesia: A Study of Highly Successful Women." In *Women in Indonesian Society: Access, Empowerment and Opportunity*, edited by M. Atho Mudzhar, Sajida S. Alvi et al., 111–133. Yogyakarta: Sunan Kalijaga Press.

Amīn, Aḥmad. 1964. *Ḍuḥá al-Islām.* Cairo: Maktabat al-Nahḍah al-Miṣrīyah.

Amīn, Qāsim. 1899. *Taḥrīr al-Mar'ah.* Cairo: Madbūlī.

______. 1900. *al-Mar'ah al-Jadīdah.* Cairo: n.p.

An-Na'im, Abdullahi. 1990. *Toward an Islamic Reformation: Civil Liberties, Human Rights and International Law*. Syracuse: Syracuse University Press.

Anjum, Mohini. 1992. "Behind Burqa." In *Muslim Women in India*, edited by Mohini Anjum, 112–18. New Delhi: Radiant Publishers.

Ansari, Muhammad Abdul Haq Ansari. 1986. *Sufism and Shari'ah: A Study of Shaykh Ahmad Sirhindi's Effort to Reform Sufism*. London: The Islamic Foundation.

Arberry, A.J. 1970. *Fifty Poems of Ḥāfiẓ*. Cambridge: Cambridge University Press.

Armstrong, Karen. 2000. "Smiting the Enemies of God." *The Globe and Mail* (Saturday, April 22), Section A.

Aṣbahānī, Abū al-Faraj. 1983. *Kitāb al-Aghānī*, 20 vols. Beirut: Dār al-Thaqāfah.

Aswad, Barbara C. 1991. "Yemeni and Lebanese Muslim Immigrant Women in Southeast Dearborn, Michigan." In *Muslim Families in North America,* edited by Earle Waugh, Sharon McIrvin Abu-Laban and Regula B. Qureshi, 256–281. Edmonton: University of Alberta Press.

Ayāzī, Muḥammad 'Alī. 1414 AH/1993 CE. *Al-Mufassirūn: Ḥayātuhum wa-Manhājuhum*. Tehran: Mu'assasat al-Ṭibā'ah wa-al-Nashr.

Aziz, Razia. 1992. "Feminism and the Challenge of Racism: Deviance or Difference?" In *Knowing Women: Feminism and Knowledge*, edited by Helen Crowley and Susan Himmelweit, 291–305. Cambridge: Polity Press.

Azmeh, Aziz Al. 1988. "Hanbalite Fideism." *Arabica* 35: 253–66.

______. 1993. *Islams and Modernities*. London: Verso.

Badawi, Jamal A. n.d. *The Muslim Woman's Dress According to the Qur'an and Sunnah*. London: Ta-Ha Publishers.

Badran, Margot. 1995. *Feminists, Islam and Nation: Gender and the Making of Modern Egypt*. Princeton: Princeton University Press.

Bāhū, Sulṭān. 1998. *Death Before Dying: The Sufi Poems of Sultan Bahu*. Translated into English by Jamal J. Elias. Berkeley: University of California Press.

Baker, Patricia L. 1997. "Politics of Dress: The Dress Reform Laws of 1920/30s Iran." In *Languages of Dress in the Middle East*, edited by Nancy Lindisfarne-Tapper and Bruce Ingham, 178–192. London: Curzon.

Bamdad, Badr ol-Moluk. 1977. *From Darkness into Light: Women's Emancipation in Iran*. Translated and edited by F.R.C. Bagley. Smithtown, NY: Exposition Press.

Barnes, Ruth, and Joanne B. Eicher. 1992. *Dress and Gender: Making Meaning in Cultural Contexts*. New York: BERG.

Benhabib, Seyla. 1986. "The Generalized and the Concrete Other: The Kohlberg-Gilligan Controversy and Feminist Theory." *Praxis International* 5(4): 401–429.

Berkes, Niyazi. 1964. *The Development of Secularism in Turkey.* Montreal: McGill University Press.

Bloul, Rachel. 1996. "Engendering Muslim Identities: Deterritorialization and the Ethnicization Process in France." In *Making Muslim Space in North America and Europe*, edited by Barbara Metcalf, 234–250. Los Angeles: University of California Press.

Boullata, Issa A., ed. 2000. *Literary Structures of Religious Meaning in the Qur'an*. Richmond, Surrey: Curzon Press.

Brewer, Jahm, and Roy Porter. 1993. *Consumption and the World of Goods*. London: Routledge.

Brown, Daniel W. 1996. *Rethinking Tradition in Modern Islamic Thought*. Cambridge: Cambridge University Press.

Cainkar, Louise. 1991. "Palestinian-American Muslim Women: Living on the Margins of Two Worlds." In *Muslim Families in North America*, edited by Earle Waugh, Sharon McIrvin Abu-Laban and Regula B. Qureshi, 282–308. Edmonton: University of Alberta Press.

Canadian Islamic Congress. 1999. *Anti-Islam in the Media: A Six-month Study of Six Top Canadian Newspapers*. Internet, http://www.cicnow.com.

Casgrain, Thérèse. 1972. *A Woman in a Man's World.* Translated by Joyce Marshall. Toronto: McClelland & Stewart.

CEQ (Centrale de l'enseignement du Québec). 1995. *Communiqué de Presse* D10156 NC 057. Montreal: CEQ.

Chatty, Dawn. 1996. *Mobile Pastoralists: Development Planning and Social Change*. New York: Columbia University Press.

Commission des droits de la personne du Québec. 1996. *Religious Pluralism in Quebec: A Social and Ethical Challenge* (February). Quebec: La Commission.

Crawley, E. 1931. *Dress, Drink and Drums*. London: Methuen and Co.

Dawood, N.J. 1995. *The Koran, with a Parallel Arabic Text.* London: Penguin Books.

al-Dāwūdī, Shams al-Dīn Muḥammad ibn ʻAli. 1972. *Ṭabaqāt al-Mufassirīn.* Edited by ʻAlī Muḥammad ʻUmar. 2 vols. Cairo: Maktabat al-Qāhirah.

Dickey, Melissa. 1994. "Images of Muslim Women in Occidental Consciousness: Reality vs. Fiction." Honours thesis, Department of Sociology and Anthropology, Concordia University.

Diop, Moustapha, and Laurence Michalak. 1996. "'Refuge' and 'Prison': Islam, Ethnicity and the Adaptation of Space in Workers' Housing in France." In *Making Muslim Space in North America and Europe*, edited by Barbara Metcalf, 74–91. Los Angeles: University of California Press.

Doi, Abdur Rahman I. 1989. *Women in Shari'ah (Islamic Law).* London: Ta-Ha Publishers.

Durkee, Noura. 1987. "Primary Education of Muslim Children in North America." *Muslim Education Quarterly* 5:53–81.

El-Guindi, Fadwa. 1981. "The Egyptian Woman: Trends Today, Alternatives Tomorrow." In *Women in the World*, edited by L. Iglitzin and R. Ross, 225–242. Santa Barbara, CA: ABC-Clio Press.

Eliade, Mircea. 1957. *Myths, Dreams and Mysteries.* New York: Harper.

Engineer, Asghar Ali. 1986. *Islam in Asia: India, Bangladesh, Sri Lanka, Indonesia, Philippines, Malaysia.* Lahore: Vanguard Books.

______. 1992. *The Rights of Women in Islam.* Lahore: Vanguard Books.

______. 1999. *Equity, Social Justice, and Muslim Women.* Sri Lanka: Muslim Women's Research and Action Forum.

Esposito, John. 1982. *Women in Muslim Family Law.* Syracuse: Syracuse University Press.

______. 1988. *Islam: The Straight Path.* New York: Oxford University Press.

______. 1995. *The Islamic Threat: Myth or Reality?* New York: Oxford University Press.

Fadel, Mohammad. 1997. "Two Women, One Man: Knowledge, Power and Gender in Medieval Sunnī Legal Thought." *International Journal of Middle East Studies* 29(2):185–204.

Fandy, Mamoun. 1998. "Political Science Without Clothes: The Politics of Dress or Contesting the Spatiality of the State in Egypt." *Arab Studies Quarterly* 20(2):87–104.

Fernea, Elizabeth. 1965. *Guests of the Sheik: An Ethnography of an Iraqi Village.* New York: Anchor Books.

______. 1985. *Women and Family in the Middle East*. Austin: University of Texas Press.

Gaffney, Patrick D. 1994. *The Prophet's Pulpit: Islamic Preaching in Contemporary Egypt*. Berkeley: University of California Press.

Geadah, Yolande. 1996. *Femmes voilées, intégrismes démasqués*. Montréal: VLB.

Gerholm, Tomas, and Yngve Georg Lithman, eds. 1988. *The New Islamic Presence in Western Europe*. London: Mansell.

Gowlett, Gerald Darren. 1995. "Perceptions of Islam in Canadian Print Media, 1983–85, with Reference to Islamic Resurgence." Master's thesis, McGill University.

Haddad, Yvonne Yazbeck. 1978. "Muslims in Canada: A Preliminary Study." In *Religion and Ethnicity*, edited by Harold Coward and Leslie Kawamura, 71–100. Waterloo: Wilfrid Laurier University Press.

Haddad, Yvonne, ed. 2002. *Muslims in the West: From Sojourners to Citizens*. New York: Oxford University Press.

Haddad, Yvonne Yazbeck, and Adair T. Lummis. 1987. *Islamic Values in the United States: A Comparative Study*. New York: Oxford University Press.

Ḥālī, Alṭāf Ḥusain. 1997. *Hali's Musaddas: The Flow and Ebb of Islam*. Translated by Christopher Shackle and Javed Majeed. Delhi: Oxford University Press.

Hallaq, Wael B. (Forthcoming). "Can the Sharī'a be Restored?" In *Arab Legal Systems in Transition*, edited by Barbara Stowasser and Yvonne Haddad.

Hallett, Mary, and Marilyn Davis. 1994. *Firing the Heather: The Life and Times of Nelly McClung*. Saskatoon: Fifth House.

Halliday, Fred. 1999. *Islam and the Myth of Confrontation: Religion and Politics in the Middle East*. London: I.B. Tauris.

Halstead, Mark. 1991. "Radical Feminism, Islam, and the Single-Sex School Debate." *Gender and Education* 3:263–278.

______. 1993. "The Case for Single-Sex Schools: A Muslim Approach." *Muslim Education Quarterly* 10:49–69.

Hambly, Gavin, ed. 1998. *Women in the Medieval Islamic World: Power, Patronage and Piety*. New York: St. Martin's Press.

Harding, Sandra. 1992. "The Instability of the Analytical Categories of Feminist Theory." In *Knowing Women: Feminism and Knowledge*, edited by Helen Crowley and Susan Himmelweit, 338–354. Cambridge: Polity Press.

Hashem, Mazen. 1991. "Assimilation in American Life: An Islamic Perspective." *American Journal of Islamic Social Sciences* 8:83–97.

Hassan, Riffat. 1994. *Selected Articles*. Montpellier, France: Women Living under Muslim Laws.

Haw, K.F. 1994. "Muslim Girls' Schools: A Conflict of Interests?" *Gender and Education* 6: 63–76.

Hendrickson, Hildi. 1996. *Clothing and Difference: Embodied Identities in Colonial and Post-colonial Africa*. Durham, NC: Duke University Press.

Herald, Jacqueline. 1981. *Renaissance Dress in Italy 1400–1500*. London: Bell and Hyman.

Hewer, Christopher T.R. 1992. "Muslim Teacher Training in Britain." *Muslim Education Quarterly* 9:21–34.

Hogben, Murray. 1983. "The Socio-Religious Behavior of Muslims in Canada: An Overview." In *The Muslim Community in North America*, edited by Earle H. Waugh, Baha Abu-Laban and Regula Burckhardt Qureshi, 111–123. Edmonton: University of Alberta Press.

______. 1991. "Marriage and Divorce Amomg Muslims in Canada." In *Muslim Families in North America*, edited by Earle H. Waugh, Baha Abu-Laban and Regula Burckhardt Qureshi. Edmondon: University of Alberta Press.

Hood, Hugh. 1971. "Moral Imagination: Canadian Thing." In *Canada: A Guide to the Peaceable Kingdom,* edited by William Kilbourn, 29–38. Toronto: Macmillan.

Hoodfar, Homa. 1991. "Return to the Veil: Personal Strategy and Public Participation in Egypt." In *Working Women: International Perspectives on Labour and Gender Ideology*, edited by Nanneke Redclift and M. Thea Sinclair, 104–124. London: Routledge.

______. 1995. "Situating the Anthropologist: A Personal Account of Ethnographic Fieldwork in Three Urban Settings: Tehran, Cairo, and Montreal." In *Urban Lives: Fragmentation and Resistance*, edited by Vered Amit-Talai and Henri Lustiger Thaler, 206–226. Toronto: McClelland & Stewart.

______. 1997a. *Between Marriage and the Market: Intimate Politics and Survival in Cairo*. Berkeley: University of California Press.

______. 1997b. "The Veil in Their Minds and on Our Heads: The Persistence of Colonial Images of Muslim Women." In *Other Circuits: Intersections and Exchanges in World Theory and Practice*, edited by David Lloyd and Lisa Lowe, 248–279. Durham, NC: Duke University Press.

______. 2000. "Iranian Women at the Intersection of Citizenship and Family Code: The Perils of 'Islamic Criteria.'" In *Women and Citizenship in the Middle East,* edited by Joseph Suad, 287–313. Syracuse: Syracuse University Press.

______. 2001. *Le voile comme espace de négociation de l'identité et de la modernité: du Moyen-Orient au Canada.* Cahiers des conférences et séminaires scientifiques No. 7 et No. 8. Chaire Concordia-UQAM en études ethniques, Université du Québec à Montréal et Concordia University.

______. (Forthcoming[a]). *Everyday Forms of Resistance in Iran.* Montpellier, France: Women Living under Muslim Laws.

______. (Forthcoming[b]). *Women's Movement and Gender Debates in the Muslim World.*

Huntington, Samuel P. 1993. "The Clash of Civilizations?" *Foreign Affairs* 72(3):22–49.

———. 1993. "Crash of Civilization." *Foreign Affairs* 72, no. 3: 22–49.

Husaini, Zohra. 1990. *Muslims in the Canadian Mosaic: Socio-Cultural and Economic Links with Their Countries of Origin.* Edmonton: Muslim Research Foundation.

Ḥusayn, Ṭāhā. 1971. *Min Tārīkh al-Adab al-'Arabī.* 2 vols. Beirut: Dār al-'Ilm lil-Malāyīn.

Ibn al-Athīr, 'Izz al-Dīn. 1979. *al-Kāmil fī-al-Tārīkh.* 20 vols. Beirut: Dār Sādir.

______. 1997. *Usd al-Ghābah fī Ma'rifat al-Saḥābah.* Edited by K. Shihah, 5 vols. Beirut: Dār al-Ma'rifah.

Ibn al-Jawzī, Abū al-Faraj Jamāl al Dīn 'Abd al-Raḥmān ibn 'Alī. 1989. *Kitāb Aḥkām al-Nisā'.* Edited by Z. Ḥamdān. Beirut: Dār al-Fikr.

______. 1992. *Kitāb Aḥkām al-Nisā'.* Beirut: Mu'assasat al-Kutub al-Thaqāfīyah.

Ibn Ḥabīb, 'Abd al-Mālik. 1992. *Kitāb Adab al-Nisā'.* Edited by 'Abd al-Majīd Turkī. Beirut: Dār al-Gharb al-Islāmī.

Ibn Ḥanbal, Aḥmad ibn Muḥammad. 1986. *Aḥkām al-Nisā'.* Edited by A. 'Aṭā'. Beirut: Dār al-Kutub al-'Ilmīyah.

Ibn Hishām, Muḥammad 'Abd al-Mālik. 1987. *al-Sīrah al-Nabawīyah.* Edited by U. Tadmurī, 4 vols. Beirut: Dār al-Kitāb al-'Arabī.

Ibn Kathīr, Abū al-Fidā' Ismā'īl 'Umar. 1978. *al-Sīrah al-Nabawīyah.* Edited by M. 'Abd al-Wāḥid, 4 vols. Beirut: Dār al-Fikr.

Ibn Khallikān, Ibn al-'Abbās Shams al Dīn. 1978. *Wafayāt al-A'yān wa-Anbā' Abnā' al-Zamān*. Edited by Iḥsān 'Abbās, 20 vols. Beirut: Dār Ṣādir.

Ibn Manẓūr, Muḥammad. n.d. *Lisān al-'Arab*. 20 vols. Beirut: Dār Sāḍir.

Ibn Sa'd, Muḥammad. 1990. *al-Ṭabaqāt al-Kubrá*. Edited by Muḥammad 'Aṭā, 8 vols. Beirut: Dār al-Kutub al-'Ilmīyah.

Ibn Taymīyah, Aḥmad ibn 'Abd al-Ḥalīm. 1985. *Ḥijāb al-Mar'ah wa-Libāsuhā fī al-Ṣalāh*. Edited by Muḥammad Naṣīr al-Dīn al-Albānī. Beirut: al-Maktab al-Islāmī.

Iqbāl, Muḥammad. 1973. *Rumūz-i Bīkhudī*. In *Kulliyāt-i Iqbāl, Fārsī*. Lahore: Shaikh Ghulam Ali and Sons.

______. 1989. *The Reconstruction of Religious Thought in Islam*. Edited by M. Saeed Sheikh. Lahore: Institute of Islamic Culture.

______. 1999. *Poems from Iqbal*. Reprint. Translated by V.G. Kiernan. Lahore: Iqbal Academy and Oxford University Press.

Jabbra, Joseph G. and Nancy W. Jabbra. 1987. *Lebanese of the Maritimes*. Tantallon, Nova Scotia: Four East Publications.

Jāhiẓ, Abū 'Uthmān 'Amr. 1980. *Risālat al-Qiyan: The Epistle on Singing-Girls of Jahiẓ*. Edited with translation and commentary by A. Beeston. Warminster: Aris & Phillips Ltd.

Jehl, Douglas. 1999. "Arab Honor's Price: A Woman's Blood." *The New York Times* (Sunday, June 20), Section 1.

Joly, Jacques. 1996. *Sondage d'opinion publique québécoise sur l'immigration et les relations interculturelles*. Québec: Ministère des Relations avec les citoyens et de l'immigration.

Kabbani, Rana. 1986. *Europe's Myths of Orient: Devise and Rule*. Bloomington: Indiana University Press.

Kadi, Joanna, ed. 1994. *Food for Our Grandmothers*. Boston: South End Press.

Kashmerier, Zuhair. 1991. *The Gulf Within: Canadian Arabs, Racism and the Gulf War*. Toronto: J. Lorimer.

Keddie, Nikki. 2002. "Women in the Limelight: Some Recent Books on Middle Eastern Women's History." *International Journal of Middle East Studies,* 34(3):553–573.

Keddie, Nikki, and Beth Baron. 1991. *Women in Middle Eastern History: Shifting Boundaries in Sex and Gender*. New Haven: Yale University Press.

Keddie, Nikki, and Lois Beck. 1978. *Women in the Muslim World*. Cambridge: Harvard University Press.

Kelley, Ron. 1994. "Muslims in Los Angeles." In *Muslim Communities in North America*, edited by Yvonne Yazbeck Haddad and Jane Idleman Smith, 135–167. Albany: State University of New York Press.

Kelly, Patricia. 1997. "Integrating Islam: A Muslim School in Montreal." Master's thesis, Institute of Islamic Studies, McGill University.

______. 1998a. "Muslim Canadians: Immigration Policy and Community Development in the 1991 Census." *Islam and Christian-Muslim Relations* 9(1):83–102.

______. 1998b. "The Ethnolinguistics of Immigration: The Social Functions of Language in a Muslim School in Montreal." Paper presented to seminar "Langues en Contact," Département d'anthropologie, Université de Montréal, March 10.

______. 1999. "Integration and Identity in Muslim Schools: Britain, United States, and Montreal." *Islam and Muslim Christian Relations* 10: 197–217.

Khalaf Allāh, Muḥammad Aḥmad. 1977. *Dirāsāt fī al-Nuẓūm wa-al-Tashrī'āt al-Islāmīyah.* Cairo: Maktabat al-Anjlū al-Miṣrīyah.

Khan, Shahnaz. 2000. *Muslim Women in North America.* Gainesville: University Press of Florida.

Khanum, Saeeda. 1992. "Education and the Muslim Girl." In *Refusing Holy Orders: Women and Fundamentalism in Britain*, edited by Gita Sahgal and Nira Yuval-Davis, 124–140. London: Virago.

Khaṭīb al-Baghdādī, Abū Bakr. 1931. *Tārīkh Baghdād.* 14 vols. Cairo: Maktabat al-Khanji.

Khomeini, Ruholla. 1984. *A Clarification of Questions: An Abridged Translation of Resaleh Towzih al-Masael.* Translated by J. Borujerdi. Boulder: Westview Press.

Kristeva, Julia. 1989. *Étrangers à nous-mêmes.* Paris: Fayard.

Lane, Rose Wilder. 1997. *Islam and the Discovery of Freedom.* Beltsville, MD: Amana Publications.

Lavigne, Marie. 1995. "Ce hijab qui nous interpelle." *La Gazette des Femmes* (janvier–fevrier). Publication bimestrielle du Conseil du statut de la femme.

Lemu, B. Aisha, and Fatima Heeren. 1978. *Women in Islam.* Leicester: The Islamic Foundation.

Lenk, Helle-Mai. 1998. *Emilie Ouimet: Race and Reading the Quebec National Narrative.* Toronto: Ontario Institute for Studies in Education, University of Toronto.

______. 2000. "The Case of Emilie Ouimet: New Discourse on the Hijab and the Construction of Quebecois National Identity." In *Anti-Racist Feminism: Critical Race and Gender Studies*, edited by Agnes Calliste and George J. Sefa Dei, 73–90. Halifax: Fernwood.

Leveau, Remy, and Gilles Kepel. 1985. *Culture islamique et attitudes politiques dans la population musulmane en France: Enquête effectuée pendant le mois du Ramadan.* Paris: Fondation nationale des sciences politique.

Lewis, Philip. 1994. *Islamic Britain: Religion, Politics, and Identity among British Muslims*. London: I.B. Tauris.

Lindisfarne-Tapper, Nancy, and Bruce Ingham, eds. 1997. *Languages of Dress in the Middle East*. London: Curzon.

Mabro, Judy. 1991.*Veiled Half-Truths: Western Travellers' Perceptions of Middle Eastern Women*. London: I.B. Tauris & Co.

McDonough, Sheila. 1994. "Muslims of Montreal." In *Muslim Communities in North America,* edited by Y. Haddad and J.I. Smith, 317–334. Albany: State University of New York Press.

McDonough, Sheila, and Sajida S. Alvi. 2002. "The Canadian Council of Muslim Women: A Chapter in the History of Muslim Women in Canada." *The Muslim World* 92, nos. 1 and 2 (Spring): 79–98.

McGowan, Rima Berns. 1999. *Muslims in the Diaspora: The Somali Communities of London and Toronto*. Toronto: University of Toronto Press.

McLaren, Peter. 1993. *Schooling as a Ritual Performance: Towards a Political Economy of Educational Symbols and Gestures*. New York: Routledge.

MacLennan, Hugh. 1971. "After 300 Years Our Neurosis Is Relevant." In *Canada: A Guide to the Peaceable Kingdom,* edited by William Kilbourn, 8–13. Toronto: Macmillan.

MacLeod, Arlene Elowe. 1991. *Accommodating Protest: Working Women, the New Veiling, and Change in Cairo*. New York: Columbia University Press.

Mas'ūdī, Abū al-Ḥasan 'Alī ibn al-Ḥusayn. 1982. *Murūj al-Dhahab wa-Ma'ādin al-Jawāhir.* 5 vols. Beirut: Dār al-Kitāb al-Lubnānī.

Mawdūdī, Abū al-A'lā'. 1972. *Purdah and the Status of Woman in Islam*. Translated and edited by al-Ash'ari. Lahore: Islamic Publications.

______. 1973. *Tafhīm al-Qur'an*, vol. 1. Lahore: Maktabah-i Ta'mīr-i Insānīyat.

Mawsū'at al-Ḥadīth al-Sharīf. n.d. 2nd ed. Cairo: Ṣakhr.

Mernissi, Fatima. 1987. *Beyond the Veil: Male-Female Dynamics in Modern Muslim Society*. Bloomington: Indiana University Press.

______. 1990. *The Forgotten Queens of Islam*. Translated by M.J. Lakeland. Cambridge: Polity Press, 1990.

______. 1991a. *The Veil and the Male Elite: A Feminist Interpretation of Women's Rights in Islam*. Translated by M.J. Lakeland. Reading, Mass.: Addison-Wesley.

______. 1991b. *Women and Islam: An Historical and Theological Enquiry*. Oxford: Blackwell.

______. 1992. *Islam and Democracy: Fear of the Modern World*. Translated by M.J. Lakeland. New York: Addison-Wesley.

______. 1993. *The Forgotten Queens of Islam*. Translated by M.J. Lakeland. Cambridge: Polity Press.

______. 1996. "The Jariya and the Caliph: Thoughts on the Place of Women in Muslim Political Memory." In *Women's Rebellion & Islamic Memory*, edited by Fatima Mernissi, 77–91. London: Zed Books.

Metcalf, Barbara. 1996. "Sacred Words, Sanctioned Practice, New Communities." In *Making Muslim Space in North America and Europe*, edited by Barbara Metcalf, 1–27. Los Angeles: University of California Press.

Moussali, Ahmad S. 1992. *Radical Islamic Fundamentalism: The Ideological and Political Discourse of Sayyid Qutb*. Beirut: American University of Beirut.

Mudzhar, Atho M., and Sajida S. Alvi et al., eds. 2002. *Women in Indonesian Society: Access, Empowerment and Opportunity*. Yogyakarta: Sunan Kalijaga Press.

Muḥammad, Abū Sar'ī. 1985. *Zīnat al-Mar'ah wa-Libāsuhā fī al-Kitāb wa-al-Sunnah*. Edited by Muḥammad Naṣīr al-Dīn al-Albānī. Cairo: Maktabat al-Turāth al-Islāmī.

Mumtaz, Khawer, and Farida Shaheed, eds. 1987. *Women of Pakistan*. London: Zed Press.

Mutahhari, Murtaza. 1989. *The Islamic Modest Dress*. Translated by Laleh Bakhtiar. Albuquerque, NM: Abjad.

Nader, Laura. 1989. "Orientalism, Occidentalism and the Control of Women." *Cultural Dynamics* 2(3):323–355.

Nasr, Seyyed Vali Reza. 1996. *Mawdudi and the Making of Islamic Revivalism*. New York: Oxford University Press.

Nielsen, Jorgen S. 1995. *Muslims in Western Europe*. Edinburgh: Edinburgh University Press.

Norton, John. 1997. "Faith and Fashion in Turkey." In *Languages of Dress in the Middle East*, edited by Nancy Lindisfarne-Tapper and Bruce Ingham, 149–177. London: Curzon.

Ohan, Farid E., and Ibrahim Hayani. 1993. *The Arabs in Ontario: A Misunderstood Community*. Toronto: Near East Cultural and Educational Foundation of Canada.

Paidar, Parvin. 1995. *Women and the Political Process in Twentieth-Century Iran*. Cambridge: Cambridge University Press.

Parker-Jenkins, Marie. 1992. "Muslim Matters: An Examination of the Educational Needs of Muslim Children in Contemporary Britain." *American Journal of Islamic Social Sciences* 9:351–369.

______. 1995. *Children of Islam: A Teacher's Guide to Meeting the Needs of Muslim Pupils*. London: Trentham Books.

Parker-Jenkins, Marie, and Kaye Francis Haw. 1996. "Equality Within Islam, Not Without It: The Perspectives of Muslim Girls in a Muslim School in Britain." *Muslim Education Quarterly* 13:17–34.

Parkington, A. 1992. "Popular Fashion and Working Class Affluence." In *Chic Thrills: A Fashion Reader*, edited by J. Ash and E. Wilson, 145–161. Berkeley: University of California Press.

Payne, Blanche. 1965. *History of Costume: From the Ancient Egyptians to the Twentieth Century*. New York: Harper and Row.

Perrot, Philippe. 1994. *Fashioning the Bourgeoisie: A History of Clothing in the Nineteenth Century*. Translated by Richard Bienvenu. Princeton: Princeton University Press.

Pinault, David. 1998. "Zaynab bint 'Ali and the Place of the Women of the Household of the First Imams in the Shi'ite Devotional Literature." In *Women in the Medieval Islamic World*, edited by Gavin R.G. Hambly, 69–98. New York: St. Martin's Press.

Pulcini, Theodor. 1995. "Values Conflict among American Muslim Youth." In *Muslim Minorities in the West*, edited by Syed Z. Abedin and Ziauddin Sardar, 178–203. London: Grey Seal.

Qayrawānī, Abū Isḥāq Ibrāhīm al-Ḥuṣarī ibn 'Alī. 1953. *Zahr al-Ādāb wa-Thamar al-Albāb*. Edited by Z. Mubārak and M. 'Abd al-Ḥamīd. Cairo: Maṭba'at al-Sa'ādah.

Quataert, Donald. 1997. "Clothing Laws, State and Society in the Ottoman Empire, 1720–1829." *International Journal of Middle East Studies* 29(3):403–425.

Qifṭī, Jamāl al-Dīn Abū al-Ḥasan ʻAlī ibn Yūsuf. 1326 AH/1908 CE. *Kitāb Akhbār al-ʻUlamā' bi-Akhbār al-Ḥukamā'*. Cairo: Maṭbaʻat al-Saʻādah.

Rahman, Fazlur. 1962. "Sunna and Hadith." *Islamic Studies* 1(2):1–36.

———. 1965. *Islamic Methodology in History*. Karachi: Central Institute of Islamic Research.

______. 1980. *Major Themes of the Qur'an*. Minneapolis: Bibliotheca Islamica.

______. 1982. "The Status of Women in Islam: A Modernist Interpretation." In *Separate Worlds: Slaves of Purdah in South East Asia*, edited by H. Papanek and G. Minault, 285–310. Delhi: Chanakya.

Rahman, Yusuf. 2001. "The Hermeneutical Theory of Naṣr Ḥāmid Abū Zayd: An Analytical Study of His Method of Interpreting the Qur'ān." Ph.D. dissertation, McGill University.

Raza, Mohammad. 1993. *Islam in Britain: Past, Present, and Future*. Leicester: Volcano Press.

Rāzī, Fakhr al-Dīn. 1976. *al-Tafsīr al-Kabīr.* 32 vols. Cairo: ʻAbd al-Raḥmān Muḥammad.

Roded, Ruth. 1994. *Women in Islamic Biographical Collections: From Ibn Saʻd to Who's Who*. Boulder, Colorado: Lynne Rienner.

Rostom, Kamal A., ed. 1989. *Arab-Canadian Writing: Stories, Memoirs, and Reminiscences*. Fredericton, NB: York.

Rugh, Andrea. 1986. *Reveal and Conceal: Dress in Contemporary Egypt*. Syracuse: Syracuse University Press.

Said, Edward. 1978. *Orientalism*. New York: Random House.

______. 1981. *Covering Islam: How Media and the Experts Determine How We See the Rest of the World*. New York: Pantheon.

______. 1997. *Covering Islam: How Media and the Experts Determine How We See the Rest of the World*. Revised Edition. New York: Vintage Books.

______. 2001. Interview with *The Progressive Magazine*. Interview by David Barsamain. November 2001. http://www.progressive.org/0901/intv1101.html.

Saqib, M.A.K. 1986. *A Guide to Prayer in Islam*. London: Ta-Ha Publishers.

Sarwar, Ghullam. 1994. *British Muslims and Schools*. London: The Muslim Educational Trust.

Schimmel, Annemarie. 1987. *And Muhammad Is His Messenger: The Veneration of the Prophet in Islamic Piety*. Lahore: Vanguard Books.

______. 1997. *My Soul Is a Woman*. New York: Continuum Publishing.

Selby, Karen. 1992. "The Islamic Schooling Movement in the United States: Teachers' Experiences in One Full-Time Islamic School." *Muslim Education Quarterly* 9:35–48.

Shadid, W.A.R., and P.S. Van Koningsveld, eds. 1996. *Muslims in the Margin: Political Responses to the Presence of Islam in Western Europe*. Kampen, The Netherlands: Pharos.

Shaḥrūr, Muḥammad. 1993. *al-Kitāb wa-al-Qur'ān: Qirā'ah Mu'aṣirah*. Beirut: Sharikat al-Maṭbū'āt.

Shahshahani, Soheila. 1995. *A Pictorial History of Iranian Headdresses*. Tehran: Modabber Press.

Shirazi, Faegheh. 2001. *The Veil Unveiled: The Ḥijab in Modern Culture*. Gainesville: University Press of Florida.

Singerman, Diane, and Homa Hoodfar. 1996. *Development, Change, and Gender in Cairo: A View from the Household*. Bloomington: Indiana University Press.

Sisters in Islam. 1991a. *Are Muslim Men Allowed to Beat Their Wives?* Bangi, Selangor, Malaysia: Sisters in Islam.

______. 1991b. *Are Women & Men Equal Before Allah?* Bangi, Selangor, Malaysia: Sisters in Islam.

Sponsler, Clair. 1992. "Narrating the Social Order: Medieval Clothing Laws." *Clio,* (Spring), 280.

Stanton, Elizabeth Cady. 1970. *Eighty Years and More*. New York: Sources Books.

Stowasser, Barbara. 1987. "Liberated Equal or Protected Dependent? Contemporary Religious Paradigms on Women's Status in Islam." *Arab Studies Quarterly* 9(3):260–283.

______. 1993. "Women's Issues in Modern Islamic Thought." In *Arab Women: Old Boundaries, New Frontiers*, edited by Judith E. Tucker, 3–28. Bloomington: Indiana University Press.

Ṭabarī, Abū Ja'far Muḥammad ibn Jarīr. 1987. *Jāmi' al-Bayān fī Tafsīr al-Qur'ān*. 30 vols. Beirut: Dar al-Ma'rifah.

______. 1997. *Tārīkh al-Umam wa-l-Muluk*. 30 vols. Beirut: Dār al-Kutub al-'Ilmīyah.

Tarlo, Emma. 1996. *Clothing Matters: Dress and Identity in India*. Chicago: University of Chicago Press.

Tibi, Bassam. 1998. *The Challenge of Fundamentalism: Political Islam and the New World Order*. Berkeley and Los Angeles: University of California Press.

Tougas, Claudette. 1995. "Horreur à Oklahoma City." *La Presse,* Montreal (avril 21).

Turenne, Martine. 1997. "Ce qui se cache." *Chatelaine* (juillet), 27–33.

Vakili, Valla. 1996. *Debating Religion and Politics in Iran: The Political Thought of Abdolkarim Soroush.* New York: Council on Foreign Relations.

Waardenburg, Jacques. 1988. "The Institutionalization of Islam in the Netherlands, 1961–86." In *The New Islamic Presence in Western Europe*, edited by T. Gerholm and Y.G. Lithman, 8–31. London: Mansell.

Wadud Muhsin, Amina. 1992. *Qur'an and Women: Reading the Sacred Text from a Woman's Perspective.* New York: Oxford University Press.

Wāḥidī al-Nīsābūrī, Abū al-Ḥasan 'Alī. n.d. *Asbāb al-Nuzūl*. Riyad: Maktabat al-Riyāḍ al-Ḥadīthah.

Wahidur Rahman, A.N.M. 1993. "Modernist Muslim's [*sic*] Approach to *Ḥadīth*: Aligarh School." *Hamdard Islamicus* 16(4):13–26.

Wāqidī, Muḥammad ibn 'Umar. 1984. *Kitāb al-Maghāzī*. 3 vols. Edited by Marsden Jones. Beirut: 'Ālam al-Kutub.

Waugh, Earl H. 1991. "North America and the Adaptation of the Muslim Tradition: Religion, Ethnicity, and the Family." In *Muslim Families in North America*, edited by Earle H. Waugh, Sharon McIrvin Abu-Laban and Regula Burckhardt Qureshi, 68–95. Edmonton: University of Alberta Press.

Webb, Wilfred Mark. 1912. *The Heritage of Dress*. London: Times Book Club.

Wheatcroft, Andrew. 1993. *The Ottomans: Dissolving Images*. London: Penguin Books.

Wikan, Unni. 1982. *Behind the Veil in Arabia: Women in Oman*. Chicago: University of Chicago Press.

Wollstonecraft, Mary. 1982. *Vindication of the Rights of Women.* New York: Whitsun.

Yousif, Ahmad F. 1993. *Muslims in Canada: A Question of Identity*. Ottawa: Legas.

Zaman, Sadia, ed. 1999. *At My Mother's Feet: Stories of Muslim Women.* Kingston: Quarry Women's Books.

Zaydān, Jurjī. 1958. *Tārīkh al-Tamaddun al-Islāmī*. Edited and with commentary by H. Mu'nis. Cairo: Dār al-Hilāl.

Zuhur, Sherifa. 1992. *Revealing Reveiling: Islamist Gender Ideology in Contemporary Egypt*. Albany: State University of New York Press.

Contributors

Sajida S. Alvi is Professor of Indo-Islamic History, and holder of the Chair in Urdu Language and Culture at the Institute of Islamic Studies, McGill University. Her major publications include: *Mir'āt al-'Ālam: History of Awrangzēb,* 2 vols. (1979); *Advice on the Art of Governance: An Indo-Islamic Mirror for Princes* (1989); and *Urdu for Children: Book One*, 4 vols. (1997). On women's issues her publications include: *Women in Indonesian Society: Access, Empowerment and Opportunity*: *Conference Proceedings*, co-edited with M. Atho Mudzhar (2002); "Career Development of Women in Indonesian Society: A Study of Highly Successful Career Women," co-authored with Sabir Alvi, in *Women in Indonesian Society: Access, Empowerment and Opportunity* (2002); "The Canadian Council of Muslim Women: A Chapter in the History of Muslim Women in Canada," co-authored with Sheila McDonough, in *The Muslim World,* vol. 92 (2002); edited "Muslim Women and Society," in *An Anthology of Islamic Studies*, edited by H. Federspiel, vol. 2 (1996); "Polygamy," "Evidence," "Inheritance," in *International Conference on Islamic Laws and Women in the Modern World* (1996); and "Unpacking the Symbolism of the Muslim Veil," co-authored with Sheila McDonough, in *Ecumenism (Women of Faith in the World's Religions)*, no. 115 (September 1994).

L. Clarke is Assistant Professor of Religion and Islam in the Department of Religion, Concordia University, Montreal. She has also taught in the department of Oriental Studies at the University of Pennsylvania, and at Bard College, New York. Her most recent publication is an edited volume entitled *Shī'ite Heritage: Essays on Classical and Modern Traditions* (2001).

Soraya Hajjaji-Jarrah is a Ph.D. candidate at the Institute of Islamic Studies, McGill University, and has served as an Assistant Professor in the Faculty of Education, University of Libya. She is the author of "The Enchantment of Reading: Sound, Meaning and Expression in Sūrat al-'Ādiyhāt," in *Literary Structures of Religious Meaning in the Qur'ān*, edited by Issa Boullata (2000).

Homa Hoodfar is Associate Professor of Anthropology in the Department of Sociology and Anthropology, Concordia University. Her latest research focuses on the lives of Afghan refugee women in Iran and Pakistan. She has also conducted field research in Iran, Egypt, Pakistan and Canada. Among her more recent publications are: *The Women's Movement in Iran: Women at the Crossroads of Secularization and Islamization* (1999); *Between Marriage and the Market: Intimate Politics and Survival in Cairo* (1997); and *Development, Change, and Gender in Cairo: A View from the Household*, co-edited with Diane Singerman (1996).

Patricia Kelly Spurles is a doctoral candidate in Anthropology at the Université de Montréal. She is the author of "Integration and Identity in Muslim Schools: Britain, U.S., and Montreal," in *Islam and Christian-Muslim Relations* 10, no. 2 (1999) and "Muslim Canadians: Immigration Policy and Community Development in the 1991 Census," ibid. 9, no. 1 (1998).

Sheila McDonough is Professor Emeritus in the Department of Religion at Concordia University. Her publications include *Gandhi's Responses* *to Islam* (1994), and *Muslim Ethics and Modernity* (1985). She has written numerous articles and chapters in books relating to Islam in South Asia, and to issues relating to Muslim women. Among the latter are: "The Canadian Council of Muslim Women: A Chapter in the History of Muslim Women in Canada," co-authored with Sajida S. Alvi, in *The Muslim World* (Hartford) (Spring Issue, 2002); "A Gender Hierarchy in Islamic Thought," in *Life Ethics in World Religions*, edited by Dawne McCance (1998); "The Impact of Social Change on Muslim Women," in *Gender, Genre and Religion*, edited by Morny Joy (1995); and "Unpacking the Symbolism of the Muslim Veil," co-authored with Sajida S. Alvi, in *Ecumenism (Women of Faith in the World's Religions)*, no. 115 (September 1994).

Reem Meshal is a doctoral candidate in Islamic Studies at McGill University where her research focuses on *sharī'ah* and practice in Muslim legal history. Her previous research on the international law of the sea was published in the proceedings of the United Nations' 10th Conference on International Law, Qatar (1994).